MECCA IN MOROCCO

Edinburgh Studies of the Globalised Muslim World

Series Editor: **Frédéric Volpi**, Director, Prince Alwaleed Bin Talal Centre for the Study of Contemporary Islam, University of Edinburgh

This innovative series investigates the dynamics of Muslim societies in a globalised world. It considers the boundaries of the contemporary Muslim world, their construction, their artificiality or durability. It sheds new light on what it means to be part of the Muslim world today, for both those individuals and communities who live in Muslim-majority countries and those who reside outside and are part of a globalised ummah. Its analysis encompasses the micro and the macro level, exploring the discourses and practices of individuals, communities, states and transnational actors who create these dynamics. It offers a multidisciplinary perspective on the salient contemporary issues and interactions that shape the internal and external relations of the Muslim world.

Forthcoming and available titles

Salafi Social and Political Movements: National and Transnational Contexts
Masooda Bano

A Political Theory of Muslim Democracy
Ravza Altuntaş-Çakır

Literary Neo-Orientalism and the Arab Uprisings: Tensions in English, French and German Language Fiction
Julia Wurr

Why Islamists Go Green
Emmanuel Karagiannis

Islamic Modernities in World Society: The Rise, Spread and Fragmentation of a Hegemonic Idea
Dietrich Jung

Islamists and the Global Order: Between Resistance and Recognition
Hanna Pfeifer

Mecca in Morocco: Articulations of Muslim Pilgrimage in Moroccan Everyday Life
Kholoud Al-Ajarma

edinburghuniversitypress.com/series/esgmw

MECCA IN MOROCCO

Articulations of Muslim Pilgrimage in Moroccan Everyday Life

Kholoud Al-Ajarma

EDINBURGH
University Press

Edinburgh University Press is one of the leading university presses in the UK. We publish academic books and journals in our selected subject areas across the humanities and social sciences, combining cutting-edge scholarship with high editorial and production values to produce academic works of lasting importance. For more information visit our website: edinburghuniversitypress.com

First published in hardback by Edinburgh University Press 2024

Edinburgh University Press Ltd
13 Infirmary Street
Edinburgh EH1 1LT

Typeset in 11/15pt EB Garamond by
Cheshire Typesetting Ltd, Cuddington, Cheshire

A CIP record for this book is available from the British Library

ISBN 978 1 3995 2071 3 (hardback)
ISBN 978 1 3995 2072 0 (paperback)
ISBN 978 1 3995 2073 7 (webready PDF)
ISBN 978 1 3995 2074 4 (epub)

CONTENTS

List of Figures and Tables vii
Acknowledgements ix
Note on Translation xiii
Series Editor's Foreword xv

Introduction 1

1 Theoretical Framework and Methodology 7

PART ONE THE PILGRIMAGE TO MECCA: A TRIPARTITE PROCESS OF PREPARATION, PILGRIMAGE AND AFTERMATH

2 Before Departure: Motivations for Hajj Performance and the Creation of a Muslim Moral *Habitus* 47

3 In the Hajj: A Sensory Experience that 'Cannot be Described in Words' 74

4 After Hajj: Refashioning of the Self as *al-Ḥājj/al-Ḥājja* 102

PART TWO IDENTITY AND POLITICS

5 Hajj and Moroccan National Identity 123

6 Contesting Pilgrimage: Moroccan Perspectives on Saudi Control of the Hajj 145

7 Intersecting Power Structures in Moroccan Women's Narratives of the Hajj 173

PART THREE THE PILGRIMAGE: INFORMING EVERYDAY LIFE

8 '*Ḥajj al-Miskīn*': Moroccan Local Pilgrimage 193

9 Constituted Everydayness: Singing of Mecca and the Pilgrimage in Morocco 213

10 *The Pilgrimage of the Cat* and Other Hajj Stories: Performing Piety and Moral Transformation through Storytelling 232

Conclusion – Mecca in Morocco: Manifestations of the Hajj in Moroccan Everyday Life 251

Bibliography 265

Index 302

FIGURES AND TABLES

Figures

1.1 Pilgrims performing *ṭawāf* around the Kaʿba (Mecca, 4 February 2018) 9

1.2 Mount Arafat during Hajj, as documented by one of the research participants (Mecca, 20 August 2018) 11

2.1 *Qurʿa* winners vis-à-vis Hajj applicants, 2015–18 52

3.1 Living room in a house with wall hanging of the Kaʿba (Fes, 4 August 2015) 82

3.2 The scale model of the Grand Mosque of Mecca displayed in Morocco Mall (Casablanca, 30 July 2015) 84

3.3 Pilgrims documenting their experience and sharing it via social media (Mecca, 7 February 2018) 85

3.4 Women waiting to enter the Rawḍa, 8:30–10:30 p.m. (Medina, 1 February 2018) 93

3.5 Men drinking Zamzam water at the Grand Mosque of Mecca (Mecca, 8 February 2018) 94

4.1 Pilgrims welcomed at the airport (Casablanca, 3 October 2015 and 28 September 2016) 104

5.1 Facebook post shared by a pilgrim 139

6.1 Report about *'umra* fees in the daily newspaper (Casablanca, 5 October 2016) 147
6.2 Image from Christiaan Snouck Hurgronje's *Mekka* (1888) 152
6.3 Recent image of Mecca showing the *abrāj al-bayt* project (2016) 152
6.4 Two women sitting in front of a new construction advertisement (Mecca, 9 February 2018) 153
6.5 Worker at a hotel in Mecca offering guests cardamom-flavoured Zamzam water (Mecca, 10 February 2018) 154
6.6 Picture of the Paradise Garden of al-Baqīʿ in 1907/8 by Muhammad ʻAli Effendi Saʻudi) 158
6.7 Signs indicating behaviour guidelines near Uḥud cemetery (Medina, 1 February 2018) 158
6.8 Hop-on-hop-off bus stops (Medina, 1 February 2018) 159
6.9 Flyers distributed in the Grand Mosque of Mecca about women's dress code (Mecca, 7 February 2018) 165
8.1 The site of Sīdī Shāshkāl and images from the Pilgrimage of the Poor (11 September 2016) 199
8.2 The day of the Pilgrimage of the Poor at the site of Sīdī Bū Khiyār (21 August 2018) 201

Tables

2.1 Annual number of Hajj pilgrims to Saudi Arabia, 2015–18 49
2.2 Documentation required from female pilgrims (according to civil status) 53
6.1 Previous accidents during Hajj 162

ACKNOWLEDGEMENTS

I extend my heartfelt gratitude to the numerous individuals who have contributed to my academic journey that led to the completion of this book. Their valuable support and contributions merit sincere recognition and appreciation. The book is based on five years of research that investigates the sociocultural embeddedness of Hajj in contemporary Morocco. It was part of the research project 'More Magical than Disneyland: Modern Articulations of Pilgrimage to Mecca', thanks to a grant provided by The Netherlands Organization for Scientific Research (NWO).[1] I would like to express my sincere gratitude to the project's lead who supervised and accompanied me throughout my PhD journey, Marjo Buitelaar; to my second supervisor, Clare Wilde; and to friends and former colleagues at the Faculty of Theology and Religious Studies at the University of Groningen. I am grateful for having been able to write my research in such an inspiring environment.

At the University of Edinburgh, I wish to extend my heartfelt gratitude to my colleagues and friends at the Alwaleed Centre for the Study of Islam in the Contemporary World and the Department of Islamic and Middle Eastern Studies. The Centre's vibrant academic environment has provided a nurturing space where engaging with other scholars, collaboration and participation in discussions within this esteemed community have immensely enriched my understanding of the contemporary study of Islam and Muslim societies.

My sincere appreciation goes to various scholars who have read and commented on my work, including Simon Coleman, Thijl Sunier, Hetty Zock and Kim Knibbe, to name but a few. Their feedback and scholarly work have helped me develop the analysis presented in this book. I would like also to acknowledge the team of the research project 'More Magical than Disneyland' in addition to Marjo Buitelaar: Richard van Leeuwen, Khadija Kadrouch-Outmany and Ammeke Kateman.

I am grateful for the support of several academic institutions during this journey: the Dutch Institute for Higher Education in Scientific Research (NIMAR), which facilitated my research permit and remains an inspirational presence in education; Netherlands Interuniversity School for Islamic Studies (NISIS), where I gained much knowledge, including in their summer schools, seminars and conferences; and the Oxford Centre for Islamic Studies (OCIS), where I spent six months as a Chevening Fellow.

My heartfelt gratitude extends to my Moroccan friends and interlocutors who opened their homes and hearts to me, enabling my fieldwork and research. To guarantee their anonymity and privacy I have used pseudonyms, which unfortunately prevents me from being able to thank them by name. Nonetheless, my deep gratitude goes out to each one of my interlocutors, and I hope that this work will live up to the expectations and trust that these individuals have placed in it. Without the people I have mentioned or alluded to, my time in Fes, Rabat, Mohammedia, Casablanca, El Houseima, Marrakech, Ourzazate, Safi and many other places would have been much impoverished.

I would like to acknowledge that some of the data woven into the fabric of this book has also found its place in the scholarly tapestry of other publications, including book chapters such as 'Saudi Hajj Management through Moroccan Pilgrims' Eyes' in *The Politics of the Hajj in a Comparative Perspective: States, Entrepreneurs, and Pilgrims*, ed. Marie Brossier, Muriel Gomez-Perez and Cédric Jourde (Palgrave Macmillan, 2024); "Beyond Words": Moroccan Pilgrims' Narrations about their Ineffable Hajj Experiences through Stories about the Senses', in *Narrating the Pilgrimage to Mecca: Historical and Contemporary Accounts*, ed. Marjo Buitelaar and Richard van Leeuwen (Brill, 2023); and 'Power in Moroccan Women's Narratives of the Hajj', in *Muslim Women's Pilgrimage to Mecca and Beyond. Reconfiguring Gender, Religion, and Mobility*, ed. Marjo Buitelaar, Viola Thimm and Manja

Stephan-Emmrich (Routledge, 2020). In addition, my exploration of the 'Pilgrimage of the Poor' was previously (2022) published in a peer-reviewed article in the journal *Anthropology of the Middle East*, and my reflections on the post-Hajj transformation of Muslim pilgrims in the journal *Religions* (2021). I hope that these publications, together with this book, may contribute to the enrichment of the scholarly discourse on pilgrimage, presenting a view of the diverse dimensions of this sacred journey.

Finally, my family's immeasurable role in this journey deserves special mention. Their love, encouragement and unwavering support have given me the strength to persist in the face of circumstances that have sometimes been challenging.

Note

1 Grant number: 360-25-150; programme leader: Prof. Dr M. W. Buitelaar, University of Groningen.

NOTE ON TRANSLATION

Since all the conversations, narratives, stories, etc. in the book occurred in Arabic, I have taken responsibility for translating them into English. Arabic words and phrases have been rendered in the simplest manner recognisable by the Arabic speaker while being faithful, as much as possible, to the Moroccan dialect, *dārīja*, in which these words were spoken. I have chosen to adopt a simplified version of the transliteration used by the *International Journal of Middle East Studies (IJMES)*, as shown in the table below. When translations of Qur'anic verses are given, the interpretation of Muhammad A. S. Abdel Haleem (2004) is adopted. This translation of the Qur'an is written in contemporary language, making the text understandable while providing an accurate rendering of the original Arabic.

ء	=	ʾ	د	=	d	ض	=	ḍ	ك	=	k
ب	=	b	ذ	=	dh	ط	=	ṭ	ل	=	l
ت	=	t	ر	=	r	ظ	=	ẓ	م	=	m
ث	=	th	ز	=	z	ع	=	ʿ	ن	=	n
ج	=	j	س	=	s	غ	=	gh	ه	=	h
ح	=	ḥ	ش	=	sh	ف	=	f	و	=	w
خ	=	kh	ص	=	ṣ	ق	=	q	ي	=	y

Vowels:	Long	ا/ى = ā	و = ū	ي = ī
	Short	َ = a	ُ = u	ِ = i
	Diphthong		وَ = aw	يَ = ay

SERIES EDITOR'S FOREWORD

The *Edinburgh Studies in the Globalised Muslim World* is a series that focuses on the contemporary transformations of Muslim societies. 'Globalisation' is meant here to denote that although the Muslim world has always interacted with other societal, religious, imperial, or national forces over the centuries, the evolution of these interconnections constantly reshapes Muslim societies. The second half of the twentieth century has been characterised by the increasing number and diversity of exchanges on a global scale bringing people and societies 'closer', for better and for worse. The beginning of the twenty-first century confirmed the increasingly glocalised nature of these interactions and the challenges and opportunities that they bring to existing institutional, social and cultural orders.

The series is not a statement that everything is different in today's brave new world. Indeed, many 'old' ideas and practices still have much currency in the present, and undoubtedly will continue to in the future. Rather the series emphasises how our current globalised condition shapes and mediates how past worldviews and modes of being are transmitted between people and institutions. The contemporary Muslim world is not merely a reflection of past histories, but it is also a living process of creating a new order on the basis of what people want, desire, fear and hope. This creative endeavour can transform existing relations for the better, for example by reconsidering the relations between society and the environment. They can equally fan violence and hatred as illustrated in the reignition of cycles of conflicts over sovereignties, ideologies, or resources across the globe.

The *Globalised Muslim World* series arrives at a challenging time for any inquiry into Muslim societies. The new millennium began inauspiciously with a noticeable spike in transnational and international violence framed in 'civilisational' terms. A decade of 'war of terror' contributed to the entrenching of negative mutual perceptions across the globe while also reinforcing essentialist views. The ensuing decade hardly improved this situation, with political and territorial conflicts multiplying in different parts of the Muslim world, and some of the most violent groups laying claim to the idea of a global caliphate to justify themselves. Yet, a focus on trajectories of violence gives a distorted picture of the evolution of Muslim societies and their relations with the rest of the world. This series is very much about the 'what else' is happening as we move further into the twenty-first century.

Kholoud Al-Ajarma's *Mecca in Morocco* provides a most insightful contribution to the debates on the contemporary significance of the Hajj in Muslim lives from the perspective of the anthropology of Islam. The transnational construction and perception of the *umma* has long been linked to the experience of this pilgrimage that brings together Muslims from all over the world to Mecca, previously a once-in-a-lifetime religious experience for most. As the subtitle of the book, *Articulations of Muslim Pilgrimage in Moroccan Everyday Life*, indicates, Al-Ajarma approaches this issue from the bottom up through the factual and imagined encounters of Moroccan citizens with this event. Considering the insertion of the Hajj into the lives of the participants, the book highlights how the perception and significance of this experience is shaped by its socio-historical context, its socio-economic and politico-administrative constraints and its gendered dimension, as well as by its central religious narrative. In her perceptive analysis, Al-Ajarma details and elucidates the agency of individuals and communities in creating a discourse and practice that are directly meaningful to their everyday life, while at the same time making them part of a global religious community and ideal.

Considering the different approaches, experiences and consequences of the pilgrimage to Mecca for a group of Moroccans, the book highlights how the *umma* and the idea of the *umma* are instantiated and diffused by the participants. The lived religion perspective adopted by Al-Ajarma enables her to bring into focus the strengths and tensions of this unique religious experience. In particular, the analysis shows how the Hajj simultaneously constitutes a mode of integration into a wider transnational and global community and a means of re-assertion of national identity. These encounters enable those individuals to articulate a stronger religious worldview, while at the same time leading them to question the political, administrative and economic management of the pilgrimage by the Saudi authorities and their own government. Importantly, Al-Ajarma also sheds light on the insertion of the Hajj into the lived religious experience of the individuals and the community over time. As storytelling, and creative visual and oral representations of this experience, are communicated in interpersonal relations, they shape the dynamics of local religious practices, including those national pilgrimages performed by individuals unable to travel to Mecca. The richness of the details analysed in the book constitutes a most welcome addition to the literature on both contemporary pilgrimages and lived religion in the Muslim world. Al-Ajarma's insights into the anthropology of Islam will undoubtedly encourage more research on the contemporary significance and evolution of these practices, which are at once unfolding within the *umma* and making a globalised Muslim world.

Professor Frédéric Volpi
Chair in the Politics of the Muslim World
The University of Edinburgh

To my beloved parents and siblings, whose unwavering
love and support have been the greatest blessing.

INTRODUCTION

Fatima, a Moroccan woman in her sixties and a mother of seven, took me to visit Fes el Bali, the old city of Fes, the day after my arrival in Morocco. Our tour started at Bab Boujloud, a blue gate that gives access to the start of *ṭalʿa kibīra*, the main souk street that crosses the *medina* (old city) and leads to the Qarawiyyin mosque at its heart. As we walked down in the *medina*, we passed street vendors and restaurants offering traditional cuisine; we encountered both locals and tourists in a mixture of traditional and modern clothes. The *medina* was vibrant with life, sounds, smells and colours. The scent of fresh herbs mixed with the odour of freshly dyed animal skins from the tanneries, accompanied by a rich soundtrack of artisans at work, with laughter and conversation between people on the street.

Fatima walked confidently through the alleys of the *medina* that appeared to me to be a maze of workshops. On our way, we stopped at several shops: at one to buy almond sweets, at another to get a mixture of green and black olives, and at a third where Fatima purchased spices. The shops were excitingly buzzing with life; Fatima seemed happily familiar with everyone and everything.

As she entered each of the shops, Fatima would start a conversation with '*al-salāmu ʿalaykum*', to which the reply was '*wa-ʿalaykum al-salām*', followed with 'Welcome, *al-ḥājja!*'.[1] In the market, in the neighbourhood, and even among relatives, friends and family members, Fatima is known as *al-ḥājja*, an honorific title which is given to a Muslim who has successfully completed the Hajj, the (major) pilgrimage to Mecca. Fatima had performed the Hajj some twenty years earlier, yet, through this title, the legacy of having completed the religious duty has accompanied her ever since, and was also reflected in her position in society, as I saw it. In turn, she herself often referred to her pilgrimage to Mecca, underscoring the personal and societal significance of the journey. She often spoke about how the pilgrimage to Mecca had helped her develop as a Muslim.

I lived in Fatima's house in Fes for several weeks at the commencement of my fieldwork in Morocco, a home that became both a refuge during fieldwork and a substitute family. Fatima would talk to me, and, at other times, to friends and family members in my presence, for hours about her memories of Mecca and her wish to visit it again. Witnessing her conversations, I saw how the pilgrimage had become part of her everyday life. Her main living room had a framed photograph of the Grand Mosque of Mecca. On the wall, two portraits dominated the view: one of Fatima's parents and the other of her in-laws. Both the two men and the two women in the portraits were dressed in *iḥrām* clothing, garments worn by Muslims during the pilgrimage to Mecca.[2] Fatima told me stories of her parents' pilgrimage, and of the tradition of having a portrait photograph taken in *iḥrām* clothing, often in a studio in Mecca or Morocco, before leaving for the Hajj.

I accompanied Fatima in several family gatherings and celebrations, where people showed her much respect. When we visited relatives coming from Mecca or when she heard of friends going on Hajj, she would react with '*sa'dāthum*' ['Lucky them!'].[3] In conversations about Mecca, Fatima or her many friends would say '*Allah lā yiḥrimna min dhāk al-maqām*' ['May God never prevent anyone from those holy places'].[4]

While Fatima and I were walking out of the *medina* that very first day of my fieldwork, we passed by two young men standing near a pottery shop. I overheard the older man say, 'When will you find a wife?' The second man replied, 'I want to get married to a good woman, and I will send her mother to Mecca for Hajj so she will know how much I value her!' A casually overheard comment, but a significant one.

From the very inception of my research in Morocco, the religious and social significance of the Hajj was underscored by seemingly minute details, encapsulated in the details of people's interactions. Through these details,

I came to appreciate the way in which Hajj permeates every level of a person's life after their pilgrimage; its long-lasting legacy for the individual; and the myriad ways in which it infuses people's interactions, social structures, community values and everyday life in Morocco, the topic of my study.[5]

This ethnographic study examines the socio-cultural embeddedness of the Hajj, the annual pilgrimage to Mecca, in present-day Moroccan society.[6] It approaches the Hajj as both a sacred religious rite and a human and logistical feat that plays a vital role for Muslims in crafting their religious selves. Approaching pilgrimage from the perspective of its role in a lived religion, this book examines the overarching questions: how does the Hajj pilgrimage feature in the everyday lives of Moroccans?; and how are Moroccan views of Hajj reflected in the micro-practices of pilgrims and their wider networks?

To address these questions, I will address three key sub-themes. Firstly, I will explore the connection between the desire to undertake the Hajj pilgrimage, the transformative experience of performing Hajj, and the role of becoming a pilgrim (*ḥājj* or *ḥājja*) in the process of self-fashioning within the context of everyday life. Secondly, I will examine the significance and meanings Moroccans ascribe to the pilgrimage, considering how these meanings are shaped by various forms of identity politics and intricate webs of power relations that encompass various categories of pilgrims and non-pilgrims. Lastly, I will investigate the integration of the Meccan pilgrimage into the social practices and cultural fabric of everyday life in Morocco, illuminating its broader influence on the society and the many ways it finds expression in everyday customs, rituals and artistic expressions. By addressing these sub-themes, we can gain a comprehensive understanding of the multifaceted roles and impacts of the Meccan pilgrimage in the lives of Moroccans and its implications for self-identity and broader societal dynamics.

Following Chapter One, in which I briefly outline the theoretical debates and methodological insights guiding this study, the first part of the book consists of three empirical chapters. The first part focuses on the everyday lives of pilgrims, before, during and after they perform the pilgrimage. I begin by exploring the experiences of pilgrims before they embark on the journey to Mecca, scrutinising the bureaucracy involved in the application, as well as considering both the religious and the logistical preparations necessary for the performance of the Hajj. I then discuss the narratives of pilgrims concerning their actual experience of the Hajj, viewed through the lens of the Hajj as a 'sensational form', and reflect on the Hajj as an emotional experience. In the chapter that follows, I look at the everyday lives of pilgrims once they return from Mecca, and consider how their everyday experiences and self-fashioning are inextricably intertwined with their new honorific title *al-ḥājj* (for male pilgrims) or *al-ḥājja* (for female pilgrims).

The second part of the book opens with a chapter discussing the significance of the Hajj for Moroccans, both within the wider political domain of the Moroccan government and within the individual sphere, exploring how Moroccans express their sense of national belonging. The subsequent chapter examines another political dimension by zooming in on how Saudi politics affects the organisation of the Hajj. I sketch in it how Moroccans, as pilgrims who experience the new regulations and politically influenced changes in Mecca, reflect on the power exercised over them. The third chapter of the second part looks specifically at women, whose Hajj experiences in some respects differ from those of their male counterparts because of their gender.

For the third and final part of this book, I shift the focus from pilgrims to wider situations in Moroccan society where references to the pilgrimage or to Mecca are made in the context of everyday social and cultural practices. The first practice is a local pilgrimage known in Morocco as the 'Pilgrimage of the Poor', a local pilgrimage rooted in religious observation. I then look at songs and stories related to the Hajj that feature both on special occasions and in everyday situations.

In the subsequent chapters, I engage in an analysis of my own observations and the narratives of my research participants regarding their pilgrimage experiences, focusing on unravelling the diverse expressions of the Muslim tradition as it finds articulation and enactment within the context of Morocco. This examination illustrates how the Islamic tradition in Morocco is adapted and influenced by local historical and cultural inheritances. The purpose of this book is to provide a comprehensive illustration of how this diversity manifests in the context of Moroccan pilgrimage practices. My hope is that it may contribute to the expanding body of academic literature that reveals the diversity and nuance of Islam as a religious tradition. This will be further illustrated in Chapter One, which situates this work in relation to the existing literature on the topic and focuses on the centrality of the Hajj in Muslims' everyday lives.

Notes

1. *Al-salāmu ʿalaykum* is a greeting in Arabic that means 'Peace be upon you'. The typical response to the greeting is *wa-ʿalaykum al-salām*, meaning 'And peace be upon you too'. The complete greeting in Islam is *al-salāmu ʿalaykum wa-raḥmatu Allāhi wa-barakātuhū*, meaning 'Peace be upon you, as well as the mercy of God and His blessings' (Arendonk and Gimaret 2012).
2. *Iḥrām* clothing includes men's and women's garments worn by Muslims while performing the rites of pilgrimage, during either the major pilgrimage (Hajj) or the minor pilgrimage (*ʿumra*) (Peters 2007).
3. *Saʿdāthum* (sing. *saʿdātik*) is an expression often used by Moroccans to mean 'Good for you' or 'How lucky you are'. It conveys happiness, compliments, and sometimes envy.
4. *Allah lā yiḥrimna min dhāk al-maqām* ('May God never prevent anyone from going to that holy place') is a common expression shared among pilgrims. For further discussion on religious formulas in everyday Arabic language, see, among others, Migdadi, Badarneh and Momani (2010); Farghal (1995); Gregory and Wehbe (1986).
5. Fieldnotes, 2 August 2015. All the grey-shaded vignettes in the book are based on the author's fieldnotes.
6. Given that Morocco's Muslim community is predominantly Sunni, the author assumes that it is Sunni perspectives which are centred and foregrounded in this study.

Notes

1

THEORETICAL FRAMEWORK AND METHODOLOGY

Introduction

This chapter is divided into four parts. The first includes a description of the rites of the Muslim pilgrimage and their significance. This is followed by a brief history of the pilgrimage from Morocco to Mecca. Then, I provide an overview of the anthropological framework of pilgrimage, including some anthropological contributions to the study of Hajj in particular. Finally, I provide a methodological reflection on the 'story' of this research and my own position as a participant observer.

The Rites of Hajj

The Hajj is one of the Five Pillars of Islam, and a duty which Muslims must perform – once in a lifetime – if they are physically and financially able.[1] The Hajj takes place during a five-day period from the eighth to the thirteenth of Dhū l-Ḥijja, the last month of the Islamic lunar calendar, at the city of Mecca (and its surroundings) in Saudi Arabia. During the days of Hajj, pilgrims perform a series of symbolic, religious and emotional rites, following in the footsteps of the prophets Abraham and Muhammad (Bowen 2012).[2]

The first of the Hajj rites is entering *iḥrām*, or the state of consecration, which takes place when pilgrims approach the surroundings of Mecca at the *mīqāt*, one of five official locations that mark the boundaries of the sacred area around Mecca.[3] Here, pilgrims perform a ritual ablution. Then, men dress in two seamless white sheets that are wrapped around the waist and the left shoulder and women are free to dress in any manner they find proper, if they cover their whole body apart from their hands and faces.[4] The uniformity and simplicity of the *iḥrām* symbolise the humility and equality of all believers before God, regardless of worldly differences in race, nationality, class, age, gender or culture (Bianchi 2013, 25). Entering *iḥrām* also symbolises detachment from everyday material life and entrance into the sacred time and space of the pilgrimage (Haq and Jackson 2009; Cooke and Lawrence 2005). The *iḥrām* at the *mīqāt* locations also includes announcing the *niyya* (intention) to perform the Hajj, the *ʿumra*, which is a lesser optional pilgrimage, or both. The *niyya* often involves performing two *rakʿa* of *salāt* (ritual prayers).[5] Upon completing their *iḥrām*, pilgrims proceed to Mecca while reciting the *talbiya*:

Here I am at Your service, O Lord,	*Labbayka Allāhumma*
here I am;	*labbayk;*
Here I am; You have no partners,	*Labbayka lā sharīka laka;*
Yours alone is all praise,	*Inna al-ḥamda,*
and all bounty;	*Wa al-niʿmata;*
Yours alone is the sovereignty;	*Laka wa-l-mulk;*
You have no partners.	*Lā sharīka lak.*

In addition to *talbiya*, pilgrims can also perform unprescribed *duʿāʾ*, supplication prayers.

From the moment pilgrims complete their *iḥrām*, they should refrain from lewdness, abuse or hostile argument (Peters 1994). Indeed, Muslims should not commit any of these offences at any time, but they are even more sinful during Hajj. Pilgrims must also refrain from any form of sexual activity and from contracting marriage, and they must not use perfume, no animal may be hunted or killed, and they must not cut their hair or clip their nails until the pilgrimage rites are over and pilgrims can then remove their *iḥrām* (Abdel Haleem 2012, 1). When pilgrims reach the Kaʿba, the cubic building in the centre of the courtyard of the Grand Mosque of Mecca, they raise their hands, ask God for His grace and then start performing the first *ṭawāf*, known as *ṭawāf al-qudūm*, a sevenfold anti-clockwise circumambulation around the Kaʿba.[6] The *ṭawāf* starts from the black stone, which pilgrims should touch,

Figure 1.1 Pilgrims performing *ṭawāf* around the Kaʿba (Mecca, 4 February 2018)

if possible, otherwise they should point towards it every time they pass it.[7] As the Kaʿba is often called an earthly counterpart of God's throne in Heaven or *Bayt Allāh al-Ḥarām* (House of God), the *ṭawāf* is seen by most Muslims as a human imitation of angels' circulation of the throne in worship (Bianchi 2013, 25).

After *ṭawāf*, pilgrims proceed to the Place of Abraham or *maqām Ibrāhīm*, a glass-covered stone that is said to contain the footprints of the prophet, where pilgrims perform two *rakʿa* of *ṣalāt* prayers. They are then recommended to drink from the water of Zamzam and proceed to perform the next rite of *saʿī*, which includes walking and running between two hillocks, Ṣafā and Marwā (Matthews and Matthews 1996).[8] The *saʿī* between the two hillocks commemorates the search for water by Abraham's second wife, Hagar, for her baby son Ishmael (Tagliacozzo and Toorawa 2015, 32–4). When Abraham, on God's command, left the mother and infant alone in the desert, Hagar anxiously searched for water for her thirsty son and discovered the sacred water of Zamzam, the water from which pilgrims continue to drink during the pilgrimage and which they carry home to share with their dear ones upon return (Tagliacozzo and Toorawa 2015, 34; Katz 2004; Peters 1994). By running or walking seven times between the hillocks of Ṣafā and Marwā, pilgrims commemorate Hagar's ordeal and her trust in God to save her baby and herself (Peters 1994).[9] When performed outside the season of Hajj, the rites of *ṭawāf* and *sa'ī* are considered as *'umra*, the Muslim voluntary pilgrimage which can be undertaken at any time of the year.[10]

On the eighth of Dhū l-Ḥijja, the first night of the Hajj proper, pilgrims travel to the tent camps of Minā, some eight kilometres from Mecca, where they spend the night (Matthews and Matthews 1996). Following their night in Minā, pilgrims travel a distance of 14.4 km the next morning (known as *Yawm 'Arafat* or the Day of Arafat) to Mount Arafat and its plain, where the most important rite of the Hajj takes place: *wuqūf* (the standing [before God]). Without this rite, the Hajj is considered void and unacceptable (Sardar 2014).[11] On the plain of Arafat pilgrims perform the *ẓuhur* and *'aṣr* prayers together at midday at Masjid Namira and continue with individual and group *du'ā'* supplication prayers from the afternoon until sunset.[12] In these prayers, they ask God to forgive their sins and accept their pilgrimage. They also read from the Qur'an and make *du'ā'* prayers for family, friends and humanity at large.

In Arafat, some pilgrims stay in the shade of tents sheltered from the midday sun while others scale the sides of the Mount of Mercy.[13] During the *wuqūf* hours, pilgrims commemorate a similar gathering that took place when the prophet Muhammad performed the 'Farewell Pilgrimage' and delivered his last sermon during his own Hajj in 632 CE (Zadeh 2015). The gathering at Arafat is seen as an assembly which is also a symbolic reminder of Judgement Day (Mols and Buitelaar 2015, 4).

At sunset, all pilgrims hasten out of the valley (this departure is sometimes called *nafra*), and inch their way through the narrow mountain pass of Muzdalifa. In Muzdalifa, the pilgrims spend the night praying in the open under the desert sky. Here, pilgrims also collect pebbles that are 'ammunition' for the following day when they perform the next rite of Hajj: *rajm* (stoning [the Devil]) (Maqsood 2008). The rite of *rajm* or *ramī* starts at sunrise on the tenth day of Dhū l-Ḥijja taking place at the *jamarāt*, which constitute three walls (formerly pillars) symbolising the Devil. This rite commemorates Abraham's chasing away the Devil when the latter tried to persuade him to disobey God

Figure 1.2 Mount Arafat during Hajj, as documented by one of the research participants (Mecca, 20 August 2018)

and refrain from offering his son Ishmael (Matthews and Matthews 1996).[14] Pilgrims hurl seven pebbles, one by one, at the largest of these pillars, representing the Devil. After the stoning, each pilgrim offers an animal sacrifice commemorating the sacrifice that God ultimately accepted from Abraham in place of his son.[15] Simultaneously with the pilgrims who perform the Hajj near Mecca, Muslims around the world celebrate *ʿīd al-aḍḥā* or *ʿīd l-kbīr* as it is often called in Morocco (the Feast of Sacrifice), making their own sacrifices of sheep, goats, cattle or camels (Al-Sawydani, Badarinath and Douglas 1995).[16]

Following the first stoning of the Devil, men have their hair and beards shaved off (*ḥalq*) or shortened (*taqṣīr*) and women cut off a lock of their hair (Hammoudi 2006). This rite concludes the Hajj proper. Pilgrims may then take off their *iḥrām* clothing if they wish to do so and return to Mecca, where they perform another *ṭawāf* known as *ṭawāf al-ifāḍa*, which includes seven anti-clockwise circumambulations around the Kaʿba. Then, they must return to Minā to spend two more nights. Many pilgrims, however, for practical reasons of transport and time, stay in Minā for two more days, during which they repeat the rite of stoning and then return to Mecca, whilst others choose to stay in the comfort of the Mecca hotels and commute to Minā for the two days. Before leaving Mecca, pilgrims are advised to visit the Ka'ba one last time and perform a farewell *ṭawāf*: *ṭawāf al-wadāʿ*.

In addition to the mandatory rites of Hajj, many pilgrims pay a visit to Medina for a few days either before or after their pilgrimage. Some 240 km north of Mecca, Medina was the city where the prophet Muhammad lived for ten years, where the first Muslim community was established and where the prophet is buried. While Mecca is imagined as the religious centre for Muslims, Medina is considered the second holiest city in Islam and occupies a significant role in the social and religious imagination of Muslims (Kenny 2007). In Medina pilgrims visit the Mosque of the prophet Muhammad, where they can visit his grave along with the graves of his companions and successors Abu Bakr and Omar. For many people, the visit to the Prophet's tomb is a highly emotional aspect of the pilgrimage experience, although not a rite of the Hajj itself. While the rites of the Hajj take place on five specific days each year, pilgrims often spend three to four weeks in Mecca and Medina where, in addition to the performance of pilgrimage, they engage in visiting the sites where the Prophet and his companions once lived.

Strictly defined, the Hajj is required once in a lifetime for adult Muslims who are physically and financially able (Bianchi 2004; Aziz 2001; Robinson 1999; Peters 1994; Murata and Chittick 1994). However, the significance of the Hajj, and the impact of its rites, live on, and assume significant importance in the lives of pilgrims and in their wider life-worlds, which can be seen in numerous accounts of pilgrims (Bianchi 2004; Wolfe 1997; Peters 1994; Scupin 1982). The Hajj, then, is not only an individual religious undertaking of devotion for Muslims but is also a global annual event that embraces political, social, economic and intellectual aspects (Ryad 2017). In addition, the Hajj itself often represents the culmination of years of spiritual preparation and planning (Gatrad and Sheikh 2005, 133). As if to mark its personal and social significance, once they have completed the pilgrimage, pilgrims are given the honorific title *al-ḥājj* for males, or *al-ḥājja* for females, and the legacy of Hajj manifests itself in their everyday lives.[17]

A Brief History of the Pilgrimage to Mecca from Morocco

As the Muslim pilgrimage to Mecca and Medina is considered the most important travel event for Muslims on both communal and personal levels (Sardar

2014; Sijapati 2020; Bianchi 2004), Moroccan history of the Hajj is as old as Islam in the region. Ever since its arrival in what is now Morocco, Islam has been an important aspect of people's culture and identity (Sadiqi 2018).[18] Probably the earliest Muslims from Morocco made the journey to Mecca on foot, or mounted on a horse or a camel (Murata and Chittick 1994, 41). The first documented African pilgrimages to Mecca, however, were from Cairo during the era of the Fatimid dynasties (909–1171) (Ochsenwald 1980). These early Muslims, travelling in camel caravans across the Sinai Peninsula to the Hijaz region of Arabia where Mecca is located, established a route that was used continuously until the twentieth century (ibid.). The Moroccan historian Muhammad Al-Manuni (1953) mentions that the history of the Moroccan journeying to Mecca (*rakb al-ḥājj* or *rakb*) dates back to the middle of the times of the Almohads, the Moroccan Amazigh Muslim empire founded in the twelfth century.

By the thirteenth century, pilgrim routes across North Africa from as far west as Morocco linked up with the Cairo caravan to Mecca (Sardi 2013, 169–74). Pilgrims from Morocco either travelled in small groups or, ideally, accompanied the great Hajj caravan which carried merchants and pilgrims every year from Morocco to Cairo (Al-Manuni 1953). Composed of pilgrims, merchants and guards, the great caravan often had a thousand or more camels (El Moudden 1990). Covering perhaps twenty miles a day and visiting the famous Islamic mosques of Tlemcen (Algeria) and Kairouan (Tunisia), before reaching Egypt, the journey to Mecca in its essence entailed moving with ease beyond borders that today exist between North African countries. In the thirteenth century, few West African pilgrims completed the pilgrimage in less than two years, and the average time was eight years (Birks 1977, 47; Al-Manuni 1953).

Several Moroccan scholars and travellers documented their journey to the Hijaz, including their accounts, news and the performance of the Hajj, like Ibn Qunfud al-Qusnaṭīnī and Muhammad al-ʿAbdarī (Al-ʿAbdarī 1999; El Mouadden 1990).[19] Al-ʿAbdarī, for example, started his journey from the Haha tribe (near Saoira) on the 25th of Dhū l-Qiʿda 688/1289. He travelled from the west to the east of Morocco to Talmisan. Talmisan was a central location for Moroccan travel, where pilgrims gathered to start their journey. Al-ʿAbdarī estimated that around one thousand pilgrims departed on the same journey to Mecca (Al-ʿAbdarī 1999). The journey meandered from Morocco through Algeria and Tunisia, Qairawan and Trablus to Alexandria and Cairo before reaching the Hijaz (ibid.). In the fourteenth century, Ibn Battuta travelled from Morocco to the Hijaz with the main purpose of carrying out the Hajj in the holy places of Mecca and Medina. He arrived in Mecca in 1326, a year and four months after leaving home, and was able to complete his pilgrimage (Al-Manuni 1953). His *Rihla* documents the extensive travels and adventures across the Muslim world and beyond, providing insights into the diverse cultures, customs and societies he encountered during his travels (Tolmacheva 1993; Waines 2015). It provides valuable information, spanning regions such as North Africa, the Middle East, Central Asia, the Indian subcontinent, Southeast Asia and even parts of Europe (Waines 2015).

The journey to Mecca, by either land or sea routes, involved months of hardships and dangers, including sea – or sand – storms, pirates and bandits as well as diseases and other dangers to health (Murata and Chittick 1994, 21; Sijapati 2020, 37–8). Despite these difficulties, more pilgrims continued to join the journey to Mecca, especially during the fifteenth and sixteenth centuries, through trans-Saharan caravans travelling from Morocco to Egypt. From the sixteenth century onwards, the volume of pilgrims increased as the Ottomans fortified the route of the Egyptian caravan (Shair and Karan 1979, 600). By the seventeenth century, travellers often reached Egypt after a voyage on a French ship or by travelling with a caravan which traversed North Africa from west to east, and they then would join the annual pilgrimage caravan from Cairo (Faroqi 1994, 142). However, frequent Bedouin attacks on pilgrim caravans and political instability arising from the involvement of the Ottomans in regional conflicts resulted in a declining trend in the number of pilgrims in the nineteenth century (Shair and Karan 1979, 599–60).

Beginning in the nineteenth century, Moroccan pilgrims began traveling via a sea route through the southern Mediterranean to Alexandria on their way to Mecca (Kateman 2023). By the early 1900s railways were transporting thousands of affluent pilgrims, while the less affluent simply walked along the tracks (Ochsenwald 1984, 1980).[20] In the 1950s, Moroccans started travelling by air. However, land routes continued to be popular. On the one hand, this was due to poverty; on the other, it was due to the desire of pilgrims to visit the famous places of Islam in North Africa. Later, closed borders, conflicts and other post-colonial factors limited over-land travel.

The long historical tradition of travel to Mecca in Morocco shows little sign of abating. In 2019, the population of Morocco was estimated at 36.66 million, of whom 99 per cent are Sunni Muslims.[21] On average, some 32,000 Moroccans perform the Hajj every year, in addition to those who visit Mecca for *ʿumra* outside the season of Hajj.[22] Especially since the conditions of the pilgrimage, such as the means of transportation, have evolved over the years, allowing a greater number of Moroccans to travel to Mecca, the pilgrimage continues to be extremely popular among Moroccans, and many still describe it as a 'dream-wish' today. It remains true, however, that for most Muslims, including many Muslims in Morocco, the Hajj is beyond reach because of their gender (see Chapter Seven), their financial situation, health issues, or the imposed quota system that allows only a small number of applicants to be issued with a Hajj visa (Bianchi 2004, 11).

Many Moroccans try to substitute for the Hajj by performing the lesser pilgrimage, the *ʿumra*. According to a local official, during the years 2015 to 2019, an average of 140,000 Moroccans visited Mecca every year for *ʿumra*.[23] Throughout Morocco, as for Muslims in general, Hajj holds a prominent place in everyday life and popular culture (Boissevain 2012, 21–30; Haq and Jackson 2009), and this will be the theme of the remaining chapters of this book.

Theoretical Framework

Pilgrimage, in Islam (and in other religions), is often discussed in terms of a central aspect of religion that includes both beliefs and practices (Rahimi and Eshaghi 2019). In personal accounts of the Meccan pilgrimage, Moroccans speak about how they see themselves as Muslims, a matter which plays a key role in their self-narratives and becomes an indicator of who they are (Buitelaar and Zock 2013). Thus, the pilgrimage as a practice is not limited to a number of rites that pilgrims engage in when they visit Mecca, but is also related to how people bring to it their understanding of pilgrimage, framing the ways in which they engage with other religious, social and cultural practices. Therefore, it is important to situate this book in the larger framework regarding the study of both pilgrimage and Islam from an anthropological perspective.

The Anthropology of Pilgrimage

Émile Durkheim's 1912 classic, *The Elementary Forms of the Religious Life*, provides a starting point for looking at 'the sacred' and at pilgrimage from a social-scientific point of view. Durkheim characterises religious festivals in small-scale, aboriginal societies as unifying, morally re-energising institutional moments. The transition that pilgrims experience is what makes pilgrimage a '*rite of passage*', a term coined by Arnold van Gennep (Gennep et al. 1977; Gennep 1960). According to Gennep, 'rites of passage' mark life stages or seasonal transitions and are characterised by three phases: a separation or detachment from the ordinary, leading to an ambiguous 'outsider' status; a 'between' phase of ambiguity or 'liminality' which is finally resolved into a new stability (aggregation); and the resumption of ordinary life. These three stages of separation, transition and incorporation can be recognised in the activities that pilgrims undertake preceding, during and after the Hajj. The experience of Moroccan pilgrims fits neatly into this overview of the whole experience: before leaving for Mecca, pilgrims engage in settling their debts, asking forgiveness from family and friends and collecting requests for special prayers (Murata and Chittick 1994, 41). These and other such activities can be seen as part of the first, separation stage.[24] The transition to the liminal phase arguably starts as soon as pilgrims embark on their journey. Entering the state of *iḥrām* marks another important transition that continues until pilgrims conclude the rites of Hajj, after which they enter the incorporation phase (Gennep 1960, 185). The incorporation phase is often concluded when pilgrims return home as new pilgrims (*ḥujjāj*).

The work of Gennep on rites of passage was taken up by Victor Turner, who developed, in the late 1960s, a theoretical model of pilgrimage. In his work, Turner recognises pilgrimage as a movement from familiar structure and the everyday to highly ritualised life, characterised by 'anti-structure' or the absence of structure (King 2023). Through the journey to a distant place, the pilgrim is separated from the rule-governed structures of mundane social life, becoming both geographically and socially marginal. Travelling away from one's home on pilgrimage offers an opportunity to shed one's conventional roles. As pilgrims distance themselves from the structure of normal, everyday life, they simultaneously move away from established hierarchies into a 'liminal' status, freed from the normal bonds of structure (Kapferer 2019, 1–2; Wegley 2006). In *Image and Pilgrimage in Christian Culture* (1978), Victor Turner and Edith Turner argue that liminality produces a sensation of unity, *communitas* and anti-structure as integral features of pilgrimage. The concept *communitas* is used to refer to 'a relational quality of full unmediated communication, even communion' with other individuals, 'which combines the qualities of lowliness, sacredness, homogeneity, and comradeship' (Turner and Turner 1978, 250).

The rites of Hajj contain many elements that can be recognised as attributes of liminality, such as pilgrims bidding farewell to their beloved ones; entering the state of *iḥrām*, during which they refrain from clipping nails or cutting hair and breaking away from routines of daily life in order to dedicate oneself fully to worshiping God. Hajj rites also contain many elements that can be recognised as generating *communitas*. What is experienced by Hajj pilgrims can be referred to as a unity of the global imagined *umma*, the community of believers (Makris 2007, 137; Malcolm X 1965).[25] Further, many scholars focus on the unity and cohesion of the Hajj (Clingingsmith et al. 2009; Haq and Jackson 2009; McLoughlin 2009; Coleman and Elsner 1995). For example, in the study carried out by Clingingsmith et al. (2009) among Pakistani pilgrims, the findings show that attending the Hajj leads to feelings of unity, equality and harmony with fellow Muslims, as well as more favourable attitudes towards women. The study also reflects increased belief in peace and harmony with adherents of different religions. In line with aspects of this theoretical framework, in Chapter Three I offer examples of Moroccan pilgrims' own narratives about their Meccan experiences in which some aspects of *communitas* can be recognised.

Turner's model had a significant impact on the anthropological study of pilgrimage and remained dominant throughout much of the 1970s and 1980s, focusing on the shared sense of community associated with pilgrimage (Mols and Buitelaar 2015). Many studies, however, critiqued the Turnerian approach for being too totalising in its depiction of pilgrimage rather than taking into account the variety of pilgrimage experiences and the range of motivations for performing a pilgrimage (Dubisch 1995; Eade and Sallnow 1991; Eickelman and Piscatori 1990; Crumrine and Morinis 1991; Sallnow 1981; Werbner 1989). For example, Michael Sallnow, studying group pilgrimage among Quechua Indians in the Andes, finds that pilgrims do not encounter one another in the manner described by Turner and might rather be characterised by nepotism, factionalism, endemic competition and inner-community conflict (Sallnow 1987, 1981). In their edited volume *Contesting the Sacred* (1991), Eade and Sallnow challenge the *communitas* paradigm by arguing that the empirical study of pilgrimages shows a marked presence of competing discourses on all levels and phases of pilgrimage. Thus, *communitas* cannot be assumed to exist in all pilgrimages. Eade and Sallnow further argue that social boundaries are not annihilated but reinforced throughout the pilgrimage experience (Eade and Sallnow 1991; Sallnow 1991, 1981). They argue that if an essential, universalistic character of a pilgrimage site had to be identified, it would have to be the capacity of pilgrimage to absorb and reflect a multiplicity of religious discourses. Therefore, they suggest an alternative theory of pilgrimage as a realm of competing discourses which should be analysed in specific social settings according to specific historic and cultural meanings.

Studies on the Hajj rarely examined aspects of contestation. An important exception is Robert Bianchi's 2004 work that focuses on the politics of the Hajj in different Muslim-majority states. Moroccan scholar Abdellah Hammoudi, in his book *A Season in Mecca: Narrative of a Pilgrimage* (2006), details many moments of tension that occurred during his pilgrimage experience in 1999. Hammoudi acknowledges that his pilgrimage was radically different from those historically carried out by earlier pilgrims. While narratives of those earlier trips focus on the hardships and difficulties of the road, these are somewhat different challenges from the difficulties faced by pilgrims today (most of whom stay in hotels). Nevertheless, the author makes a case for continuity of experience, both in relation to the physical challenge of the journey, albeit modified because of the passage of time, and to the transformation he experienced during the pilgrimage. Other examples of competing discourses can be seen in studies focusing on local pilgrimages (*ziyāra*) to a *zāwiya* or a lodge of a saint or local shrine (Flaskerud and Natvig 2018; Tapper 1990; Fox 1989). I shall reflect on the findings of these studies as I analyse the findings of my research among Moroccan pilgrims.

Simon Coleman (2002) also discusses the issue of the contrast between the theory of *communitas* and contestation paradigms. Coleman (and others) sought to move the field of pilgrimage studies beyond the binary opposition between *communitas* and contestation, pointing out the potential for useful insights from both approaches. *Communitas* failed to consider the mundane conflicts inherent in pilgrimage and the fact that pilgrimage as an institution cannot actually be fully understood as a universal or homogeneous phenomenon but should be deconstructed into historically and culturally specific instances, which encompass the person, place and story. In the Introduction to their edited volume *Reframing Pilgrimage: Cultures in Motion*, Coleman and Eade argue for an approach that considers both the behavioural patterns that may be observed in pilgrimage and the embeddedness of pilgrimage in the everyday social world of pilgrims (Coleman and Eade 2004).

Within the Muslim pilgrimage experiences, several studies have examined the pilgrimage of Muslims in the West, especially in relation to diaspora communities. Examples include the work of Seán McLoughlin (2013, 2010, 2009) on the pilgrimage of Pakistani Muslims in Great Britain and the research of Farooq Haq and John Jackson on the Hajj experiences of Pakistani and Pakistani-Australian pilgrims (Haq and Jackson 2009), as well as Carol Delaney's study on the pilgrimage of Turkish migrants in Germany (1990). Several collective volumes also exist on the Muslim pilgrimage, including the edited volume of Luitgard Mols and Marjo Buitelaar (2015), which includes several case studies on the Hajj, the more recent volume *Muslim Pilgrimage in the Modern World* edited by Babak Rahimi and Peyman Eshaghi (2019), the volume *Muslim Women's Pilgrimage to Mecca and Beyond: Reconfiguring Gender, Religion and Mobility* edited by Marjo Buitelaar, Manja Stephan-Emmrich and Viola Thimm, Francis Edward Peters' *The Hajj* (2021), and the most recent volume, *Narrating the Pilgrimage to Mecca: Historical and Contemporary Accounts* (2023) edited by Marjo Buitelaar and Richard van Leeuwen. There is also a range of academic studies that look at pilgrimage through various lenses, for instance in relation to tourism (Jamal et al. 2018; Timothy and Olsen 2006) and historical encounters (Ryad 2016), as well as pilgrimage and globalisation (Quinn and Keely 2018; Hyndman-Rizk 2012; McIntosh, Reader 2007; Bianchi 2004).

Out of all the complex theoretical analyses existing in the scholarly literature, one can conclude a simple truism that the Hajj is both an individual and a social experience, historical and contemporary, religious and mundane, and includes aspects of both *communitas* and contestation. In the words of Barbara Metcalf:

> By undertaking the Hajj, the pilgrim in principle affirms his individual responsibility for obedience to God and claims his place among the community of faithful people. (1990, 100)

In summary, there has been a shift in the study of pilgrimage over time from ideas of *communitas* to those of conflict and contestation, and, more recently, towards looking at the experience from the perspective of its embeddedness in everyday life. It is also important to situate this study within the broader framework of the anthropology of Islam, since it takes an anthropological/ethnographic approach when looking at the lives of pilgrims and the socio-cultural dimensions of the everyday lives of Muslims.

Islam as a Lived Religion

This work falls within the broader scholarship of the 'anthropology of Islam' (as opposed to being strictly a study of the Hajj, or an anthropology of pilgrimage). An obvious starting point in the study of the anthropology of Islam is the work of Talal Asad as represented by his article 'The Idea of an Anthropology of Islam' (Asad 1986). Asad argues that studies should take Muslims seriously on their own terms, and calls for anthropologists to examine Islam as 'a discursive tradition that connects variously with the notion of moral selves, the manipulation of populations (or resistance to it), and the production of appropriate knowledges' (ibid., 7). He argues that Islam 'is neither a distinctive social structure nor a heterogeneous collection of beliefs, artefacts, customs, and morals. It is a tradition' (1986, 14). This article, together with Asad's wider body of work (Asad 2003, 1993, 1986), has been influential for many anthropologists who have taken up his enquiries about religion and the mundane, as well as studies of morality, piety and Muslim practices of everyday religiosity (Schielke 2010).

Employing Asad's framework, which views practices of (self-) discipline as a defining aspect of the formation of religious subjects (Asad 1993), scholars such as Saba Mahmood (2005), Charles Hirschkind (2006), Lara Deeb (2006) and Humeira Iqtidar (2011) have foregrounded pious practices and Islamic revivalist organisations and lifestyles as a locus of agency. Mahmood (2005) and Hirschkind (2001, 2006), for example, with different emphases, take Asad's work further and argue for an anthropology of morality that focuses on the ways in which moral personhood and responsibility are created and practised. Mahmood, in her study *Politics of Piety* (2005), highlights the micro-social ethical practices of women in the Egyptian piety movement. Hirschkind follows a similar line of reasoning in his work on cassette-tape sermons in Cairo. Cassette ethics, Hirschkind argues, are conceived as part of the moral reform of society, of creating Islamic ethical sensibilities and dispositions in open competition with profane ideals and practices (Hirschkind 2006).

The focus on the cultivation of religious virtues and dispositions of ethics and piety by Mahmood and Hirschkind has been inspirational for many anthropologists (with acknowledgement of the heterogeneity of approaches in each one of these) who focus on the cultivation of piety through the study of deliberate and habituated acts of ethical self-formation. However, later researchers have critiqued the way the project of moral reform and the prioritising of piety excludes the plurality of ethical registers with which religious actors engage (Deeb 2011; Schielke 2010). Instead, scholars such as Magnus Marsden (2005) and Samuli Schielke (2015, 2010) have highlighted the ambivalent and unpredictable ways in which ordinary Muslims navigate between religious considerations on the one hand, and non-religious concerns, aspirations and passions on the other. In Schielke's words, there is 'too much Islam in the anthropology of Islam' (2010, 2). The risk Schielke identifies is that of essentialism, presenting a single aspect of the life of a Muslim, those pious moments, as standing for the whole. For most people, Schielke argues, moral subjectivities are characterised more by ambiguity and a diversity of referential frames than by a neat coherence. Anthropologists like Deeb and Schielke call for attention to be paid to the 'everyday' lives and experience of people who happen to be Muslim, so as to recognise the 'humanity of people on their own terms', to develop a 'grounded and nuanced understanding of what it means to live a life' (Schielke 2010, 5). This move has resulted in an approach that privileges the study of everyday Islam.

A point of departure for the study of everyday life – in general – might be Michel de Certeau's *The Practice of Everyday Life* (1988), which examines life as it is lived and daily exchanges as a rich source of meaning for scholarly analysis. In this text, de Certeau turns his attention to what he sees as the creative poetics of the 'common man' in his patterns of interactions; he offers a micro-analysis of the daily enactments and renegotiations which people undertake. De Certeau's account of the everyday thereby foregrounds creativity and resistance while simultaneously inscribing them within, rather than dislocating them from, existing norms and values.

Other scholars have reflected and magnified this approach to the idea of 'lived religion' by focusing on what people do and say in a specific context and how they experience, express and shape their religion in everyday contexts (McGuire 2008, 12; cf. Schielke and Debevec 2012; Dessing et al. 2013; Ammerman 2007; Hall 1997). Nancy Ammerman, for example, argues that 'understanding religion will require attention both to the "micro" world of everyday interaction, and the "macro" world of large social structures' (Ammerman 2007, 234). Meredith McGuire follows a similar argument in *Lived Religion: Faith and Practice in Everyday Life*, in which she focuses on religion practised, experienced and expressed by ordinary people (McGuire 2008, 12).

Assuming that individuals continuously engage in making and remaking religion by undertaking religious activities, the religious lives of people are co-constituted by various, sometimes competing, priorities and experiences involving all dimensions of life (Ammerman 2007). People's actual everyday experiences reflect their personal understanding and daily negotiation of their religion (McGuire 2008; cf. Toguslu 2015; Mines and Lamb 2010; Ammerman 2007; Orsi 2003; Hall 1997). This makes everyday life a key tool in the study of religion (Toguslu 2015). For this research, lived religion is explored through participant observation, by following pilgrims mainly through the public and private domains which make up people's everyday realms of existence. To address the subject of pilgrimage with reference to religion in the everyday life in Morocco, and to contribute to our understanding of lived religious processes in a Muslim context, I focus on how the pilgrimage to Mecca is embedded in the specificities of social and cultural practices, as well as the everyday lives of Moroccans.

Relevant to the chosen focus of my research, the most influential proponent of the turn to everyday Islam as a crucial site for enquiry might, arguably, be Samuli Schielke, starting with his article 'Being Good in Ramadan' (2009). In this article Schielke examines the experiences and daily practices of 'ordinary Muslims' in a northern Egyptian fishing village during the month of Ramadan. This work of Schielke has been often cited by other scholars as an analytical touchstone (Debevec 2012; Khan 2006).[26] In another article, 'Second Thoughts about the Anthropology of Islam, or How to Make Sense of Grand Schemes in Everyday Life', Schielke argues for taking into consideration the complexities and ambiguities of everyday life that are informed by various cultural discourses simultaneously (Schielke 2010). Schielke argues that although people may habitually live in ways that conform to moral rules and religious conventions, it is also important to leave room for the ambiguities, contradictions, ambivalences and tensions between religion and daily life (ibid.). Indeed, the religious realm cannot be separated from other everyday practices, but rather reveals the 'plural, complex, and essentially unsystematic nature of religion' (Schielke and Debevec 2012, 3).[27]

I agree with Schielke's critique, but want to add that the paradigm of self-cultivation erases from our view not only various non-religious sensibilities, but also other modes of religiosity. Whereas Schielke seems to be of the view that there was 'too much Islam' in the anthropology of Islam (ibid. 2010, 2), I would add that there too little attention is paid to the fact that there are varied and simultaneously coexisting modes of the articulation of Islam. Some of these are geographically mediated or shaped by wider cultural discourse, whilst others vary from one individual subject to another. I want to suggest that self-identifying as a Muslim is significant in the context of the moral reasoning, whether through the directed work of ethical self-formation that a number of anthropologists have productively described, or in the process of accommodating the faith to the process of living one's life, with all its ambiguities, contradictions and multiplicity of referential frames (Beekers and Kloos 2017).

What I find in the narratives of my interlocutors in Morocco is that, although they are sometimes uncertain or doubtful, or – indeed – their daily lives show ambivalence, they nonetheless frame their religious lives in terms of an effort to be 'good Muslims'. Moroccan pilgrims sometimes acknowledge failure in this process of ethical formation. Thus, I find the work of Beekers and Kloos (2017) relevant here. In the Introduction to the edited volume *Straying from the Straight Path: How Senses of Failure Invigorate Lived Religion*, David Kloos and Daan Beekers argue that the struggles inherent in everyday life can, in fact, contribute to productive avenues in the processes of ethical formation rather than being seen as setbacks or obstacles to it, given the appropriate, constructive reading of and learning from the perceived 'failure'. Therefore, as Kloos and Beekers argue, a comprehensive approach towards the religious subject should include both questions about religious commitment, success, social mobility and progress and questions about drawbacks, doubt and sinfulness.

Since the religious lives of most Muslims are not necessarily governed by an internally coherent set of ethics or by a certainty about the place of religion in both public and private spheres, anthropologists working on Muslim societies have highlighted the prevalence of moral ambivalence, the ways in which individuals deal with conflicting 'moral registers' (Schielke 2015, 53ff), or 'multidimensional' selves (Simon 2014). I have chosen an ethnographic approach that takes into consideration the complexities in people's everyday lives and their motivations, experiences, practices and uncertainties in dealing with such complexities. As I am concerned with both the pursuits of pious self-formation and the doubt and ambivalence of pilgrims' everyday lives as part of ethical formation, I examine how – in their everyday lives – normative religiosity, moral norms and ambivalences infuse one another.

This is my chosen emphasis. However, I am cognisant of the issues signalled in an article published in *HAU: Journal of Ethnographic Theory*, in which Nadia Fadil and Mayanthi Fernando (2015) warn against the excesses they perceive in current anthropological studies of 'ordinary Islam'. Fadil and Fernando argue that the turn to everyday Islam has created a problematic opposition between 'piety' and 'the everyday'. The advocates for this turn, they continue, 'conceptualize normative doctrine and everyday practice as unconnected and, indeed, as opposed. Yet the fact that a commitment to a particular norm is often imperfectly achieved does not refute the importance attached to that norm' (ibid., 70). Although Fadil and Fernando's argument is compelling, I disagree with their claim that the focus on the everyday aspects of religion as it is lived effectively presupposes, or privileges, the view that there is a resistance to religious norms or even a conflict between such norms and daily life. I believe that the critical response to 'the piety turn' (2015, 81) does offer an important addition to the study of Islam by acknowledging the complexity and multiplicity of everyday life and the ways in which everyday life and religious perspectives and commitments interact.

I am seeking to show, through this ethnographic study, the possibility that thinking of piety, considering the search for a virtuous life, and living fully within the concerns of the everyday can coexist and be held in balance all at once. What might be most relevant to my approach is the response to Fadil and Fernando's piece by Lara Deeb (2015), who moves this debate forward by thinking of piety and the everyday together. Deeb proposes examining 'both the ways the everyday is shaped by religious discipline and normativity *and* the ways that religious discipline and normativity are themselves produced through and change via everyday social life' (ibid., 96, emphasis in the original; Elliot 2016). In this book, I follow a similar line of inquiry by tracing the ways in which experience in everyday life can be found to affect, or even stimulate, the quest for religious ideals. When one studies how Muslims 'live' the Hajj, both the plurality of moral frameworks that are at play and the ambivalence of everyday life can be noticed. For most Muslims, being a pilgrim, or a Muslim in general, is metaphorically 'a work in progress', an evolving process or a journey. People might want to live according to certain moral registers and aspire to be 'good Muslims', but their everyday lives, cultural discourses and *habitus* are characterised by complexities; the interplay of the numerous factors that inform their practices and meaning-making processes is what I seek to uncover in this study.[28]

Mecca holds profound significance for millions of Muslims worldwide as the holiest city in Islam, revered for its connection to the prophet Muhammad and the birthplace of the faith (van Leeuwen 2023, 47).[29] Practising Muslims face Mecca during their daily prayers and many cherish Hajj souvenirs brought home by pilgrims, which are viewed as carrying Meccan sacredness. The pilgrimage in the everyday life of Moroccans epitomises the meaning of Islam as 'a grand scheme' (Schielke 2010, 14). This means that the pilgrimage to Mecca becomes a guideline for life, a spiritual 'watch' and 'compass', providing meaning and direction to everyday concerns and experiences (Tweed 2006).[30] Religion can serve as a basis for the production, legitimisation and contestation of individual and group identities and social ties. Such a perspective embraces moral regimes and religious rules, but also leaves room for the ambiguities, contradictions, ambivalences and tensions between religious ideals (as an expectation of increased piety after the Hajj) and the daily lives of pilgrims. Within my research, I aim to show how the pilgrimage to Mecca might encapsulate the ultimate religious, spiritual value for Muslims and how such value may, at times, be actively operant within the realms of the mundane, as a means of reflecting, absorbing and interpreting everyday concerns, worries and other debates, blurring the demarcation between religious and non-religious aspects of life. In this way, people bring expectations of piety and guidelines for everyday life and Hajj into dialogue with each other.

During the period of my fieldwork, I was introduced to hundreds of such people, formally interviewed dozens and lived with many families. In the stories that Moroccans relate about the pilgrimage to Mecca, people are informed by their *habitus* and the cultural discourses in which they are embedded. The view of pilgrimage as a socially and culturally constructed sign of distinction and as a form of 'capital' allows for a nuanced outlook on the pilgrimage as religious practice and on Muslim identity-construction in context. I make extensive use of ethnographic analysis to show that these issues are more complex phenomena than can be conveyed by a survey or than non-ethnographic analysis is able to convey. An analysis of micro-level practices, everyday life and individual narratives is necessary for providing a multi-dimensional image of meaning-making regarding religion, on personal, national and other levels. From this perspective, this research is significant as it provides not only an ethnography of a Muslim community, but also the first single-country ethnographic study of the Hajj – regarding both its performance and its significance in everyday Moroccan life.

An emphasis on lived religion implies recognition that religious feelings and meanings are produced not only through discursive traditions but also via bodily experiences (Promey 2014; Houtman and Meyer 2012; Morgan 2012, 2010; Orsi 2005; McDannell 1995; Tweed 2006). Given the growing body of research that demonstrates the inseparable links between thinking, feeling and embodiment (including those of Smith 2013; Meyer 2012; Lakoff and Johnson 2003; Massumi 2002; Damasio 1999), I approach the Hajj as a 'sensational form': a relatively fixed, authorised mode of invoking and organising access to the transcendent. Pilgrims physically re-enact critical sacred dramas in Islamic historiography. As such, 'walking in the footsteps' of prophets Abraham and Muhammad is considered an overwhelming experience that cleanses the soul. In this sense, this book views religion through the lens of the senses, with a predominant focus on visible and audible experiences.

In the face of this multifarious approach, considerable care was needed in selecting the ethnographic methods that I used during my fieldwork in Morocco. I describe and account for my choices in the next section.

A Methodological Narrative

Ethnographic accounts of people's daily concerns can contest the assumption in the public discourse that Islam determines various dimensions of the lives of Muslims – that is by inference, *all* Muslims. The obvious problem with this commonly held, and damaging, view is that it presupposes the existence of a cultural essence; it also implies a view of culture as static. Therefore, the importance of the study of lived religion is that it looks at actual practice and belief as performed and held by people. The ethnographic mapping of the contextual presence of Islam in the everyday lives of Muslims is of crucial importance in the study of contemporary Islam. Ethnographic research provides us with insights into the wide variety of ways in which Islam is adopted in practice and defies stereotypes, expectations and rigid classifications. Simultaneously, focusing on life issues that, albeit in diverse ways, all people encounter in their everyday lives, this ethnographic research contributes to de-exceptionalising 'the Other' and looking afresh at our taken-for-granted practices and views, thus challenging the gap between Muslims and non-Muslims that is often assumed in popular debates (Buitelaar 2018).

Why Morocco?

The first detailed ethnographic information about Morocco – to my knowledge – comes from French colonial officers who administered the region – officially – from 1912 until 1956. Their reports, however, did not lead to what we would today recognise as systematic research and remained largely unpublished (Kraus 1998, 1). Obviously, they being colonial officers, their perspective was not neutral but coloured by power relations. It was only in the 1950s and 1960s, when anthropological research of Morocco began to be more serious, that a more academic dimension was adopted, an approach which was less obviously influenced by colonial perspectives. Monographs on Morocco were published starting in the late 1960s, putting the country at the centre of anthropological debates on Islam (Gellner 1981; Eickelman 1976; Geertz 1968), power relations (Bourqia and Gilson Miller 1999; Hammoudi 1997;

Munson 1993), diversity (Rosen 2016; Combs-Schilling 1989), ethnographic writing (Newcomb 2010; Buitelaar 1993; Crapanzano 1980; Munson 1984) and the nature of fieldwork (Dwyer and Muhammad 1982; Rabinow 1977). In his book *Islam Observed* (1968), Clifford Geertz argues that Moroccan and North African societies have best been viewed as consisting of unstable and temporary small social networks that are constantly created and re-created by pragmatic individuals (Geertz 1979, 235; 1971). Geertz focuses on Islam as a religion that, for at least two centuries, has experienced upheavals and cultural changes that are still under way today.

The first comprehensive studies of religion in Morocco include Dale Eickelman's *Moroccan Islam: Tradition and Society in a Pilgrimage Center* (1976), *The Aith Waryagher of the Moroccan Rif* by David Hart (1976) and Ernest Gellner's *Saints of the Atlas* (1969). Although these studies provide rich ethnographic analysis of Moroccan tribes and some of their religious practices, they nonetheless apply a structural approach that neglects history and social change and presents a static view of the Moroccan communities (Hammoudi 1974). Between 1965 and the 1970s, several anthropologists conducted research in Morocco, including Clifford Geertz, Lawrence Rosen, Paul Rabinow and Hildred Geertz. Clifford Geertz and this group of researchers conceived of culture as a system of meanings and analysed the communities they worked with accordingly. Unlike Hart and Gellner, the latter researchers stayed around Arabic-speaking towns in the lowlands and were interested in the contemporary, expressed through symbols and actions. Nevertheless, most of these studies present a coherent story of a rather static culture in Morocco (Eickelman 1985; Hammoudi 1974). In the 1970s and 1980s respectively, Combs-Schilling and Kraus conducted fieldwork in Morocco, focusing on ritual, behavioural strategies and tribal social organisation (Kraus 1998; Combs-Schilling 1989). Although relevant to this study in that they provide deep ethnographic insights into the life of the inhabitants of Morocco, as far as they address pilgrimage, these studies focus on Morocco as a pilgrimage centre and on one type of pilgrimage: saint veneration (Bowen 1993; Eickelman 1976; Geertz 1968).

Morocco has rarely – if at all – been studied in relation to the Hajj as an ethnographic endeavour. As thousands of pilgrims, individually or in groups, visit local Moroccan shrines throughout the year, also tens of thousands of

Moroccans perform the pilgrimage to Mecca. The existence of pilgrimage places, other than the holy shrine of the Ka'ba in Mecca, is a controversial subject among Muslims (Barnes 2006; Bhardwaj 1998; Eickelman and Piscatori 1990). Therefore, being both a point of departure for a pilgrimage journey and, at the same time, a pilgrimage destination is what makes Morocco an interesting case to study.

Although there is a long heritage of travel accounts and personal narratives of Moroccan pilgrims, such as Ibn Battuta's famous travel book (originally published in 1829) and Abdellah Hammoudi's *A Season in Mecca* (2006) documenting his Hajj journey of 1999, less ethnographic work – if any – has been done on the pilgrimage to Mecca from a Moroccan perspective. Arguably, for Moroccans, as for many Muslims, the pilgrimage to Mecca is one of the key fields through which religiosity is expressed, a religiosity which is a core feature of their everyday lives. Although the pilgrimage to Mecca is the fifth pillar of Islam, it is only mandatory for those who are able to perform it (*istiṭā'at al-sabīl*); there is no sense of its being an absolutely required obligation for those physically or financially disadvantaged (Tagliacozzo and Toorawa 2015; Donnan 1995, 69).[31] However, in practice, many people who might be considered exempt from this religious duty do strive to perform the Hajj as it is highly valuable as a religious achievement and as a marker of social and religious prestige in Morocco and throughout the Muslim world (Yamba 1995; Eickelman and Piscatori 1990; Baderoon 2012). Thus, in Morocco, being a *ḥājj* or *ḥājja* – someone who has performed Hajj – comes with considerable associated status, which until recently was ascribed to older people (Buitelaar 2015). It is relevant, therefore, to study this acquired prestige in relation to the micro-practices of everyday life in Morocco, assessing the added social value of Hajj in addition to its religious one. Most studies of Hajj have not featured a detailed discussion of how Hajj articulates and manifests its significance in everyday life, and this is worthy of exploration, hence this study.

Moreover, in Morocco, religion is highly valued at the official state level. As the country is predominantly Maliki- and Sunni-oriented, and the king is regarded as both the head of state and leader of the religious community (*amīr al-mu'minīn*), Islam is considered a central element in the Moroccan nationalist narrative (Sadiqi 2018; Hammoudi 1997).[32] The state bureaucracy manages and oversees the performance of the pilgrimage to Mecca, making it a matter intimately linked with national and state politics. The state, therefore, controls the process of the pilgrimage to Mecca and at the same time influences its meanings in the public sphere.[33]

Although it can be argued that the Hajj today is easier than ever due to the advent of modern technologies, new modes of transportation, and the rise of a middle class that has placed the Hajj – and *'umra* – within reach of increasing numbers of Muslim pilgrims (Mols and Buitelaar 2015), there have been heated debates concerning the management of the pilgrimage, the problems involved in the Hajj registration process, and in the Saudi control over this religious duty (Fisk 2016; Bianchi 2016, 2015, 2004; Egan 2012; Amiri et al. 2011; Roy 2010).[34] Therefore, Morocco can inform us about the ways in which the political and cultural spheres can influence, and are in turn influenced by, the pilgrimage to Mecca.

Lastly, Morocco provides an interesting case study because little has been written about the pilgrimage within the context of the everyday lives of Moroccans. Most available studies regarding Muslim societies focus on piety movements rather than the context of everyday life.[35] The studies that have appeared on the everyday lives of Muslims focus on several Muslim societies such as Egypt (Schielke 2015, 2012; Ismail 2006); Southeast Asia (Rahman 2015; O'Connor 2012; Adams and Gillogly 2011; Mines and Lamb 2010), and diaspora and Muslim communities in the West (Toguslu 2015; Sunier and Landman 2014; McLoughlin 2010). The publications that have appeared about Islam in Morocco predominantly focus on Sufism and local pilgrimages, although a few have appeared in recent years discussing aspects of the everyday life in Morocco, including Rachel Newcomb's *Everyday Life in Global Morocco* (2017) and *Women of Fes: Ambiguities of Urban Life in Morocco* (2010) as well as *Encountering Morocco: Fieldwork and Cultural Understanding* edited by David Crawford and Rachel Newcomb (2013) and Marjo Buitelaar's comprehensive study *Fasting and Feasting in Morocco* (1993). Just as Buitelaar's (1993) study of fasting and feasting in Morocco was the first comprehensive ethnography of the fourth pillar of Islam, that is, the month of Ramadan, in a specific cultural setting, my study, to the best of my knowledge, is the first ethnographic work within the societal context of one country focusing on the fifth pillar of Islam: the Hajj.

Fieldwork: First Encounters

During my first visit to Morocco in March 2015, I met Abdullah, a Moroccan researcher who in speaking about his country told me:

> Morocco is a country of rich cultural and religious diversity . . . It is influenced by Arab-Islamic, Amazigh and Saharan-Hassanic cultures, and reflecting African, Andalusian, Hebraic and Mediterranean influences . . . This diversity makes any question about religion challenging to answer . . . There is official Islam and popular Islam, Sufism, Maraboutism, political Islam, and so on; it is not easy to identify one Islam but a plural: *Islams* . . .

Indeed, Morocco has a diverse society, with people drawn from a variety of educational and social backgrounds and possessing different ethnic backgrounds, that is, identifying as Arab or Amazigh, in addition to a small number of Christian and Jewish Moroccans (Boum 2013 ; see Amster 2013; Cornell 1998; El Mansour 2020; Green 2018).[36] As my research progressed, I witnessed aspects of this diversity in addition to the central role Islam plays in the daily lives of many Moroccans. Since its arrival in the seventh century until today, Islam had influenced the social, political and cultural values of Moroccan society (Geertz 1968). This book, therefore, aims to tell numerous stories about Moroccans, their daily lives, narratives and experiences. At the same time, it tells the story of my own participation and attempt to understand the lives of these people.

When I moved to Fes for my fieldwork in the summer of 2015, I lived with a Moroccan family whose members had generously invited me into their home and integrated me into their daily rhythms and routines. Fatima, whom I mentioned in the Introduction, or *khāltī* as I called her, took me under her wing and provided me with motherly care, introduced me to her network, and invited me to join women's gatherings and family occasions.[37] In the neighbourhood, I was also welcomed by shopkeepers who accepted me as the guest of the respected *ḥājja* Fatima and her family.[38] Staying with a Moroccan family proved to be the best way to familiarise myself with Moroccan Arabic, *dārīja*, which differs considerably from Palestinian and Modern Standard Arabic. Through daily conversations, mainly with my host family, shopkeepers and taxi drivers, I managed to nearly perfect my dialect speech in a few weeks.

Within field research, the way community members see researchers influences what we will be told, how we might interact with people and places, and, ultimately, the kind of data we gather in the field. Therefore, in considering the *how* of the fieldwork, the various experiences I encountered underscore the need to scrutinise questions of ethics and the usefulness of methods to be used in the field (Fechter 2003; Davies and Spencer 2010). In Morocco, my Palestinian identity was a highly significant identifier, both for my interlocutors and for me as a researcher. My status as a Palestinian (an oppressed people that deserves aid and solidarity is the dominant discourse in Morocco about the plight of the Palestinian people), coupled with my position as a researcher at a European university (part of an elite and affiliated with former colonial powers who used ethnographic research in Morocco as an aid to control and surveillance) had different implications for and impacts on those whom I met and those with whom I worked. People displayed abundant support for Palestine, which reached beyond a sense of nationalistic belonging. I was often told that 'In Morocco, Palestine is considered a national cause', and that Moroccans supported the struggle of the people of Palestine. People often referred to the Moroccan quarter of Jerusalem or *ḥārat al-maghāriba*, which symbolises the historic relationship of Moroccans to Palestine, a connection which dates to the twelfth century. Many Moroccans referred to the time of the Ayyubids, when Moroccans volunteered in the army of Saladin and subsequently were invited or permitted to remain in Jerusalem.[39] Others referred to an ancient ritual they called *taqdīs*, which refers to Jerusalem, al-Quds, as pilgrims used to visit the city and its Al-Aqsa Mosque either before or after their pilgrimage to Mecca so as to have visited the third most sacred mosque in Islam after those in Mecca and Medina. During my fieldwork, those I met often wanted to hear about Palestine through me, creating a natural and easy starting point to many conversations. Many Moroccans told me that they wished to visit Jerusalem and wanted my opinion on how to realise that ambition. Others too were similarly sympathetic to me, such as a local governmental officer who stated that he would help me simply because I come from Palestine, which he described as a sacred place that was dear to his heart.

The significance of my Palestinian identity, then, became paramount in Morocco. When introducing me to others, Moroccans used my nationality as a Palestinian as the first identifier after my first name. People often responded to that with *miskīna*, the connotation of which is 'poor thing'; the word can be used to describe someone who is the epitome of misery. In Morocco, however, the expression is used colloquially to express sympathy and warm feelings for the other. Being the *miskīna* from Palestine allowed me to gain access to a larger number of contacts within the local community. Many Moroccans were also fascinated by the fact that I excelled in the local dialect; my dialectal accomplishments were seen very positively, and I was occasionally told that I had become a local *maghribiyya* (Moroccan) myself. This interesting combination of being distinctively Palestinian yet linguistically in harmony with the local Moroccan culture enhanced my access to research opportunities.

Studying the pilgrimage to Mecca as it features in the narratives and experiences in the everyday lives of Moroccans, as well as wishing to investigate the meanings produced around the Meccan pilgrimage in Moroccan micro-practices in broader socio-cultural dynamics, required a long-term, qualitative field-based approach (Marcus 1998). The principal method of data gathering during my fieldwork, therefore, was participant observation. I closely observed local practices as I joined my interlocutors in their workplaces, markets, shops, living rooms and kitchens. On various occasions, my interlocutors showed an interest in my research findings and my own person. They frequently asked me how I liked their country and their cultural practices, and what differences I perceived between Morocco and my home country Palestine.

Participant observation is the most effective approach for ethnographic research as it allows a deep understanding of people's lives as individuals, and at the same time allows the observer to assess the interactions they have in their social world (Marcus 1998; Marcus and Fischer 1986; Rabinow 1977). My conversations with Moroccans about the pilgrimage often took place spontaneously, in informal settings. On specific occasions, including meetings with local officials and imams, visiting returning pilgrims and meeting people I did not know previously, I organised and conducted semi-structured in-depth interviews. In total, I lived with ten families, conducted approximately fifty personal, detailed yet informal interviews with Moroccans who intended to go, or had been, on Hajj, and, of course, had innumerable informal conversations with Moroccans I met at the market, on the train, in taxis or even on the street. The families with whom I lived resided mainly in urban centres: I was first in Fes, then in Mohammedia, and, finally, in Casablanca. I also spent one month in the city of Safi and a few weeks visiting pilgrimage sites and interviewing pilgrims (*ḥujjāj*) in and near the cities of Ouezzane, El Hoceima, Meknes, Moulay Idriss Zerhoun, Marrakech, Ouarzazate, Rabat and El Jadida. Multi-sited ethnographic research proved helpful for several practical and educational reasons. First, I was able to access different personal networks and social classes, including upper-middle-class and lower-middle-class, as well as less privileged communities. This provided me with a rich social spectrum for analysis.[40] I would meet a family of limited means one day and a wealthy businessman the next. I would stay in a comfortable bedroom one night and share a bed with a friend in her parents' small house in another. I would be invited to a luxurious restaurant for a seafood meal one afternoon and on the following day would dine with another interlocutor on a cheap sardine lunch. Always, however, even the poorest people showed enormous hospitality by offering me tea, lunch or dinner. Working in different sites also allowed me to meet a larger number of people who had been on Hajj than I would have in a single-site study. Furthermore, being introduced to and becoming acquainted with various locations in Morocco enhanced my skills as a researcher by immersing me in a plethora of social contexts and milieux, making me more sensitive to cultural differences with each encounter.

Combining a range of different methods including listening, observing, and tracing techniques when carrying out research over time allowed me to test the data that I gathered and to modify my techniques when collecting further data. Long-term fieldwork also allows opportunities for discovering the 'unsaid' in everyday life (Dresch et al. 2000). Not all communication is explicit or on the surface, but is often conveyed through the interstices of spoken language (Joseph 2018; Altorki and El-Solh 1988).

When I left Morocco after my first research period, I stayed connected with many of my interlocutors mainly via social media networks. They provided me with updates about their personal lives and the situation in Morocco in general. I returned to Morocco in the summer of 2016, six weeks before the Hajj season. I stayed first in Casablanca, then in Safi, Ouezzane and Ouarzazate where I met more Moroccans and witnessed several local events like the Pilgrimage of the Poor, local celebrations of religious events like the Feast of Sacrifice, other festivals at saints' shrines, and even visited a cinematic reconstruction of the Kaʿba which had been built in the desert for the famous film al-*Risāla*, which depicts the life of the prophet Muhammad.[41]

Following my two major periods of fieldwork (July 2015 to April 2016 and June 2016 to January 2017), I travelled to Morocco for three more follow-up visits to catch up with friends and interlocutors, witness changes in the Hajj administrative procedures, and verify the data gathered in the previous research trips. I also made use of local institutions involved in the Hajj process. I met, on a regular basis, with workers at local government offices, travel agents, and Hajj and *ʿumra* trip organisers. I visited local bookstores and libraries to gain further knowledge on Moroccan culture and society. In addition, I contacted Moroccan artists, university students and researchers to discuss their Hajj-related work or aspects of Moroccan culture, history and religious practices. I found these encounters to be highly valuable, especially in broadening my perspective on Morocco and its people.

Research data also included media, such as daily printed newspapers, Moroccan TV channels and social media platforms, as well as literature, song lyrics and stories, all of which I translated from Arabic to English. In the analysis and interpretation of my empirical data, I have tried to stay close to the words and expressions used by the people whom I encountered in Morocco.

Although qualitative research does not allow one to generalise for a larger population, it does, however, provide rich, contextualised understanding of the theme of this research and it facilitates reflection on relations and patterns on a meta-level (Rabinow 1977). I want to emphasise, nonetheless, that the statements I make in this book regarding my topic only apply to my specific research settings and the respondents with whom I have spoken. Because of the abundance of observations, I selected cases that most strongly illustrate the arguments developed in this study and lend themselves to 'thick description' (Geertz 1973). Nonetheless, like any other study, this book can only offer a mere glimpse into the lives of people and their religious understandings, both of which are more complicated than the area I have been able to analyse. I am, however, convinced that the process of observing and participating in the everyday lives of Moroccans has enriched my understanding of the meanings of pilgrimage to Mecca for the people whose lives I was trying to understand, to a far greater extent than any other method would have allowed. Concurrently, through my analysis, I also hope to enrich the understanding of how religion, with its complexities and nuances, is lived within the everyday world of a group of Muslims.

In addition to the main fieldwork activities, the narratives, shared stories and experiences of research participants inspired me to join a group of pilgrims on a lesser pilgrimage trip, *ʿumra*, to experience the atmosphere of Mecca myself. I did so in 2016 and 2018. These trips allowed me to see examples of the struggles that Moroccans experienced, which they sometimes shared with me. For example, being a young woman meant that I needed a male guardian on the trip, a *maḥram*.[42] My father, aged eighty, accompanied me on the journey, together with my mother who looked after him, and my eldest sister who looked after the two of them. Despite my irritation with these restrictions, having companions during the pilgrimage proved helpful. My mother and sister are very sociable women who talked to pilgrims from various backgrounds, a fact which allowed me greater access to women, especially at the Grand Mosque of Mecca. During our two-week journey to Mecca, we joined not only Moroccan pilgrims, but pilgrims from all around the world. I witnessed the interactions between Moroccans and other pilgrims, their conversations, shopping trips and prayers.

In the end, my corpus of field notes contained the narratives of over one hundred people in over five hundred pages. What followed next was a process of thinking, sketching, designing, discarding, reading and rereading, arranging, interpreting, oscillating between field notes, interviews, analysis, literature searching, and writing and deleting first then second and third versions, details of which I will spare the reader.[43]

Inasmuch as the field researcher's subjective experience continues to shape ethnographic knowledge, however, I hope that I have been able to reflect on, and to discuss, some aspects of the way in which the field makes its imprint on the researcher and, in turn, how the researcher's identity impacts the data gathered, and other registers of fieldwork.

Conclusion

In this chapter, I introduced the rites of the Hajj and briefly presented its history in Morocco. I then discussed the central concepts that will be addressed throughout the book, drawing inspiration particularly from the field of pilgrimage studies. I emphasized the significance of studying the Hajj in the context of everyday life in Morocco, shedding light on the ways in which this examination contributes to ongoing anthropological discussions. Specifically, I examined how Islam, viewed as a broader discursive tradition operating on a macro level, is manifested and experienced in the routine micro-level practices of everyday life. This book does not (exclusively) study the pilgrimage itself, but rather its significance in the daily lives of the pilgrims and their lived experiences. As the following chapters will show, my research supports Schielke's observation that everyday life is inherently and intrinsically in flux – complex, messy, ambivalent. I argue in this book that people can still aim at developing a pious self even if not through such strictly religious 'disciplining' and orthodox discourse, but by developing a 'believing' and ethical attitude while being engaged in everyday activities.

In addition to this conceptual framework, this chapter contains the narrative of my own methodological trajectory. I mentioned some of the terminology used (e.g. 'friend' and 'interlocutor'), as well as the methodology (participant observation, in various places, and with varying degrees of familiarity with my interlocutors). On the basis of this fieldwork, I examine how for Muslim pilgrims in Morocco there is a continuous struggle to tackle the complexities of everyday social and religious existence. Not everybody has a similar understanding of religious teachings. Pilgrims are influenced in their readings of the significance of religion in general and of the Hajj in particular by multiple personal markers of identity, such as their gender, age, and social, political and educational backgrounds, all of which can overlap and interact. Thus, these various categories of identification intersect to establish a person's position in society and his or her ability to perform the Hajj. In addition to these personal factors, we all live in a culturally conditioned environment. The expression of pilgrimage experiences through cultural products, such as songs and narratives, interacts with an individual's experience of the Hajj to intensify, replicate and re-create the experience of being a pilgrim. Of course, those cultural acts affect fellow citizens who may not yet have performed Hajj, but who imbibe the narratives of those who have managed to go on pilgrimage. Everyday life is complex and full of ambiguities, and nowhere is this more apparent than in the influence of pilgrimage on a society such as that in Morocco.

Following the suggestion of Coleman and Eade not to focus on the pilgrimage site as such but on the movement of people, ideas and other elements as a bridge to studying pilgrimage, and Schielke's focus on the study of everyday life, I will, in the following chapters, discuss how the pilgrimage to Mecca features as part of the lived religion of Moroccans, by tracing, recording and analysing their everyday lives. My privileged position as the writer of this book gave me the confidence to offer my interpretations of my interlocutors' words, and I hope that I have been able to do this in a manner that does them justice.

Notes

1. The other four pillars of Islam are: reciting the testimony of faith, the *shahāda* ('There is no god but God, and Muhammad is the messenger of God'); performing ritual prayers five times a day; fasting during the month of Ramadan; and giving alms. The word 'Hajj' probably derives from an old Semitic root meaning 'to go' or 'to visit a holy place' (Mawdudi 1982; Daluw 1969, 273).
2. Views on the significance and meanings attributed to the Hajj and its rites have differed among scholars of Islam, some of whom build on al-Ghazali's emphasis on 'pure obedience', but, in different ways, extrapolate this to ritual efficacy and mythic re-enactment (Al-Ghazali 2009). Since the purpose of this book is not a discussion of scholarly Islamic interpretations of the Hajj, the discussion is restricted to conveying more general interpretations on which there might be broad, albeit not complete, consensus among contemporary Muslims (Katz 2004).
3. *Mīqāt* refers to any one of five stations in a radius bordering the sacred territory of Mecca where pilgrims purify themselves and put on the *iḥrām* before going on Hajj or *'umra* (Wensinck and Jomier 2012). Those coming from the direction of Medina and its surrounding areas have their point of *iḥrām* in a place called Dhū al-Ḥulifa, while those coming from the direction of Syria and all areas north of it use al-Juḥfah. Pilgrims coming from the direction of Najd have their *mīqāt* in Qarn al-Manazil, and those coming from the direction of Yemen use the *mīqāt* of Yalamlam. Those living near Mecca should put on their *iḥrām* where they live, while inhabitants of Mecca itself should put on the *iḥrām* as soon as they declare

their intention to perform the Hajj (Peters 1994). When flying to Mecca, it is necessary to wear one's *iḥrām* before the plane enters the *mīqāt* zone in the air; for Moroccans, this is when the plane is above Rabigh, which is roughly on the same latitude as al-Juḥfah.

4. Women are not allowed to cover their faces during Hajj, on the basis of hadith narrated in al-Bukhārī, that when prophet Muhammad was asked what clothes pilgrims may wear in the state of *iḥrām* he said: 'Do not wear a shirt or trousers, or any headgear [e.g. a turban], or a hooded cloak; but if somebody has no shoes he can wear leather stockings provided they are cut short off the ankles, and also, do not wear anything perfumed with saffron, and the *muḥrima* [a woman in the state of *iḥrām*] should not cover her face, or wear gloves' (Al-Bukhārī, book 28, hadith 18).
5. *Ṣalāt* (*or ṣalāh*) refers to ritual prayers performed by Muslims. The *ṣalāt* consists of multiple movements which include standing, bowing, prostrating oneself, sitting, and reciting Qur'anic verses and other specific words. Each occasion on which a person performs these steps is called *rakʿa* and each prayer consists of two or more *rakʿa*s. There are five mandatory prayers per day that a Muslim should perform, taking place as follows: *fajr* (at dawn before sunrise); *ẓuhur* (at midday, after the sun passes its highest point); *ʿaṣr* (in the late part of the afternoon); *maghrib* (just after sunset); and *ʿishā'* (between sunset and dawn). Muslims can also make voluntary prayers at other times of the day or on a specific occasion such as entering the state of *iḥrām*, following the *ṭawāf* around the Kaʿba, or at the time of a death, among others (Katz 2013). Throughout the book, I refer to ritual prayers as *ṣalāt* prayers to distinguish them from supplicatory prayers, which I refer to as *duʿā'* prayers following the Arabic term.
6. During *ṭawāf*, male pilgrims should also leave their right shoulder bare to demonstrate their humility (Buhl 2012).
7. The black stone is a rock set into the eastern corner of the Kaʿba. According to hadith, 'the black stone is from Paradise' (Al-Nisā'ī, vol. 3, book 24, hadith 2938).
8. The Well of Zamzam is located within the Grand Mosque of Mecca and is believed to be a source of water miraculously granted by God to Hagar, wife of Abraham and mother of Ishmael (Chabbi 2012).
9. There are three different types of Hajj, namely: *Hajj-ul-ifirād* (when a pilgrim does not combine Hajj with *ʿumra*); *Hajj-ul-qirān* (which combines Hajj and *ʿumra*); and *Hajj-ul-tamattuʿ* (which performs *ʿumra* first then Hajj) (Al-Baṣīrī 2002).
10. For both Hajj and *ʿumra*, a Muslim must first assume *iḥrām*, and both rituals end with *ḥalq* or *taqṣīr* (shaving or partial shortening of the hair). A pilgrim is

generally able to complete *ʿumra* in a few hours, as against Hajj, which has to be completed on five specific days of the year.

11. Arafat is said to contain the 'Sacred Precinct' where it is said that Adam and Eve made a sacrificial offer (to God) at al-Muzdalifa and recognised each other at Arafat (Meri 2004, 232).
12. Masjid Namira is a mosque located on the plain of Arafat.
13. Mount of Mercy is another name for the Mount of Arafat (Wensinck and Gibb 2012).
14. According to the Islamic tradition, Abraham was commanded by God to sacrifice his son as a test. The devil tried to stop God's command from being obeyed by visiting Hagar, Ishmael and Abraham. Each time the devil told them about the impending sacrifice, they responded that if it was God's command, they must obey. When Abraham finally attempted to sacrifice Ishmael, God told him that he had fulfilled the command and that Ishmael was spared. Instead, God provided an animal for the sacrifice (Qur'an 37: 101–7).
15. Animal sacrifice for pilgrims nowadays consists of symbolically buying a sacrifice coupon of, as of 2016, 460 riyals (around 112 Euros) to have a sheep, ram, etc. slaughtered on one's behalf.
16. I will refer to *ʿīd al-aḍḥā* (the Feast of Sacrifice) throughout the book as *ʿīd l-kbīr* so as to remain as close as possible to how it is often called in Morocco.
17. The terms *al-ḥājj* and *al-ḥājja* refer to those who are in the act of performing the pilgrimage. In some Muslim communities, these terms are also used to address older persons, whether or not they have performed the Hajj. In Morocco, addressing older people as *al-ḥājj* or *al-ḥājja* is a sign of respect (Peters 1994).
18. Morocco itself has been inhabited by Amazigh or Berber tribes for at least 5,000 years before the arrival of Islam. The Muslim conquest of what is now Morocco took place between 705 and 740 (Munson 1993). Musa Ibn Nusayr is believed to have established Arab rule in the territory of present-day Morocco between 705 (or 706) and 708 (or 709) (Nasr 1987). In 710, the Caliph of Damascus appointed Salih ben Mansour as the first governor of the first Muslim empire in Morocco, called Nokour after a river south of El Hoceima in the central Rif (Obdeijn, De Mas and Hermans 1999, 41). Islam has been the official religion of both Arab and Berber royal dynasties since the eighth century. The official Islamic school in Morocco is the Sunni Maliki school, itself based on shariʿa (Islamic judicial law) (Abun-Nasr 1987).
19. It was common among religious scholars of North Africa to combine pilgrimage with a visit to the major centres of the Islamic world and even produce written

accounts of their travels (Faroqi 1994). Al-ʿAbdarī, for example, travelled to Mecca in 668/1289 to perform the Hajj and documented his journey (Al-ʿAbdarī 1999). Other travellers from Morocco to Mecca include Al-Qaysī (1968) and Al-ʿAyāshī (2006).

20. A video documenting the pilgrimage to Mecca from Morocco in 1949 shows groups of pilgrims boarding a ship and others waving from quayside. The French flag on the ship leaving the port is an indicator of French colonial organisation of the Hajj as a means of legitimising French power, which can also be seen in British management of the Hajj during the same period (Cooper 2019; Fichter 2019; Low 2008; Slight 2014). The video can be viewed at https://www.youtube.com/watch?v=FCKa2T6grKE (last accessed 12 December 2023).
21. *Morocco Population*, 12 June 2019, http://worldpopulationreview.com/countries/morocco/ (last accessed 30 December 2019).
22. The number of pilgrims follows a quota system, which will be extensively discussed in Chapter Two.
23. Unpublished information gathered during fieldwork.
24. The next chapter provides a detailed description of preparations for Hajj among pilgrims in Morocco.
25. In Malcolm X's oft-cited diary, he speaks about his pilgrimage to Mecca as follows: 'We were truly all the same (brothers), because their belief in one God had removed the "white" from their minds, the "white" from their behavior, and the "white" from their attitude' (X and Haley 1965, 340).
26. Although I focus on the work of Samuli Schielke, he being the often-cited proponent of this turn to everyday Islam, more studies can be found on the topic, including Al-Muhammad (2012), Al-Muhammad and Peluso (2012), Das (2012), Debevec (2012), Khan (2006, 2012), Mittermaier (2012) and Simon (2009). I do not suggest any homogeneity in this literature and recognise the very different orientations and analytic attachments that animate these studies. I am interested in how all these works frame the everyday as a site of complexity, ambiguity or encounter.
27. Another significant edited volume on Islam as lived religion is that of Nathal Dessing, Nadia Jeldtoft, Jørgen Nielsen and Linda Woodhead, *Everyday Lived Islam in Europe* (2013). In this volume, the authors promote an approach to the study of Muslims and Islam in Europe through the avenue of the 'everyday'.
28. *Habitus* is a concept used by the French sociologist Pierre Bourdieu to refer to the physical embodiment of cultural capital. It also refers to the deeply ingrained

habits, skills and dispositions that people acquire through their life experiences (Bourdieu 1977).

29. The pilgrimage to Mecca is a deeply cherished and transformative experience for those who can undertake it (Buitelaar and Leeuwen 2023; Porter 2012; Peters 1994). However, it is essential to acknowledge that not all Muslims view Mecca through the same lens. Some individuals belonging to sects or minority groups within Islam may experience fear or trepidation when visiting Mecca, particularly if their sects face restrictions or exclusion from participating in the Hajj. For instance, some followers of the Ahmadiyya sect face restrictions and must conceal belonging to their sect due to its being banned in Mecca (Valentine 2021; Larsson and Sorgenfrei 2021). This highlights the complex interplay between religious authorities, sectarian dynamics and access to sacred spaces, prompting us to recognise and address the diversity of experiences within the Muslim community concerning Mecca's significance.
30. Tweed argues that religiosity is the itinerary and compass that guides people's journeys and orientation (Tweed 2006, 85).
31. Several verses in the Qur'an speak of the duty to perform the Hajj (Qur'an 2, 196 and 3, 97). The performance of the Hajj in these verses is conditioned on the ability and well-being of the prospective pilgrim. Verse 97 of the third chapter of the Qur'an, for example, after reaffirming that Mecca is the destination of pilgrimage, reads 'Pilgrimage to this House is an obligation by Allah upon whoever is able among the people' (Qur'an 3, 97). Ideally, a pilgrim should perform the Hajj if he or she is financially able and when all other debts have been discharged. Money should also not be borrowed for the purpose of the pilgrimage, and all financial matters and social obligations should be settled prior to a pilgrim's departure to Mecca (Donnan 1995, 69).
32. For more information on the importance of Islam in the national imaginary of the Moroccan diaspora, see Timmerman et al. (2017) and Toguslu (2015).
33. See Chapter Five.
34. The contention for authority over Mecca, Medina and the pilgrimage is not a contemporary phenomenon. Historical instances of this struggle can be found in scholarly works such as Teitelbaum's study 'Hashemites, Egyptians, and Saudis: The Tripartite Struggle for the Pilgrimage in the Shadow of Ottoman Defeat' (2020), where several relevant examples are explored, offering insights into the complex dynamics surrounding these sacred sites (see also Chapter Six).
35. For examples from Egypt, see Anani (2016), Winegar (2006) and Mahmood (2005).

36. Historically, Morocco was home to a thriving Jewish community numbering some 240,000 people (2.7 per cent of the total population) before the Second World War (Boum 2013, 1). By 2013, however, fewer than 3,000 Jews resided in Morocco, principally due to their migration to Israel, Europe and the Americas (ibid.). In 2019, Pope Francis visited Morocco and pointed out the importance of religious diversity in Morocco, addressing some 10,000 members of Morocco's Catholic community (which is around 30,000 in total, with sub-Saharan Africans making up a large part of the overall number of Christians in the country).
37. The word *khāltī*, literally meaning 'my (maternal) aunt', is generally used as a term of endearment and respect towards older women with whom one develops a kind of relationship. Throughout the book, I refer to different people in the same way I addressed them during my fieldwork. I addressed older women with *khāltī* ('my maternal aunt') or *al-ḥājja* as a sign of respect, and older men as *'ammī* ('my paternal uncle') or *al-ḥājj*. I refer to those I met once or twice for interviews, for example, as interlocutors, and to those I knew for longer periods as friends, although the two categories sometimes overlap (Berger 2018; Driessen 1998). Peter Berger finds that making friends in the field is a natural process caused by the situation in which ethnographers find themselves (Berger 2018). He also points out that interlocutors themselves sometimes frame relationships in terms of kinship or friendship with the ethnographer (ibid.).
38. The definite article 'al-' in the Arabic language, whose function is to render the noun which it prefixes definite, is sometimes omitted in transliteration (from the words al-*ḥājj/al-ḥājj*) to conform with Arabic grammar rules.
39. The Moroccan quarter was established in 1193 by Saladin's son al-Malik al-Afḍal Nurud-Dīn 'Ali as a *waqf* (a charitable trust), and was dedicated to all Moroccan immigrants (Al-'Ulaymī 1973; cf. Peters 2017, 357–9).
40. According to a Moroccan government study dating from 2008, 'the middle class is constituted of individuals whose consumption, expenditure or income levels are in the middle range of the social distribution of those indicators' (quoted in Boufous and Khariss 2015, 3). In this book, I measure the middle class in two ways: by the interlocutor's self-identification and by their income. Self-identification was based on people's family conditions and background, and income levels depended on the type of employment and education of household members. For discussion of class issues in Morocco see Bogaert (2018), Cohen (2004), Crawford Newcomb (2013), Newcomb (2017) and Sadiqi (2018; 2003).

41. *Al-Risāla*, originally known as 'Mohammad, Messenger of God', is a 1976 historical drama directed and produced by Moustapha Akkad, chronicling the life and times of the prophet Muhammad.
42. Under Saudi Arabia's male guardianship system, every woman applying for a visa must have a male guardian – a father, brother, husband or a son – to accompany her during the visit. When this research was conducted, the 'maḥram' provision was only relaxed for women over 45 years of age travelling in organised groups. In 2021, Saudi Arabia allowed women to register to perform the Hajj without being accompanied by a maḥram. For further elaboration and implications of the Saudi regulations on the matter, see Chapter Two.
43. For more details of my research experience in Morocco and other places see Al-Ajarma 2022.

PART ONE

THE PILGRIMAGE TO MECCA: A TRIPARTITE PROCESS OF PREPARATION, PILGRIMAGE AND AFTERMATH

Continuity of Imagery: The Linguistic Search for the Essence of Hajj

'The Kaʿba appeared . . . saying to us: "Come to me, oh lovers of my beauty. This time cannot be overcome. Where would you find a beauty like mine? There is no other to love in the universe. Those who have seen [the Kaʿba] find happiness. Those who have not [seen it] find sorrow!"' (Al-Qaysī 1632 [1968]; my translation from the Arabic).

'The Hajj took us back to our will to exist beyond the worlds we ascribed to ourselves, in our differences – race, class, nation, gender – called us to bring forth our pasts and the pasts we had to summon in the form of something to come. Its story – or rather, its stories, since there were several – took hold of our lives. They made us retell the Qur'anic narratives that retraced our past and anticipated its conclusions' (Hammoudi, Hajj season 1999 [2006], 284).

'I completed the Hajj . . . Being at the Kaʿba was a meeting; an encounter with my inner self . . . Does all this have a meaning? Suddenly I stopped, saying, yes . . . Is life not an answer to God's call? Only to Him . . . In every place, in every time' (Aourid Hajj season 2007 [2019], 90 ; my translation from Arabic).

2

BEFORE DEPARTURE: MOTIVATIONS FOR HAJJ PERFORMANCE AND THE CREATION OF A MUSLIM MORAL *HABITUS*

O God,
how I long to complete my wish
on Mount Arafat;
O my Lord how I wish
to visit the chosen Prophet . . .
(lyrics of Moroccan song)

Introduction

It was around 3 p.m. when I arrived at Qassim's dentistry clinic in a crowded neighbourhood of Casablanca. As I entered the clinic, I noticed that the waiting area was full of women and children waiting to be seen by the doctor. At the reception, I was welcomed by a man, probably in his seventies, who sat behind a wooden counter. He smiled generously as he welcomed me in. He was wearing a yellow *jellaba* and had a red cap on his platinum-white hair. Earlier, when I had called to make an appointment by phone, I had been answered by a female secretary. I explained this to the man, who told me that the secretary had had to leave, so that he had taken her place, as he was the father of the dentist. From behind his chair, he pulled out a grey plastic side table, placed it in front of the counter and invited me to sit and chat with him.

Soon, a young woman carrying a child entered the clinic. The woman greeted the man: 'Blessed is your safe return, *al-ḥājj*! How was your Hajj?'

The older man thanked her politely, and answered: 'Thank God, all went well...' As he registered the woman's name at the bottom of the list of patients, she commented: 'May God never prevent anyone from [accessing] these holy places ...' She then added: '*Allāh yaʿṭīnā al-ḥajj* [May God grant us all the Hajj]', to which the man replied: 'Amen!' After writing the woman's name in a large notebook in front of him, he asked her to sit in the waiting area.

The man – *al-ḥājj* Jamal was his name – had been to Hajj together with his wife and their son, the dentist. Our conversation was private, although I could not tell if the women in the waiting room could overhear our dialogue. When I asked Jamal about his experience, he shared his thoughts:

> God, the Almighty, commanded prophet Abraham in Sūrat al-Hajj: 'And proclaim unto mankind the pilgrimage'[1] ... An entire chapter [in the Qur'an] is specially named after this sacred duty ... Ever since this proclamation, the hearts and minds of Muslims have been longing for that House of God, and crowds of visitors come to it from every distant place in response to the call of God ... However, a person can perform the Hajj only when they hear that proclamation ...

According to *al-ḥājj* Jamal, no one can go to Mecca, or perform the pilgrimage, unless they hear God's proclamation, the *nidā'* or *ādhān*. 'When you hear the call, the *ādhān*, you should go to Mecca and perform the pilgrimage': *al-ḥājj* Jamal pointed to his ear as he said these words, indicating the sense of hearing.

When we talked more, I learned about the application process which, like all Moroccans, *al-ḥājj* Jamal had had to go through before being able to perform the pilgrimage. He said:

> Originally it was four of us: my wife, my son, my son's wife, and I ... We applied twice for Hajj before we were finally selected ... We were accepted last year and went to Hajj this year [as is the procedure in Morocco].[2] We prepared our papers, had medical tests done and paid for our trip, then prepared for the trip ... Before leaving [Morocco], we said farewell to family and friends, and finally went on Hajj ... The process took around one year ...

The period between *al-ḥājj* Jamal's Hajj application and the time of the family's departure was a busy one, filled with both religious and mundane practices. Even if a person was fully prepared, however, according to *al-ḥājj* Jamal he (or she) would only depart on the Hajj journey if God had made a proclamation and destined him (or her) to visit the holy places.[3]

The Meccan pilgrimage is considered the world's largest human gathering, with almost 2.4 million people performing the pilgrimage in 2018 (Table 2.1). In Morocco, as in other Muslim-majority nations and communities, Muslims perform several national and family rituals before they can perform the Hajj. In this chapter, I will discuss the necessary preliminaries to Hajj, both religious and mundane. In the process, I show how the religious imperative to perform this pilgrimage is interwoven with material considerations and concerns. These do not necessarily detract from the spiritual aspects of preparation but are natural and inevitable considerations undertaken to maximise the second phase – the experience of pilgrimage itself. I additionally illustrate the reservoir of spiritual consolation on which people draw should they fail to undertake the Hajj, and I consider the lengths to which some are prepared to go to make their dream of Hajj a reality.

Table 2.1 Annual number of Hajj pilgrims to Saudi Arabia, 2015–19

Year	Number of pilgrims	Number of Moroccan pilgrims
2015	1,952,817	25,600
2016	1,862,909	25,600
2017	2,352,122	32,000
2018	2,371,675	32,000
2019	2,489,406	32,000

Pilgrimage starts with the application process, followed by a selection procedure referred to in Morocco as the *qurʿa* (national lottery), and then the registration procedures, all of which are carefully managed by the state. In addition, once selected to perform the Hajj, Moroccans must prepare themselves both financially and socially, involving family, friends and relatives. These ritualised contexts become the locus of negotiation between mundane and religious commitments.

The period before a person can travel to Mecca, perform the pilgrimage or be addressed as *al-ḥājj*/*al-ḥājja* is lengthy. In her discussion about preparing for the Hajj in Tunisia, Katia Boissevain (2012) describes this period as one containing both administrative procedures and religious rituals. Taking Boissevain's descriptive analysis one step further, I will show how the religious aspect of the application process, such as the 'hearing of God's proclamation', is intimately and inseparably entwined with mundane aspects, such as the administrative parts of the application process.

Indeed, from the time a pilgrim formulates their intention of performing the pilgrimage, through the application and selection process, and on to the departure from Morocco to Mecca, both the pilgrim and the state are involved in a series of activities that include a pilgrims' social network and the larger community (Hammoudi 2006). Therefore, this chapter demonstrates that the material preparation for this ritual represents an important aspect of the pilgrimage; this phase of pilgrimage reveals to the outside observer both its roundedness in Moroccan society and the personal importance of the pilgrimage in the everyday lives of Moroccans. Although some aspects of the preparation for Hajj might seem mundane for some people, they are still vitally important in ensuring that the Hajj, as a religious duty, is performed well.

The chapter is organised as follows. It starts with a description of the *qurʿa* and its significance in Morocco, accounting for both the administrative and the religious aspects of the process. This is followed by a discussion of the reflections of Moroccans on the administrative process and the means used to avoid the *qurʿa*, including possible alternatives to this approved method; these alternatives include some that border on the illicit. Finally, I reflect on the importance of both religious and mundane preparedness before undertaking of the pilgrimage, which is for many Moroccans the journey of a lifetime.

Between the Quota and the *Qurʿa*: Managing Desires and Hurdles

My conversation with *al-ḥājj* Jamal revealed the lengthy process through which each Moroccan wishing to perform the pilgrimage to Mecca must go. Initially, prospective pilgrims must visit local governmental offices where they can complete a registration form. Applicants should carry with them their national identification cards so that their name and number are registered in the electronic system. An applicant must not have completed the Hajj within the preceding ten years, and women must have a male companion registered with them at the same time.[4] Once the details of applicants are entered into the system, they need to wait for the national draw, the *qurʿa*, which takes place some weeks following the end of the registration process.

The *qurʿa* was initiated as a mechanism for dealing with the ever-growing number of Moroccan Hajj applicants, whose number far exceeds the Hajj quota allocated for Moroccan pilgrims. The quota system was initiated by Saudi Arabia in 1987, as a result of the country's being overwhelmed by the growing numbers of pilgrims, and due to fears of losing control over the pilgrimage.[5] In 1988, the Organization of Islamic Cooperation (OIC) decided to set a Hajj quota for each country at 1,000 pilgrims per million of the total (Muslim) population (Bianchi 2004, 51).[6] As a result, Morocco has a total allocation of some 32,000 pilgrims per year.[7]

In Morocco, the application and the *qurʿa* take place one year before the performance of the Hajj.[8] This means that those who performed the Hajj in 2015 were successful in the *qurʿa* of 2014. According to the Moroccan regulations, the oldest 15 per cent of all applicants automatically qualify for the pilgrimage without having to go through the process. The *qurʿa* is organised by each municipality (*ʿamāla*) individually and takes place in a public venue, normally a large hall that can accommodate the many applicants who wish to witness the procedure. During the *qurʿa*, envelopes with the names of applicants are drawn from a large box, and the names in the envelopes are announced aloud. Although these moments are ones of anticipation and excitement for those whose names are called, they are also moments of disappointment for others.

Many people make sure they attend the draw, and *al-ḥājj* Jamal's son was no exception, according to his father:

> My son called me and said: 'Congratulations! We are going on Hajj!' . . . Then a friend who also attended the *qurʿa* called. He said: 'You are lucky! Congratulations! I heard that hundreds of people attended [the lottery], yet only tens were selected . . .' Hajj is indeed so dear to the hearts of Moroccans . . .

According to a local government officer, 264,522 Moroccans applied for the Hajj in 2014, compared to 27,000 people who were selected to perform Hajj from Morocco the following year (2015).[9] This means that only around ten per cent of the applicants get selected to perform the Hajj (Figure 2.1). More than two hundred thousand Moroccans and their families were left

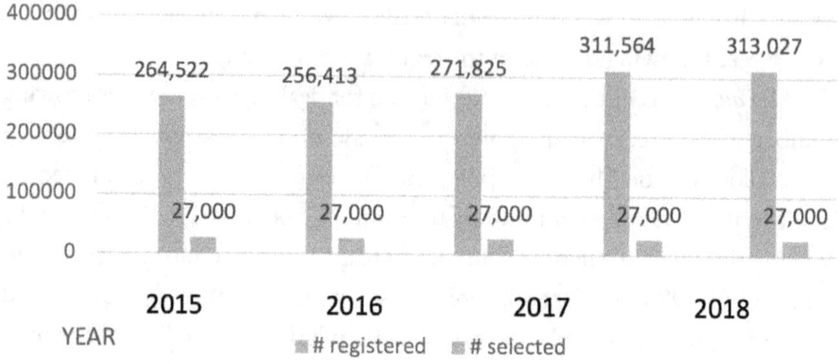

Figure 2.1 *Qurʿa* winners vis-à-vis Hajj applicants, 2015–18

disappointed, not being selected to perform religious duty. It is important to note that the total quota is larger than the number of visas allocated in the *qurʿa*, as the remaining thousands are reserved for government purposes. Some of those visas would be given to officials accompanying pilgrims as delegates of groups of religious scholars, governors, guides, doctors, nurses and other professionals. Visas are also given to officials such as ambassadors and councillors, or as royal favours, as was the case in 2019 when the king of Morocco sent a delegation of twenty blind Moroccans on Hajj.[10] In addition, for several years in a row – before 2015 – the allocated quota was reduced by 20 per cent due to the expansion project of the Grand Mosque of Mecca. As a point of interest, among the pilgrims I met during my fieldwork, the average number of attempts in the *qurʿa* before success came was four. Very few (around two in a hundred) stated that they had won the *qurʿa* upon their first registration. One Moroccan told me that his sister had applied eight times for Hajj before being finally selected in the *qurʿa*.[11]

Although being selected to perform the Hajj in the *qurʿa* is hugely significant for Moroccans, it is only one step in the arduous process. Once accepted to perform the Hajj, future pilgrims are given a period during which they should fulfil their Hajj-related financial duties by depositing the complete Hajj fees in an allocated bank account. Failure to pay those fees in time means that the applicant might lose her/his opportunity to perform Hajj and would subsequently be replaced by another person from the long waiting list. Once payment has been verified by the administration, the prospective pilgrim is required to deliver a 'visa file' to the relevant authorities, which consists of pilgrim's passport, two personal photographs and copies of the national identification card. Women must submit other documents proving their civil status (Table 2.2). Then, the prospective pilgrim is required to undergo a full medical examination, which also involves tests for infectious diseases, as well as compulsory vaccination, which is free for pilgrims, but should be carried out in assigned hospitals or health centres at a specific period before the Hajj. Should the aspiring pilgrim be unable to travel during the allocated year for any reason, these formalities are required again for subsequent applications.

Table 2.2 Documentation required from female pilgrims (according to civil status)

Single	Married	Divorced	Widow
Civil status certificate*	Copy of marriage contract	Marriage certificate	Husband's death certificate
Certified proof of male companion	Husband's consent	Divorce certificate	Civil status certificate
	Companion's approval	Civil status certificate	Companion's approval
National identification card and a photocopy of it			
National passport			
Two passport-size images			

*According to a local official, the civil status certificate can be obtained from the relevant civil authorities and women are required to submit it.

The procedures after selection are many and varied. To illustrate and reflect on these aspects of the pilgrimage, I will give as an example the experience of *al-ḥājja* Zahra, a retired teacher from Salé.

A Pilgrim's Trajectory: Administrative Procedure and a Test of Faith

Al-ḥājja Zahra performed the Hajj in 2006. This was the first year Morocco had adopted the *qur'a* as a way of dealing with the growing numbers of pilgrimage applications. Being a widow over 45 years of age, Zahra decided to apply for Hajj alone, dispensing with the male family supporter required by younger women. She followed the assigned procedure, filled in applications, prepared all the required documents and waited for the draw. The drawing of names itself was a tense ceremony, attended by hundreds of potential pilgrims, some of whom had brought family members along too. Local officials, mosque imams and representatives of travel agencies were present to witness the process. Then, the names were pulled from a large box, one by one. The first was that of *al-ḥājja* Zahra, who was joyous, thanked God for this blessing and immediately called her three daughters to deliver the good news.

As the names were read aloud by one of the officials, she could easily identify those selected as they received complimentary words, congratulating them on the good news. Some men would say 'Congratulations', and others would say '*sa'dātik*', meaning 'Lucky you', or 'How happy you must be now!'. Some women expressed their joy with strident ululations. However, as the reading out of the names of those accepted came to an end, and the official continued to draw out the names that would be on the waiting lists, Zahra could also see disappointment, and heard people telling each other 'God willing, you will be selected next year', and 'Maybe God is hiding for you a greater good'.

Once selected, Zahra began preparing herself for the journey. She ordered a local tailor to prepare a white *jellaba*, which she planned to wear for her *iḥrām*. She went to the market and bought various necessities. Then, she sought information from people who had been on Hajj, asking about the rites, what to carry from Morocco, and what to expect to see in Mecca. Zahra's daughter bought her a book called *The Guide to Performing Hajj and 'umra*, which included instructions for pilgrims and some historical narratives about each site to be visited.

Weeks after the draw, Zahra was required to continue the Hajj procedures. She had learned that she would need to take blood tests, have vaccinations and prepare her passport for the visa procedure. When she went for vaccination in Salé, however, she learned that her name was not on the lists they had received of pilgrims. Expecting that a mistake had occurred, she went to the hospital in Rabat, where she was told that her name was not on their lists either, and she was advised to ask at the local government office. There, to her dismay, it was confirmed that her name was not mentioned in the pilgrimage list. Zahra believed that the error was not an innocent accident. She was convinced that there was an attempt to replace her with another pilgrim by some kind of subterfuge. Given the fact that she had submitted all papers in a timely manner, she complained about this.

Although Zahra had learned that she would be going to Hajj a year earlier in the *qurʿa*, once she realised that there was an administrative issue she became more fearful of not being able to go on Hajj after all. I learned from Zahra's daughter that her mother was deeply affected by the experience and went from extreme happiness to depression. To save expenses, she walked back and forth between Salé and Rabat, five kilometres each way, almost daily, to ask about any developments in her case. She complained at the local office and went to the ministry, which, after considering her case, found that her name needed to be put back on the list. By the time Zahra's problem had been resolved, however, groups of pilgrims had already left Morocco for Saudi Arabia. Her passport had not been returned and she was still tied up with the visa procedure. Zahra was profoundly worried that she would miss her chance of going to Hajj. However, two days before the last group of pilgrims left for Mecca, she received good news. Her passport was ready along with the Hajj visa, and she was placed on the last flight leaving Morocco.

Although the process was lengthy and highly bureaucratic, Zahra nonetheless saw what happened to her as a good sign, especially when she learned that her group – including many people from the state delegation – had been placed in one of the best hotels, a five-minute walk from the Grand Mosque in Mecca. Under normal circumstances, Zahra would have had to pay extra fees to enjoy such a privilege. Had she left earlier, she could have been accommodated at a more distant location, several kilometres away from the mosque. Before leaving for Mecca, Zahra said farewell to her friends and neighbours. If she had learned the good news earlier, she could have invited family and friends for a meal, as is the normal custom, but time constraints prevented this. She asked her daughters and siblings for forgiveness, or *musāmaḥa*, a customary procedure for those leaving on Hajj; she also asked them if they wished for specific *duʿāʾ* prayers to be made on their behalf in Mecca, and enquired about special requests for gifts or souvenirs to be brought back from the holy places.[12] On the day of travel, her daughters and her brother accompanied her to the airport. Mecca being the first destination meant that Zahra should not forget to wear her *iḥrām* clothes before leaving Morocco.

Although Zahra's story had a successful conclusion, it illustrates that the *qurʿa* process can be stressful, especially as most Moroccans can only perform the Hajj if they are selected in the draw. The official bureaucratic mechanisms can be perceived as placing an obstacle in the path of the pilgrim, and may potentially create stress, which displaces spiritual preparations, substituting instead pragmatic, mundane worries. Therefore, some Moroccans try to find alternative ways to avoid the lengthy procedure. In the next section, I reflect on some of these alternatives, as I learned about them during my fieldwork in Morocco.

Avoiding the *Qurʿa* Procedure

During my fieldwork, I learned of several ways in which people manage to avoid the draw, or, when not selected in the process, still manage to find a way of performing the Hajj. People who can afford extra expenses sometimes resort to the black market to obtain a special type of visa. These are referred to in Morocco as *mujāmala* visas; the Arabic term can be translated as 'gratis' or 'courtesy' visas.[13] The source of this type of visa is often unknown. In Morocco, however, I heard rumours that these visas are issued by the government of Saudi Arabia as gifts (hence the name *mujāmala*) to Muslim-majority countries in addition to those issued to the people allowed by the quota system. The reason for this gift is to allow government officials or people with exceptional circumstances (like the elderly) to be able to perform the Hajj without being subjected to the *qurʿa* process. In principle, these visas are meant to be free of charge. Therefore, those receiving them should pay only for transport and accommodation, in addition to Hajj services. In practice, however, these visas reach special dealers in the black market, who sell them at unaffordable prices to those desperate to perform the Hajj, subverting their original purpose and opening an avenue for abuse.

Another story that I heard in Morocco about the source of these visas indicated that they can be granted through Saudi embassies in countries where the quota is not met. *Al-ḥājj* Salim, a man who works at a tourist agency in Casablanca, told me about two pilgrims who had travelled with him from

Morocco to Mecca in 2012, carrying visas that had been issued in Nouakchott, the capital of Mauritania. *Al-ḥājj* Salim learned from the two men that they had paid around three thousand Euros each for the visa only. According to him:

> In some countries where people are extremely poor and cannot afford Hajj, their visas are taken by those corrupt dealers. If Mauritania, for example, had a quota of four thousand people and only three thousand could afford the expenses, then the rest of the visas would be sold.

According to *al-ḥājj* Salim this procedure was terminated in 2015, when the Moroccan government deemed it illegal and denied departure to those holding Hajj visas not issued in Morocco. If people holding such visas were allowed to leave Morocco, they would have been banned from entering at the Saudi side.

Although significant and rigorous procedures have been introduced by the Moroccan government to regulate such illegal visas, there are still stories of corrupt dealers, involved not only in selling visas to aspiring pilgrims, but also in forging visas while claiming they are *mujāmala* visas. In 2018, for example, dozens of people, from Casablanca and Agadir, discovered that they had fallen victim to such practices after having paid large sums of money to three dealers.

As desperate pilgrims paid vast amounts to obtain a Hajj visa, a dispute took place in June 2018 in the Moroccan parliament, which was granted five-hundred courtesy visas by the Saudi government.[14] This dispute, news of which reached official and social media and subsequently became a topic of conversation on the streets, concerned the controversial decision to allow parliamentarians or their family members or friends to have visas for Hajj without the troublesome procedure of the *qurʿa* with which ordinary Moroccan citizens must comply.

In Morocco, I witnessed several conversations and disputes regarding the *mujāmala* visas. As an example of these disputes, in the following section, I offer a conversation between two men from the city of Mohammedia: *al-ḥājj* Yassin, who had been on Hajj in 2014, and Ayyub, who had yet not performed the Hajj. The conversation took place at Yassin's small factory where Ayyub and I were invited for tea on 28 October 2015. The two men had been friends for many years and the conversation was lengthy; I will therefore cut directly to the part of their discussion that relates to the theme of this chapter:

Yassin: I am planning to go on *'umra* next Ramadan . . . I would not be able to register for Hajj again for ten years; yet I miss those holy places. What about you? Are you planning to apply?[15]
Ayyub: You know how expensive the Hajj has become . . . Not only the fees for the pilgrimage, but also the cost of gifts, parties and other commitments, these are all so costly . . . I need to take these costs into consideration. But I might apply for the *qur'a* next year.
Yassin: It would be good if you apply. You know, it is difficult to be selected in the *qur'a* anyhow.
Ayyub: Yes, I know! I heard that some people avoided this lottery in previous years by looking for *mujāmala* visas.
Yassin: They are more expensive. I heard from friends that one might pay up to nine million centimes [around nine thousand Euros] just to get the visa.
Ayyub: But I heard that doing such things [buying a *mujāmala* visa] is taboo [*ḥarām*].
Yassin: The halal [permissible] and the *ḥarām* [taboo] are both specified in the Holy Qur'an.[16] I do not think it is *ḥarām*! If a person is blessed to have enough money, why would they not go? Especially if they do not get selected by the state's *qur'a*! A person can go to a travel agency which has relationships with people in Saudi Arabia who offer visas as gifts . . . It is fine; if people are blessed from God to have enough money, they can go that way . . . We all go for a major purpose: [God's] forgiveness of our sins . . . Pilgrims use money, sacrifice their time, and leave their families behind to go to that place and be closer to God.

The conversation between *al-ḥājj* Yassin and Ayyub reflects the two contrasting opinions regarding the *mujāmala* visas among Moroccans. Some people, like Yassin, do not see the harm in such a procedure. The pilgrimage becomes possible for those 'who can afford it'. Many people, however, find the procedure highly unjust, disadvantaging the poor, and unfair to those who comply with the official procedures of Hajj application. From a religious point of view, many people consider it *ḥarām* to involve oneself in such a questionable activity, even if one can afford the costs. In the words Ayyub said to me in private following our meeting with Yassin: 'Would God accept a pilgrimage based on corruption and deceit?'

The *mujāmala* visas, and the dubious methods of acquiring them, are, it seems, often available to those who can afford to pay. However, people with limited funds, who have also been unlucky in the draw but who desperately wish to perform the pilgrimage, may try to find other means of fulfilling their ambition. Those means might also be considered unethical or even illegal, but they are under less popular scrutiny than the stratagems adopted by the rich. As an illustration, one trick is to travel to Saudi Arabia to undertake an *'umra* during the period leading up to the Hajj (before the tenth month of the lunar calendar).[17] In recent years, the latest dates for *'umra* trips have been during the month of Ramadan, after which there is a period of approximately two months until the start of the Hajj season. Those wishing to perform the Hajj could remain in the country illegally, extending their visit until the time of the Hajj.

According to *al-ḥājj* Salim, only a small number of Moroccan pilgrims performed their Hajj using this tactic in recent years, as the Saudi control measures have become stricter. If detected by the Saudi authorities during the period leading to the Hajj season, the aspiring pilgrims would be arrested and then deported back to Morocco; they would also be subjected to large fines and would be denied entry to Saudi Arabia for ten years. A tiny number of Moroccans, however, manage to break the Saudi regulations. To evade being captured by the police, these people have to hide and live through difficult conditions until their Hajj is finally complete. When I interviewed *al-ḥājj* Salim about this practice, he told me:

> The Saudi authorities have made it much harder for those who stay for Hajj illegally by adopting new procedures including having intensive inspections and checkpoints in the Mecca and Jeddah areas. However, some might endure two months of suffering . . . [and] if they manage to stay, they return to Mecca seeking concealment among more than two million pilgrims . . . Once they decide to return to Morocco, however, they must deal with the consequences at the airport . . . But whatever these [consequences] are, it is over! They are now pilgrims . . .

Here again, one can see how the religious practice of Hajj is tightly framed by social conditions, financial ability and the way Hajj policies and regulations are being managed. The sacred duty of pilgrimage and the mandatory practices related to the application procedure are inextricably intertwined, and pilgrims cannot separate the spiritual aim from the mundane constraints placed upon its realisation. During my fieldwork, I did not meet any Moroccan who openly acknowledged having performed an illegal action so as to perform the Hajj, or proudly admitted that they paid extra for a pilgrimage visa. The reason for this, according to *al-ḥājj* Salim, is that no one would admit engaging in illicit practices that would compromise the validity of their pilgrimage. Some research participants indicated that they had performed the Hajj when they lived in Saudi Arabia using their labour contracts and residence permits to undertake the pilgrimage, or even that they had applied to work in the Kingdom so as to be able to perform the scared duty. Lücking's research on migrants from the Indonesian island of Madura who journey to Mecca sheds light on the close interconnection between work and pilgrimage. For those Indonesian migrants, some of whom are on pilgrimage waiting lists that can stretch to twenty years or even more, obtaining an *ʿumra* visa has emerged as a popular strategy for entering Saudi Arabia, providing them with an opportunity to work while anticipating the Hajj season.[18] Upon arriving in Saudi Arabia they resort to hiding, and a significant number engage in illegal work as they await the pilgrimage season (Lücking 2017, 261–3). These anecdotes offer a glimpse into the possibility of individuals clandestinely staying in Mecca to fulfil their pilgrimage aspirations. The discreet nature of these practices, coupled with the sensitivity of the topic, make it challenging to acquire concrete data to substantiate the extent of such occurrences in the Moroccan context, but the existence of these narratives underscores the need for further investigation and recognition of potential irregularities in the pilgrimage process.

For Moroccans who cannot fulfil the pilgrimage to Mecca, either legally or illegally, an alternative religious avenue is sought, such is the urge of many to travel to Mecca. Performing the *ʿumra*, therefore, is a popular way of dealing with the disappointment of not being selected by the *qurʿa*. In the following section, I offer the story of Yasir, a man in his sixties, as an example.

ʿUmra as an Alternative Pilgrimage to Hajj

For many Moroccans who cannot perform the Hajj due to the various conditions, going on *ʿumra* seems a suitable alternative. According to local travel agents with whom I spoke, more than one hundred thousand Moroccans performed the *ʿumra* in 2018 and more than thirty thousand people in the month of Ramadan alone. The numbers were even higher in 2019, as according to a local official, one hundred thousand Moroccans performed the *ʿumra* in Ramadan and some eighty thousand at other times of the year.[19] When I met Yasir, a fabric shop owner from Fes, he told me that he had undertaken five *ʿumra* trips. He performed his first *ʿumra* in 2005, together with a group of friends, all of whom had failed to be selected in the *qurʿa*. The second trip was in 2008 with his wife, the third in Ramadan of 2011, and he had gone once every two years since then. He explained to me that on each occasion when he had applied for Hajj he had wished to be accepted, yet he believed it was God's will that he had not been. Yasir told me that he would go to Mecca every year if he could, so great was the call, and so intense was his longing for the holy places. He could not imagine that any Moroccan would not wish to visit those places.

Yasir had applied for Hajj – and had failed – five times. He believed that not being selected was a test of his faith, and that when he was ready God would surely reward him with Hajj. For him, pilgrimage

> is like marriage. One might think, I want to get married when I am thirty-five years old, wiser, and have the financial means; but if that man meets the right woman and God helped him, they might get married at twenty-five . . . Pilgrimage is similar . . . When the opportunity comes, I do not want to miss it . . .

Yasir used the simile of marriage to clarify his point. For him, one should perform the Hajj whenever one is able to do so. Like marriage, however, one might be ready for it on a personal level, but, if a person's destiny were to be married later, then they would have to wait until the right time. Yasir feared, however, that he would grow older without being able to perform Hajj. For him, the pilgrimage demands that one is healthy and strong enough to perform the rituals to optimum effect. Driven by a different imperative, many Moroccans still wish to perform the Hajj when older. They long to be able 'to cleanse themselves from sins and get ready to meet God', Yasir told me. I saw Yasir frequently during my stay in Fes; I greeted him whenever I passed by his shop and stopped to chat frequently. Despite the passage of time, he remained hopeful that he would be able to go on Hajj.

The Pilgrimage Process and Motivations, Encompassing the Religious and the Mundane

During my interactions with prospective pilgrims in Morocco, they often spoke about their motivation for applying for the Hajj. Like *al-ḥājj* Jamal, many Moroccans portrayed their motivations in religious terms, speaking of 'renewal of one's faith', 'connecting with God at the most holy place for Muslims', or simply referring to 'a religious duty' and 'one of the pillars of Islam'. *Al-ḥājj* Yassin encapsulated people's motivations during his conversation with Ayyub when he said:

> Hajj is always present in all Moroccan houses . . . Everyone who can perform Hajj should apply, and go . . . Hajj is not an extra thing; it is an obligation . . . Who would not like to answer the call of God or visit the Prophet? Through Hajj, one can address God, recognize His oneness, thank Him for His blessings, seek His forgiveness for the sins one has committed and repent of one's wrongdoings . . .

The words of *al-ḥājj* Yassin echo those of many of the Moroccans I met. Referring to their selection in the *qurʿa*, my interlocutors used expressions such as 'It was God's will', 'God's blessing', or 'God's favour' (*bi-faḍli-llāh*). Interestingly, the Arabic expression *faḍl* also refers to preference, connoting a sense of being 'chosen' by God, or favoured by Him. On the other hand, people who were not selected often considered this to be a sign of a different nature, that it was not the right time to perform the pilgrimage, and that 'when the right time comes, one would certainly answer God's proclamation', as Ayyoub stated. Success or failure in the *qurʿa* is ascribed to God's will, and the devout are more able to accept the outcomes because of this deeply rooted belief.

There is a period of one year between the time of registration, passing through the *qurʿa* and preparing for the Hajj, and the actual time of travel to Mecca. In this period, various material factors might hinder a person from performing the pilgrimage. A person might fail to meet the financial fees of the pilgrimage; a woman could become pregnant; one might fall sick or even die. In those cases, Moroccans often interpreted such situations in religious terms, however worldly or mundane the roots of the obstacle might be. According to *al-ḥājj* Salim: 'If a person really wished to perform the pilgrimage, and for any reason were not able to make the journey, God would accept one's intention and still reward him/her.' According to many Moroccans, one's intention (*niyya*) is recognised by God, and therefore one may be rewarded even if one does not manage to perform the pilgrimage.

One example of such interference in the pilgrimage is provided by the case of Sarah, the daughter-in-law of *al-ḥājj* Jamal. Sarah was selected in the *qurʿa* together with her husband and parents-in-law. However, following the draw, Sarah found out that she was pregnant. She was due to give birth only two weeks before the pilgrimage to Mecca would take place. The news of her pregnancy was a source of both joy and regret. The family were grateful to receive the news of the pregnancy; however, they, and Sarah specifically (according to her father-in-law), were disappointed that she was not able to perform the pilgrimage with her family. For *al-ḥājj* Jamal, the pregnancy was a sign that God's proclamation for Sarah's Hajj was yet to be made. He hoped that in the coming years she could apply for the *qurʿa* once more, and if she were selected her husband would accompany her as male guardian.[20]

During my fieldwork, I noticed that Moroccans often spoke about the pilgrimage as a practice that strengthens one's faith and solidifies one's relationship with God. Hajj, it seemed, was not just an obligation that a Muslim has to perform once in a lifetime. Rather, engaging in Hajj helped to constitute and solidify moral commitment to one's faith over time. As *al-ḥājja* Zahra put it:

> I wanted to perform Hajj to experience that feeling of belonging, of being a member of a bigger Islamic community; Hajj *renews* one's faith and cleanses the pilgrim from all sins one might have committed during his life . . . I grew up hearing stories from my parents and grandparents about the Hajj, looking at the Kaʿba on TV, and learning about it from the Qur'an and religious texts . . .

The collective narratives, widely circulated in Moroccan society, about people who have already been to Mecca to perform the Hajj and *ʿumra* seem to provide a further motivation for the performance of the Hajj. People were often encouraged to apply for Hajj, as *al-ḥājj* Yassin did when he conversed with

Ayyub. Moreover, performance of the Hajj includes an aspiration to transform one's status both on a religious and a social level. On the personal level, the performance of pilgrimage is an opportunity for self-development and for transformation into a better Muslim. As *al-ḥājj* Jamal said, when I met him, the Hajj is a school (*madrasa*):

> When people go on Hajj people learn a lot: about life, other Muslims, and about their faith . . . People should not go empty-handed and return empty . . . People should return with good hearts and deeds; never lie, never cheat and stay faithful . . . Their children and wives should witness that change and they too should benefit from the Hajj.

Although Moroccans mainly state religious reasons for performing the pilgrimage, I learned of other motivations that are sometimes debated whenever the pilgrimage topic is discussed. One motivation for pilgrimage was related to the social status a pilgrim often enjoys upon the completion of this religious duty. In comparison with the past, there are now greater numbers of people who successfully perform the Hajj. Yet the title *al-ḥājj* or *al-ḥājja* remains highly significant at both personal and social levels as a form of social, religious and moral capital.[21] In their family and in daily life in their wider community, pilgrims are highly respected and well-regarded.[22]

Nonetheless, when declaring their own Hajj motivations, people often avoid reference to such acquired personal 'kudos' as a motive, and only put forward the religious reasons related to strengthening one's faith and religious transformation. When speaking about others who make or have made Hajj, however, non-religious and perhaps even questionable motives also come to the fore. This sort of motivation would be frowned upon and openly criticised. During my fieldwork, I noticed that women were often the ones subjected to such criticism.[23] This might be related to stereotypical views of women, assuming them to be attracted to social status more readily than their male counterparts, and to be driven more by desires and less by religious motives (Sadiqi 2003; Ennaji 2008; Buitelaar 1993).[24]

Before leaving Morocco for Mecca, would-be pilgrims say farewell to their friends and neighbours. Such events are an interesting combination of spiritually, religiously observant practices and far more mundane habits. It is a religious expectation that pilgrims will settle their disputes and, if in debt, meet their financial obligations before departing for Mecca. In return, often family members and friends visit those leaving on Hajj, and ask for *duʿā'* prayers to be said on their behalf in Mecca, either in front of the Kaʿba or on the day when pilgrims are at Arafat. In addition, they might ask for gifts and souvenirs to be brought specifically from Mecca. Some of these objects may have religious connotations, including the water of Zamzam, prayer mats or scarfs, while others are less obviously religious, such as henna and a herbal plant known as 'the tree of the virgin Mary', a plant that is believed to cure infertile women (Al-Ajarma 2018). This combination of religious and material or mundane requests can also be seen in the types of prayers that relatives and friends ask of a departing pilgrim. As I witnessed the departure of pilgrims many times, either in their houses or at the airport, I heard a variety of requests for prayers, ranging from asking for God's forgiveness and blessings, and praying that God would help the person in being selected for pilgrimage, to God's assistance in finding a good husband or success in passing university or school exams. As for the pilgrim, all the requests are met with a single promise: *in-shā'-Allāh* ('If God wills!').

Another customary practice observed by many Moroccans before leaving for Mecca is one that was referred to as voluntary charity, *ṣadaqa*, or a banquet, *walīma*, a meal for family and friends that takes place at the house of the prospective pilgrim. Such gatherings are often organised upon a pilgrim's return from Mecca. Yet many Moroccans also have a get-together, often a smaller one, before leaving for Mecca. In addition to sharing food, the gathering sometimes includes Qur'an recitation, listening to music (mostly with religious themes but sometimes also non-religious), or singing and dancing. Although this practice is still popular in Morocco, many people criticised the profane or worldly aspects of the gathering, particularly the singing and dancing. In addition, some people were disapproving of the *ṣadaqa*. As the name *ṣadaqa* indicates, the purpose of the meal is to stage an act of charity, an act provided by the pilgrim's family. Those invited to this charitable meal, however, are rarely the poor or the ones in need of charitable giving. Therefore, many Moroccans consider it an unnecessary expenditure before the Hajj. Instead, those not in favour of this practice suggest, a prospective pilgrim should undertake 'moral preparation', such as increasing praying or fasting, taking pilgrimage lessons at local mosques, and solving disputes (which might be old or new) in preparation for the sacred journey. In the next section, I focus on the pilgrimage lessons at the local mosques as one aspect of the preparation of the pilgrimage journey.

A Pilgrimage Lesson in Fes

Pilgrimage lessons have become a common phenomenon in recent years in Morocco. Some are organised by the Ministry of Religious Affairs at mosques and others by travel agencies. Information about the dates and times of the lessons are advertised on the Ministry's website or through travel agencies, as was the case with the lessons I attended in Fes. The lesson described here was the second in a series of ten lessons which took place in Al-Baraka Mosque every Sunday after *ʿaṣr*, late afternoon prayer, in the weeks leading up to the Hajj.

I arrived half an hour early for the prayer, to find that the doors of the mosque were still locked. Outside on the stairs leading to the women's section of the mosque, I joined a woman in a brown dress and blue headscarf who waited for the doors to be opened. Soon, a young man showed up, opened the door and left. At that point two other women joined us. The three women were there for the lessons. One of them told us that she had learned about the lessons by chance and had missed the first one. One woman reported that what she had learned in the previous lesson related to performing the *niyya* of the Hajj, 'O God, I intend to perform *ʿumra* and Hajj. So, make them easy for me and accept them from me.' Then she listed the rituals to be performed once at the Grand Mosque of Mecca, including *ṭawāf*, the *saʿī* between the hills of Ṣafā and Marwā, and completing the *ʿumra* (for women, by cutting off a short lock of hair). From a notebook that she carried she read:

> Remember, when you drink the water of Zamzam you can say a specific *duʿāʾ* prayer, of '*Allāhumma innī asʾaluka ʿilman nāfiʿan wa rizqan wasiʿan wa shifāʾan min kullī dāʾ* [O God, I seek beneficial knowledge, wide sustenance and cure from all ailments from You]',[25] then say *bismi-llāh*,[26] and drink the water.

While waiting for the call for prayer, the women discussed practical Hajj arrangements, such as the health reports they were preparing in order to carry along in case of health emergency, and necessary travel documents to bring to Mecca. They then spoke about their expectations of the Hajj conditions in Mecca and Medina. One of the women said that she watched TV programmes about the Hajj, which recommended prospective pilgrims not to be frightened when they see the number of people they would meet during the Hajj. A second woman had heard in a radio programme that pilgrims were recommended to be at the airport six hours before the time of the flight to avoid any complications.

The women also discussed the dress code in Mecca. One of the women stated that she would carry one Moroccan *jellaba* and buy others in Mecca to wear during the Hajj; those would be black dresses, *ʿabāya*s, like those worn by women in Saudi Arabia. The other two women disagreed and stated that they would wear Moroccan dresses, which they had made specifically for Hajj, at all times. The women then discussed their financial needs during the Hajj. One said that she had been warned by previous pilgrims to beware of thieves. One should not carry a lot of money and should leave valuables in the hotel safe.

The conversation continued, dominated by practicalities, tips, and advice of a relatively worldly and practical nature. Some discussions did relate to religious matters. The women discussed the best times to perform *ṭawāf* and prayers. One of them advised the others to perform *ṭawāf* between prayers, especially in the early morning or evening hours when the heat would be less harsh. The women noted that it would be better to sleep less and pray more. The women agreed to meet again the following Sunday, once they had discovered where their accommodation in Mecca would be, to arrange a meeting with each other during the Hajj.

One of the women declared that she had agreed with some other women travelling with the same agency to Mecca to carry specific food items from Morocco including potatoes, tomatoes, olive oil and herbs. She feared that the food in Mecca would be too foreign or unsuitable. Those women were travelling to Mecca for the first time and were uncertain of what they would find there. Another woman, who had heard through former pilgrims that there were plenty of familiar food stuffs available in Mecca and Medina and that there was no need to carry food from Morocco, told the others that women, herself included, should focus on the rituals of worship rather than thinking about food or shopping. They all agreed, but mentioned that it would still be their responsibility to prepare the food during the pilgrimage.

At that point, the imam recited the *iqāma*, the announcement that prayer was about to commence. The women stopped their conversation and stood in line in preparation for the communal prayer that was about to take place. Around eighty women had gathered at the mosque for prayer and nearly all remained for the lesson that followed. For this purpose, they moved to the men's section of the mosque, where the imam giving the lesson and some sixty men sat in the front; the women took their places at the back. Some women took notebooks out of their bags and took notes during the lesson. The imam had a PowerPoint presentation installed on a small computer screen next to him. On his other side, a large box was painted in black to give an idea of the structure of the Kaʿba. Some of the women moved closer to be able to see the PowerPoint presentation, yet keeping an acceptable distance from the men.

Carrying two pieces of white cloth, the imam first showed the men how to wear the *iḥrām* clothes. He then instructed the women to wear any comfortable clothes as long as they were modest and covering their full bodies. Next, the imam circumambulated the black box to show the future pilgrims how to perform *ṭawāf* around the Kaʿba. He explained that pilgrims should perform each rite of the Hajj to the best of their ability. 'Hajj is performed once in a lifetime for most people; therefore, there is no chance to repeat the rites if they are performed in a wrong manner', he concluded. Following his explanation of the rituals, the imam advised the pilgrims to start their journey by reciting the *duʿā'* prayer of travel.[27] Several women noted the prayer in their notebooks.

The lesson lasted around one and a half hours. People had the chance to ask questions during the last half hour. One man asked whether the Hajj rites varied according to different *madhhab*s (schools of Islamic jurisprudence).[28] The imam explained that the main rites were the same for all Muslims, although there were minor differences. He gave an example of *ṭawāf al-wadāʿ*, the last circuit of the Kaʿba which pilgrims perform before leaving Mecca, and explained that the last *ṭawāf* is considered obligatory by the Hanafi and Hanbali schools but simply *mustaḥabb*, desirable, and not obligatory, by the Maliki school that is followed in Morocco. This explanation meant that if pilgrims were not able to perform the last *ṭawāf*, no penalty would be incurred for the default. Towards the end, he indicated that Moroccan pilgrims should follow the Maliki *madhhab*, in accordance with what he taught them about the Hajj.

At the end of the lesson, the women left the room first. Some left immediately while most stood outside the mosque to discuss what they had heard from the imam, further preparations for the journey and arrangements for travel. Again, many women discussed food necessities, clothing and housing arrangements. Although all these issues might seem mundane in relation to the religious aspect of the Hajj, nonetheless, according to one of the women outside the mosque, 'It is necessary to arrange those things so they would not be a source of distraction during the Hajj'. For her, managing issues related to food, clothing and accommodation is an essential foundation for a better Hajj experience. As the women said goodbye to each other to go home, I had the impression that they were content about what they had learned that afternoon.

Conclusion

The focus of this chapter has been on the preparatory rituals preceding the performance of the Hajj in Morocco. I began by unpacking the administrative and religious practices that take place, starting from the time a Moroccan declares their intention to perform the Hajj, up until their physical departure to Mecca. Reflecting on the procedures a pilgrim must adopt before being able to perform the Hajj, I showed how in these steps religious and mundane factors are inextricably intertwined as part of the daily lives of Moroccans, and how, in the process, people's personal desires and spiritual hopes are combined with their fears about the *qurʿa* itself and their nervousness about other practical steps they need to overcome before being allowed to go to Mecca. Thus, awaiting the *qurʿa* involves much anticipation and even stress, especially for those who may have failed in previous applications.

The *qurʿa* is the most problematic of the procedures preceding the Hajj. If selected at the *qurʿa*, a person is considered lucky, and this is often seen as a sign of God's approval of the pilgrimage intention. However, the spiritual elation is quickly followed by concerns about more mundane and trivial details and considerations, including travel, food, clothing, etiquette, and social customs, before departure. Those who have been rejected, although frustrated, take consolation in religious responses to their situation, including embracing the concept of God's will and their own destiny.

Due to the limitations imposed by the *qurʿa* system, some Moroccans look for alternatives enabling them to perform the Hajj, including purchasing expensive visas or committing actions that may be considered illicit or illegal, such as overstaying in Mecca outside the pilgrimage season until the time of the pilgrimage. In this grey area between legal and illegal practices, one can detect corruption in the administrative process governing Hajj. Besides the prospective pilgrims themselves, many others are involved in the process, opening opportunities for abuse.

Preparation for the Hajj is nearly as much a social as a personal affair. This comes to the fore in the passing on of advice, or in terms of people helping others to iron out troubles or obstacles which can arise, including missteps in the bureaucratic process itself (as was the case with Zahra, the woman who fell off the pilgrim list). Even relative strangers, such as the women I met at the mosque, become involved in discussions of a quite detailed nature, and are assumed to be a legitimate and helpful source of support. This reflects the way in which Hajj and all its stages seem to be fully integrated into the fabric of life in Morocco.

Many of the preparations that take place before the pilgrimage are far from spiritual. There are a great many 'travellers' tips', and many such tips might seem not to be related at all to the spiritual impetus behind the Hajj. However, as the women in the mosque asserted, being well-prepared means that pilgrims can fully immerse themselves in the religious aspects of the pilgrimage experience once they arrive in Mecca, having dealt with all potential material distractions beforehand. In the narratives of Moroccan pilgrims, there are still strongly religious threads running through this mass of worldly anxieties. Often these manifest themselves in quasi-ritual expressions of hope, faith and blessing.

Thus, the period of preparation may seem to be awash with mundane matters, but these act as hand-servants to the still-to-come spiritual experience. This spiritual experience will be discussed in the next chapter.

Notes

1. The full verse from the Qur'an reads: 'Proclaim the Pilgrimage to all people. They will come to you on foot and on every kind of swift mount, emerging from every deep mountain pass' (Qur'an 22, 27). According to Ibn Kathīr, Abraham said to God: 'But my voice cannot reach all peoples.' God responded: 'You make the call, and We will deliver the invitation to all' (Ibn Kathīr 1986 vol. 3, 216–17).

2. Square brackets are used to indicate where I have added words for clarification which were not included in the original quotation or text.
3. Fieldnotes, 22 October 2015.
4. For women under the age of 45, a *maḥram* (first-degree male companion: father, brother, uncle or husband) is mandatory for Hajj registration. Women aged over 45 can travel without a *maḥram* but need to be registered with a *rafīq*, a male companion who can accompany a group of women to Hajj and is appointed by the government for women who do not have a first-degree male companion.
5. Following a major clash with Iranian pilgrims in 1987, the Saudi government feared attempts to politicise the pilgrimage (Fischer and Abedi 1990).
6. The Organization of Islamic Cooperation (OIC) (formerly known as the Organization of the Islamic Conference) was established in 1969 and is made up of fifty-seven member states (Peterson 2003).
7. During my fieldwork, rumours circulated in Morocco and elsewhere that the *ʿumra*, which can be undertaken at any time of year, might also be subjected to similar quota rules in the future, at least during times of greater influx such as the month of Ramadan and the period of *al-mawlid al-nabawī*, the prophet Muhammad's birthday.
8. Each Muslim country has the freedom to manage its quota. Some countries, like Indonesia, do not have a Hajj *qurʿa*. Indonesians wishing to perform the pilgrimage have to register their names via a government registration system and wait their turn (Saudi Gazette 2016). According to a report by the Cabinet Secretary of the Republic of Indonesia, the wait time is on average around twenty years, depending on the province (2019). Other countries, like Jordan, use the *qurʿa* system and at the same time manage the numbers of applicants by age. For example, those who registered for Hajj in 2018 had to be born in or before 1970. The *qurʿa* in Jordan takes place in the same calendar year as the Hajj for which people are applying.
9. Unpublished information provided through personal connections with a local official.
10. Several Moroccan news agencies covered this event thoroughly (https://mamlakatona.com/archives/107288 [in Arabic], last accessed 25 December 2019).
11. Unpublished information provided through personal connections with a local official. Out of all successful applicants, 8,000 people can register to perform the Hajj with authorised travel agencies and the rest must travel under state management.

12. Musāmaḥa, literally 'forgiveness', refers to the act of seeking the forgiveness of relatives and friends before a pilgrim leaves to Mecca. This practice is said to date back to the times when a potential for physical harm or death on the long journey was high, serving as spiritual preparation for 'meeting God' during the pilgrimage, or in case of death (Murata and Chittick 1994, 21; Sijapati 2018, 109).
13. *Mujāmala* – meaning courtesy – visas refer to guest visas which can be issued outside of the protocol of the quota scheme. According to local travel agents, these visas are sold on the black market by a few Moroccans who benefit from the process (unpublished information).
14. The dispute in the parliament was reported in in the media with headlines including 'Free Hajj visas ignites war in the parliament' (*Al-'usbū'*, 7 June 2018).
15. The pilgrimage guidelines state that once a pilgrim has been to Mecca for the Hajj, they cannot apply to again for at least ten years.
16. Sometimes Moroccans would allude to the Qur'an (or the Prophet) – as popular knowledge – without specifics being provided. In relation to the permissible or taboo argument, the Qur'an has several related verses, mainly concerning food and consumption activities, such as 'You who believe, eat the good things We have provided for you and be grateful to God, if it is Him that you worship. He has only forbidden you carrion, blood, pig's meat, and animals over which any name other than God's has been invoked. But if anyone is forced to eat such things by hunger, rather than desire or excess, he commits no sin: God is most merciful and forgiving' (Qur'an 2, 172–3). Other examples can be found in the Qur'an, including verses 5, 3; 5, 5; 6, 121; 7, 33.
17. According to the Saudi regulations, *'umra* visas stop after Ramadan, the ninth month of the lunar calendar. The period following Ramadan aims at preparing for the Hajj season. *'umra* reopens at the new lunar year (unpublished information provided by a Moroccan travel agent).
18. Foreign Muslim migrant labourers who already possess a Saudi residence permit are required to acquire an official permit to partake in the Hajj. However, they have the flexibility to perform the pilgrimage either individually or in self-organised groups (Buitelaar 2023, 28; Lücking 2017).
19. Unpublished information provided by a local official through personal connections. According to the same official, an average of 140,000 Moroccans performed *'umra* annually between 2015 and 2019.
20. Despite the ten-year prohibition imposed on those who successfully perform the Hajj, a male pilgrim who has been on Hajj less than ten years previously can still accompany a female first-degree relative to the Hajj as a male guardian (*maḥram*).

21. On forms of capital see Bourdieu 1986.
22. The honorific title *al-ḥājj* or *al-ḥājja* comes with significant social and religious significance, which I discuss in Chapter Four.
23. For examples of women's experiences as pilgrims see Chapters Four and Seven.
24. See Chapter Four.
25. This *du'ā'* prayer is said to have been recommended by the prophet Muhammad in hadith (Ibn Mājah, Vol. 1, book 5, hadith 925).
26. *Bismi-llāh* is a short version of *bismi-Allāh al-raḥmāni al-raḥīm* (In the name of God, the Merciful Benefactor), which is also called *basmala* or *tasmiya*. The invocation of the *basmala* is recommended as a blessing for Muslims at the beginning of every important act such as reciting the Qur'an, eating, drinking, etc. (Carra de Vaux and Gardet 2012).
27. Muslims are encouraged to perform a *du'ā'* prayer when travelling, according to one hadith: 'O God, we seek virtue and piety from You in this journey of ours and the act which pleases You. O God, lighten this journey of ours, and make its distance easy for us. O Allah, You are (our) companion during the journey, and guardian of (our) family. O God, I seek refuge with You from the hardships of the journey, gloominess of the sights, and finding adverse changes to property and family on return' (Muslim, book 15, hadith 479).
28. A *madhhab* refers to a school of thought within *fiqh* (Islamic jurisprudence). Most Sunni Muslims follow one of the four major Sunni school (Hanafi, Maliki, Shafi'i, Hanbali). Moroccans follow the Maliki *madhhab*.

3

IN THE HAJJ: A SENSORY EXPERIENCE THAT 'CANNOT BE DESCRIBED IN WORDS'

Let us walk in paths of safety,
God, the Prophet and the Qur'an are with us;
with God, and lights of certitude before us,
and with our faith,
we will overcome every oppression

(Lyrics of Moroccan song)

Introduction

A few days after my arrival at Fes, I met Hanan, a local tailor whose shop was across the street from the house where I lived. Hanan spent most of her time at the shop. She had performed the Hajj in 2006, and ever since she has visited Mecca for *'umra* at least once a year. When I visited Hanan's shop, she was often busy guiding the work of two women and three men who would spend their day designing and preparing Moroccan traditional dresses, *qafṭāns* and *ṭaqshiṭas*.[1] Hanan herself was very stylish, often wearing elegant skirts with matching shirts and colourful head scarves that revealed some of her dyed hair. When I visited Hanan's shop, I expressed my interest in learning about her experience in Mecca. Hanan's first reaction was a sigh, followed by a few seconds of silence. She then told me that if I wanted to learn about the experience of being in Mecca, I should go to visit it myself, since for her that was the only way one could understand the importance of the journey. In her words, 'the pilgrimage was an unforgettable experience', and 'a chance of a lifetime to experience a place that was better than any other place'. As my visits to Hanan's shop continued, I got to hear more about her trips to Mecca, the places she visited, her prayers and thoughts, and the people she met during the pilgrimage, both Moroccans and foreigners.

One afternoon, I sat with Hanan and the two women workers in the front room of the shop, which had a desk and five chairs. The front of the shop was made of glass so that those inside could see the passers-by in the street, while those passing could see the new dresses displayed on two mannequins. Hanan was telling us that she had prayed that she could make the pilgrimage to Mecca:

> I wished for a pilgrimage in which the Day of Arafat [when pilgrims perform the rite of *wuqūf*, or stand on or beside Mount Arafat] would be on a Friday. I would say: 'O Lord! Grant me the Hajj in which the standing on the Day of Arafat is a Friday . . .' If so, it would be considered *al-ḥājj al-akbar* [a greater pilgrimage]. Then, I would have two celebrations: one for Hajj and another for Friday.[2]

Hanan believed that a pilgrimage in which the Day of Arafat fell on a Friday was more blessed than any other, and she was grateful that her prayers had been heard.

Upon hearing Hanan's story, one of the women who worked for her commented: 'It is the dream of every Muslim! May God never prevent anyone from [accessing] these holy places.' Reconfirming her prayer, the others said: 'Amen!'

At that moment, Hanan saw someone she knew passing by the shop. '*Al-ḥājja* Amina! *Al-ḥājja*!', Hanan called, and raised her voice to get the attention of the woman outside. The woman raised her hand in greeting and walked towards the shop, which she entered, greeting us before she spoke to Hanan briefly. Hanan wanted her to choose a fabric for a new *jellaba* that she had asked her to make in pink or green – she had to make a choice. While Amina tried the two pieces of fabric, I learned that she had been to *'umra* with Hanan. She had been on Hajj in 2003 and on *'umra* once every year for the past seven years. Hanan suggested that Amina join us to tell me about her experience, a suggestion to which Amina answered: 'What is there to say? That experience cannot be described with words!'[3]

As my fieldwork in Morocco progressed, I often heard words like those spoken by Hanan and Amina describing the pilgrimage to Mecca as a journey beyond words, a journey that one has to experience personally to understand its importance and effect. On several occasions, pilgrims told me that the experience cannot be fully grasped by others without their experiencing, feeling and sensing what they themselves had experienced, felt and sensed.

In their narratives about their pilgrimage experiences, Moroccan pilgrims spoke of the importance of the Hajj as a sacred journey which freed them from sins and, importantly, gave them the opportunity to ask for God's forgiveness and mercy. Furthermore, pilgrims often described what they had seen and heard, the food that they had eaten and the prayers they had recited. They expressed their bodily reactions during the pilgrimage, including the tears they had shed at different sites, with reference to 'goose bumps' and 'pounding hearts' to convey profound excitement and awe. In a way, the pilgrims were sharing their pilgrimage experience by 'seeking the senses' (Sparkes 2009).

Taking the narratives of Moroccan pilgrims as my point of departure in this chapter, I shall discuss the pilgrimage experience through its capacity to address the physical senses of pilgrims, through which their emotions are evoked (de Witte 2011; Meyer 2009, 2006; Hirschkind 2006). I will analyse how pilgrims reflect on their experience in Mecca and Medina through expressions of bodily sensations and spiritual feelings. Building on the theoretical perspectives of the anthropology of emotions and the senses, I will reflect on how, in the narratives of Moroccan pilgrims, the pilgrimage comes to the fore as a religious experience that has the capacity to influence the body and the senses. I will argue that sharing the experience of the Hajj with others – through oral narratives – reflects the richness of the experience. At the personal level, the use of senses in descriptions of the pilgrimage allows for the expression of the continuous awareness of, and presence in, the time and place of the pilgrimage for the individual. At the group level, sharing the experience allows the audience to develop their own religious sentiments, so that Hajj narratives trigger stimulation of feelings and emotions in the audience, both those who have been to Hajj and those who have not, as was the case with the women described earlier.

In this sense, sharing the experience is a cultural act that conditions people's expectations of certain physical and emotional reactions which they might expect to experience during the pilgrimage. Both those who have performed the Hajj and prospective pilgrims may thus – consciously or unconsciously – anticipate certain emotions related to the various rites enacted during the pilgrimage. Moreover, what pilgrims experience later becomes a point of reference in their everyday lives. While in what follows I describe references to the five senses, my aim is to move beyond these descriptions and incorporate them ethnographically into an analysis of everyday practices, experiences and communications (Schielke and Debevec 2012; Howes 2003).

Engaging with the anthropologist Fiona C. Ross's call (2004, 41) to take 'seriously the ways that we engage in and with space/place, filling it with activity, relations, sensual engagements, interpretive activity, [and] emotions', I use the narratives of Moroccan pilgrims and my own observations during two *ʿumra* trips to understand how performing the pilgrimage is, inter alia, a sensory experience (Hemer and Dundon 2016; Stoller 1997, 1989). Therefore, this chapter is structured as follows. First, it outlines some theoretical insights into the sensorial aspects of the pilgrimage. Next, there is a discussion of how Moroccan pilgrims express their pilgrimage experience through the five dominant senses: the visual, the olfactory, the aural, the haptic and the taste-related. The senses have an immediacy that we all experience and share, making them ready channels through which we can communicate and experience, hoping that others will readily grasp our meaning. They also offer an approach to other, more ineffable, abstract or spiritual meanings. Thus, the visual and the oral/aural, as well as smell, taste and touch, offer meaningful insights into the pilgrimage experience that allow for continuous awareness of the time and place of the pilgrimage. By way of a conclusion, I reflect on the influence of the narratives on both the narrators themselves and the listeners.

Pilgrimage as a Sensory Experience

Since the 1980s, several scholars have advocated for a research perspective that considers the role of the senses and emotions in understanding how social worlds are shaped (de Witte 2011; Meyer 2009, 2006; Howes 1991; Feld 1991, 1982; Stoller 1989). Anthropological writings on the senses initially tended to explore specific sensory domains, such as sound, taste, smell or touch (Feld 1991; Stoller 1989), and critiqued the predominantly visual focus of much anthropology. However, in more recent work, the emphasis has been on the combination of different senses, taking into consideration everyday practices, experiences and communications (Howes 2003). Birgit Meyer, for example, calls for an approach that pays attention to the entanglement of a person's cognitive, visceral and emotional appraisal in the sense-making of affective situations (Meyer 2015). Addressing the role of aesthetic and sensory experiences in the formation of religious subjectivities and communities, Meyer explains that sensational forms make sensory involvement with, and access to, the transcendental possible:

> Sensational forms . . . are relatively fixed, authorized modes of invoking, and organizing access to the transcendental, thereby creating and sustaining links between religious practitioners in the context of particular religious organizations. Sensational forms are transmitted and shared, they involve religious practitioners in particular practices of worship and play a central role in forming religious subjects. . . . [T]he notion of 'sensational forms' can also be applied to the ways in which material religious objects – such as images, books, or buildings – address and involve beholders. Thus, reciting a holy book such as the Qur'an, praying in front of an icon, or dancing around the manifestation of a spirit are also sensational forms through which religious practitioners are made to experience the presence and power of the transcendental. (Meyer 2011, 160)

In their ability to make the transcendental sensible, Meyer argues, sensational forms play a key role in constructing religious subjects and communities as 'experiences of the transcendental and the ways in which they are invoked in the here and now underpin individual and collective identities' (ibid.).

The pilgrimage experience is fluid and pervasive, transcending boundaries and weaving across a spectrum of experiences, narratives and practices (Coleman 2023, 422). The sensory experiences – as described by pilgrims – might appear to be beyond comprehension or awe-inspiring (Meyer 2015). During my fieldwork, the pilgrimage was often described as an emotionally powerful experience because of the impact it could leave on the senses of both those who performed the pilgrimage and the audience that listened to their narratives and accounts. Most pilgrims tended to speak about their religious or spiritual experience by describing its effect on their bodies. For example, one pilgrim spoke about her hair standing on end when she saw the Ka'ba or feeling shivers on her skin when she visited the Prophet's Mosque.

Marjo Buitelaar (2015) points out the importance of understanding specific instances of Hajj performances within their wider historical and cultural contexts, each of them testifying to the Hajj as part of Islam as a living tradition. In this sense, it is important to take into consideration socio-cultural contextualisation of the pilgrims in addition to the emotional affect and 'awe-filled' perspectives in their narratives. Bodily responses, as well as emotional experiences evoked during the pilgrimage, do not exist separately from the more abstract meanings attributed to the pilgrimage experiences that have been structured by socio-cultural contexts (ibid.). The role of sensational forms in the construction of religious subjectivities and communities is described by Meyer via the term 'aesthetic formation'. According to Meyer, aesthetic dimensions of religion are central in generating shared sensory experiences, which are not to be seen as mere expressions of a community's beliefs and identity, as in Benedict Anderson's notion of the 'imagined community', but are also actively involved in an ongoing process of constructing or making religious subjectivities and communities:

> 'aesthetic formation' captures very well the formative impact of a shared aesthetics through which subjects are shaped by tuning their senses, inducing experiences, molding their bodies, and making sense . . . (Meyer 2009, 7)

The sensory experiences provide a framework for emotions, but at the same time cultural discourses and expectations about emotions also shape the sensory experience, as I shall argue (Davies 2011; Schielke 2010, 10). By looking at the sensory dimension of the pilgrimage experience, I am 'emphasizing the lived and emergent nature of the senses' and 'the cultural embeddedness of sensory experience' (Porcello et al. 2010, 53). I will now shift my discussion towards embodiment and the sensuous experience, starting with sight and then continuing with soundscapes, smell, taste and touch. I start with another conversation that I witnessed between Amina and Hanan.

Sight and the Pilgrimage Experience

> **Amina:** The first time I went to Mecca, I could not believe that I was going to see the Kaʿba. When we approached Mecca in the bus, I asked my husband 'Where is the Kaʿba? Where is the Kaʿba?' He said: 'Be patient! Be patient!' I could not wait to see it.

> **Hanan:** When I saw the Kaʿba I cried and cried. I thanked God for that moment.
> **Amina:** I cried too. I cried every time I visited the Kaʿba . . . I often saw the Kaʿba before going in person, but it is not the same . . . Seeing is different!
> **Hanan:** It is never the same; to be there is unique . . . The first time was different from the second, and from the third . . . But always very overwhelming . . .
> **Amina:** I felt like I was flying in the air! I forgot everything . . . I looked around at the people and places; people circling the Kaʿba . . . I felt . . . [sigh] . . . One should go there and experience it to understand [the feeling]. When you go, you will understand . . .

Like Amina and Hanan, pilgrims often spoke of what they had seen during the pilgrimage. For most pilgrims I met, the sight of the Kaʿba was the most iconic. Encountering the Kaʿba for the first time provided what were among the most iconic and 'totemic' images of the pilgrimage, ones often mentioned in Hajj narratives. A totemic object is, of course, a physical one, but one that has acquired symbolic representational and even spiritual qualities and connotations, which convey a spiritual relationship that pilgrims assume with the Kaʿba.[4] In my conversations with Amina, Hanan and many other pilgrims, they described their first sight of the Kaʿba as an unforgettable moment. They described its cube-shaped stone structure, the black silk *kiswa* with golden and silver embroidered calligraphy with which it is covered, and the sea of Muslims surrounding it and performing their *ṭawāf*. Hanan and Amina both mentioned how, upon seeing the Kaʿba, they were overwhelmed with emotions that brought tears to their eyes. In addition to tears, for many pilgrims the sight of the Kaʿba resulted in bodily reactions, including shivering, cold skin or instant feelings of strength. For example, Ruqayya, a pilgrim from Fes, described her experience as follows:

> My legs could not carry me any more; my whole body refused to move. I was like a stone . . . I sat down, my head on the shoulder of my sister-in-law . . . Then I felt something bunching my skin . . . It was like I was struck by energy and could not tell where it was coming from. Then I stood, I was strong, and I circled the Kaʿba in full strength.

The sight of the Kaʿba had a physical impact on Ruqayya, as she did not feel the usual pain in her legs when she walked. Like Ruqayya, many pilgrims spoke to me about feeling sudden strength, increased heartbeats and seeing flashes of colours, all of which reflected how one sensory experience, sight of the Kaʿba, stimulated physical responses for those pilgrims.

When Ruqayya described being pinched on her skin, she pinched my leg as a way of conveying the bodily sensation to me. Many Moroccans could relate to Ruqayya's experience. At a family gathering, a female cousin confirmed Ruqayya's words. She commented that the Kaʿba had a special magnitude. In her words: 'When we went to the Kaʿba, I felt that it has unnatural gravity and that I was attracted to it.' A second cousin also commented: 'One would forget all one's sadness and daily concerns.'

When pilgrims spoke about the sight of the religious place, they sometimes pointed out the spiritual rewards of their experience. *Al-ḥājj* Sami, an older pilgrim I met in Casablanca, told me about the importance of looking at the Kaʿba:

> God, the Almighty, looks each night upon the people of Earth. The first He sees are the people of the *Ḥaram* . . .[5] He forgives those He sees circumambulating, those He sees praying, and those standing in front of the Kaʿba.[6]

Al-ḥājj Sami mentioned a hadith of the prophet claiming that God has put 120 blessings that descend every day on the Kaʿba and the people around it: sixty blessings for those who do *ṭawāf*, forty for those who pray and twenty for those who look at the Kaʿba.[7] The mere sight of the Kaʿba, then, is believed to be a central element of the ritual for which people receive blessings. In a way, the religious texts through which pilgrims learn about religious sites are brought to life for them when they perform the pilgrimage, and may contribute to the construction of their experience.

The sight of the Kaʿba is both iconic for the individual and becomes a significant social experience, shared within the wider community. As in discussions of the Hajj between Ruqayya and her cousins, the pilgrimage in general, and particularly the spaces seen during the pilgrimage, were the subject of much conversation in social gatherings. For example, when people visit a pilgrim to congratulate her on her safe return, they often ask about her experience, emphasising the importance of the sight of the Kaʿba. On several occasions, I noted that the returning pilgrim would be asked first by family members if she had cried when encountering the Kaʿba. Then, they would ask about the performance of the rites of Hajj. Often in social gatherings, one of those present would make a prayer that echoed Hanan's prayer of 'May God never prevent anyone from [accessing] these holy places'.

The importance of the visual experience is often reflected in the souvenirs and artefacts that Moroccans brought from Mecca and Medina or – less frequently – purchased locally. Images of the Kaʿba or the Grand Mosque of Mecca were displayed in every house that I visited in Morocco. In the house of one of the pilgrims I visited in Fes, for example, there was a large wall hanging depicting the Ka'ba and pilgrims circumambulating it. The wall hanging was at least a hundred inches wide. It was a reproduction of a photo taken with a slow shutter speed, blurring the collective pilgrims into one unified mass, a stylistic feature which seems to me intended to convey much more than a visual impression: it attempts to capture the unifying effect, and the collective reverence and dedication felt by the pilgrims towards the Hajj.

Figure 3.1 Living room in a house with wall hanging of the Kaʿba (Fes, 4 August 2015)

Framed pictures of the Grand Mosque of Mecca or the Prophet's Mosque in Medina, or both, were hung in people's places of work, bus stations, restaurants, and sweetshops in the market. These photographs captured both the strength of the personal experience and the shared community experience.

The visual aspect of the pilgrimage was also apparent in the work of Osama, a forty-year-old artist from Casablanca who designed a wooden model of the Grand Mosque of Mecca that I found displayed in a shopping mall in in the city. The model occupied a large area of the ground floor of the shopping centre facing the main entrance. It depicted many aspects of the Grand Mosque's structure, including four of its doors, nine minarets, the Kaʿba at its centre, the space of the *ṭawāf*, and the hills of Ṣafā and Marwā, where the ritual of *saʿī* is performed during the pilgrimage. At the mall, many visitors stood in front of the model, some taking pictures and others posing for pictures. A woman who came with her two daughters stopped and shared with strangers a memory of her *ʿumra* trip, assuming a collective interest in her personal pilgrimage, an assumption that was well-founded. Then, she stopped for a commemorative picture. I found it noteworthy that in a shopping mall, a mundane space, there was such a physical and spiritual icon of religious significance which might be taken as a reference to the commercialisation of the Hajj (Bianchi 2004).

I contacted Osama, the designing artist, and managed to meet him shortly afterwards. He shared the following insights:

> The idea imposed itself on me. Every year, I see unsuitable models of the Kaʿba that imams use in Hajj lessons at the mosque . . . They use a black box, unsuitable . . . I thought then, God's House is the most important of models . . . I made the structure together with two friends . . . When I finished the design, I wanted to give it to a mosque where Hajj lessons take place; but first, I thought if I put it in the mall for a few weeks, many people would be able to see it . . .

Osama wanted to counter visual misrepresentations of the Kaʿba and planned to replicate his model so that, in every mosque where pilgrimage lessons take place, prospective pilgrims could prepare themselves for what they would see in Mecca. Osama also told me about the reactions he had had from people who had seen the model. Like those at the mall, many took pictures and others

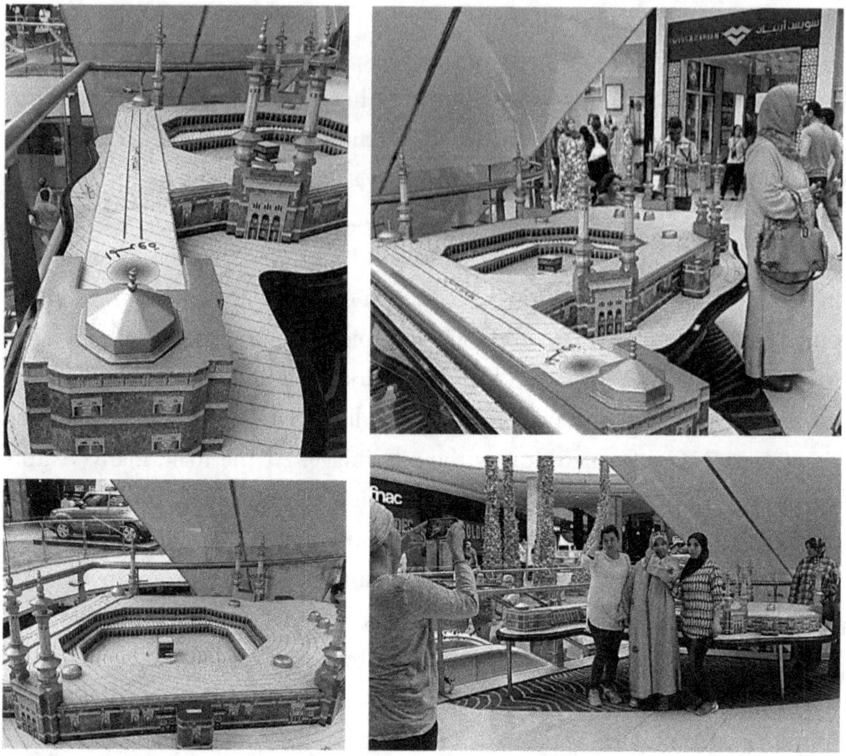

Figure 3.2 The scale model of the Grand Mosque of Mecca displayed in Morocco Mall (Casablanca, 30 July 2015)

spoke about memories the sight of the model evoked in them. Khawla, a friend of Osama who had helped in the 3D digital modelling of the design, told me that before the model was put in the mall, it was placed at the entrance of their design company in Casablanca. Every day, many people would come into the company's office to see the model closely after spotting it through the glass window. She would invite people in and take their pictures with the model. Jokingly she would tell them: 'Now you have seen the Kaʿba and the mosque, touched them and took pictures with them . . . You do not need to go to Mecca any more . . .' According to Khawla, visitors were responsive to the joke, and affected and touched by the quality of the depiction of the design, sometimes sharing their emotions of longing for the holy sites, and they often commented that although the design was impressive, 'seeing the real thing was like nothing else'.

Figure 3.3 Pilgrims documenting their experience and sharing it via social media (Mecca, 7 February 2018)

Sharing the experience of what they saw, not only did pilgrims evoke personal feelings and memories, but the narrative reconstructions were also a social activity that touched the senses and emotions of others. Nowadays, pilgrims can tweet, share or post photos of their Hajj experiences whilst in Mecca and Medina (Caidi, Beazley and Marquez 2018, 9–10; Al-Ajarma and Buitelaar 2021). The act of sharing is significant for both the pilgrim and those at home waiting for a picture from those in the holy places.

The visual dimension of the pilgrimage experience and its multiple effects in the narratives of Moroccan pilgrims do not only revolve around the Kaʿba, although it is fair to say that this is a focal point. The images committed faithfully to memory extend to other sacred points associated with the Hajj, including the plain of Arafat and the Mosque of the Prophet, among others (Fischer and Abedi 1990; Hammoudi 2006; McLoughlin 2009; Mols and Buitelaar 2015). I will try to touch on the significance of those locations in the narratives of pilgrims in relation to other senses, in addition to sight, in the remaining parts of this chapter.

Soundscapes and Feelings

In the previous chapter, I showed how Moroccans refer to the performance of the Hajj as 'hearing the calling of God'. During the pilgrimage itself, multiple sound-environments contribute to constructing the experiences of pilgrims. First and foremost, vocal practices form a crucial element in the performance of the pilgrimage rites. For example, once dressed in their *iḥrām*, all the pilgrims participate in the same sound creation process as they recite the *talbiya* until they enter Mecca. According to the Moroccan pilgrims with whom I spoke, the aural patterns of the *talbiya* helped in arousing or stimulating their feelings in preparation for the performance of the central elements of the pilgrimage. In addition, the sound of pilgrims together reciting the *talbiya* was a reminder of being part of a larger Muslim community, the *umma*. In the words of *al-ḥājj* Mousa, a pilgrim from Fes:

> People start the *talbiya* as soon as they enter their *iḥrām* . . . *Labbayka Allāhumma labbayk* . . . they chant together . . . When a pilgrim raises his voice with the *talbiya*, he remembers that he has answered the call of the Almighty and that there will be another call on the Last Day, when people will be either accepted or refused, punished or rewarded, elevated or cast down . . .

In this sense, the hearing and the aural imagination of pilgrims are key sites for creating the pious Muslim subject (Schulz 2006, 2003; Hirschkind 2001).[8] With around two and a half million people performing Hajj, sounds such as the recitation of the *talbiya*, as well as other supplication prayers that pilgrims murmur, produce increased feelings of harmony and unity among pilgrims.

During the pilgrimage, pilgrims engage with other soundscapes such as the call for prayer in Mecca and Medina and Qur'an recitations during prayers, as well as collective supplication prayers made during *ṭawāf* around the Kaʿba and *saʿī* between the hills of Ṣafā and Marwā. The sounds pilgrims experience, according to many pilgrims, have a direct capacity to engage both their body and their soul; the sensory experiences acquire an abstract, spiritual dimension for the pilgrims, quite unlike most day-to-day sensory experiences.

When performing the rites of Hajj, pilgrims imitate supplication prayers that they hear around them; some repeat *duʿāʾ* prayers after a leading man or from their phones, while others read *duʿā*'s from small booklets that they hold between their hands. Some people say their prayers aloud and others in silence. In the following conversation, Hanan and Amina reflect on the prayers they made when entering the Grand Mosque of Mecca:

Hanan: When Amina reached the mosque, she raised her two hands and said in a very loud voice: 'Thank you . . . Thank you, my Lord . . . Thank you.' *[As she imitated Amina, Hanan stood up and raised her hands in a prayer gesture.]*
Amina: I did not feel anyone around me . . . I left it to my mouth to say whatever it wanted. Thank God for that . . .
Hanan: You cried a lot too!
Amina: Yes! You did too! Do you remember? I cried, too. And I thanked God, prayed, and made *du'ā'* prayers [loudly] . . .

The recitation of prayers contributes to the production of a certain ambience for pilgrims, melding the many languages spoken by separate and collective voices, all raised in devout murmurings that may influence the nature and intensity of the inner experiences of the pilgrims.

Fascinated by the diversity of the languages spoken by fellow pilgrims and the different dialects of Arab pilgrims coming from various countries, Hassan, a pilgrim from Safi, shared with his sister short messages from fellow pilgrims that he had recorded every day during his *'umra* trip. In the clips which his sister, Fatiha, shared with me, I saw pilgrims from Indonesia, Sudan, Egypt, Palestine and Jordan greeting her in their language or local dialect and wishing she would visit Mecca. The clips were each less than a minute long, yet Fatiha cherished them and saved them on her phone. In recording the short messages and sending them to his sister, Hassan aimed at sharing the diversity of the Muslim global community beyond Mecca, an action that deeply touched her and stimulated her own longing for the holy places.

It is worth mentioning here that language does not often stand as a barrier between pilgrims. Pilgrims communicate through non-verbal signals, smiles, nods, frowns and hand gestures. The social and ethnic boundaries are dissolved in a mutually understood deep connection: the quest for spiritual fulfilment.[9]

Another aural experience that influenced the pilgrims was that of engaging in ritualised communal prayers. Particularly significant in this respect is the *janāza* (funeral) prayer.[10] This prayer takes place five times a day after every mandatory prayer. For Hassan, for example, the *janāza* prayer was a constant reminder of death, that life was short and that he should be more pious in his actions and deeds.

In addition to the aural patterns in which pilgrims engaged, some pilgrims related auditory experiences that were beyond the natural. For example, at a women's gathering in Fes, Ruqayya told a group of female relatives that during her pilgrimage she had had the following heightened and inexplicable experience:

> I was performing my *ṭawāf* around the Kaʿba when I heard someone calling . . . 'Faiza . . . Faiza' . . . That is the name of my daughter! I looked around trying to identify where the sound might be coming from. But everyone was performing their *ṭawāf*. . . Could it have been my imagination? Was it a divine call? I did not know what that meant!

For Ruqayya, what she had heard was a key message that would haunt her thoughts for a long time afterwards. Upon asking a religious scholar in Mecca, she learned that this might be a *karāma*, an expression that means an extraordinary favour from God.[11] Ruqayya was told that the meaning of her experience was that good fortune awaits her daughter. Two years later, Faiza performed Hajj with her father, being the youngest in the family to do so – something that Ruqayya related back to her own extraordinary auditory experience in Mecca.

Smell

Of the five senses, Moroccan pilgrims spoke about smell the least. Although it never went into detail, the discussion among Moroccan pilgrims about smell was limited to three subjects: the mosque's cleanliness, the unhygienic conditions in Minā, and perfumes or scents brought home as gifts. Several pilgrims commented on the cleaning process that takes place at the Grand Mosque of Mecca, where they saw large groups of workers daily cleaning the entrances to the Mosque, bridges, minarets and columns. Pilgrims told me that rose water was used to perfume the passages and hallways of the mosque. A few incense burners also perfume the mosque with *bukhūr* between sunset and evening prayer, while the mosque's officials perfume the Kaʿba's *kiswa* and black stone five times a day.[12]

Contrasting with their comments about the cleanliness of the Grand Mosque, several pilgrims complained about their experience in Minā where piles of garbage built up during the days of the pilgrimage. A video recording shared by Moroccan pilgrims at Minā showed pilgrims complaining about the standards of hygiene in the tent camp in 2015. Nonetheless, only a few pilgrims openly complained about these troubles upon their return home. I would argue that the difference between the dissatisfaction and how they presented their experiences in narratives may be related to a hegemonic collective discourse in which it is mostly positive connotations that are ascribed to the pilgrimage experience. It may similarly be related to the idea that pilgrims should tolerate slight discomforts or negative experiences during the pilgrimage and should refuse to be distracted from their main purpose (Buitelaar and Kadrouch-Outmany 2023). On the other hand, some pilgrims expressed not having had great expectations of the stay in Minā and had anticipated the standards of hygiene being lower there than in the hotels of Mecca. Of course, pilgrims' social backgrounds can also be a factor in differential experiences of matters such as cleanliness and hygiene issues (Kadrouch-Outmany and Buitelaar 2021).[13]

The third aspect connected to smell in the narratives of pilgrims was the gifts pilgrims brought from Mecca. Many Moroccans brought back to Morocco scented bricks, *bukhūr*, mixed with musk or agarwood, *ʿūd*.[14] Some pilgrims gave *bukhūr* to family members and friends, an action which signified the social aspect of sharing the experience with those at home. Other pilgrims, like Ruqayya, liked to burn *bukhūr* in their houses, and stated that all was good, but that the one which came from the holy sites was particularly so.

Taste and Touch

Touch and taste are two senses that I will discuss together, for two reasons. The first of these is that they both require the tactile engagement of the physical body with objects around it, their only significant difference being the site of a bodily link, that is, either the skin or the mouth. Second, Moroccan pilgrims often spoke of more than one sensory experience that took place at the same time, particularly mentioning taste and touch simultaneously. That said, however, touch and taste were sometimes emphasised separately. Especially important for the pilgrims was trying to reach and touch the Kaʿba and the black stone.

Pilgrims discussed at length the types of food that were available during the pilgrimage. Since the meals were either provided in packages or prepared by pilgrims themselves, during the Hajj, comments on the food were limited to expressions of liking or disliking its flavours, spices, quality or amounts. During the *'umra*, however, pilgrims have more time to explore food options, as most meals need to be arranged by the pilgrims themselves (depending on the package bought through travel agencies). Pilgrims performing *'umra* in Ramadan were specifically vocal about their experience as they often shared breaking their fast at the Grand Mosque of Mecca (or in Medina). For example, Hassan, the previously mentioned pilgrim from Safi, expressed his enjoyment in spending Ramadan in Mecca. In addition to the spiritual dimension of the experience, he explicitly enjoyed sharing food with other pilgrims from Egypt, Palestine, Malaysia, Bangladesh and Turkey. Every sunset in the month of Ramadan (he spent all thirty days in Mecca), he would sit with a new group of people, putting his food next to theirs, enjoying conversations during *iftār* when everyone broke their fast. He relished both the food and the interactions, and in a way he was tasting the global Muslim community.

The sensory experience most talked about in relation to both taste and touch related to Zamzam water. During the pilgrimage, pilgrims drink Zamzam water and use it to wash their hands, faces and heads in a purifying ritual. Like the reciting of the *talbiya*, drinking from the water of the well of Zamzam is considered part of the rites of the pilgrimage. During their entire time in Mecca and Medina, but especially after their *ṭawāf*, pilgrims are advised to drink Zamzam water, which is consumed in large quantities.[15]

In Morocco, pilgrims often discuss the taste of Zamzam water, some saying that it is distinct from tap or mineral water and others commenting on its ability to quench both thirst and hunger. Moroccan pilgrims – on various occasions – described it to me as 'pure and colourless' and 'odourless', or remarked that 'it has an authentic taste', is 'mildly salty', or 'clean'. Here is how Ruqayya put it:

> In the Qur'an, God stated: 'We made every living thing from water.'[16] Zamzam is not just any water; it is the most sacred and miraculous water . . . It has [blessings]; just think of how long it has existed, and it still satisfies millions of people . . .

Like Ruqayya, many pilgrims emphasised the religious character of Zamzam water. Pilgrims believed that it possessed *baraka*, blessings or divine power from God. *Baraka* is believed to be found within physical objects, places and people chosen by God (Eickelman 1976; Buitelaar 1993). Believing that 'Zamzam water is what one intends it to be drunk for',[17] pilgrims assume that when one drinks it in order to be healed, God will heal; when one drinks it to quench the thirst, God will quench the thirst.

According to my interlocutors, the *baraka* of Zamzam water is further believed to be capable of being transmitted to those who did not personally visit Mecca for the pilgrimage. Consequently, those who visit Mecca carry some water back for relatives and friends in Morocco. When pilgrims return from Mecca, family members, neighbours and friends visit them and congratulate them on having completed the Hajj or *'umra*. Traditionally, visitors are then offered some Zamzam water and dates (Al-Ajarma 2018). The Moroccan etiquette for drinking it is strict: before drinking one says *bismi-llāh*, then one takes three sips, followed by saying *du'ā'* prayers. Then, on completion of the ritual, the *baraka* of the water is transmitted to the receiver. In a sense, Zamzam water is considered a doorway to the spiritual, or to other religious dimensions beyond the sensory.

Despite the centrality of the sensory experiences in the narratives of Moroccan pilgrims about Hajj, the limitation of these narratives might reside in the fact that time has passed between the experience itself and the narration, so that memories of the experiences may have undergone change. Therefore, I will now offer a narrative from my own *'umra* experience in order to provide some reflections on the senses, feelings and spaces experienced during a pilgrimage. I will focus on the experience of pilgrims when visiting Medina, specifically at the Mosque of the Prophet.

The Rawḍa: Experiencing 'a Piece of Paradise'

The heart of the prophet's mosque in Medina houses a very special but small area named *al-rawḍa al-nabawiya* or *riyāḍ al-janna*.[18] Following a famous hadith narrated by the prophet Muhammad, 'That which is between my house and my pulpit is a garden from the gardens of Paradise' (Muslim, book 15, hadith 572), many Muslims consider *al-rawḍa al-nabawiya* (or 'the Rawḍa' for short) as a highly significant place which they wish to visit and in which they strive to perform prayers. The Rawḍa is also where the prophet is buried. I was also told by Moroccan pilgrims that supplications uttered in the Rawḍa are never rejected. However, entrance to the Rawḍa is limited. This is especially the case for female pilgrims, who are allowed into only a small section of the Rawḍa, for shorter periods of time than those designated for men.

During my participant observation of the *ʿumra* in Medina, I attempted to enter the Rawḍa along with my mother and sister. I learned that it was open to women for two hours in the early morning and again after the *ʿishāʾ* – evening – prayers. Thus, before the *ʿishāʾ* prayers, we joined a group of women at the entry point near Gate 25 of the mosque. Inside the mosque, but still outside the Rawḍa, women were divided into groups on the basis of the region from which they came. Also, one side was reserved for women with disabilities, which was where my sister and I stood, behind our mother in her wheelchair. On my mother's right side, an old woman sat with her daughter. Later, I would learn that the woman was from Egypt. Shocked by the loss of her nineteen-year-old son who had drowned in a pool in upper Egypt, her daughter and husband had decided to take her on *ʿumra*, hoping that the trip would assist in healing her wounds. On my mother's left was a young boy in another wheelchair and next to him stood his mother. The boy, suffering from autism, had been brought to the pilgrimage by his parents, who hoped for blessings and healing. An old woman standing next to us kept asking her blind daughter to go to the hotel, as she was sleepy. Yet the daughter insisted on waiting, asking her mother to be patient.

We spent about two hours in front of the wooden barriers that separate the area designated for women from the Rawḍa, waiting for them to open. When the first gate was opened, everyone started to run. I pushed my mother's wheelchair and followed the crowd. When we reached the Rawḍa, we had to stand in another line, where women were allowed only in small numbers, as the space (reserved for people with disabilities) could house no more than twenty women at a time, that is around ten women with their wheelchairs and their female companions. Each group was given five minutes to pray two *rakʿas* at the assigned spot on the Rawḍa carpet, which is of the same pattern as the other carpets in the mosque except that it is light green instead of red. The experience was highly fragmented, interrupted by the sounds of the women, the shouts of the female guards and the pushing of other women.

Although the women who entered the Rawḍa were able to pray there, some even adding two more *rakʿa*s or extra *duʿāʾ* prayers before being pulled out by

Figure 3.4 Women waiting to enter the Rawḍa, 8:30–10:30 p.m. (Medina, 1 February 2018)

the guards, they could not reach the tomb of the prophet. A five-foot wall prevented the women from reaching the tomb or even seeing it. Some women tried to get a glimpse of the top part of the pulpit and the tombs. Many tried to take photos of the part they could see; taller women were fortunate in this regard. When they reached the Rawḍa, some women started ululating as a sign of joy. Although they were rebuked by the female guards they did not stop. 'We were only expressing joy. In our country when you are happy you make trills of joy', I was told by one of the women later. The intensity of the brief time women are allowed to spend at the Rawḍa made their expressions similarly intense. In addition to their ululation, many women made *du'ā'* prayers in a loud voice whilst others cried as they raised their hands in prayer. Some women gathered around marble pillars, touching them with their hands and kissing them, and, using the tip of their index finger, some women wrote the outline of their names as a kind of 'meaningful movements' (Davidson and Milligan 2004, 524). It was as if those women were seeking to leave a mark of themselves in that place before the female guards noticed and pushed them out.

The Rawḍa is a place about which Moroccan pilgrims talk extensively and with great admiration. Many Moroccan women with whom I spoke, however, expressed resentment at not being able to see the tomb of the prophet there. Men, privileged by their gender, were able to see the tomb of the prophet and

Figure 3.5 Men drinking Zamzam water at the Grand Mosque of Mecca (Mecca, 8 February 2018)

often took pictures of it to share with their female relatives. The gender privilege of men, the time limits placed on women's visits and the control by the guards seemed to militate against a spiritually satisfying experience.[19] Yet the women spoke of their spiritual elation at being in such a place.

In *A Season in Mecca: Narrative of Pilgrimage*, the Moroccan anthropologist Abdellah Hammoudi focuses on the treatment of women during the pilgrimage, as well as other restrictions on the behaviour of pilgrims, when visiting the tomb of the prophet, which he calls 'Wahhabi virulence' (Hammoudi 2006, 80). Male dominance in the Rawḍa manifests itself not only in the fact that men are able to reach and see the tomb of the prophet, but also in the significantly longer time slots available to them to visit it, and the larger space they have at their disposal in the mosque even though the numbers of male and female pilgrims do not differ much. Men, however, can cross the boundaries between male and female domains more easily than women.

In places with less surveillance, including Mount Arafat, Jabal al-Nūr where the cave of Ḥira' is located and Mount Uḥud, I witnessed people writing their names and those of their family members and loved ones on the stone using pens and markers.[20] They also wrote specific prayers for health and blessing and the date of their visit. Inscribing one's name or leaving behind messages at sacred sites can be interpreted by reference to the work of Charles Taylor, who wrote, in relation to religious experience, that 'Many people are not satisfied with a momentary sense of wow! They want to take it further and they are looking for ways of doing so' (Taylor 2002, 116).[21] What is sometimes seen as destructive can be interpreted as a cry for recognition: 'I was here too!'

More generally, Hajj narratives testify to the fact that language can be an important medium for emotional expression. Retelling and representing the experience becomes something greater than a mere narrative, but generates a spiritual quality (Meyer 2015). Therefore, pilgrims seek to relive the experience through the senses and the narratives they use to describe their pilgrimage. The retelling may also regenerate afresh what they felt. Furthermore, for the individual, the Hajj is, in a way, never over. Retelling its history revives it; stories fix the experience in the minds of the tellers and become a lingering legacy to be savoured throughout life and passed on as a desirable occurrence to others. Thus, these accounts of the Hajj have meaning and resonance far beyond their surface language. Narrations of Hajj experiences, in all their sensory diversity, preserve what is regarded as hugely significant beyond the 'momentary sense of "wow!"' (Taylor 2002, 116).

In their narratives, the words of the Moroccan pilgrims become central in describing their experience, their feelings of longing for the holy sites and the performance of the pilgrimage. Fatima Sadiqi, who studied gender and language in Morocco, points to the importance of orality as a principal component of expressing sensory experiences in everyday Moroccan speech culture. Sadiqi discusses the power of *lkelma*, the 'oral word' that is attested in many deep aspects of Moroccan culture (Sadiqi 2003, 43). One example of such orality was expressed by *al-ḥājja* Zahra, a woman in her seventies, who had performed the Hajj many years ago and wished to visit Mecca again. Her husband, however, did not approve of her wish. In a women's gathering at her house, I heard her whisper to a younger cousin: 'I miss those places, I want to see the Kaʿba again, and to visit the prophet . . . I feel fire [of longing] burning in my chest; right here [hitting her chest].' *Al-ḥājja* Zahra used references to her physical body and her sensory data metaphorically to express her longing, dramatising her message further with sighs and tear-filled eyes.[22] *Al-ḥājja* Zahra's words evoke the argument of Davidson and Milligan (2004,

523), that the 'most immediate and intimately felt geography is the body', a space of emotional and sensuous articulation and experience. In that sense, Zahra's expression of the 'burning chest' can reflect a 'bodily way of knowing' (Howes 1991, 3).

Bodily ways of knowing are further stimulated through the objects and souvenirs pilgrims bring home from Mecca. These concrete objects appeal to and stimulate the senses, including sight (like the previously mentioned pictures and posters), hearing (audio players and *adhan* or *talbiya*-making toys), touch (prayer beads and mats), smell (perfumes and scents) and taste (Zamzam water and dates), among others. Pilgrims purchase objects that they can wear on their bodies (such as T-shirts, jewellery and dresses) and use daily (like coffee cups and key fobs) as well as house decorations and items for private collections. The sharing of tactile objects, photos, water and souvenirs spreads the spiritual experience to those who have not performed the pilgrimage and helps to rekindle memories in those who have. It is a cohesive agent in society.

One aspect of the sensory experience that still merits reflection is the spontaneity of these reported experiences. How are they related to the collectively shared expectations of a pilgrim's behaviour? How are they related to previously acquired collective knowledge and the stories of previous pilgrims? And what does it indicate about a person's religiosity if she does not share the most common sensory experiences with other pilgrims? My intention here is not to question the authenticity of the sensory experiences of pilgrims, nor the meanings they relate to those experiences, but to reflect on these aspects in relation to the pilgrimage to Mecca. In their accounts of the pilgrimage experience, many pilgrims state that crying, for example, is a sign of being stunned by what pilgrims are experiencing. How does that then reflect on those who do not cry when they see the Kaʿba, for example? If crying was typically seen as a positive quality that reflects the longing to visit holy places, would refraining from crying be understood as a negative quality?

Expected Sensations and Feelings in the Holy Spaces

During my fieldwork in Morocco, I noticed that expectations concerning the sensory experience were stimulated by four media: pilgrimage accounts (both historical and contemporary, written and oral), one's religious education, the media (both audio-visual and social media) and memories of previous experiences. All these media are too broad and varied to be discussed in depth here; therefore, I will only touch on some aspects of them.

First, Moroccans often hear stories about the pilgrimage, including stories about how people experienced Mecca and Medina, and narrations about their performance of the pilgrimage rites. There are numerous historical accounts describing the pilgrimage experience, including senses and emotions. Early travellers and pilgrims from North Africa to Mecca left accounts expressing such sensational forms, in the shape of poetry and storytelling. Travelogues of Moroccan voyagers point to the emotional impact of being in Mecca. For example, Ibn Jubayr, who performed the Hajj in 1183, wrote:

> The full moon has sent its light, and the night has taken its mask off, and the sounds come from everywhere carrying the *talbiya*. The tongues are busy with *du'ā'* prayers, praying for God's grace . . . It was the night of all nights . . . The Ka'ba was a bride, beautiful as a paradise and full of the guests of the exceedingly Compassionate . . . . The sight of *bayt al-Ḥarām* makes one amazed; you would not see anything apart from devout moments and tears, and tongues that are asking for God's blessings. (Ibn Jubayr 1981, 65–73)[23]

Such Hajj accounts indicate that the culturally-conditioned expectation that the pilgrimage will stimulate strong emotions in pilgrims has a long history.

Further, the conversations I have had with people about Mecca indicate that a person's education (both formal and informal) is likely to inform his or her expectations about the sensory experience. Many Moroccan pilgrims, for example, reported that, from childhood, they have learned – from their parents, grandparents and schoolteachers – about the sacredness of Mecca and Medina, which inspired their longing to visit these places.

Furthermore, the pilgrimage to Mecca is often featured in audio-visual media platforms including TV and radio. Documentaries, news reports and TV programmes often feature aspects of the pilgrimage or discuss the importance of the holy sites. Satellite TV channels, for example, provide easy access to the pilgrimage. There are even two specialised channels providing podcasts all day every day from the two holy cities. Many pilgrims often watch these two channels to listen to Qur'an recitations and see the pilgrims as they circumambulate the Ka'ba or pray at the two holy mosques.

The use of social media as a means of sharing pilgrims' experiences facilitates the inclusion of those individuals who are not physically present in Mecca, allowing them to virtually partake in the personal journey of those experiencing the sacred space (Coleman 2023, 423; cf. Al-Ajarma and Buitelaar 2021). Exposure to these forms of media provides an opportunity to remember the pilgrimage, connect with those in Mecca and Medina, and at the same time stimulate feelings of longing for the holy sites (Al-Ajarma and Buitelaar 2021; cf. Stanton 2022). In the words of Hanan:

> Listening and seeing are different things . . . When one is in the moment and lives an experience, they have feelings that only they can understand, if they even can! Pilgrimage makes you experience different feelings . . . You must live it, see for yourself, and experience it, to understand . . .

Conclusion

In this chapter I have reflected on the emphasis on sensory experiences and emotions in the stories of pilgrims. In their narratives, Moroccan pilgrims often provided descriptions of the places they visited, people they met, rituals they performed, and feelings they encountered, which were often articulated through the senses. Yet most of the Moroccan pilgrims I met during my fieldwork would insist that the experience is beyond comprehension through words alone, and that one must go through the experience to understand the pilgrimage. A pilgrim's ability to see, listen, touch, smell and taste at the holy places becomes part of the narratives they share, expressing feelings like happiness and longing for those places.

When Moroccan pilgrims talk about sensory experiences, their words give access to a meaning that operates at a deeper level. The complexity of the sensory experiences people spoke about is intricately connected to the spiritual experience of the pilgrimage. Descriptions of the pilgrimage to Mecca as the experience of a lifetime, as something that is beyond comprehension and a magical experience transmitted in the narratives of pilgrims and through the previously-mentioned media, inevitably convey something that others may wish to replicate. Having such wishes, and in particular expressing them, contributes to a socially approved idea of being a good Muslim. In a similar vein, through narrations about strong emotions and sensory experiences, pilgrims may augment the reputation of the pilgrim as being a highly religious person. Being overwhelmed upon seeing the Ka'ba, for example, can be valuable as it could be seen to indicate a person's being chosen by God to visit His House – something also mentioned in the previous chapter.

For the individual pilgrim, narration of the pilgrimage experience is something they are prone to repeat again and again, since the Hajj is, in a way, never over. Retelling it revives it; stories fix the experience in the minds of the tellers and become a lingering legacy to be savoured throughout life and passed on to others as a desirable experience. The experience is also socially constructed, as pilgrims often spoke of sensations and emotions that are, in a way, expected. Being overwhelmed by the site of the Ka'ba, crying at the Rawḍa, feeling stronger and forgetting bodily pains are some examples of such emotions.

For the pilgrims, many moments remain significant and seem to be held dear in their stories, such as the first moment of seeing the Ka'ba, the pilgrims standing at the plain of Arafat, the moment of the completion of the rites of Hajj, and the feelings that one's sins have been forgiven. Those moments inspire many pilgrims to decide to make a fresh start and lead a more meaningful life upon their return home where a new chapter of their life starts, one that is intuitively connected with their experience in Mecca, their everyday life, and their future as *al-ḥājj* or *al-ḥājja*. In the next chapter, I shall discuss aspects of the everyday lives of pilgrims upon their return to Morocco.

Notes

1. *Qafṭān* in Morocco is commonly used to mean a one-piece dress worn exclusively by women, both as an everyday outfit and as haute-couture attire, depending on the material. A *taqshiṭa* (a loan word from Tamazight) is a two-piece version of the *qafṭān* that is worn with a large belt, primarily on formal occasions (Sellam and Dellal 2013, 165).
2. People in Morocco had told me that if the Day of Arafat, which is the highlight of the Hajj, occurred on a Friday, then it would be called *al-ḥājj al-akbar*. I could not find such a reference in any *fiqh* book that I read on the topic. However, the *fiqh* and hadith books state that Hajj itself is *al-ḥājj al-akbar* (greater Hajj) while *'umra* is *al-ḥājj al-asghar* (lesser Hajj) (Muslim, book 15, hadith 491).

One interpretation of this hadith is that the phrase *al-ḥājj al-akbar* is used in contrast to *al-ḥājj al-asghar*, which the Arabs used for *'umra*. Another interpretation is that *al-ḥājj al-akbar refers* to the tenth day of the last month of the lunar calendar and is also known as *yawm al-nahr* (day of sacrifice), which is also the first day of the Feast of Sacrifice (Al-Bukhārī, book 58, hadith 19).

3. Fieldnotes, 10 August 2015.
4. Spirituality in this book is understood as the feeling of personal connectedness with God, which includes reflection or thinking about the self that would bring one closer to God (Ahmad and Khan 2016).
5. *Ḥaram* (meaning sanctuary) is sometimes used to refer to the Grand Mosque of Mecca (al-Masjid al-Ḥarām) including the Kaʿba and other structures such as maqām Ibrāhīm, the hijr and the Zamzam Well.
6. I traced Sami's narrative to a paragraph by al-Ghazali (1853, vol 1. 307); see also Campo (1991).
7. A reference to this hadith can be seen in *Al-Muʿjam al-Awṣaṭ*, a hadith anthology of Ṭabarānī (1995, vol. 4, 381). Also, Azraqī in *Kitāb Akhbār Makka* [Book of Reports about Mecca] states that 'whoever looks at the Kaʿba with faith and belief, his sins will drop as leaves drop from a tree' (1964, vol. 2, 9).
8. Hirschkind (2001) argues that Islamic reform movements incorporate the use of mass-reproduced cassette sermons into an 'ethics of listening', which emphasises the importance of the ear as a key site for raising the consciousness of the pious Muslim subject (Schulz 2003).
9. Pilgrims also reported getting confused or irritated when confronted by the customs of other pilgrims, particularly in very crowded places or when they had to wait for a long time to perform prayers or use rest rooms (Aourid 2019; Hammoudi 2006).
10. *Janāza* prayer is part of the funeral ritual in Islam (Kadrouch Outmany 2016).
11. *Karāma* (pl. *karāmāt*) refers to the extraordinary favour shown by God towards a human being, often elicited by Muslim mystics and saints (Gardet 2012).
12. *Bukhūr* is a blend of natural ingredients, mainly wood chips, that is used as perfume or incense.
13. See also Aourid (2019), Saad Ali (2010) and Hammoudi (2006).
14. *'ūd* is the Arabic name for agar wood/aloes wood soaked in fragrant oils and mixed with other natural ingredients (resin, ambergris, musk, sandalwood, essential oils and others).
15. For example, in 2018, pilgrims consumed 8.5 million litres of water outside the pilgrimage season alone, according to a Saudi newspaper; http://english.alara

biya.net/en/News/gulf/2018/08/16/Hajj-pilgrims-consume-8-mln-liters-of-Zamzam-water.html (last accessed 22 May 2021).

16. Referring to Qur'an 21:30.
17. Referring to a saying of the prophet Muhammad: 'The water of Zamzam is for whatever it is drunk for' (Ibn Mājah, vol. 4, book 25, hadith 3062).
18. *Riyāḍ al-janna* (the Rawḍa) is the area between what was the house of the prophet Muhammad and his pulpit. The Rawḍa is floored with green carpet simply to identify it, and the entire mosque is floored with red carpet. It holds the tomb of the prophet Muhammad and two of his companions, and of the first caliphs, Abu Bakr and Umar ibn al-Khattab (Peters 1994, 103–5).
19. Gender bias in pilgrimage is not limited to the Hajj but was noted by scholars who studied other pilgrimages as well (Gemzöe 2005; Hermkens et al., 2009; Jansen and Notermans 2012). See also Chapter Eight.
20. Jabal al-Nūr (Mount of Light) is a mountain near Mecca which houses the Grotto/Cave of Hira' (*ghār ḥirā'*) where the prophet Muhammad is said to have spent a great deal time meditating. It is widely believed that it was in this cave that he received his first revelation (Peters 1994). Mount Uḥud lies around five kilometres north of Medina and the site of the Battle of Uḥud, which occurred between the early Muslims and Qurayshi Meccans in 625 CE in the valley located near the mountain (Robinson 2012).
21. In his approach, Charles Taylor criticised William James, who understood 'pure experience' to be a non-reflexive, non-verbal notion of feeling that grasps the 'immediate flux of life' in terms of its undifferentiated unfolding in the field of sensory immediacy, prior to its organisation into distinctive contents, forms and structures (James 2012, 58; cf. Taylor 2002; Laughlin and McManus 1995).
22. There is more information related to Zahra's story, to which I return in Chapter Eight.
23. From Arabic, my translation.

4

AFTER HAJJ: REFASHIONING OF THE SELF AS *AL-ḤAJJ/AL-ḤAJJA*

It was narrated that the prophet Muhammad said: 'An 'umra is an expiation for the sins committed between it and the next, and Hajj which is accepted will receive no other reward than Paradise.' (hadith)[1]

Introduction

On a warm Sunday afternoon, in early October 2015, large crowds of people were strolling around the grounds of Muhammad V Airport in Casablanca: women, dressed in long colourful dresses, large groups of men standing near the exit area of the terminal, and countless children running about.[2] Some people carried flowers and others held trays with dates and small glasses of milk. Everyone was excited and anxiously waiting for their loved ones to arrive, including the family of Abu Bakr, who had left for Mecca around a month earlier.

On that day, just before leaving Mecca to return to Morocco, *al-ḥājj* Abu Bakr had made a prayer: 'O God, I pay You farewell with my tongue, but not with my heart.' He then performed his farewell *ṭawāf* and left Mecca. At the airport in Casablanca, his family waited in anticipation of his safe return. At home, food was prepared for a banquet, *walīma*, for family and friends. The living room was cleaned and scented, and plates of sweets were placed on a centrally positioned, large round table. In the kitchen, fresh mint was ready for a pot of traditional Moroccan tea and glasses were cleaned and dried. The outside of the house had been cleaned and splashed with water. The preparations taking place at home seemed akin to a purification ritual, preparing the house to welcome the returning pilgrim and the many visitors who would come to the house to congratulate him on his safe return.

At the airport, one of Abu Bakr's daughters carried a tray laden with walnut-filled dates, a bottle of milk and five glasses. When Moroccan pilgrims come home, custom and tradition dictate that these are the first foods they will taste upon return.[3] The flight was an hour late, yet people waited. Then, a woman's phone rang and after exchanging a few words she shouted: 'The airplane has landed!' Several people around her cried out '*mubārak . . . mubārak* [Congratulations!]' and '*al-ḥamdu li-llāh* [Thank God!]'. It was not for another hour that the first pilgrim emerged from the airport building: an old woman, wearing a white *jellaba* and a matching headscarf, pushing a trolley with two suitcases and clutching a box containing a five-litre bottle of Zamzam water. Around her neck the woman had a golden plastic flask, a typical souvenir in which *ḥājjī*s also carry Zamzam water.

At the first glimpse of the returning female pilgrim, all those gathered at the arrivals area applauded. The woman raised both her arms, greeting the welcoming crowd. She looked around for her relatives, who upon recognising her shouted: 'Here! Here . . . *al-ḥājja* . . . Welcome back . . . Thank God for your safe return!' Two young women ululated in honour of the arriving pilgrims. People greeted the other pilgrims who started to appear with '*mubārak*' [Congratulations] and '*'alā slāmtik*' [Thank God for your safe return].

A young man ran to welcome an arriving pilgrim, hugging her and kissing her forehead three times. Another man ran to welcome another older woman. He passed his phone to a relative and asked her: 'Take a photo of me and *al-ḥājja*', as he posed for a picture while kissing her forehead. At another corner three women, two men and several children gathered around another pilgrim in her white *jellaba*. They gave her dates to eat, and she had one sip of milk, which was then handed to a young man who drank the rest. A young woman filmed the welcoming event and initiated a recitation of the words '*ṣlāt wa-slām 'lā rasūl Allāh; lā jāh illa jāh sayyidnā Muhammad, Allāh m'ahu jāh al-'alī*' [Prayer and peace be with the prophet of God. There is no glory but the glory of our prophet Muhammad; God, with him is the highest glory].[4] After the woman had recited the first couple of words, many people in the airport picked up the rest, which resulted a collective recital of this prayer, followed by a loud cheering and ululation by people in the crowd. At this point, dozens of people were ululating, crying, laughing, shouting, filming and taking group pictures as more pilgrims came out into the arrivals hall. At that moment, *al-ḥājj* Abu Bakr appeared; his wife and daughters ran to greet him. They then offered him some milk to drink and posed for a group photo before leaving the airport. At home, more people would be waiting to welcome his safe return.

In a later conversation I had with Abu Bakr, he used a telling image to describe the condition of those who perform a pilgrimage, saying: '[Pilgrims] now are like new-born babies: cleansed from sins and full of goodness.' This state of purification is preceded by the moral disciplines expected during Hajj itself. During Hajj, pilgrims are expected to demonstrate piety and morality,

Figure 4.1 Pilgrims welcomed at the airport (Casablanca, 3 October 2015 and 28 September 2016)

abstaining from all temptations, showing tolerance when dealing with others and avoid disputes. However, according to Abu Bakr's wife, once pilgrims return home, the real test begins: would they have been transformed so fully and now live up to the moral principles developed during Hajj? Pilgrims would be accorded the honorific title *al-ḥājj* or *al-ḥājja*: would they honour these titles? The social, moral and religious expectations placed on a person who has performed the Hajj are elevated above those of 'normal life'. The expectation is that Hajj precipitates a major transformation in selfhood, a change on a spiritual and moral level which can be traced back to the spiritual gifts associated with – and developed during – Hajj.[5]

To address the question implicit in the minds of pilgrims and non-pilgrims alike about the transformative qualities of Hajj, one must examine in some detail what happens on return to the mundane rhythms of daily life. All major experiences have a metaphorical second life in terms of their personal, material consequences and emotional resonance and – in the case of the Hajj – their spiritual significance. Additionally, the effects may reverberate in the wider community, altering the perceptions of family and friends and adding to the collective identity of the group. While much attention has, quite rightly, been focused on the deep significance of the Hajj pilgrimage itself, my research has also highlighted the ramifications of the experience, both for the individual and the community, as well as underscoring some of the more complex issues related to becoming *al-ḥājj* or *al-ḥājja*.

In this chapter, I examine how the Hajj is seen by Moroccan pilgrims as a transformative experience which on a personal level is meant to encourage cumulative acts of goodness that pilgrims strive to maintain, and on a societal level redefines their position within the community on the basis of the *ajr*, or religious merit, of being a *ḥājj*/*ḥājja*.[6] Religious merit can be understood as a form of personal capital, gained after the pilgrimage. Christopher M. Joll, in his study of Muslim merit-making in Thailand, refers to the Hajj as the biggest merit-making event of a lifetime (Joll 2011, 171–80). Pilgrims also believe that religious merit will help them reach Paradise in the afterlife (Buitelaar 1993, 121). Nonetheless, religious merit is not automatically conferred simply by virtue of having completed the pilgrimage. To maximise spiritual benefit, pilgrims must strive to lead pious lives, honouring their new status, amid the ambivalences, contradictions and inconsistencies of their normal everyday lives. Although pilgrims are meant to strive to lead a morally good life, the benefits they have accrued from pilgrimage inevitably continue to be influenced by their wider social and cultural environments. In their everyday lives, pilgrims operate within several socio-cultural settings, each with its own frames of reference, each of which can have an impact on the continuing process of merit-making (Schielke 2010).

Being a *ḥājj*/*ḥājja* offers a complex network of possibilities for change, contributing to shaping the religious imagination of pilgrims, their self-identity and their daily practices, which, in turn, are influenced by social and cultural discourses as well as having a materialist dimension (Eickelman and Piscatori 1990; Tagliacozzo and Toorawa 2015). As in other Muslim societies, the sociocultural meaning of the performance of Hajj or *ʿumra* is embedded in contemporary Moroccan society (Hammoudi 2006). On the worldly level there are benefits associated with increased knowledge, and such benefits might impact matters related to a pilgrim's work, business or other worldly benefits. Many people, much like the pilgrims themselves, seem to have lofty expectations of the pilgrims' comportment in their daily lives after their return, whilst, at the same time, admitting a realistic sense of human imperfection.

In this chapter, I explore the putative spiritual benefits of the Hajj that people who have performed it experience upon their return and address some of the more complex ambiguities encountered by pilgrims. I do this by referring closely to the testimonies of my interlocutors and using my own observations. The daily lives of those who have successfully completed the pilgrimage involve an array of practices to which pilgrims are expected to be dedicated. Once the obligation of Hajj has been fulfilled, pilgrims can turn their attention to other demands placed upon them within their daily lives. At the same time, however, pilgrims must live up to expectations concerning enhanced morality and religiosity within those diurnal contexts. This enactment of what is deemed to be a correct performance of religious duties involves specific ideals or normative expectations, which are dictated by a religious authority or, alternatively, by a faith community's understanding of Islamic tradition. The pilgrims I worked with strove to become pious, virtuous or 'correct' Muslims, as they understood that term, in a practice which becomes the continuous crafting of a religious self.

Many researchers have focused on devotional practices related to pilgrimage (Porter 2012; Hammoudi 2006; Peters 1994). Their publications, however, give little coverage to or consideration of what happens when the pilgrimage is over and the pilgrim returns home to his or her everyday life. Therefore, by examining how pilgrims are 'living' Islam, I try to address this gap in the discussion (Marsden 2005). Therefore, this chapter continues as follows. First, I refer to the ideals of constructing of a moral self in everyday life as related to the Moroccan pilgrimage experience. Then, I reflect on the return of pilgrims from Mecca and how the completion of the pilgrimage is viewed as a new beginning and a quest for perfection by many Muslims. The third section deals with the ambivalences and tensions arising from the pilgrimage within the everyday life of Moroccans, and then reflects on the expectations placed on a pilgrim within their personal social networks and in the wider society, scrutinising matters relating to social and cultural capital. The last section reflects on the politics of everyday life and questions of self-cultivation as a *ḥājj*/*ḥājja*.

Cultivating a Religious Self: the Moral Quest of a Pilgrim

Many Muslims consider pilgrimage to Mecca to be the ultimate realisation of one's religious development and a way of achieving moral fulfilment or becoming a good, or a better, Muslim. David Clingingsmith, Asim Ijaz Khwaja and Michael Kremer (2009) estimate the impact of performing the Hajj on pilgrims by comparing successful and unsuccessful applicants in a lottery used in Pakistan to allocate Hajj visas. The accounts of pilgrims in their study indicate that the Hajj generates feelings of unity with fellow Muslims, increases observance of global Islamic practices such as prayer and fasting, and increases belief in equality and harmony among ethnic groups, in addition to fostering favourable attitudes towards women. When asked about the impact of Hajj on their religiosity, the Moroccans I talked to gave similar responses. It must be borne in mind, however, that the actual experience of everyday life may be significantly at variance with one's statements about it in a survey or even in an interview setting. Participant observation, by contrast, is an analytical tool which provides a clear focus on the perceived reality of the daily lives of pilgrims, and on their behaviour, interactions and other discourses, both personal and social.

Becoming a pilgrim brings about different forms of theological understanding of Muslim subjecthood. Fatima Sadiqi argues that within the Moroccan context the concept of self (or personhood) is constructed within the Moroccan socio-cultural context; that context is rooted in the community rather than the individual (Sadiqi 2018). Therefore, the self-image of a pilgrim is constructed within his or her socio-cultural community, where religiously-defined ideals of the pilgrimage to Mecca – and of those who perform it – are presented. In my examination of how pilgrims define ideals and norms, I analyse how fellow citizens and family members living in proximity to pilgrims situate those pilgrims in relation to expected religious norms and perceptions of them being *ḥājj* or *ḥājja* within the public sphere, and how the pilgrimage contributes to crafting a religious self.

My inquiry into the crafting of a religious self takes place within a Foucauldian inquiry into how different social spaces and times produce different ideas and ideals of the subject, in relation to which the subject seeks to craft herself. Being and becoming a 'good pilgrim' includes, for many people, the perfection of virtuous behaviour, a process akin to the Foucauldian concept of 'techniques of the self' which

> permit individuals to effect by their own means or with the help of others a certain number of operations on their own bodies and souls, thought, conduct and way of being, so as to transform themselves in order to attain a certain state of happiness, purity, wisdom, perfection or immortality. (Foucault 1988, 18; cf. Mahmood 2005; Foucault 1993)

Saba Mahmood's work, for example, demonstrates how participants in the women's mosque movement in Egypt struggle to follow a particular ideal to construct themselves as religious subjects. Analogous with this, the continuous process of becoming a good Muslim for pilgrims in Morocco includes adopting behavioural patterns that are considered correct. A pilgrim is often seen by the community as a person who should apply the highest ideals possible to achieve the ideal religious selfhood within the context of their everyday life.

With these nuances and concepts of what constitutes a religious self in mind, and with an awareness of the real-life context in which the pilgrim develops that sense of selfhood, I will now consider how being a pilgrim is experienced and debated within one's path to piety (Schielke 2010). Hence, put simply, I ask what kind of father or mother, daughter or son, brother or sister, friend, neighbour or employee a pilgrim tries to become, as well as how a pilgrim is expected to behave so as to be a pious person.

Return and Questions of Life and Death

Traditionally, some Moroccans expressed the view that the optimum time to undertake the pilgrimage is later in life, when a person can be expected to have already honoured all other commitments. The pilgrimage to Mecca, from this perspective, is seen as a person's last significant act in preparation for dying. Having fulfilled all obligations at home, the pilgrim can depart for Mecca with a clear conscience and there be cleansed of all their other sins before death. Thus, it is common – as with Muslims in many other parts of the world – that some returning pilgrims bring with them the *iḥrām* which they wore in Mecca, so that they can use these two plain white sheets as their shroud (Peters 1994). In this view the Hajj is understood principally as signalling the end of material existence, and the expectation is that a returned pilgrim will be prepared for death, and be of a mind to behave accordingly.

Linked to this idea are Moroccan attitudes relating to the possibility of dying in Mecca, especially to dying after the completion of the Hajj rites. Rashid, a seventy-year-old shop owner from Mohammedia, shared a story from his pilgrimage in 1988:

> [An old woman] was performing the Hajj with her son. However, that year Hajj was difficult. It was so hot that the streets melted. I saw that with my own eyes. The old woman – she was Pakistani – was tired and sick. I spoke to her son and said: 'Why did you bring your mother? She looks very tired!' The son said that his mother insisted on coming to Mecca; *she wanted to die there*!

In the story of the Pakistani pilgrim, Rashid understood why the woman had wanted to die after Hajj, 'sinless and ready to meet God', as he explained. Moreover, when the Minā stampede of 2015 took place, causing deaths estimated at well over 2,000 pilgrims, 42 of whom were Moroccans, some people saw the disastrous event in a positive manner.[7] I heard several Moroccans say '*sa'dāthum*!', which can be translated as 'How happy they must be!' or 'Lucky them!', which in Morocco is a clear expression of admiration towards those whose death took place at the optimal spiritual moment, albeit in such a tragic context. Rashid, however, did not wish to die in Mecca. He – like many other Moroccans – preferred to die in his own home. Nonetheless, he recognised the spiritual imperative of completing the pilgrimage successfully and its role in renewing one's faith. He explained:

> Pilgrimage is an opportunity to cleanse oneself from sins . . . When one returns home, it is like being a new-born . . . it is an opportunity for a new way of life and a renewed faith [*īmān*].

Provided that the pilgrimage has been performed correctly and with honest intentions, as Rashid – and earlier Abu Bakr – said, 'a pilgrim returns free of sin. In this sense, the Hajj, as a rite of passage, marks the transition to a new life that starts upon return from pilgrimage (Werbner 2003). For Rashid, 'the real test starts when one returns home'. It is upon return that one is tested. Therefore, like Abu Bakr, Rashid had said prayers to God to strengthen his faith and asked for stability, *thabāt*, in the context of the new status he would acquire when returning to Morocco.[8]

Furthermore, the idea of completing one's faith, in an act of total consummation, is central to the performance of the Hajj. The idea itself is linked with the belief that a Muslim should complete the Five Pillars of Islam if capable. The Five Pillars of Islam – the profession of faith, performing daily prayer, almsgiving, fasting during the month of Ramadan and the Hajj – are considered the foundation of one's faith. Pilgrims themselves often describe their experience of pilgrimage within these parameters and talk about the pilgrimage in terms of changed internal states. In the words of Abu Bakr:

> One's faith is complete [when Hajj is performed] in keeping with the words of the Almighty, 'This day have I perfected your religion for you, completed My favour upon you and have chosen for you, Islam as your religion.'[9]

These ideas about rebirth and purification are central to the spiritual transformation which the returning pilgrim hopes to undergo. Many Moroccans spoke to me about their expectations that those who have been to Mecca will come back spiritually rejuvenated, displaying a new enthusiasm for a religious life upon their return home. In the words of one Moroccan woman:

'When pilgrims return from Hajj, they come back a blank sheet of paper . . . They should be careful what to write on that sheet . . .' The image of the pilgrim as a *tabula rasa* suggests that all past misdeeds are obliterated, purged and forgiven, so that the returned pilgrims begin their spiritual journey again, with no sins weighing them down.

Pilgrims try to protect and preserve their new spiritual state of purity whilst, at the same time, navigating their daily lives and interactions with others. Here, the 'performance of piety' can be observed in action. The word 'performance' is related to external factors that are visible and can, as a result, be assessed and evaluated. This is not to suggest that there is any insincerity in the performance of piety, but it may be that the returned pilgrim feels impelled to demonstrate the spiritual benefits of the Hajj through external speech markers and behavioural characteristics which connote devotion. Society may expect to perceive the outward signs of inward change. In the next section, I reflect on these expectations in relation to the daily lives and experiences of pilgrims.

A New Person? A Pilgrim's Religious and Social Life after Hajj

According to Rashid, when they return home, pilgrims focus on having the 'correct' character traits, deemed by tradition to be associated with a good pilgrim, a topic that recurred frequently in discussions of pilgrimage with Moroccans. In conversations relating to the Hajj, Moroccans often focused on describing what is expected of a pilgrim, both in terms of external behaviour and interior expressions of piety. Interior piety is linked to the idea of cultivating, and having cultivated, the sense of a close relationship with God, a feeling highly prized by pilgrims, a state achievable through the devout performance of religious duties.

This was illustrated in my interactions with pilgrims in Morocco, when I asked what, if anything, had changed in their lives since they had returned from Hajj. First, those returning to Morocco after having performed the Hajj told me that the pilgrimage had resulted in transformations that were manifested in behaviour relating to religious rituals, most notably in the realm of prayer and other kinds of religious activity. According to Samiya, a pilgrim in her sixties from Fes:

> Before going on Hajj, I used to pay less attention to my religious duties . . . I could not wake up for *fajr* prayers [at dawn], for example, and rarely fasted outside of the month of Ramadan . . . Now, I make sure to pray on time, wake up for *fajr* prayers, fast regularly and help others . . . A pilgrim should never lie, should not cheat, and should be a good neighbour . . . [A pilgrim] should stay on the right path [*al-ṣirāṭ al-mustaqīm*] . . .

Although such practices are expected of pious Muslims in general, and not necessarily only of those who performed Hajj, for people returning from pilgrimage these matters acquire an even greater insistence; an obligatory zeal informs their desire to cultivate moral selves and lead devout lives, and their practices aimed at achieving this.

Pilgrims strive towards what they consider to be a pattern of Islamic perfection. Although they may oscillate between this ideal and the realities of daily life (Beekers and Kloos 2017; Ahmed 1988; Robinson 1986), observable evidence suggests that they try to be faithful to their pilgrimage, and 'stay on *al-ṣirāṭ al-mustaqīm* [the straight path]', to quote the words of Samiya.[10] Furthermore, the daily lives of Muslims involve an array of religious obligations, regardless of whether the person has completed Hajj. But for the pilgrim, these devotional rituals acquire new resonance. Therefore, pilgrims assert a conscious belief that that they have become more mindful of religion in their daily life.

For many pilgrims, life after returning from Mecca was about the development of a new moral self, one that differentiates more closely than before between what is good and bad, right and wrong, sacred and profane, in their everyday lives. Upon return, many pilgrims felt the need to improve their social image, and their social status, through their individual behaviour. Pilgrims exhibit a determination to perform other acts, including extending hospitality and giving alms to the poor. Other aspects of external behaviour, operating on a lower level but nonetheless having great significance for pilgrims, included smiling, being kind to others, solving disputes, and adopting a positive demeanour in public. Many pilgrims organise and participate in a variety of religious gatherings including collective recitations of parts of the Qur'an. In addition, many pilgrims are invited as witnesses to marriages and to act as judges in cases of dispute. Such conduct is not exclusively the province of the devout, but pilgrims saw it as a daily manifestation of spiritual grace acquired, or intensified, during Hajj. The returning pilgrim may relish this status, and the desire to maintain that status might in turn enhance the desire to exhibit greater piety.

Social Capital and a 'New Status': Expressions of Public Religiosity

The significance, for Moroccans, of having undertaken the Hajj is determined not only by the fact that it is one of Islam's Five Pillars, but by a range of factors, which include local values, the web of relationships in which they are embedded and the social expectations of pilgrims. Most notably, there is a change in a pilgrim's social status, indicated both by perceptions of how the pilgrim should now behave, and by the deference which others should show them (Donnan 1989). In Morocco, the honorific title *al-ḥājj* or *al-ḥājja* carries social significance, in the sense that the community expects a pilgrim to be respected and honoured. The significance of the title may be explained through the words of Nisrin, a young Moroccan woman whom I met in Casablanca. Nisrin used to address one friend of her mother as *khāltī*, a term that means 'maternal aunt' but is applied – as a mark of respect – to other older women. However, when this woman returned from Hajj she demanded to be addressed differently. In Nisrin's words:

> *Khāltī*, a friend of my mother, went on Hajj last year. When she returned, we visited her and I said: 'Congratulations on your Hajj, *khāltī*.' The woman looked at me and said: 'Do not call me *khāltī* any more! Instead, call me *al-ḥājja*!'

Nisrins's aunt clearly wanted deferential recognition for her status, a recognition which superseded her previous form of address. Nisrin believed that the friend of her mother was seeking social recognition for religious merit, pursuing prestige rather than spiritual recognition.[11] More than once, Nisrin mentioned, the aunt called attention to her pilgrimage, by bringing the topic up when she visited relatives; for example, when she referred to the wintry weather she insisted on comparing it with the dry heat of Mecca during her pilgrimage. Nisrin, and many other Moroccans, questioned the automatic use of the title for those who have performed the Hajj.

In days past, the prestige of the title *al-ḥājja/al-ḥājja* hinged on its relative rarity. Formerly, the trip to Mecca was perilous, arduous, costly and often long. These factors made the Hajj a rare ideal attainable only by a few people, and rendered its completion a significant achievement (Scupin 1982). Therefore, those who had successfully completed the Hajj acquired a higher social status in their home communities. More recently, matters have changed. As a result of the fact that more people are nowadays financially able to perform the Hajj (despite difficulties and restrictions such as the quota system and visas), the prestige linked to the title *al-ḥājj* or *al-ḥājja* has diminished. When I asked Nisrin if she called her aunt by the title *al-ḥājja*, she answered: '*Allāh yismaḥli* [May God forgive me], but when I see her, I call her *khāltī* on purpose . . . I can see it on her face that she does not like it!' The fact that Nisrin began her answer with *Allāh yismaḥli*, however, was an indication that she believed her behaviour towards her mother's friend might not be appropriate, considering the latter's age and social status as a female pilgrim. Being recognised as a pilgrim still carries high social significance among Moroccans, although the greater frequency of completion of the Hajj has introduced a modern ambivalence towards the title, albeit a muted one.

When Moroccans discuss the issue of ascribing high status to pilgrims, many people draw a clear distinction between religion, culture and tradition. Abu Bakr, for example, asserted that the practice of naming is more a cultural than a religious practice. Upon my asking him about the title *al-ḥājj* by which he is known, he commented:

> When the prophet performed the Hajj in Mecca, no one called him *al-ḥājj* Muhammad. His companions also performed the Hajj. But no one says *al-ḥājj* Ali, *al-ḥājj* Umar or *al-ḥājj* Uthman . . . Those were the leaders of the Muslim community; yet none of them was called *al-ḥājj*.

The reason a person should perform pilgrimage, according to Abu Bakr, is simply that God commands pilgrimage, and therefore it is not obligatory for them to be given the title *al-ḥājj* upon their return from Mecca. Rashid expressed a similar view:

> When someone prays, he performs an obligation. Yet, he would not be called *al-muṣallī* [the one who prays]. When he fasts, he performs an obligation,

> yet he would not be given the title of *al-ṣāʾim* [the one who fasts] . . . Pilgrimage is the same; it is an obligation and those who perform it are lucky and hopefully God accepts their pilgrimage; but there is no need for them to be called *al-ḥājj*.

Thus, both Abu Bakr and Rashid believed that it is for the community to confer upon them the honorific title of one who has completed the Hajj, and is not something pilgrims themselves should ask for (Buitelaar 2018).

Although pilgrims assume an automatic entitlement to an honorific title on their return from Mecca, this, however, does not mean that a person necessarily receives respect and social status. In fact, family, friends and others actively assess the behaviours and religious conduct of the returned pilgrim. They assess the changes which have occurred (even if perhaps not consciously), such is the expectation of transformation that people are attuned to. The following discussion illustrates how being a pilgrim affects the perception of that person within a family context. The case relates to Abu Bakr and his wife Najla.

Flaws in Perfection: the Ambivalences of Everyday Life

Najla, her daughter Yusra and I were looking at some pictures which documented Abu Bakr's pilgrimage journey from two years earlier. Several hundred pictures were saved in a special folder on the daughter's computer, downloaded from her father's phone, documenting his journey in Mecca and Medina. With every picture, mother and daughter narrated what they remembered about Abu Bakr's pilgrimage experience. They told me about the application process, preparations for the journey, and his departure. Several family pictures were taken at the airport, recording his departure and safe return. Remembering her husband's departure for Hajj, Najla commented:

> Before he left for Mecca, at the airport, he cried and asked for forgiveness for every moment of anger and every unjust action during our life together . . . I felt like he was paying the last farewell. I felt that he would not return and wanted to be cleansed from his sins before meeting God . . . We all cried and to myself I thought that he would return as *al-ḥājj*, a completely new person!

Najla described her husband as being, upon his return from Hajj, the kindest she had ever known him. 'How long do you think that lasted?', Najla asked me. She then answered her own question: 'Three months!' Describing the change in his behaviour, Najla clearly remembered the words of her husband upon his return from Mecca:

> He told me that being on Hajj reminded him of the prophet, especially of the deeds of the prophet who was a gentle man, a kind and a loving husband, and a good father and neighbour . . . [My husband] wanted to be a loving husband just like the prophet . . . And he was! He was the perfect husband; never angry, always smiling and speaking nicely and gently . . . For three months! After three months, he returned to his old self . . . He is not a bad person, but he easily gets angry and gets irritated often . . . I have to say, those three months [immediately following his return] were the best months of our twenty-five years of marriage . . .

In the three months that followed her husband's return, Najla recognised him as 'truly *al-ḥājj*', as one who was spiritually transformed. The husband worked hard to demonstrate piety and reverence and to evince qualities such as open-mindedness and readiness to be a good husband. This change is a state brought about through the pilgrim's own efforts. However, the transformation, in this case, was not held to be permanent, revealing that the experience of pilgrimage alone is considered insufficient, in itself, to bring about total and lasting change.

The life of pilgrims after Hajj reflects the reality that moral selfhood remains a compelling struggle for people, because of the complex and contradictory sources from which selfhood is built, and also because of the contradictory demands placed on the self when one is simply living. Thus, the new moral status acquired after pilgrimage becomes a site of struggle for the returning pilgrim, a fact observed within the family, and evaluated by those closest to the pilgrim. Rashid expressed this dilemma when he told me:

> When people go on Hajj and return, their behaviour might change between themselves and God with more prayer, fasting and almsgiving. However, what is between themselves and people might not change a lot . . . We are just humans; [a pilgrim] might return to treat people badly, cheat, or gossip . . . [That's part of] a human's daily life!

For many Moroccans a good pilgrim is a person who fully and comprehensively applies the teaching of the Qur'an and the prophet's instruction for moral action (Schielke 2009). This idea, however, is complex; it does not mean that people can live in this way, and therein lie the ambiguous consequences of the ideals represented by religious expectations. As Najla put it: 'At the end of the day, a pilgrim is only human; humans do right and wrong. They might try not to, but it is difficult.' Thus, the benefits of pilgrimage in terms of their 'legacy' are held to be equivocal. The honorific title rings hollow when the expected transformation seems unfulfilled, and members of the community are reluctant to ascribe the title to flawed individuals.

However, these judgements are not universally shared; as Najla's view shows, some take a more nuanced perspective regarding expectations of pilgrims on return from Hajj. In this alternative view, there is a recognition that to fail and err is human; people holding this view consequently moderate their expectations of pilgrims.

Straying from the Right Path

It is, of course, pilgrims themselves who must deal with their own sense of failure. They may provide different explanations for the change, or lack of change, in themselves after Hajj. Rashid, for example, told me that he believed that one's character does not significantly change after Hajj but that the outcome of Hajj depends on one's upbringing, *tarbiya*. He optimistically estimated that 90 per cent of Moroccans change positively after Hajj and try to follow the straight path. He insisted that, although a pilgrim might return to his old habits, the change in his or her heart would remain consistent after Hajj. In his words: 'after Hajj, a pilgrim's heart is filled with faith [*yiʿmar bil-īmān*].'

Some pilgrims insisted that in a Muslim's life there are always pathways for ethical improvement which exist independent of Hajj. Thus, the pilgrimage to Mecca is not the end of that improvement but a step, and for some, even a beginning. There seemed to be a shared ethical mode among pilgrims that enabled my interlocutors to see their moral shortcomings as an opportunity for learning from experience rather than as occasions of sin which damage their personal religious development. Beekers and Kloos (2017) reflect on the dialectical relationship between the pursuit of religious adherence on the one hand and the experience of moral fragmentation on the other; they do this by focusing on self-perceived senses of failure. They argue that experiences of a sense of failure offer an important and productive entry point for the study of lived religion in today's world, a world in which religious commitments are often volatile, and where believers are regularly confronted by alternative lifestyles, worldviews or desires as they strive to become self-reflexive religious subjects. The acknowledgement of moral failure, they argue, is part of the formation of one's ethical compass (Koning 2017, 48; Sunier 2017, 113). Taking this argument one step further, it could be argued that explicitly acknowledging one's sense of failure can be a 'technique of the self' in the sense of formulating and rechannelling that sense of failure as a learning moment. Reflecting upon and 'testifying' about such moments thus actually contribute to and stimulate one's development and enhance the presentation of a religious self (Buitelaar 2019).[12] For example, although pilgrims admitted failure in the performance of humility, they continued to talk about this very failure as an avenue to a more reflective state of mind, a fact which they often vocalised. In other words, recognising and responding to one's lack of capacity to realise certain ideals becomes a mode of self-cultivation.

Serious attempts to persist in developing a pious self-formation are evidenced by many of the pilgrims with whom I talked, as they described daily activities. One significant feature of the demeanour of pilgrims is that they try, if they are able and where possible, to return to Mecca again for *'umra*. Several pilgrims among my interlocutors performed *'umra* once a year following their Hajj, a considerable investment of time and resources. However, the business of everyday life made my interlocutors aware that their religious endeavours were perpetually incomplete projects that required ongoing work and investment of time, attention and spiritual energy. Their practices of worship were part of such ongoing, forever imperfect, moral and spiritual work on the self, aimed at becoming closer to God. In this way, the pilgrimage, and its aftermath, constituted an attempt at coming to terms with self-perceived imperfections and inadequacies, without ever fully resolving them.

Conclusion

In this chapter I have discussed how pilgrims relate to a particular religious ethos that they are expected to embrace, negotiate and practise within the social spaces they inhabit. The focus has been on how religious discursive practices and ideals operate in the everyday lives of pilgrims, and how these practices are incorporated into the crafting of a religious self that matches the aspirations associated with a new honorific. Pilgrims, just like everybody else, live their everyday lives laden with ambiguities and contradictions. There are several contradictions between, on the one hand, how a pilgrim is expected to behave in a religious moral register and, on the other, the reality of his or her actual behaviour and daily interactions with others.

While Moroccans recognise that pilgrimage to Mecca can have certain transformative properties, enabling returning pilgrims to pursue a more spiritual life and leading them to a better understanding of Islam, they do not always consider the outcome to be perfect or lasting. Thus, my research reveals that the construction of a virtuous self and religious persona is far from straightforward. Despite the aspirations of and manifestly sincere efforts made by returned pilgrims, there was a general realisation that the performance of the Hajj is no guarantee, per se, of a life transformation and an elevation to a higher religious standard. The process is not simply an individual enterprise with a guaranteed outcome.

If piety, religious self-fashioning and conviction constitute one aspect of what pilgrims strive to achieve, then imperfection, uncertainty and ambivalence are undeniably competing elements of the everyday lives they live. Self-perceived failure is, in many cases, part of religious practice and experience. To navigate, or negotiate, the complexities of life as it is lived, while still maintaining a sense of striving for spiritual improvement, is a laudable religious pathway. To accept human frailty and yet sustain a religious endeavour, even if not perfectly realised, could provoke a sense of failure which might, in turn, militate against that sustained religious practice. The recognition that spiritual 'improvement' is the target, rather than perfection, allows pilgrims to embrace the facts of daily life as they find them.

Notes

1. *Hajj al-Mabrūr* refers to an accepted pilgrimage (Muslim, book 15, hadith 493).
2. Security measures in 2015 were not as strict as in the years that followed, allowing non-travellers to enter the airport freely. However, in 2016, following three suicide bombings in Belgium (two at Brussels Airport and one at Maalbeek metro station in central Brussels), security measures were significantly heightened. Information provided through personal contact with a local official.

3. Dates and milk have different meanings depending on the occasion on which they are served, I learned from Moroccans. When guests are received, milk and dates are signs of honour and welcome; at weddings, the bride and groom share milk and dates which signify peace, happiness and welfare.
4. Moroccans use this prayer, and other versions of it, on different occasions, including engagement parties, weddings, birthday parties and other celebrations (Dessing 2001, 126).
5. Fieldnotes, 3 November 2015.
6. In Morocco (and other places), the title *ḥājj*/*ḥājja* is often used to address older people, mainly as a sign of respect regardless of whether or not the person in question has actually performed the Hajj.
7. On 24 September 2015, an event described as a crush and stampede caused deaths estimated at over 2,000 pilgrims suffocated or crushed in Minā. The accident was widely covered by the Moroccan and international press; https://apnews.com/3a42a7733a8b476889bb4b7b3be3560e/ap-count-over-2400-killed-saudi-hajj-stampede-crush (last accessed 23 March 2021).
8. *Thabāt* means stability or constancy. It is considered a quality of the Muslim in belief, worship and morals (Abu-Rabiʿ 1996, 150). In Muslim tradition, it is believed that, after a person dies, their soul passes through a stage called *barzakh*, where it exists in the grave. The dead person is then questioned by two angels, who ask about their beliefs. A righteous Muslim is believed to respond by saying that their Lord is God, that Muhammad is their prophet and that their religion is Islam. The action of holding to this test is referred to as *thabāt*, endurance or stability (Coward 1997).
9. Quoted from Qur'an 5:3. It has been said that this verse was revealed during the farewell pilgrimage on the Day of Arafat (Al-Bukhārī, book 64, hadith 429).
10. *Al-ṣirāṭ al-mustaqīm* or the straight path is mentioned in the opening chapter of the Qur'an in the form of a supplicatory prayer offered by humans to God: 'Guide us to the straight path: the path of those You have blessed, those who incur no anger and who have not gone astray' (Qur'an 1, 6–7). The historian Michael Cook notes that *ṣirāṭ* in Arabic is only ever used in a religious context. Also, it has no plural form, indicating that there can be only one *ṣirāṭ*, which is living through the way to God (Cook 2000, 25).
11. For more information on Moroccan women's experience of the Hajj, see Chapter Seven.
12. Buitelaar, personal communication (15 November 2019).

PART TWO

IDENTITY AND POLITICS

Illustrative Anecdote: Prayers for the Hajj

Passing through the old medina of Rabat, Rue Souika was buzzing with the business of buying and selling. I moved along with the crowd, hearing along the way a young man imploring passers-by to buy colourful winter blouses that he sold. A woman passed in front of me looking at the young man's wares. I heard the man saying: 'Allāh yaʿṭīk al-ḥajj' [May God grant you the Hajj] (20 July 2016).

I joined an organised trip to the Merzouga desert as I wanted to visit this iconic region in the southeast of Morocco. Alongside a Moroccan friend and a bus full of fellow Moroccans from Rabat and Casablanca, we departed on Friday with the intention of returning on Sunday night after spending a night in the desert. Our journey began with a morning arrival in Errachidia, where we took a tour of the local market and enjoyed a relaxed lunch before proceeding to what appeared to be the edge of the desert. Upon arrival, we were greeted by local guides with camels ready for us. Mounting the camels, we ventured deeper into the vast expanse of sand dunes. After some time, we had to dismount and continue on foot, climbing one of the tallest sand dunes in Morocco amidst a line of fifty people. I found myself out of breath from the exertion. As the sun began to set, the anticipation of reaching the summit and beholding the magnificent view intensified among all of us. Despite the physical challenge, a young woman at the front of the line encouraged everyone to persevere: 'Come on! Keep it up; imagine you're on Hajj!' Her words reached all of us. In response to the woman's encouragement, another woman further back replied, 'Pray for me that *Allah 'yaʿṭīnī al-ḥajj'* [May God grant me the Hajj]'.

5

HAJJ AND MOROCCAN NATIONAL IDENTITY

Up! my brethren,
Strive for the highest;
We call to the world
That we are here ready;
We salute as our emblem
God, Homeland and King

(national anthem of Morocco)

Introduction

Samiya is a woman in her sixties, a widow, and a mother of four, all of whom are married and live away from home. When I visited Samiya one evening in her house, she invited me to watch a daily Turkish drama with her. She volunteered to tell me the plot of the Moroccan-Arabic-dubbed drama that has been podcast in Morocco for at least two years. Samiya lives in a well-decorated house. In the living room where we sat, there were three large sofas, a round dining table and a couple of antique wooden coffee tables. The walls were decorated with two frames containing Qur'anic calligraphy and an image of the Ka'ba. A golden decorated copy of the Qur'an rested on a wooden table next to the large TV, which was showing the Turkish drama.

As soon as the drama finished, Samiya changed channel to *al-'ūlā* or Channel 1, the first national Moroccan TV channel, to watch the evening news. The first news segment was about the anniversary of 'The Revolution of the King and the People', the independence movement that had led to the end of the French protectorate.[1] Addressing the Moroccan public on an occasion celebrating the Moroccan nation-state, Mohammed VI, the king of Morocco, spoke to the nation with the following words:

> Dear citizens, it is God's will that, this year, the commemoration of the Revolution of the king and the People should coincide with the celebration of the blessed Feast of Sacrifice. Although the two events differ in essence – one being national, and the other religious – they nonetheless arouse similar emotions in the hearts and minds of Moroccans, given the values of sacrifice and loyalty underpinning them.[2]

The king's rhetoric was far from accidental, but was engineered specifically to unite the national and religious aspects of Moroccan identity. Despite insisting that the two occasions – one national and the other religious – are different, the king's uniting of the two events reveals how the religious and mundane are interwoven in Morocco. Religion, here, is used as a tool for promoting national identity and unity. In this chapter, I investigate the link between pilgrimage to Mecca and national identity in Morocco. I will argue that while the pilgrimage is fundamentally important for a Muslim religious identification, it is also an occasion that contributes to the construction of a nationalistic discourse on both national and personal levels.

Though the gathering in Mecca of millions of pilgrims for the Hajj is an expression of Islam's global, transnational Muslim community (Clingingsmith, Khwaja and Kremer 2009; Eickelman and Piscatori 1990; Sijapati 2020), even the possibility of and experience of the Hajj are shaped and influenced by national belonging. For example, the Hajj is carefully managed through national policies. Throughout the Hajj journey, pilgrims are marked by their national identity: they are provided with name tags, backpacks and other paraphernalia which are often embossed with national flags or printed in their colours. Guides have national flags attached to their clothing, and housing allocated to pilgrims is based on where they come from, such as the tents in Minā where accommodation is divided on the basis of nationality. Pilgrims are also guided in their local languages and services are provided to Moroccan pilgrims in Arabic.

National identity is not a pre-existing concept, but is very largely constructed and produced by people as they develop and express their understandings of situations, events and other people (Shatzmiller 2005). Therefore, individuals define themselves in terms both of individual uniqueness and of specific group memberships. The following, therefore, addresses two formulations of national identity in Morocco: Moroccan nationalism seen from a state perspective, and being Moroccan as perceived and expressed by citizens themselves. To address this complex process, I will first analyse the speeches of King Mohammed VI addressing Moroccan pilgrims in the four years to 2018; secondly, I shift focus to how pilgrimage is portrayed in mosques and state-media coverage; and thirdly, I consider the symbolic importance of being Moroccan in Mecca, where that national identity itself is contested. Finally, I turn to the narratives of Moroccan pilgrims regarding their pilgrimage journey after they return home. For necessary background, I first briefly introduce the historical context in which the question of Morocco's national and religious identity is embedded.

National Identity and Religion in Morocco

Religion and religious identifications feature prominently in many everyday discussions about politics or national belonging in Morocco. The national ideology has always combined what is presented as traditional culture and religious adherence combined with modernity; thus, religion and politics are barely separable (Sadiqi 2011). Although the modern nation-state is a recent creation, Islam has been a factor of identity in what is present-day Morocco and has been so ever since the establishment of the ninth-century Idrisid dynasty, the first Moroccan Muslim dynasty, which founded the city of Fes (Abu Nasr 1975, 78). Since then, Islam has taken various forms, which have had different effects on the character of Moroccan society, from peripheral to mystical, and in the twentieth century have involved more modern visions of Islam (Wyrtzen 2016; Spiegel 2015; Zeghal 2008; Geertz 1971; Hagopian 1963).[3]

The Moroccan constitution of 1996 describes the Kingdom as a sovereign Muslim state, *al-dawla al-islāmiyya*. The constitution introduces Morocco as an Islamic country with a legislative body and political parties. In the hierarchal structure of the government, however, the monarch represents the core of religious power. The Moroccan 'Alawi ruling dynasty (1666–present) continues to claim heritage as genealogical descendants of the prophet Muhammad, as part of a narrative that legitimises their claims to authority (Nelson 1978, 207–9). The 'Alawi family bears the title *sharifian* (noble) family, which has a considerable influence in Moroccan culture and society (Zeghal 2008; Howe 2005).[4]

Furthermore, the religious significance of the king is illustrated by his title *amīr al-mu'minīn* or Commander of the Faithful, the highest religious and political authority (Sadiqi 2018, 46).[5] The religious status of this title was codified by King Hassan II in the 1962 constitution (Biagi 2014; Waterbury 1970). Of independent Morocco's eight constitutional reforms, seven were made during the reign of Hassan II.[6] All constitutions ensured the religious and legal legitimacy of the king and the political power of the *makhzen* (Sater 2016).[7] For example, article 19 of the Moroccan constitution of 1996 states:

> The king, *Amīr al-Mu'minīn* (lit. 'Commander of the Faithful'), shall be the supreme representative of the nation and the symbol of the unity thereof . . . As Defender of the Faith, he shall ensure respect for the constitution. He shall be the protector of the rights and liberties of citizens, social groups and organizations.[8]

Post-1963, King Hassan II used Islam to both ensure the authority of the royal palace and legitimise his own power (Benomar 1988, 544). He secured his authority by appropriating to himself control of religious affairs, which had formerly been managed by three distinct institutions: the 'ulama' or religious clergy, the *zāwiya* or lodge for religious authority and the monarch, establishing hegemony over both the political and religious realms in Morocco (Zeghal 2008, xii).

One example of the cementing of the power of the royal family is the principle of the *bay'a*, the oath of allegiance to the leader.[9] Every year, on 3 March, at the Celebration of the Throne, a pledge of allegiance is made, in which ministers, mayors, deputies and all local representatives of the government present themselves before the king and renew their *bay'a* in an official ceremony. The *bay'a* symbolically affirms the authority of the ruling monarch as a leader who is not only a political leader but is also a direct descendent of the Prophet, and who thus deserves the title 'commander of the faithful' (Eickelman and

Salvatore 2022, 92–115). Among Moroccans, the status of the king is assured in the hierarchical formula declared in the national motto: God, homeland and the king (Touhtou 2014).

The process of political and religious influence that Hassan II left behind was extended when Mohammed VI ascended the throne in 1999. Mohammed VI introduced new policies that resulted in an administrative restructuring regarding the way in which religion is managed in Morocco. There was a strong push for a distinctively Moroccan form of Islam to be achieved by organising the religious field and pursuing the training of religious scholars inside and outside the country (Hissouf 2016).[10] For example, in 2013, Morocco launched an internationally-oriented imam training policy in line with moderate 'Moroccan-style' Islam, based on the Sunni Maliki school of thought (Hlaoua and Baylocq 2016).[11] In 2015, Morocco inaugurated the Mohammed VI Institute for Imam Training in Rabat, thus institutionalising the training of Moroccan, African and European preachers and religious scholars (Hmimnat 2020).[12]

This supreme and all-embracing status has not been without challenge. In the popular uprisings that swept across North Africa starting in Tunisia in December 2010 (Harb and Atallah 2015), approximately 150,000–200,000 Moroccans in fifty-three cities and towns across the country marched, in a call for greater democracy and change, on 20 February 2011: hence it was called the 20 February Movement (Madani, Maghraoui and Zerhouni 2012; Fernández Molina 2011). Those marching called for democracy and change, symbolised by the popular Arabic call *al-shaʿib yurīd dustūr jadīd* ('The people want a new constitution').[13] The response to the 20 February Movement was a rapid drafting and adoption of a new constitution in July 2011. Compared to earlier constitutional texts, which promote a selective identity (Arabic and Islamic), the new constitution was more open. The preamble states that national unity is forged by the convergence of Arab-Islamic, Amazigh and Saharan-Hassani components and enriched by 'African, Andalusian, Mediterranean and Hebrew' heritage (Morocco's Constitution of 2011).[14]

Although the 2011 constitution includes important departures from the previous one, in the new constitution the king effectively remains at the centre of political and constitutional life, and he continues to concentrate all powers in his hands.[15] He remains at the centre of political and constitutional life particularly because he alone can revise the constitution.[16] In addition to the constitution, over the years the public speeches of the king have become a prime reference for political and religious life in Morocco (Madani, Maghraoui and Zerhouni 2012). For example, political parties use the speeches of the king as guidelines for the government. Most political leaders refer to them, and no one can disagree with their substantive content (Maghraoui 2011).[17] The speeches are the dynamic behind every change, the blueprint for various actions, and the centre around which the politics of consensus are constructed (Kaye 2008, 148–50).

During my fieldwork, I observed how the king of Morocco actively cultivated the image of himself as a pious Muslim. For example, every year in Ramadan, he presides over a series of religious lectures known as *durūs al-Ḥassaniyya* (Porter 2001, 25).[18] This Ramadan tradition was begun in 1963 by the late King Hassan II (hence its name), and has hosted prominent Muslim scholars and jurists from diverse Islamic branches and ideological backgrounds to discuss issues and concerns of the Muslim *umma* (Porter 2001, 35). The lectures are attended by the king, other members of the royal family, religious scholars, high-ranking state officials, and members of Muslim countries' diplomatic missions to Morocco. The king also attends Friday prayers, which are podcast on national TV (Roberson 2014, 67). During the prayers, the king appears in special garb reserved for religious events that emphasise his status as king and religious leader (Landau 1962, 25). During the Feast of Sacrifice he ritually slaughters two rams, one of them symbolically on behalf of Moroccans as a nation. Traditional culture, religion and modernity are all presented in the state discourse as integral parts of a single composite of Moroccan identity (Hissouf 2016). Therefore, the Hajj offers a central opportunity for the consolidation of beliefs, for ensuring the religious legitimacy and responsibility of the king, and for enforcing religious, national and other identities of Moroccans in general.[19] The pilgrimage to Mecca is a pivotal moment when the king addresses the nation by addressing the pilgrims.

In the next section, I provide a translation and analysis of the annual farewell speech, as it is often called, offered on behalf of the king to pilgrims on their first day of departure from Morocco to Saudi Arabia.

The Official Discourse on the Hajj and the Role of the King

When the first group of Moroccan pilgrims headed to Saudi Arabia to perform pilgrimage for the hijri year 1437 on 31 August 2015, they received an official farewell message from the king at Rabat – Salé Airport. The message was read out to the Moroccan pilgrims by the Minister of Endowments and Islamic Affairs, Ahmed Toufiq. A similar tradition was in evidence every year during my fieldwork between 2015 and 2018. In general, the speeches focus on four areas: the importance of Hajj as a religious duty for Muslims, the significance and role of the government and the king, the roles and responsibilities of Moroccan pilgrims in Mecca, and specific messages relating to the year or time of year at which the speech is made.

The speeches all begin with the King congratulating Moroccans performing Hajj, and mentioning its importance for Muslims at large and for him himself. For example:

> I am sure you are aware, honourable pilgrims, of the importance I attach to the pilgrimage and the attention I devote to this pillar of Islam, which is the culmination of a lifetime of worship. Through Hajj, we make sure our faith is complete, in keeping with the words of the Almighty: 'Today I have perfected your faith for you, completed My favours upon you, and chosen Islam as your way.'[20] (20 August 2016)

The role of the king is heavily emphasised throughout the speeches, in which he is presented as the Commander of the Faithful and protector of faith and religion. The king's descent from the prophet Muhammad is emphasised here, such as in the following statement from the 2018 speech:

> I realize how eager you are to visit the holy sites and the blessed tomb of my ancestor, prophet Muhammad – may peace and blessings be upon him. I pray that the Almighty God may fulfil your wishes and answer your prayers. I invoke His blessings upon you and pray that you may return safely to your homeland and your loved ones . . . It goes without saying that the Hajj season is a time to remember a part of the blessed life of our most exalted prophet, *my ancestor prophet Muhammad* – may peace and blessings be upon him. (26 July 2018)[21]

Such statements function to create authority by association and underscore the power of the king through his claimed connection with the prophet.

In his message, the king of Morocco also emphasises his role in ensuring that pilgrims receive the correct religious guidance. Such interest in religious orthodoxy can be seen in statements such as 'My message to you illustrates my concern to ensure the preservation of religious tenets and to show how much I care about them' (26 July 2018). The message also emphasises the fact that the king spared no effort to facilitate pilgrimage for those able to perform it, by instructing the Minister for Islamic Affairs to take whatever measures might be necessary for the performance of this pillar of Islam, and to provide pilgrims with the assistance and guidance they need through the appropriate religious, health and administrative delegations accompanying them, making sure they receive all the necessary services in the Holy Land.

The king further refers to the duties of Moroccan pilgrims during the Hajj, including acting in accordance with the guidelines given by Moroccan and Saudi officials and being on their best behaviour in front of other pilgrims. The king asks Moroccans to serve as ambassadors for their country, conveying a positive image of its cultural heritage. He addresses pilgrims, saying:

> I . . . want you to serve as ambassadors for your country, conveying a fine image of its cultural heritage. I also want you to understand that our country owes its security and stability to the ideals and immutable values. Under my guidance, our country is continuing its successful march towards further progress and accomplishments. (26 July 2018)

> I must now remind you of your individual and collective obligations towards your beloved country . . . Chief among these is your commitment to the immutable, sacred values of the Moroccan State – a nation which is based on moderate Islam and the Sunni doctrine, as represented by the Maliki doctrine and the Ash'ari rite . . . I therefore want you to be ambassadors for your country during that great gathering and reflect the characteristic, long-standing traditions of Moroccans, namely those of brotherhood, solidarity, moderation, and openness. (8 August 2017)

Being ambassadors, pilgrims are responsible for presenting an image of Morocco when away from the homeland. In relation to their behaviour in

Mecca, the king instructs pilgrims to be patient, to show restraint and self-control and to avoid any inclination towards selfishness, as those are 'the virtues Islam wants Muslims to comply with' (2015).

Another responsibility for Moroccan pilgrims, according to the king, is their reciprocal duty towards him in his capacity as the Commander of the Faithful. The duty includes prayers for the king, who, according to the 2015 message, provides comfort for pilgrims, protects the unity of the nation, and ensures the country's stability and development. The message includes clear instructions for pilgrims to perform *duʿā'* prayers for the king at the holiest of the sites:

> When you are at that most impressive place and at other sites as well – especially when you stand on Mount Arafat – remember your duty to pray for your king, who provides for your comfort and security, for the unity of the nation and for the betterment of your lives. Ask God to help me perform good deeds, to grant me and all members of the royal family good health, to make me ever pleased and satisfied with our beloved Crown Prince, His Royal Highness Prince Moulay El Hassan, and to shower His blessings upon my esteemed grandfather, his late majesty king Mohammed V, and upon my revered father, his late Majesty king Hassan II – may they rest in peace. May the Almighty forever protect and safeguard our homeland.

The monarch then urges pilgrims to comply with the ministry's arrangements and to abide by the instructions provided by the Saudi authorities concerning the organisation of the Hajj season.

Among their duties, Moroccan pilgrims should strive to behave and show manners that are advocated as part of the Moroccan cultural narrative: a spirit of genuine tolerance and brotherhood in which Islam is seen as

> a middle-of-the-road religion, without extremism, reclusiveness, or intransigence – a faith based rather on cooperation, solidarity, and commendable conduct [aiming] to erase that stereotyped image circulated by the enemies of Islam, by radicals and religious zealots. (31 August 2015)

The symbolic message of the king's speech represents an opportunity to promote a 'moderate Moroccan Islam' that is presumed to be inspired by the mystical Sufi heritage. The messages also suggest a collective national identity which is characterised by 'brotherhood, solidarity, moderation and openness' (8 August 2017). The message has a third audience, the wider world. In this reading, the pilgrimage is appropriated as a symbol for promoting a narrative of tolerance and for stressing the power and influence of the monarchy, ensuring that those listening understand Morocco to be a peaceful, pluralistic and tolerant nation. A quasi-ritual status has become attached to the monarch's speeches, enhancing their significance and making them, in a sense, an integral part of the Hajj experience.

State-affiliated institutions – such as mosques, television, newspapers and radio – participate in the process of confirming the role of the state in the nationalistic discourse of the pilgrimage. Friday sermons, for example, which are often attended by large numbers of Moroccans, feature stories about the Hajj, the Prophet's life and his experiences in Mecca and Medina, among other topics. In a Friday sermon I attended at a mosque in the coastal town of Essaouira, the imam pointed out that pilgrims were performing the Hajj in Mecca, and stressed that 'we are connected with them in our hearts' in Morocco.[22] He advised people to connect with those in Mecca by fasting, sacrifice and celebration:

> On the Day of Arafat, we can connect further with those performing the duty on the plain of Arafat near Mecca. We connect with them as we fast the Day of Arafat in faith; we connect with them when we slaughter the sheep on the day of *ʿīd*; we connect with them as we celebrate the Hajj in Morocco. (16 September 2016)

The imam explained the spiritual and religious significance of the Hajj, in addition to the importance of harmony and good citizenship among all Moroccans, stressing the need for solidarity and unity through shared religious observation. He finished his sermon by praying for God's forgiveness and blessings for Moroccans performing their Hajj in Mecca, for all Muslims, and for Muslims in Morocco, before extending the prayer to the king, the royal family, the prince, and the late kings Muhammad V and Hassan II.

Friday sermons featured not only religious messages but also ethnic, cultural and political ones. In a small town near Rabat, I met an imam of a mosque to learn more about Friday sermons. He told me that imams of every Moroccan mosque registered at the ministry receive and read out to

Friday congregations the exact same sermons. These sermons are written and disseminated by a central committee of the Ministry of Endowment and Islamic Affairs. He also mentioned that the sermons are explicitly managed so that they correspond with both the religious calendar and the national agenda.

After the Hajj proper was concluded, I attended a Friday sermon in Casablanca where the theme of the sermon was 'citizenship and patriotism'. The sermon focused on the importance of the homeland as a gift from God to man. 'The link between man and land is like that between a child and his mother who carried him, fed him, and raised him . . . Therefore, love of homeland is part of one's faith', the imam explained. When the imam illustrated the importance of citizenship and patriotism, he used examples from the prophet Muhammad's life and his feelings of love and belonging towards Mecca. The imam spoke about the night of *hijra*, when the prophet left Mecca for Medina, and discussed how difficult it was for him to leave his homeland:

> The prophet stood on the border of Mecca and said: 'By God, you [Mecca] are the best and most beloved land to God, and the dearest of the land to me. By God, had I not been expelled from you, I would never have left you.'[23]

The importance of Mecca was further highlighted by the story of the prophet Abraham, who prayed to God to protect Mecca and make it a place of safety and abundance.[24] By referencing the two examples from Mecca, the imam illustrated that loving one's homeland is a duty, part of one's faith and of primordial human nature, *fiṭra*.[25] Through these stories, the imam defined 'real patriotism' as contributing to the development of one's country and ensuring its safety and stability. When this sermon was delivered, Hajj was still fresh enough for Mecca to be a timely and powerful symbol to use.

In Morocco, I witnessed how Moroccans follow the Hajj events in Mecca with keen interest. During the Hajj season, local channels report news from Mecca. The images on TV channels, including Channel 1, Channel 6, which is dedicated to religious education, and even the primarily entertainment channel 2M, showed pilgrims around the Kaʿba, praying in the Grand Mosque of Mecca and standing on the plain of Arafat. These broadcasts emphasised that pilgrimage revealed Islam to be 'a religion of tolerance, brotherhood and humanity' and 'a faith which rests on principles like unity of Muslim communities, equal rights and obligations, peace, respect for others, and the protection of Muslims' (Channel 1 news report, 2 September 2015).

During the Hajj season of 2016, Channel 1 of Moroccan national TV had daily reports reflecting the experience of pilgrims in Mecca. One report explored the living conditions of pilgrims. It began by showing two middle-aged men reading the Qur'an on their beds in a room overlooking the Grand Mosque of Mecca. From the window of the room, the footage showed the Kaʿba and the minarets of the mosque. Then, the reporter interviewed four women who sat on a bed in a similar room to the first overlooking the Kaʿba. One of the women prayed to God to protect the pilgrims and help them in performing the rituals, to protect all Muslims and to protect the king, to which the other women responded: 'Amen!'

Although Moroccan state channels showed positive reports from Mecca, there are other channels of communication through which the official media claims were contested (Eickelman and Anderson 1999, 1–18; Schulz 2012; Al-Ajarma and Buitelaar 2021). In Rabat, for example, a Moroccan friend shared a video showing Moroccan pilgrims complaining about the unhealthy conditions they had suffered during the 2017 Hajj season in Saudi Arabia. This incident created controversy on Moroccan social media. One video showed a group of people carrying the Moroccan flag in a demonstration against the management of the accommodation of Moroccans near the site of Minā. In a report that a Moroccan pilgrim published on social media, a man wrote: 'all Moroccans are standing together in Mecca' (18 August 2017).

In their edited volume on new Muslim media, Eickelman and Andersen (1999) speak about the fragmentation of religious authority due to the creation of alternative sites of religious discourse beyond the traditional methods. Pilgrims actively use social media and other communication platforms to voice their opinions and challenge the discourse the state puts forward in its official media (Al-Ajarma and Buitelaar 2021). Another example of such contestation is a video I received via WhatsApp from Lubna, one of my interlocutors whom I will introduce in Chapter Seven. The video featured a group of pilgrims as they complained about the quality of food served during the Hajj, as well as about having to stay in unsanitary accommodation in the holy city. 'This is the dinner offered to the Moroccan pilgrims: an expired juice box', says a man as he shows the camera the offending item. 'Moroccans, if you are planning to come on Hajj next year, you need to speak for your rights. There is only hunger and dirt', the man continued. Thus, the positive construction of national and religious identity, which is initiated at the topmost level of Moroccan society, is not without its challenge or counterpoint in the modern age of digital technology.

The next chapter will discuss various stories connected with the pilgrimage in relation to the management of the Hajj. In the next section of this chapter, I move on to discuss personal reflections on the Hajj experience in relation to Moroccan national identity and belonging.

Moroccans' Reflections on the Hajj Experience and National Identity

During my fieldwork in Morocco, thousands of Moroccans performed the pilgrimage to Mecca every year, together with nearly two million Muslim pilgrims, representing every nation in the world. Many Moroccans would make the point that the Hajj represents a kind of ideal society, free from the biases and divisions that dominate the profane world. They shared personal stories of bonds forged and strengthened during pilgrimage, of friendships that defied national boundaries through a sense of harmony or *communitas* (Turner and Turner 1978, 13; Turner 2012, 4). And yet, despite this harmony, many pilgrims judge one another, and the experience stimulates individual reflections on national belongings, and differences between Moroccans and Muslims of other nations. The following includes an excerpt from a conversation I had with Samiya, the woman mentioned at the beginning of this chapter, and two of her neighbours one Thursday afternoon in Casablanca.

I joined Samiya to visit her neighbour, Muna, who had returned from Hajj a few days earlier. As we walked side by side towards Muna's house, I helped Samiya carry a bag full of sugar cones, a frequent practice when visiting those returning from Hajj. The gift of sugar, according to a local friend, is a long-standing tradition which dates to a time when sugar was rarely available and such a gift reflected respect and appreciation. At Muna's door, we met with Zaynab, another neighbour who came to visit. In Muna's living room, the new pilgrim welcomed us and immediately asked her two young daughters to bring sweets and drinks.

The girls disappeared for a couple of minutes and returned carrying two trays containing plates of dates, three small glasses of Zamzam water and a pot of Moroccan tea, which they placed on a round table where two more trays were readily available with a rich variety of traditional marzipan sweets. Once the women had enquired about Muna's health, trip conditions and the pilgrimage experience, they wanted to learn more about the journey:

Samiya: How did you perform the rites? How was the journey?
Muna: Thank God! It was a wonderful journey. All the rites were fine . . . I am thankful to be back home with my daughters . . . and I am finally back in my country!
Zaynab [who had not been on Hajj] May God grant all Muslims a visit to those holy places.
[The two other women said 'Amen!' in agreement with Zaynab's supplicatory prayer.]
Zaynab: . . . How was your experience?
Muna: . . . I cried, prayed, did *du'ā'* prayers . . . I learned a lot about the people I travelled with . . . I made friends with people from many countries.
Samiya: . . . I still remember how those Indonesians were so organised, always clean and polite . . .
Muna: Yes, especially those of Indonesia and Malaysia . . . But us Moroccans, we are not unbelievably bad either. We are not as organised as these people or even Turkish people, but we are more developed than many other pilgrims . . . We are more organised . . . I thanked God that I am Moroccan!
[The two guests looked puzzled by Muna's last comment and asked for explanation.]
Muna: This experience made me think about our life in Morocco. Our traditions are different from other people, our culture is genuinely nice, our food is good, our land is beautiful. Compared to many people, we were organised . . . [and] behaved better than many others . . . I thank God that I am back home . . . I thanked God that I am Moroccan . . . Thank God I am Moroccan!
Samiya: The life in Morocco feels good when one is away and when comparing with other people.
Muna: Even people's looks are different. Seeing so many men, during Hajj, I now think my husband is good-looking, which is something I never thought!
[The two women laugh at Muna's comment.]

Muna: Seriously! I see my husband as a handsome man now . . . Our country is beautiful, and its people are good.

The Hajj serves as a vivid lens through which to perceive distinctly differences between one's native culture and community and the diverse communities encountered during the pilgrimage journey (Sijapati 2020, 36). For Muna, the pilgrimage offered an opportunity for her to reflect on her Moroccan identity and to compare Moroccan culture, practices and national heritage to those of pilgrims from other nations. The encounters with other people, their ways and traditions served to reinforce a sense of contentment with the traditions of home. The same newly restored appreciation applied to food, culture, and even her husband. Muna's observations about the diverse looks of people during Hajj, followed by her new-found perception of her husband as handsome, highlights how the physical appearances of individuals from diverse backgrounds are being scrutinised and compared, and how Moroccans are perceived as individuals within the broader Muslim community. Her observation reflects how diverse experiences and encounters during the pilgrimage can lead to new-found appreciation and admiration for those from one's own cultural background. For Muna, the experience evoked a sense of pride and connection to her national identity. However, by remarking on the physical attractiveness of her husband in comparison to that of others she had encountered during Hajj, Muna also underscores the potential for comparative judgements based on physical appearances after being exposed to other pilgrims from diverse backgrounds.

Other Moroccans reflected an appreciation of Moroccan unity during and after the pilgrimage to Mecca. For example, Maysa, a woman in her thirties who went on Hajj with her elderly father, told me that she had enjoyed meeting, in Mecca, Moroccan women from various places in Morocco. In the tent camp in Minā, where women are separated from men, both women and men get the opportunity to become acquainted with those staying in their tent. Even though pilgrims come from all around the world and gather in Minā, the tent camp is organised in sections accommodating people in groups with the same national background, but within each group people may never have met their compatriots from other regions or social classes. Some interlocutors said their tents had contained around twenty-five pilgrims whilst other tents accommodated more than a hundred people each. When they stay in Minā, pilgrims have the opportunity to learn about each other's lives and develop friendships. Here is what Samiya told me about meeting other Moroccans in Mecca:

> During Hajj, I met with Moroccans from all around the country. I realized how those from Rabat are different from those of Marrakech or Fes . . . We are not only Arabs, but we mingled with different Amazigh groups: *riyafa* [the Riff people inhabiting the plains], *jebala* [the mountain people] and *soussi* [people of the Middle Atlas] . . . It is rare to see in one place, even in Morocco, a mixed group of people like that . . .

Although Samiya recognised the diversity of Moroccans she met with in Mecca, like several other Moroccans she pointed out that Moroccans were distinct from other groups of pilgrims (Jenkins 2008, 1997; Polletta and Jasper 2001). The appreciation of national diversity and belonging was often manifested in the conditions that Moroccans face during Hajj. In another visit to Muna in Casablanca, she told me about an incident that occurred in Mecca:

> One day, as I was trying to return to my hotel, I lost the way. It was after *ʿishāʾ* [evening prayers] and I was alone. As I walked down one dark street, I got worried that I had lost my way . . . Suddenly, a man stopped his car next to me and approached me in Moroccan *dārīja*. 'Sister, do you need help?', he said . . . He recognized me by my white *jellaba* . . . He was Moroccan! I felt relieved . . . He showed me the way back to the hotel and made sure I was safe.

For Muna, Moroccan dress was a mark of distinction, a way to identify as Moroccan among people from diverse backgrounds. When in Mecca, many Moroccans ensure their distinctiveness primarily through their dress code. Moroccans can easily be identified by the *jellaba*, a long, hooded coat worn by men and women.[26] Women's *jellaba*s, often white, are worn during the Hajj and *ʿumra* rituals and during the rest of the time they spend in Mecca. Nonetheless, some women told me that on their way to Mecca they were encouraged to buy a black *ʿabāya* to wear instead of their white *jellaba*s.[27] While some women followed this recommendation, the majority remained in their traditional clothes. Even Muna, who had bought a black

ʿabāya to wear in Mecca after she performed the Hajj, decided to carry a Moroccan *jellaba* in her bag and put it on before getting on the flight back to Morocco.

In my conversations with Moroccan pilgrims, there seemed to be a clear suggestion that some pilgrims of other nationalities are praiseworthy. To illustrate this point, Hassan, whom I met in Safi, shared photos of the Hajj, including that presented in Figure 5.1 along with its Arabic caption, which I translate as follows:

> We return one more time to the Muslims of Southeast Asia who are well-organised, well-mannered, and performed the rites with humility. Even when they left hotels, they were impressive in their organisation, their bags organised, and they sit in the buses while their bags get organised without disorder or troubles. Salute to those individuals whose leaders have shown dedication to the well-being and development of their people. May God help those with whose language the Qur'an was revealed.

Figure 5.1 Facebook post shared by a pilgrim (shared via Facebook, Safi, 28 November 2018)

Moroccan pilgrims often reflected on which groups had behaved more appropriately, who enjoyed better services, and which groups were less fortunate than the Moroccan pilgrims. Such debates tend to resolve themselves with the conclusion that Moroccans are positioned somewhere in the middle. Upon their return from Mecca, many Moroccans would say, in gatherings with family members or friends, 'Thank God I am Moroccan!'

As if conscious that others will also be making evaluations and comparisons, whilst in Mecca the pilgrims seek to present a bright, positive image of their country. Many Moroccans told me that the once-in-a-lifetime Hajj is not only a religious duty, but also a unique opportunity to present a positive image of Morocco to the world. Muna, for example, spoke about how her behaviour was meant to be exemplary because she was in the state of *iḥrām* and because her behaviour reflected the image of her country. In this way, she echoed the message of the king by being an 'ambassador' of Morocco in Mecca.

Following the completion of the Hajj rituals, many pilgrims expressed their longing to return home. This was how Rashid from Mohammedia – whom I introduced in Chapter Four – put it:

> When you go somewhere away, you miss your mother . . . You might be at the best place in the entire world but still, nowhere would compensate for your mother . . . My homeland is like my mother. I recognise the importance of going to Mecca; I always long to go and perform Hajj and *'umra*, yet I always rush back to my family here . . .

Longing for Morocco is not necessarily a longing for the same Morocco as is propagated through state messages. Expressing opinions about the monarchy and the state is very risky in Morocco, so to protect my interlocutors I have not pursued the issue of what dimensions of Moroccan identity they valued, and had missed, so dearly. It is safe, however, to quote Hassan, who asserted that the noblest of people are the ones who are the most pious. In a way Hassan was referring to a verse from the Qur'an: 'People, We created you all from a single man and a single woman, and made you into races and tribes so that you should recognize one another. In God's eyes, the most honoured of you are the ones most mindful of Him: God is all knowing, all aware' (Qur'an 49, 13).

Conclusion

In this chapter, I have argued that the pilgrimage to Mecca is not only an enormous religious event in Morocco but also an occasion for reinforcing the sense of national identity in the official discourse of the Moroccan government, and an opportunity for Moroccans to reflect on their own identity and their sense of belonging to their homeland.

At the level of official discourse, Morocco is ruled by a constitutional monarchy which claims legitimacy through its genealogical descent from the prophet Muhammad, implying overtly that its ruling representative is also *amīr al-mu'minīn*, the successor to the Prophet's religious and secular authority. In the official discourse, the pilgrimage is a force that is used to help strengthen national unity and is seen as an opportunity to reassert the religious authority of the monarchy. Moroccan pilgrims are urged to see themselves as the ambassadors of their country, embodying its identity and civilisation as well as the values in which they are grounded, namely, the unity of the *umma* and epitomising communal coherence and a commitment to the ideals of moderation and balance.

Most pilgrims willingly accept the ambassadorial role because it resonates with their pre-existing sense of national identity and therefore is not an imposition so much as a validation of national pride. This role also provides an opportunity to demonstrate the qualities of Morocco to the wider *umma* while relishing encounters with people of other regions, who may even speak other languages. Moroccan pilgrims, then, seek to communicate with other pilgrims as best they can, exemplifying their commitment to religious unity. Thus, although the Hajj gives pilgrims the opportunity to express, produce and reinforce Muslim unity on the one hand, on the other the pilgrimage also stimulates its own subtle reflections on the question of belonging, on both a national and a personal level.

Notes

1. 'The Revolution of the King and the People' or *thawrat al-malik wa-l-sha'b* refers to the independence movement in Morocco. This nationalist movement grew from protests regarding the Berber Dahir of 16 May 1930. On 20 August 1953 (the eve of the Feast of Sacrifice), the French authorities forced Mohammed V

along with his family into exile in Corsica and then to Madagascar. Mohammed V returned from exile on 16 November 1955, and was again recognised as Sultan after active opposition to the French protectorate. Morocco became independent in 1956, and in 1957 Mohammed V adopted the title of King (Wyrtzen 2015).

2. Fieldnotes, 20 August 2018.
3. Morocco was ruled by the ʿAlawi dynasty since the seventeenth century. Many Amazigh tribes were, however, not submissive to the ruler (Sultan). This led at the beginning of the twentieth century to two different regions: *bled es-Siba* (areas outside central government control) and *bled al-makhzen* (areas under central government control) (Hoffman 1967; Zeghal 2008).
4. In addition to the ruling family, several Moroccan families claim to be descendants of the prophet Muhammad, something which also comes with certain symbolic prestige (Bazzaz 2010).
5. In Sunni Muslim tradition, *amīr al-mu'minīn* ('prince of the believers' or 'commander of the faithful') originally referred to Caliph Umar, a companion of the prophet Muhammad, and was used by subsequent caliphs. It is also one of the titles of the caliphs, successors to the prophet Muhammad, as both heads of states and (honorary) religious leaders, and it can also have military connotations as commander in chief (Wyrtzen, 2015). According to Shiʿi tradition, the label refers exclusively to Caliph Ali, the son-in-law of the Prophet. No other current head of state assumes the title apart from the king of Morocco.
6. The first constitution was that of 14 December 1962. Since then, Morocco has experienced eight constitutional amendments, the first in 1970 and the last in 2011 (Ruchti 2012; Touhtou 2014).
7. The notion of *makhzen* refers to the central power and political authority of the state including the close entourage of the king as the effective centre of power and political control (Maghraoui 2001). When speaking about the *makhzen*, what is implied is generally an authoritarian practice of government without any form of accountability (ibid.).
8. In addition to article 19, the following articles give the king additional powers: articles 23 (The person of the king shall be sacred and inviolable); 24 (The king shall appoint the Prime Minister. Upon the prime minister's recommendation, the king shall appoint the other Cabinet members, just as he may terminate their services. The king shall terminate the services of the Government either on his own initiative or because of their resignation); 27 (The king may dissolve the two houses of parliament or one thereof by royal decree, in accordance with the conditions prescribed in articles 71 and 73); and 30 (The king shall be the

commander-in-chief of the Royal Armed Forces. He shall make civil and military appointments and shall reserve the right to delegate such a power) (Ruchti 2012).

9. The *bay'a* (investiture or oath of allegiance) is a pre-Islamic tribal allegiance system that was incorporated into Islamic tradition. Initially in Islam, the *bay'a* was sworn to the prophet Muhammad as an oath of allegiance (Khel 1981, 227–38). Anybody who wanted to enter Islam did so by reciting the basic statement of the faith expressing his faith in the oneness of God and the prophethood of Muhammad. The Prophet also formally took *bay'a* from the people and tribes of Medina. Through this formal act they entered the Islamic community, showing their willingness to follow and obey the Prophet (ibid.). Since then, the *bay'a* has become an act by which a certain number of persons, acting individually or collectively, recognise the authority of another person as the head of a Muslim state or community (Podeh 2010, 117–52).
10. The training of religious scholars initiative was a response to the terrorist events that occurred in Morocco on 16 May 2003. The policy aimed to deal with extremism by advocating a modern Islam that rejects extreme Salafism, including Jihadism (Hissouf 2016).
11. Information provided by a local official via personal communication.
12. For more information on Morocco's transnational religious policy, see, among others, Hmimnat (2020; 2018), Werenfels (2014), Munson (1993) and Sparkes (2022).
13. Although the 20 February Movement was inspired by the revolutions in Tunisia and Egypt and had similar characteristics in terms of the role of the Internet and protests bringing together thousands of young people, the movement cannot be interpreted as simply part of the Arab Spring, since Moroccan civil society has been active over many years before the Arab Spring demanding changes in the constitution (Maghraoui 2008; 2002).
14. Also in the 2011 constitution, the Arabic language is no longer the only official language of the state, and the Amazigh language has also become an official state language and part of a common heritage of all Moroccans, without exception, as stated in article 5.
15. The 2011 constitution has gone through several changes relative to the 1996 text, including the recognition of new rights, recognition of the Amazigh language as an official language and the promotion of human rights. However, the constitution continues to be criticised, for example for not establishing a 'true parliamentary monarchy' (Newcomb 2017; Madani, Maghraoui and Zerhouni 2012).

16. The king appoints the head of government and other cabinet members following a proposal by the head of government (Madani, Maghraoui and Zerhouni 2012).
17. The constitutional basis for this authority of the speeches of the king was formulated in article 28 of the 1996 constitution, which stated: 'The King shall have the right to deliver addresses to the nation and to the parliament. The messages shall be read out before both houses and shall not be subject to any debate' (Maghraoui 2011). The same constitutional basis that forbids debating the King's speeches is now part of article 52 of the 2011 constitution.
18. Moroccan TV, Channel 1, 1 June 2018.
19. In *Fasting and Feasting in Morocco,* Marjo Buitelaar refers to national identity politics in relation to the fasting month of Ramadan (Buitelaar 1993).
20. Verse quoted from the Qur'an (5: 3).
21. From the Hajj farewell speeches of 2018, 2017 and 2016 (italics mine).
22. Documented Friday sermon (fieldnotes, 16 September 2016).
23. I could trace this hadith to the hadith collection of Ibn Mājah (vol. 4, book 25, hadith 3108).
24. The prayer was mentioned in the Qur'an in two places: 'Remember when Abraham said, "Lord, make this town safe! Preserve me and my offspring from idolatry" (Qur'an 14, 35); 'Abraham said, "My Lord, make this land secure and provide with produce those of its people who believe in God and the Last Day." God said, "As for those who disbelieve, I will grant them enjoyment for a short while and then subject them to the torment of the Fire – an evil destination"' (Qur'an 2, 126).
25. *Fiṭra* refers to the state of purity and innocence in which, so Muslims believe, all humans are born. It is usually translated as 'natural constitution' or 'innate nature' (Macdonald 2012).
26. Moroccan men often wear traditional clothing and leather slippers outside the period of *iḥrām*.
27. The *ʿabāya* cloak is a simple, loose over-garment, essentially a robe-like dress, often black in colour, worn by some women in some Muslim societies including Saudi Arabia.

6

CONTESTING PILGRIMAGE: MOROCCAN PERSPECTIVES ON SAUDI CONTROL OF THE HAJJ

For you [Medina] I have ardent love,
And a yearning in my heart;
I have a vow – if I fill my eyes with those
walls and places where [the Prophet] walked . . .
Had it not been for obstacles and enemies,
I would always visit them,
even if I were to be dragged upon my feet

(Qadī ʻAyyāḍ)[1]

Introduction

At the henna party of Nuha's cousin, I found myself sitting at a table with seven women sharing food and drinks.[2] Henna parties are a time of festivity when women enjoy a gathering characterised by singing, dancing, food and celebration at the house of the bride before the day of the wedding. During the party, the bride is visited by a traditional henna artist who paints intricate designs on her hands and feet. Close family members and friends, including Nuha and I, were invited to come together to celebrate and share a meal.[3] On the same table sat Hajar, the mother of the bride, Salma, a relative in her sixties, Latifa, an aunt in her seventies, and Samira, the bride's sister; and I was introduced to the others. We were first offered some milk and dates followed by salads. Soon, large plates of cooked chicken and more salads were brought. Samira asked her eldest aunt if she had heard about the new visa charges for Hajj and *ʿumra*. The conversation went something like this:

Samira: Auntie, have you heard that extra fees have been imposed on any pilgrim travelling to perform *ʿumra* for a second time?
Latifa: Yes! I heard in the news. The rule applies to you if you have been [to Hajj or *ʿumra* in the past].
Nuha: It seems that the Saudi [government] is using that holy place for business now!
Salma: I remember when I went to *ʿumra* last year; I was bothered by the evil look of that clock tower. It makes the mosque look tiny.
Samira: It is the only thing one notices when entering Mecca; I thought the mosque would be the most iconic monument . . . I was wrong!
Latifa: I remember when I went to Hajj many years ago, we stayed in a simple hotel, now there are big fancy hotels . . .
Salma: Some people say that if you stay at one of the hotels in the clock tower, you do not even need to leave your room; you can pray there, and it is considered part of the square of the Grand Mosque . . .
Hajar: But only the rich can enjoy these hotels! . . . They claim that they want to make Hajj better; but they are not! All these destructions of sites where the prophet lived in Mecca and Medina, where the Companions lived, and where the history of Muslims was . . . All destroyed!
Samira: A neighbour of mine was in Mecca when a crane collapsed [on 11 September 2015] in the Grand Mosque . . . There were a lot of deaths . . . She was saved and thanked God that nothing happened to her . . .
Salma: The sight of these cranes over the heads of pilgrims is scary . . .
Samira: . . . Pilgrims [are put] in danger for the sake of these plans. *ḥshūma . . . ḥshūma* [Shame . . . Shame on them!]
Nuha: They behave as if Hajj is only theirs . . . Hajj belongs to all Muslims . . .
Hajar: I was hoping to go to *ʿumra* next Ramadan . . . But I am afraid that I would be praying and at the same time scared that something might fall on me at any moment . . .
Samira: They claim to safeguard the holy sanctuaries; the call themselves *custodians* but at the same time they engage in the destruction of the history of Islam and replace holy sites with Western hotels . . . It just does not make sense![4]

شقيقة الرميد تعتدي

شرطي ضمن شبكة للنصب

المنشطات تضرب ألعاب القوى من جديد

الصباح

ASSABAH

■ عمرة

فوجئت وكالات الأسفار بقرار ملكي صادر عن الملك سلمان بن عبد العزيز، برفع الرسوم عن أداء شعائر العمرة للمرة الثانية إلى ألفي ريال سعودي، أي حوالي خمسة الاف و300 درهم، إذ أصبح لزاما على المعتمر تسديد المبلغ للمصالح المختصة في المطار، قبل الشروع في أداء العمرة الثانية، الأمر الذي أثار استياء المهنيين، بسبب انعكاسات هذا القرار على أسعار تسويق منتوجات العمرة في المغرب ودول أخرى، ذلك أنه سترتفع بشكل مهم خلال الفترة المقبلة.

Figure 6.1 Report about *ʿumra* fees in the daily newspaper (Casablanca, 5 October 2016) – English translation: *ʿUmra*: A royal decree by King Salman bin Abdul-Aziz has taken Moroccan travel agencies by surprise. It imposes a fee of 2,000 riyals (roughly 5,300 Moroccan dirhams [500 Euros]) on anyone travelling to perform the *ʿumra* pilgrimage for a second time . . . Workers in this sector fear that the decree will negatively affect the sale of *ʿumra* packages in Morocco and in other countries. *ʿUmra* fees will soon increase.

This chapter deals with how, in relation to the Hajj, Moroccans reflect on Saudi Arabia not only as the country that is home to the two holy cities of Mecca and Medina, but also as a state whose governance administers and shapes the pilgrimage experience. It is well-known to Moroccans that because of Hajj, Mecca has become the spiritual centre for Muslims, who aspire to an ideal of unity and solidarity (Rippin and Bernheimer 2018; Cragg and Speight 1980, 60). When in Mecca and Medina, Muslims not only perform the rites of Hajj and *ʿumra*. They also pray, associate with each other and visit various sacred sites that are significant in the history of the Islamic tradition. The Hajj, as Bianchi puts it, is a cycle of planning and preparation which includes finance, education, transportation, accommodation and celebration (Bianchi 2004, 4). Whenever possible, travellers to Mecca combine worship with non-religious activities such as business, tourism, study and job seeking (Bianchi 2007).

Thus, the total experience of the pilgrimage is more complex and includes far more ‘profane’ matters, not just the religious duties involved. During my fieldwork, I heard many stories from Moroccans who discussed their ambivalence about the pilgrimage experience. On the one hand, pilgrims recognise the pilgrimage as a 'once in a lifetime experience' and recognise themselves as the 'guests of God' in Mecca, as they put it. At the same time, they discussed having to deal with the bureaucracy of the Hajj management and the Saudi model of governance, political authority and power whilst in Mecca (Campo 1991; Dorsey 2017; Law 2015; Pascatori 1983; Sardar 2014; Vogel 2002, 2000).[5] Moroccans often contrasted the Saudi approach to Islam with their own Maliki doctrine and with the Sufi heritage that is very much celebrated by most of those I met during the duration of my fieldwork in Morocco (Al-Rasheed 2007, 57).

In this chapter I will address how Moroccan pilgrims position themselves vis-à-vis the Saudi 'mode of domination', to use Pierre Bourdieu's term (Bourdieu 1990, 122–34). They experience Saudi control at every level of the Hajj experience, from the selection process through to the accommodation, and down to the very issue of who is permitted access to which sites. For all Muslims, Mecca and Medina are the most important sites of the *umma*, which, ideally – many Moroccans would argue – should fall under the leadership of the whole Muslim community, rather than the government of one country which imposes its own interpretation of Islam on all activities in Mecca and Medina (Bianchi 2007). In Mecca, pilgrims find themselves in a complex web of relations where they experience the domination of the state, solidarity among pilgrims, co-operation, conflict, debate and contestation. In line with Foucault's observation that *place* is fundamental in any exercise of power, Mecca is not only a spiritual and religious place for Muslims but also a location that has been politicised through various human agencies. In fact, Eickelman and Piscatori attempt to summarise this by stating that Muslim politics is a process of 'competition and contest over both the interpretation of symbols and control of the institutions, formal and informal, that produce and sustain them' (1996, 5).

Before discussing the stories and narratives of Moroccan pilgrims relating to the main theme of this chapter, I will provide a brief historical analysis of Saudi control over the pilgrimage itself and the major changes that have taken place since the 1900s in the ruling powers of the region once known as the Hijaz. I then discuss specific examples of Saudi control over the Hajj – as illustrated by Moroccan pilgrims' narratives – starting with the redevelopment of Mecca and the changes in the holy sites, before proceeding in the third section to discuss how Moroccans reflect on the Saudi control over religious practices in Mecca. In the fourth section, I discuss how Moroccans reflect on the accidents and human loss occurring in Mecca at the time of pilgrimage. Finally, I discuss how Moroccans reflect on Saudi policies and politics in relation to the management of the pilgrimage.

Contestations of the Sacred in Saudi Arabia

The origins of the modern Saudi state date back to the early 1900s, when Ibn Saud retook Riyadh to re-establish his ancestors' realm (Goldberg 2013).[6] In October 1924, the forces of Abd al-Aziz Ibn Saud captured Mecca, which inaugurated a new era in the relationship between pilgrimage and Saudi authority (McLoughlin 1993).[7] After becoming the acknowledged ruler, Ibn Saud swore that he would rule in accordance with religious law, thus offering reassurance to prospective pilgrims throughout the Muslim world and the local Meccan establishment (Hobday 1979). In 1932, Saudi Arabia was established as a kingdom by king Abd al-Aziz. Much of the Arabian Peninsula was politically unified by 1932 in the third and current Saudi state, the Kingdom of Saudi Arabia.[8] The present regime is particularly interested in the holy places, as can be seen from the change in 1986 in the honorific address of the present rulers, from only 'king' to, also, 'The Custodian of the Two Holy Mosques' or *khādim al-ḥaramayn*.[9]

Through the assertion of the authority of the king as 'The Custodian of the Two Holy Mosques', the Saudi government has been responsible for overseeing the well-being of millions of pilgrims from all countries since the end of the Second World War. Many measures were taken to facilitate the pilgrimage, including rebuilding and expansion works in and around the Grand Mosque of Mecca and in Medina. In 1962, the Ministry of Pilgrimage and Endowments was created to take primary responsibility for the organisation of the Hajj. Yet, there is hardly a ministry in the Saudi government that is not involved in the management of the pilgrimage (Bianchi 2004). Nevertheless, it is also true that other interested groups – travel agents, politicians and other institutes – contribute to the day-to-day implementation of Hajj policy and are also involved in service planning and delivery before, during and after the pilgrimage (ibid.).

For many years, Saudi claims of exclusive sovereignty over the holy cities was met with demands for reform of the Hajj management by individual pilgrims, travel groups and governments of Muslim-majority countries. Proposals for reform included the establishment of collective management of the Hajj by all Muslim countries under the auspices of the Organization of Islamic Cooperation (OIC) (Bianchi 2017). Saudi rulers seemed to agree to this proposal, considering the challenges posed by the Islamic Revolution in Iran and the Iran pilgrimage boycott in the late 1980s (Bianchi 2004).[10] However, when Iran ended its pilgrimage boycott in 1991, the Saudis backtracked on pledges to foster an international regime for Hajj management (Amiri et al. 2011). Instead, they embarked on a rapid expansion of the pilgrimage sites and a thorough remodelling of Mecca's landscape, including demolishing most of the city's ancient quarters and working-class districts and replacing them with luxury hotels and shopping malls that were beyond the reach of ordinary pilgrims (Bianchi 2004). If the intention of the changes was to lessen the risks involved for pilgrims to the site, then the results have not been conclusive: the dangers and tragedies of the Hajj have continued, including stampedes, accidents and deaths among pilgrims.

The Expansion of the Grand Mosque and the Contraction of Equality

The conversation of the women who gathered at the henna party mentioned in this chapter's Introduction revealed several aspects of the dissatisfaction the pilgrims felt with the current management of the Hajj. The first issue is the new construction around the Grand Mosque of Mecca as part of the expansion projects that make way for further pilgrimage-related infrastructure.[11] Under the redevelopment discourse, the Saudi government justifies the expansion on the grounds that improving the conditions for pilgrims is an exemplary duty of the 'Custodian of the Two Holy Sanctuaries'. The development project is justified – according to my interlocutors – under the pretext of increasing capacity, particularly for the circumambulation of the Kaʿba during pilgrimage. Pilgrims question the benefits of, and even the need for, such projects, commenting on their grandiose nature (Al-Alawi 2006, 15).

One artefact that Moroccan pilgrims often discussed was on the clock tower, the grand mark of development directly adjacent to the Grand Mosque in the *abrāj al-bayt* (Arabic for the Towers of the House [of God]) endowment complex. The construction of *abrāj al-bayt* real estate development project meant the destruction of many old buildings surrounding the Grand Mosque. Some of these buildings are considered architectural heritage sites designed by the Abbasids and the Ottomans, and, more importantly, historical sites associated with the prophet, his family and companions (Al-Alawi 2006). For example, Ajyad Fortress, an eighteenth-century Ottoman citadel, was demolished to make room for the new buildings.[12] In addition to the pilgrims, the Turkish government had protested against the destruction of the fortress, according to *al-ḥājj* Salah, a travel agent from Casablanca. Despite objections to the project, the towers were built as part of a mega-mall complex of seven skyscraper hotels, shopping centres and restaurants.

The size, significance and view of the clock tower is a continuous topic of discussion among Moroccans who have been to Mecca. For example, in the gathering of the women at the henna party, Samira expressed her dissatisfaction with the way the clock tower 'looms over the mosque', and Salma personified the edifice, possibly transferring to the building the hostility she felt towards those who caused it to be built, complaining that the tower makes the mosque look small in its shadow and has an evil appearance. For many Moroccans, the Meccan clock tower stands as a symbol of the increasing disparity between rich and poor in Islam's holiest city. In the women's conversation, Latifa expressed a fear that the new buildings, including those in the tours, target a certain class of Muslims, prioritising material wealth and position above spiritual commitment.

I also met people, however, who could afford the expenses of the new hotels and clearly benefited from their services. One example was Rashid, the businessman from Mohammedia introduced in Chapter Four who told me that he liked the modern hotels, shopping centres and restaurants. Together with his wife, he had stayed in one of the hotels in the clock tower and went to the Grand Mosque only at the time of prayers to perform them with the rest of the pilgrims. Most Moroccan pilgrims, however, shared the less favourable view expressed by the women at the henna party.

The rapid influx of capitalist investment in Mecca and Medina has led many Moroccans to believe that money and economic growth, rather than the well-being of pilgrims, are the ultimate reason for the expansion work undertaken by the Saudi authorities.[13] For example, in addition to the *abrāj al-bayt* project, a second – and even larger – real estate development project in Mecca is that of Jabal 'Umar, which is currently being constructed and will include around forty residential towers including two five-star and six three-star hotels (Egan 2013).

Figure 6.2 Image from Christiaan Snouck Hurgronje's *Mekka* (1888)

Figure 6.3 Recent image of Mecca showing the *abrāj al-bayt* project (2016)

Figure 6.4 Two women sitting in front of a new construction advertisement (Mecca, 9 February 2018)

During my second *'umra* trip to Mecca, I saw huge billboards advertising the apartment buildings of Jabal 'Umar, one of which showed a young man praying in front of a glass window with a direct view of the Ka'ba and the Grand Mosque of Mecca. As I took a picture of the billboard, two women in colourful dresses came and sat on the side of the street on the pavement in front of the picture. Next to them a woman and a child also sat on the street. Later, when I showed the picture to Fawziyya, a forty-three-year-old Moroccan woman who performed the Hajj in 2016, she asked: 'Will there be a place for those two women inside of that [apartment building]?'

Moroccan pilgrims attributed a profane motive to the new development projects: that Saudi Arabia is looking to diversify its economy so that it is not so dependent on oil revenue – particularly now that, with its war on Yemen, there is a need for additional sources of income.[14] The experiences of Moroccan pilgrims, also, accentuate the noticeable gaps in economic prosperity and available resources among pilgrims (Sijapati

2020, 36). For many Moroccan pilgrims, the new construction around Mecca stands as a symbol of the increasing disparity between rich and poor and poses questions in the minds of pilgrims about the values of equality and simplicity within the pilgrimage and its rites. 'The high-rise complexes and luxury hotels have changed the experience of Hajj for rich pilgrims, while poorer pilgrims find it increasingly difficult to afford lodgings', *al-ḥājj* Salah told me during a visit to his office at the travel agency.[15] He continued:

> In olden times, people would travel on camels for months and ran a risk of death during the Hajj journey . . . Yet, there were fewer restrictions on the Hajj . . . It felt more spiritual in the past . . . Now there is an obsession with the best tower, the tallest building, the fanciest hotel . . . They turned Mecca into a show of modernity . . .

Al-ḥājj Salah and other pilgrims told me stories about times during the Hajj when they had witnessed discrimination. During my *'umra* trip in 2018, I visited one of the luxury hotels in the clock tower to explore the view from its restaurant directly onto the Grand Mosque of Mecca. At the hotel, I was offered complimentary coffee, dates and cardamom-flavoured Zamzam water. It was ironic that Zamzam water, the most sacred water of all, available

Figure 6.5 Worker at a hotel in Mecca offering guests cardamom-flavoured Zamzam water (Mecca, 10 February 2018)

to all pilgrims, was infused with flavour for rich pilgrims and served in gold-plated bowls.

The essence of Hajj, for many Moroccan pilgrims, lies in creating equality between all people. This equality is symbolised by the act of *iḥrām* when all pilgrims dress modestly and perform the same rites. Current trends, however, are 'making equality a distant dream', as I was told by Samira when she commented on the current management of the Hajj.

Destruction of Graves and Historical Sites

In my conversations with Moroccan pilgrims, they talked about the many highly significant sites which had to be destroyed to make space for the new developments in and around Mecca and Medina. The destruction of such sites raised many questions among Moroccans: what discussion took place among religious scholars that allowed the destruction of the cemeteries and other sites to take place? Why were they destroyed? And – as many Moroccans told me – 'How would the Prophet see the current changes that the Saudis have made to his cities, Mecca and Medina?' The following passage is from a conversation I had with Yasir, the fabric shop owner from Fes whom I introduced in Chapter Two:

> When I was in Mecca, I wanted to see the places where the prophet once lived and to remember what he did . . . My father told me many stories about visiting places like saqift Banī Saʿida,[16] the place of the battle of the Trench,[17] the house of Khadija,[18] and many others. These places were significant in the history of Islam . . . All those places are now gone!

It is estimated that the construction projects have resulted in 95 per cent of the original historic buildings in Mecca being torn down (Johnson 2014; Nasrawi 2007).[19] Historical buildings that have been demolished over the last two decades include the house of the prophet Muhammad's first wife, Khadija, the historical mosque marking the Battle of the Trench, and a mosque that was linked to the prophet's grandson (Taylor 2011). At issue is whether these constructions and changes have meant that the Hajj experience has lost its true spiritual meaning for some pilgrims, and whether the destruction has reduced the heritage of the prophet Muhammad.

Pilgrims' accounts reflect concerns about the transformation of both Mecca and Medina (Al-Alawi 2006). *Al-ḥājj* Salah put it as follows:

> The house of Khadija, the wife of the prophet, was transformed into a public toilet facility . . . The house of the Companion of the prophet Abu Bakr – which I visited in the past – was replaced with a hotel . . . The sites of the main battles in Islamic history, Uḥud and Badr, which were led by prophet Muhammad, have been paved for a parking lot for cars and buses . . .

Moroccans demonstrated disagreement with what they sometimes identified as a Wahhabi, and on other occasions labelled as a Salafi, view regarding the act of visiting graves (Abou El Fadl 2001).[20] Contrary to the Saudi regulations, visiting graves of religious figures and saints is a popular practice in Morocco (Eickelman 1976). Being Sunni Muslims and highly influenced by Sufi doctrines, Moroccans honour the prophet and express love for him and his household. For example, the *mawlid* or birthday of the prophet is an occasion for celebration throughout Morocco.[21] In Morocco, profound respect is paid to figures related to the prophet Muhammad, such as Moulay Idriss I, who is believed to be the great-grandson of the prophet.[22] Other Moroccans related by a bloodline to the prophet, known in Morocco as the *Shurfa*, are also highly respected, along with the monarch, who claims descent from the prophet as shown in Chapter Five (Ouguir 2013; Rhani 2014). When I visited the shrine of Moulay Idriss I in Zerhoun with Nuha, she said:

> Look how people here visit the shrine of Moulay Idriss . . . Imagine how much more important are the places where the prophet himself – *'alayhi l-salām* – lived . . .[23] Oh how much I would have liked it to visit his house and the houses of his companions . . .

The places Moroccans like to visit in Mecca and Medina acquire spiritual status not only because of their connection to the prophet but also because they are seen as 'signs of God', according to *al-ḥājj* Salah.[24] The signs – so *al-ḥājj* Salah told me – may be places, events, personalities, catastrophes and many other things, but one thing which the holy Qur'an makes clear is that the signs, *āyāt*, are meant to remind people of God, his bounties, his mercy and his other attributes. Therefore, places, symbols and historical personalities, which serve as reminders and symbols for humanity and strengthen submission to God, are to be respected, preserved – even cherished – and revered within the context of the faith.

In a conversation with *al-ḥājj* Salah, he mentioned several other controversial issues in relation to Saudi Arabia's management of the Hajj. He referred to the Wahhabi antipathy to Sufi practices such as veneration of saints and visitation of tombs. He also questioned why the Hajj visa application asks for one's religion and sect. As for religion, it is known that Hajj visas would only be issued to Muslims. When it came to sect, *al-ḥājj* Salah thought this would be a way of monitoring Sunni and Shiʿi pilgrims. He was not happy about the boycott by Iran of the Hajj season in 2016, although he agreed with the Iranian position on the events of 2015, which will be mentioned later. Commenting on the absence of Iranians in the Hajj of 2016, one of my interlocutors quoted a female guard in Mecca who claimed that the Hajj season of the year went smoothly due to the absence of Iranians.

For Moroccan pilgrims, *ziyāra* (visits) to the places where the prophet had lived is a significant part of their experience. These places include the graveyard and cemeteries where the Companions of the prophet are buried, such as Baqīʿal-Gharqad, known as Jannat al-Baqīʿ or simply al-Baqīʿ (Munt 2014, 126). This is the cemetery where many of the most respected early figures of Islam are buried, including the third caliph, Uthman ibn Affan, the imam of Medina Malik ibn Anas (hence the Maliki schools of law followed in Morocco) and the prophet's infant son Ibrahim and grandson Hasan (Beránek and Ťupek 2018, 70–122). Historical records show that there were domes, cupolas and mausoleums in Jannat al-Baqīʿ before the twentieth century; today it is a bare land without any buildings.[25] Only men are allowed to visit the graveyard, as women are not allowed to visit graveyards in Saudi Arabia (see Chapter Eight).

Another significant cemetery which pilgrims often visit is that near Mount Uḥud. Many pilgrims visit the mountain and the cemetery as part of their *ziyāra* near Medina. According to *al-ḥājj* Salah:

> In 2013, the Saudi authorities used concrete to fill the crevice in Mount Uḥud where the prophet Muhammad went after the battle of Uḥud and put up a sign to warn visitors that this was a mountain like any other . . .

Figure 6.6 Picture of the Paradise Garden of al-Baqīʿ in 1907/8 by Muhammad ʿAli Effendi Saʿudi (Kioumgi and Graham 2009, 102–3)

Figure 6.7 Signs indicating behaviour guidelines near Uḥud cemetery (Medina, 1 February 2018)

There are signs placed near the graveyard of the Battle of Uḥud with instructions in different languages prohibiting journeying with the intention of visiting graves, supplicating the dead, wiping the walls, or picking stones from the graves. Climbing Mount Uḥud and picking stones or collecting sand from it for the purposes of seeking blessings are all prohibited.

A paradoxical yet interesting sight near Mount Uḥud, however, was that of an iconic, open-top double-decker tour bus, just like any hop-on-hop-off

Figure 6.8 Hop-on-hop-off bus stops (Medina, 1 February 2018)

bus that can be found in any of the world's tourist attractions. Mount Uḥud is stop number 5 in the hotspots of Medina, which also included al-Baqīʿ, the Mosque of the prophet and other attractions. The bus also makes stops at several shopping malls. Moroccan pilgrims often visit the mountains around Mecca and Medina and the places they can reach, even if advised not to go to those places. At the same time, some pilgrims commented on the ironic mingling of aspects of the sacred (pilgrimage) with other, conflicting purposes (such as commercial pursuits).

Martyn Egan (2013) calls the paradoxical elements of the Saudi society 'halal ignorance', applying Olivier Roy's paradigm of 'holy ignorance' (Roy 2010). According to Roy, holy ignorance removes the possibility of the profane (that is, a social and cultural domain independent of the religious) and rejects the possibility of the secular (Roy 2010, 28–9). In the Saudi context, according to Egan, this project of discoloration has resulted in a society in which practices and objects are classified exclusively according to the religious markers of halal and *ḥarām* and are thus reconstituted within a universe of religious practice, *ʿibādāt*. In that sense, a visit to a graveyard is *ḥarām* but the redevelopment of Mecca and destruction of historical sites is halal. To put it differently, halal ignorance can be applied to the selective use of religious reasoning to permit, or prohibit, actions – but always with a 'religious' justification.

Morocco itself is home to hundreds of sacred sites and pilgrimage places such as tombs, caves, cult locations and even trees that are scattered throughout its deserts, coastlines and mountains. Some of these sites are part of the indigenous Amazigh culture and others are related to Jewish and Christian as well as Islamic heritages (Amster 2013). Many such sites continue to be popular places for Moroccans to visit. Both men and women also visit local tombs and graveyards. For example, on the Day of ʿĀshūrāʾ, the custom goes that women and men go to cemeteries to visit their deceased relatives.[26] According to *al-ḥājj* Salah:

> It seems too easy for the Saudis to call anything *bidʿa* [illicit innovation] or even *ḥarām* . . . But in Morocco people visit graves; both men and women do . . . The prophet himself visited the graves of the martyrs and people wish to follow the example of the prophet . . .

The Moroccan pilgrims I spoke to expressed deep interest in following the example of the prophet in their *ziyāra* practices in Mecca and Medina (Munt 2014, 123–47).[27] Some of them explicitly compared the regulations they found when visiting Saudi Arabia for Hajj or *ʿumra* to the religious style in Morocco, stating that they find that in Morocco there is a middle path to Islam that is essentially different from that adopted in Saudi Arabia. They object to the religious reasons that are used to justify the destruction of graves and shrines and to restrict access to sites linked to historically significant religious figures.[28] Therefore, it is fair to say that Moroccan pilgrims are dissatisfied with the Saudi religious interpretation and consequent regulation of *ziyāra*.

While many of the Moroccans with whom I talked expressed their dissatisfaction with the destruction of graves and other historical sites and voiced their dissatisfaction with the policing of their experience in Mecca and Medina, the main fear of many Moroccans during the pilgrimage revolved around the kind of accidents that have occurred in Mecca, especially at the times of the pilgrimage. In the next section, I discuss the stampede that took place during my fieldwork in Morocco in 2015.

Preserving the Safety of Pilgrims between Stampedes and Disasters

The following anecdote describes the time when news of the Minā stampede which took place in September 2015 was received. It was the first day of *ʿīd l-kbīr*, which I spent with *al-ḥājj* Salim and his family in Fes. Salim, his wife and his two daughters sat watching Moroccan national TV as it showed live footage of the prayer of *ʿīd*, performed by Moroccans and accompanied by the king of Morocco, in one of the mosques in Rabat. A few minutes later, breaking news sketchily reported an accident near Mecca, the victims unknown. Around half an hour later it was reported that the accident was a stampede, and hundreds of victims were predicted. Immediately, *al-ḥājj* Salim made phone calls enquiring about a friend who was performing Hajj. When the friend did not answer, *al-ḥājj* Salim called the friend's son, who confirmed that his father was safe. *Al-ḥājj* Salim spent the afternoon enquiring about other people he knew in Mecca.

Al-ḥājj Salim followed the reports on the numbers of victims on Saudi and Moroccan TV channels, as well as online, as the number of victims continued to rise, first to 105, then to 364, and later to 717 by the afternoon. By the evening, five Moroccans were reported among the dead, including the imam of Morocco's Hassan II Mosque in Casablanca. Eight Moroccans were reported injured, and dozens were reported missing (fifteen male and nineteen female pilgrims according to *al-ḥājj* Salim).

No details were released about an investigation into the cause of the tragedy. Moroccans whom I met in the days following the tragedy would say, 'The poor people went to perform Hajj and lost their lives.' Others said, 'Lucky them! They died after the Day of Arafat, which means their Hajj is complete', 'They died totally cleansed from sins', or 'It's the mistake of bad management and arrogant government' and 'May God take revenge [on the Saudi authorities!]'. For many weeks after the tragedy, Moroccans everywhere I went talked about the stampede and discussed in detail how it had happened, the possible reasons, and the number of pilgrims who had died. The final reports stated that the number of victims reached more than 2,400 (Gladstone, 10 December 2015).[29] The figures included 41 Moroccans among the dead.[30]

The stampede in Minā was the second incident to happen in the Hajj season of 2015. A few months earlier, a crane had collapsed, leaving more than 100 dead and over 200 injured.[31] When the Minā stampede took place, many Moroccans referred to the earlier accident, suggesting that the Saudi authorities had been negligent for having a series of cranes overlooking the Grand Mosque in the first place.

These accidents were not the first in the modern history of the Hajj (Table 6.1). In 1990, for example, a crush in a tunnel in Minā killed 1,426 pilgrims. Further crushes occurred in 1994, 1998, 2001 and 2004 (Bianchi 2004, 11). In addition, over 400 people died in 1987 when Saudi security forces attacked Iranian pilgrims in Mecca, who were protesting peacefully against the USA and Israel (Kramer 1990, 190; Samman 2007, 140).[32]

Table 6.1 Previous accidents during Hajj

Year	Deaths	Explanation
2006	76	Collapse of hotel in Mecca
2006	364	Minā stampede
2004	250	Minā stampede
2003	14	Minā stampede
2001	35	Minā stampede
1998	118	Minā stampede
1997	343	Fire in the tents near Minā
1994	270	Minā stampede
1990	1,426	Minā stampede
1975	200	Fire in the tents near Minā

These accidents were a major topic of discussion, for a range of reasons. First, there is the subject of dying in Mecca. Many people spoke of the virtue of dying and being buried in Mecca. One taxi driver in Casablanca kept saying '*saʿdathum*!', an expression of admiration or even envy towards those who had died in Mecca. Nonetheless, other Moroccans voiced dissatisfaction with the Hajj mismanagement that might have been a factor in the stampede and previous accidents in Mecca. During the first week of October following the stampede Moroccan activists called on social media for a lawsuit to be filed against Saudi Arabia. Moroccan pilgrims and activists organised a sit-in outside the Moroccan parliament located on Avenue Mohammed V in Rabat to denounce what they called the mismanagement and lawlessness that had marked the 2015 Hajj.

The protest started peacefully, but the situation soon turned grim. A video shared on Facebook showed three police officers aggressively seizing a banner held by one of the protesters. In the footage, riot police were violently pushing protesters, forcing them to abandon their sit-in. One female protester shouted, as she was being forced to leave the square, 'This is shame . . . This is shame . . . Our country fears the petrodollar.' Officially, the Moroccan government did not openly criticise the Saudi authorities for the way they handled the aftermath of the crush. News reports, however, stated that King Mohammed VI had instructed a delegation composed of representatives of the Ministries of the Interior, Foreign Affairs, Health and Religious Endowments and Islamic Affairs to visit the hospitals and the morgue in Mecca and to follow up with identification of the Moroccan victims and where they came from. It proved impossible to find updates regarding the lawsuit against Saudi Arabia. Eventually, those who died were buried in Mecca and the injured were later returned to Morocco.

In response to the Minā stampede and other accidents that took place during the Hajj season, many Moroccans called for measures against Saudi Arabia. Indeed, measures were taken by the Iranian government which, due to the stampede of 2015, decided to boycott the 2016 Hajj season. In news reports, Iran announced that its citizens would not travel to Mecca, accusing Saudi Arabia of failing to guarantee their safety (Al-Tumi, 17 May 2016).[33] Moroccan newspapers reported the Iranian boycott, but opinion was divided between those who supported the move and others who agreed with the response of the Moroccan government, which supported the Saudi claim against what they called 'the politicization of the pilgrimage' (Binhda, 8 August 2016).[34] Many Moroccans, however, said that it was already 'political', as Saudi Arabia discriminated against the pilgrims of Iran.[35]

Dissatisfaction with the Saudi government does not come only from outside the Kingdom. Internally, there are voices that disagree with the management of the Hajj. For example, in 1994, the Committee for the Defence of Legitimate Rights (CDLR), a Saudi dissident group, opposed the Saudi government as un-Islamic and produced a report on the regime's management of the Hajj (Champion 2003, 212).[36] The report referred to the Saudi lack of professionalism, favouritism and interference in the management of the Hajj. Thus, catastrophic accidents such as stampedes are a catalyst for a broader discussion of the Saudi management of the holy sites, both outside the Kingdom and even within it.

For millions of people, Moroccans included, Mecca represents a place where pilgrims, regardless of their nationality, gather, emphasising the universal and inclusive nature of Islam. Consequently, most Moroccans I spoke to attempted to untangle the religious aspect of pilgrimage, separating it from those aspects superimposed by the Saudi government; for them, these Saudi additions and controls are not representative of Islam. According to *al-ḥājj* Salah:

> We are obliged to love God and His Prophet . . . We love the holy sites of Mecca and Medina . . . But we are not obliged to like the house of Saud! They do not represent Islam and the holy places do not belong to them; these places belong to all Muslims . . .

Al-ḥājj Salah and other Moroccan pilgrims nonetheless expressed an unwavering sense of loss related to a better past, mourning for their previous spiritual experiences of the holy sites. Their grief is articulated through a comparison of those remembered past pilgrimages with current experiences of the holy places.

Longing for the Past and Looking at the Future

The following conversation took place at the women's gathering mentioned earlier, where Samira complained that she could not visit the tomb of the Prophet in his mosque in Medina:

> **Samira:** I could not see the tomb of the Prophet either . . . I don't like the way Hajj is managed by the Saudis.
> **Latifa:** I remember in the past when I went on Hajj, rituals were easier even though facilities were not available . . . We were able to visit different sites where the Prophet and his Companions lived . . .
> **Samira:** Now everything is prohibited, *ḥarām*, they say! They try to control the way women dress, the places we visit, and prohibit us from visiting the grave of the Prophet . . . I wish I witnessed how these places were in the past!
> **Nuha:** It is not only the issue of halal or *ḥarām*; what do Saudis do with the money of the pilgrim? The war on Yemen?
> **Samira:** If the Saudis really followed the Qur'an and the teachings of the Prophet, they would not destroy the holy places and they would use the money of pilgrims more wisely.

An appeal to the 'glorious past' of the pilgrimage is a prominent feature of discussions about pilgrimage, especially among the older generation.

Figure 6.9 Flyers distributed in the Grand Mosque of Mecca about women's dress code (Mecca, 7 February 2018)

These nostalgic discourses are heavily mediated and contextualised by the dissatisfaction with the current management of the Hajj. Latifa, for example, spoke to the women about her longing for the simplicity of the Hajj in the past, as compared to the complications of the Hajj process today. When she performed the Hajj in the 1970s, she had not needed to register for the lottery *qur'a* process which Moroccans have to follow today if they wish to apply for Hajj.

In their discussion, the women emphasised the belief that the Saudi authorities that manage the Hajj and *ʿumra* have deviated from the right path. They spoke about the control practised by the Saudi authorities, particularly in relation to women. For example, at the Grand Mosque of Mecca female pilgrims were handed leaflets by female guards directing them about the proper dress code for Muslim women. Furthermore, the women were unable to visit the grave of the Prophet at the Rawḍa in Medina (see Chapter Three). The experiences that several Moroccan women had had in Mecca and Medina had left them disappointed. Following the 1979 siege of the Grand Mosque of Mecca, the Saudi government enacted a series of much more conservative ideas, especially regarding women (Doumato 2009, 24; Trofimov 2007).[37] What women experience during the Hajj, therefore, can be seen within a larger framework of 'segregation policy' directed at females (van Geel 2018, 77; Meijer 2010).

The recollected past, as portrayed by many pilgrims, is accurately represented; however, memory can be distorted by dissatisfaction with current reality, and a rosy glow imposed on a flawed history. The pilgrimage has always contained a mixture of religious and profane aspects. For example, there has always been a commercial component in the pilgrimage as a venue for trading: pilgrims travelling in caravans often traded along the way to finance their journey (Pearson 1994). Yet for contemporary Moroccan pilgrims, Saudi regulations and the destruction of holy sites are discussed in terms of the speed of change and the massive gap between the privileged and the rest that this change creates.

In addition to their nostalgia, Moroccans express fear for the future. Today, my interlocutors are debating ways of action and alternatives to the current situation in Mecca. Solutions were often discussed among Moroccans, including further internationalising the current Hajj regime and even boycotting the Hajj and *ʿumra* until the Saudi government respects the needs and demands of the full range of Muslim pilgrims. The call for a boycott had a financial aspect for many Moroccans. Many of them questioned the destination and use of the millions of dirhams they pay for Hajj and *ʿumra*. Most of the money, many Moroccans feared, does not go to the holy places but is spent on 'holidays in Western countries', according to Nuha, or 'financing the war of Yemen', something that was mentioned by several Moroccans.

It made more sense, for my interlocutors, to spend the financial benefits of the Hajj on poorer Muslim nations rather than on expansion projects, five-star hotels, and disputes with fellow Muslim countries. Thus, we see a sense of material and political dissatisfaction with Saudi Arabia which emerges through the religious experience of Hajj.

Conclusion

During my fieldwork in Morocco, Moroccan pilgrims often reflected on their pilgrimage experience in relation to some paradoxical elements of the Saudi handling of the Hajj. In the eyes of many Moroccans, much of the history of Islam in Mecca and Medina has been undermined by the Saudi mismanagement of the holy sites. At the same time, however, the pilgrimage to Mecca remains an important aspect of the lives of many Moroccans, and so do the religious sites in Mecca and Medina.

The socio-economic profile of the people I encountered during my fieldwork may have had an impact on their responses to the pilgrimage experiences, even though they spoke of the pilgrimage in spiritual religious terms. They were middle- or lower-middle-class and most of them had some education. Finances are a constraint for many of these people. Their religious beliefs and their reading of the Qur'an emphasise the universal nature of the religion – a religion for all people, equal before God. The inordinate wealth of the Saudi Kingdom as a geopolitical entity shapes the material experience of the Hajj, sharpening the economic burden of being a pilgrim. Many of my interlocutors experienced a sense of alienation, ironically in relation to the most holy sites of their religion, the cradle of Islam. These are the very sites where they expect to find the greatest peace, the greatest reassurance and spiritual consolation. Their feelings of displacement in relation to their spiritual home are felt by many to be a direct result of the Saudi modernisation project, in particular the vast array of new buildings and the erasure of ancient ones.

For Moroccan pilgrims, Wahhabi interpretations of Islam dominate the pilgrimage sites and exclude the possibility of diverse readings of the Qur'an. Divergent traditions regarding the veneration of graves placed Moroccan pilgrims at odds with the dominant Saudi reading of the Islamic tradition. As a result, many pilgrims have developed a deep sense of nostalgia for the way pilgrimages were conducted in the past. These feelings of loss are common and are discussed freely, thus increasing the likelihood of the emergence of a socially constructed collective memory.

Within the Hajj experience of Moroccans, the political strands were so tightly woven into the religious experience as to be inseparable, as was frequently illustrated in the comments quoted earlier. My interlocutors spoke about their faith as having a strongly social dimension – voiced through the sense of equality and inclusivity – which is at variance with the geopolitics of the Saudi Arabian regime.

The inequality issue is ever more present as a social factor as many pilgrims are excluded from activities of all kinds for financial reasons, and at other times because of their gender. This underscores the need for further examination of specific Hajj experiences, particularly those of Moroccan women, as explored in the next chapter.

Notes

1. Qadī ʿAyyāḍ was a judge and scholar of Maliki law. He is also known as one of the seven saints of Marrakech. He authored *Al-shifāʾ*, a famous handbook in which the prophet Muhammad's life, his qualities and his miracles are described in detail. The quoted passage is from a longer poem in the book.
2. A henna party refers to a ceremony held one day before a wedding, normally at the home of the bride. During the party, artists use a paste made from dried henna leaves (a reddish-brown dye) to paint intricate patterns (temporary tattoos) on the hands and sometimes also the feet of the bride. The bride's friends and relatives who are involved in the marriage can also receive henna tattoos. Henna is considered a sign of fertility and beauty (Kelly Spurles 2004).
3. For most Moroccan families this is the main meal of the day.
4. Fieldnotes, 8 October 2016.
5. For more information on Saudi politics, see e.g. Vogel (2000), Nevo (1998), Nehme (1994), Kechichian (1986), Al-Yasini (1985), Bligh (1985).
6. In 1901 King Abd al-Aziz ibn Abd al-Rahman al-Faisal al-Saud (Ibn Saud) conquered the city of Riyadh. Between 1909 and 1926, he extended his authority over most of Arabia. The Kingdom of Saudi Arabia officially acquired its present name in September 1932. In 1953, King Abd al-Aziz passed away and his son took over the leadership (Safran 1988, 73). For more on the history of Saudi Arabia, see Safran and Hobday (1979).

7. Ibn Saud chose to enter Mecca dressed as a pilgrim in 1924 to perform *ʿumra*, but on 8 January 1926 he was installed as king of the Hijaz (McLoughlin 1993).
8. A full analysis of the development of the Wahhabi doctrine and political discourse from its eighteenth-century origins up to its current incarnation(s) is beyond the scope of this book. For more information on this topic, see Al Rasheed (2007, 22–58) and Niblock (2006, 23–7), among others.
9. The first king of Saudi Arabia to assume the title was Faisal bin Abdul Aziz (1906–75). His successor, Khalid, did not use the title, but the latter's successor, Fahd, did, replacing the term 'His Majesty' with it. King Salman bin Abdulaziz Al Saud took the same title after the death of King Abdullah, his half-brother, on 23 January 2015.
10. Iran boycotted the Hajj for three years, from 1988 to 1990, following the severing of diplomatic relations after the 1987 Mecca incident when a demonstration by Iranian pilgrims resulted in a stampede after Saudi security officers opened fire on protesters (Benjamin 2018).
11. Expansion of the mosque began in 2011 with an estimated expenditure of 13 billion dollars. The plans for expansion include widening the area of the mosque by 400,000 square metres to allow for an extra 1.2 million worshippers (Ferrari and Benzo 2014, 323).
12. Information provided by Moroccan interlocutors.
13. For examples of media coverage concerning the destruction of monuments in Mecca and Medina, see Egan (2013) and Peer (2012, 74).
14. Saudi efforts to diversify the economy beyond oil revenues can also be seen within the global quest for alternatives to fossil fuel, yet this topic did not come up in the discussions I witnessed among Moroccans.
15. One can question whether Hajj was ever actually within the reach of ordinary people, given the hardships the journey would have entailed. In the past, for example, pilgrims had to travel a long time to reach Mecca, and even today the ability to perform the Hajj means mobilising significant financial resources. See also the 'Pilgrimage of the Poor' in Chapter Eight.
16. *Saqifat* Banī Sāʿida was a roofed building in Medina used by the Banū Saʿida clan and was significant as the site where, after the prophet Muhammad's death, some of his Companions gathered and pledged allegiance to Abu Bakr, electing him as the first Caliph (Lecomte 2012).
17. The Battle of the Trench (or *Ghazwat al-Khandaq*) was the site of a thirty-day-long siege of Medina by the Meccans, who lost the battle.

18. Khadija (or Khadija bint Khuwaylid) was the first wife and first female follower of the prophet Muhammad. She was a successful businesswoman in her own right and was referred to by Muslims as 'Mother of the Believers'. Khadija and her daughter Fatima are two of the most important female figures in Islam (Ali 2014).
19. The destruction of the sites around Mecca is not limited to modern times. Several battles took place around Mecca throughout history, including the destruction of the shrine built over the tomb of Fatima, daughter of the prophet Muhammad, and the tombs of many of his Companions in the nineteenth century (Al-Alawi 2006).
20. The term 'Salafi' can be confusing because it is defined in several ways. In general terms, Salafis are those who claim to follow the example of the early Muslim community (*salaf*) (Beranek and Tupek 2009, 2). When my Moroccan interlocutors referred to the Salafi thought of the Saudi government, they linked it with rejection of many religious and traditional actions such as the visitation of graves and saints' shrines. For more on Salafi views on *ziyāra* see Beranek and Tupek (2009). Wahhabi theology, the foundations of which were put in place in the eighteenth century by Muhammad ibn 'Abd al-Wahhab, use a strict literalism in the interpretation of religious texts and exhibits extreme hostility to mysticism and any sectarian divisions within Islam (Abou El Fadl 2001).
21. *Mawlid* often refers to observance of the birthday of the prophet Muhammad, which is commemorated in the third month of the Islamic calendar. It can also refer to annual saints' festivals in several Muslim countries during which saints are celebrated (Schielke 2006). See also Chapter Nine.
22. The shrine of Idriss I in Zerhoun, together with the tomb of Moulay Idriss II in Fes, are seen as primary local pilgrimage sites in Morocco (Wyrtzen 2015, 38–61).
23. *'Alayhi l-salām* (peace be upon him) is a conventionally complimentary phrase attached to the names of prophets in Islam and is often used following the mention of the prophet Muhammad as a short variant of the phrase *ṣallā-Allāhu 'alayhī wa-sallam* (God bless him and grant him peace); alternatively, there is the acronym PBUH.
24. The reference to the signs of God can be traced to the Qur'anic verse 'There truly are signs in the creation of the heavens and earth, and in the alternation of night and day, for those with understanding, who remember God standing, sitting, and lying down, who reflect on the creation of the heavens and earth: "Our Lord! You have not created all this without purpose – You are far above that! – so protect us from the torment of the Fire"' (Qur'an 3, 190–1).

25. The splendour of the al-Baqīʿ cemetery in medieval times was documented, for example, by the accounts of Ibn Jubayr and Ibn Battuta, who described the cemetery with its elevated domes and shrines. Al-Baqīʿ was demolished in 1806 and, following reconstruction in the mid-nineteenth century, was destroyed again in 1925 (Bayram 2014; Ende 2010).
26. 'Āshūrā' is the tenth day of Muharram, the first month in the Islamic calendar. The day was originally marked, according to hadith, when the prophet came to Medina and found the Jews observing the fast on the day of 'Āshūrā'. Asked about it, they said that it was the day on which God had granted victory to Moses (and his people) over the Pharaoh, and that they, the Jews, observed the fast out of gratitude to God. Upon hearing this, the Prophet commanded his followers to also observe a fast on this day (Muslim, book 6, hadith 2514–20). The day continues to be a recommended but non-obligatory day of fasting for Sunni Muslims and an occasion for celebration. For Shi'a Muslims it is a time of mourning, as the same date happens to be the date of the Battle of Karbala (680 CE), when Husayn, the grandson of Muhammad and the son of Ali (cousin and son-in-law of the Prophet and the First Shiʿa imam), was killed (Black et al. 2018).
27. The practice of *ziyāra* or visitation of graves itself has a varied history in Islamic tradition, beginning with traditions attributed to the prophet Muhammad, who denied himself a visit to graves but later allowed it (Beranek and Tupek 2009).
28. Members of the Permanent Committee for Scholarly Research and Iftā', a religious Saudi government body, have issued many fatwas relating to the presence of graves or shrines in, or under, mosques. I read some of these fatwas in a booklet which one of my interlocutors received in Mecca. The fatwa in the booklet claimed that destroying the sites and removing the graves, as well as restricting access to sites linked to religious figures, will prevent idolatry, and help Muslims to concentrate on their faith.
29. For the full report see https://www.nytimes.com/2015/12/11/world/middleeast/death-toll-from-hajj-stampede.html (last accessed 17 May 2019).
30. Information provided by a local official via personal connection.
31. See https://www.bbc.com/news/world-middle-east-34226003 (last accessed 12 September 2018).
32. In July 1987, the Civil Defence forces and Saudi police opened fire against Iranian demonstrators after arguments had escalated to fights between the two parties. It has been reported that 402 people were killed during the incident and 649 were wounded. This led to political tension between Iran and Saudi Arabia and Iranian

pilgrims were kept from entering Saudi Arabia for the Hajj seasons 1988 and 1989 (Kramer 1990).

33. See https://www.hespress.com/international/306464.html (last accessed 23 October 2019).
34. See (in Arabic) https://www.hespress.com/orbites/320337.html (last accessed 12 October 2019).
35. For more information on Saudi–Iranian relations see Ekhtiari, Samsu and Gholipour (2011).
36. The Committee for the Defense of Legitimate Rights was found in 1993 as the first opposition organisation in the Kingdom openly challenging the monarchy (Hearn 1998).
37. The 1979 siege of the Grand Mosque of Mecca was led by Juhayman ibn Muhammad al-Otaibi during the season of Hajj, in protest against what he and his followers described as the 'religious and moral laxity and degeneration' of Saudi rulers (Al-Rasheed 2002, 144). The dissenters claimed that the Saud family had abandoned Islamic principles, followed the lead of Western countries, and needed to be overthrown for true Islamic reform. The rebellion aimed to bring Arabia back to (Wahhabi) Islam. After the rebellion was violently crushed, the Saud family responded by making religion central to the state so as to quell any further dissent (Trofimov 2007). As a political protest couched in religious terms, the siege prompted the government to enforce a much more conservative agenda (Doumato 2009, 24; Trofimov 2007).

7

INTERSECTING POWER STRUCTURES IN MOROCCAN WOMEN'S NARRATIVES OF THE HAJJ

A happy woman was one who could exercise all kinds of rights, from the right to move to the right to create, compete, and challenge, and at the same time could be loved for doing so.

(Fatima Mernissi)[1]

Introduction

I joined Najat in visiting her parents in their house in Temara, a small coastal city to the south of Rabat, where we would spend the weekend. In a small living room, Najat, her father and I sat on two mattresses facing a flat-screen TV and talking about the father's job as a mosque imam. Soon, Najat's mother entered the room carrying a brown clay dish. Najat brought to the middle a small round table, on which the mother placed the dish and said: 'Here is your share of the seven vegetables *siksū*.'[2] The couscous dish in front of us was composed of semolina grains and granules of durum wheat, topped with cabbage, potato, turnip, carrots, courgette, pumpkin and chick-peas, along with two pieces of meat. Najat commented that her mother prepares couscous lunch every Friday, a tradition that is kept by many families in Morocco.

Whilst enjoying the home-made food, Najat's mother left the room, to return shortly with a pot of mint tea and some glasses. She sat next to us and made space for her mother-in-law, who joined us shortly afterwards.

Najat introduced me to her grandmother – Ḥanna,[3] as she referred to the older woman. Ḥanna was 82 years old when I met her and had lived with her son and his family since the death of her husband three years earlier.

Ḥanna went on Hajj seven years earlier, together with her son, who went as a religious guide with the pilgrims of his area. She remembered her pilgrimage especially in relation to the stories she had heard when she was younger and living in the village. She told me that when she was little, she knew only three people from the whole village who were lucky enough to travel to Mecca, all men, one of whom was the *faqīh* of the mosque, the one who taught the Qur'an to the children of the village.[4]

As we were speaking, Ḥanna started to sing:

The *ḥājja* is leaving with the pilgrims;
She is wearing her Mellali *ḥāyik*;[5]
How lucky you are, *al-ḥājja*!
Going to Hajj while young, *shābba*;
She tells you: 'Look after the girls!'
She tells you: 'Look after the lands!'
I am praying to God, my Master . . .
The ship is leaving;
Each has an intention;
My grave and night are coming . . .[6]

The lyrics of Ḥanna's song refer to various aspects of the Hajj, including its history, its social and symbolic significance and the gendered aspects of the journey. The song starts with a declaration that a female pilgrim, *ḥājja*, is leaving with other pilgrims for Mecca. In the past, Moroccan women leaving for Hajj used to wear a *ḥāyik*, a white cloak that covered their entire body, their head and part of their face. In the song, being able to go on Hajj is a subject of envy. This is linked to the fact that it was rare for women to perform the pilgrimage in Morocco relative to men. Therefore, women were indeed envious of female pilgrims who were able to make the journey to Mecca. It was a social expectation that one would express a desire to go on Hajj, pronouncing longing for it and a wish to join those leaving for Mecca. The song then addresses other aspects of Hajj in Morocco, such as the importance of saying farewell to those who stay behind, begging family members and friends for forgiveness and asking them to look after the girls and lands.[7] This farewell is linked to the next lines of the song, which function as a reminder of death and the grave. Mentioning death has a religious significance as a prompt for Muslims who can perform the Hajj to do so.

For Ḥanna, who had learned it from her mother, this song has been transmitted orally from generation to generation for a long time. It is uncertain how old the song is, but it alludes to the means of transport current at the time when Ḥanna learned the lyrics: ships.[8] Ḥanna's song represents a creative account of various social, religious and emotional dimensions of the Hajj. Taking it as a starting point, in this chapter I explore the meanings of Hajj for Moroccan women on both a personal and a social level. Many authors have discussed the significance of the Hajj for specific groups within the Muslim community, including converts, women, and individuals with lower social and economic status, discussing how their pilgrimage serves as a powerful counterbalance to the assumptions, and the social norms and prejudices, that they might face within their societies (Baderoon 2012, 240; Buitelaar, van Leeuwen 2023; Buitelaar, Stephan-Emmrich and Thimm 2020; Cooper 1999). The Hajj could also be seen as a mark of success on the social, spiritual and financial levels. Through Hajj, Moroccan women negotiate different forms of capital, including social, cultural and religious capital, which are also informed by their *habitus* and everyday practices (Bourdieu 1986).[9]

Examining the socio-cultural implications of women's growing access to various forms of capital related to Hajj, I use Pierre Bourdieu's concepts of *habitus* and capital as tools to explain and analyse women's narratives and the ways in which these stories are embedded in women's daily lives. Depending on the field in which it functions, according to Bourdieu, capital (or power) can present itself in economic, cultural or social forms (Bourdieu and Wacquant, 1992, 119).[10] Several anthropologists have argued for the existence and recognition of other forms of capital, including symbolic capital, moral capital and audible capital, among others (Cooper 1999). Moreover, I shall highlight how the mobility of Moroccan women is an aspect of their social diversity which is influenced by geographical origin, class, education, financial means and marital status. I will demonstrate that these variables have a direct impact on women's desire to go to Mecca, their ability to perform the Hajj and the experiences of those who have been on pilgrimage, examining the phases before, during and after they have concluded the pilgrimage.

Moroccan Women's Participation in Hajj

In general, not much information from past times is available on women's participation in Hajj journeys from Morocco to Mecca. As in other parts of the world, narratives of the Hajj often exhibit a conspicuous absence of women, a trend well-noted by scholars such as Tolmacheva (2013, 1998, 1993) and Fewkes (2020) among others. The exclusion of women's perspectives and narratives from many medieval Muslim writings on Hajj and travel, according to Fewkes (2020, 130), is indicative of the prevailing societal perceptions of gender within the cultural milieux where these narratives were constructed. The absence of women's experiences and their Hajj journeys within historical accounts in Morocco might be related to the idea that men were seen as the transmitters of tradition in the public sphere while women were seen to be connected to the private (Sadiqi and Ennaji 2006; Sadiqi 2003). It might also have been related to the limited access of women to education, which meant that most women had no access to writing their accounts. As a result, women passed on those accounts that have reached us through oral means, such as Ḥanna's song. In the past, both in rural and in urban areas, Moroccan women lived in a *ḥarīm* or in enclosed households where extended families lived together as one unit and women required permission from their husbands or other male family members before leaving a household (Sadiqi 2003). This was the case in Morocco at least up until the declaration of independence from the French protectorate in 1956. As Ḥanna explains, the tradition of female seclusion strongly affected who could perform the Hajj:

> The man who went to Hajj from our village was a *faqīh*. He was an educated teacher who worked at the mosque . . . Few people went to Hajj then, and as little girls Hajj felt way beyond our reach.

Further, although the requirement of pilgrimage to Mecca is an obligatory ritual for Muslim women and men alike, women may be excused from the obligation for reasons such as a lack of an appropriate male companion for the journey (Tolmacheva 2013; Hendrickson 2016).[11] Therefore, the pilgrimage, and other public activities like education and mosque attendance, were associated with men (Mazumdar and Mazumdar 1999; 2002; Kandiyoti 1991). Paradoxically, women did constitute many of the practitioners of everyday religion. They were highly active in the local pilgrimages, such as in visiting local saint shrines (Davis 1983; Smith 1980).

For women, right up to the present time, the performance of the Hajj remains more difficult than it is for men. One reason for this is that, in line with the Wahhabi interpretation of Islamic law, in Saudi Arabia it is considered unlawful for a woman to perform the Hajj in the absence of her husband or a close male relative.[12] These views have been integrated into Hajj regulations, restricting the opportunities to perform Hajj for all Muslim women, regardless of their nationality or Islamic denomination (see Chapter Six). This provision is only relaxed for women over 45 years of age; they are allowed to travel in groups particularly organised for women without a *maḥram*, but each group of women falls under the responsibility of a male escort, known as *rafīq* (see Chapter Two).[13]

Another obstacle that women may be confronted with concerns their responsibilities towards their families, including husbands, children and, often, parents. This issue comes to the fore in the story of Mariam (Najat's mother and Ḥanna's daughter-in-law), who told me about her own Hajj experience:

> My husband went to the Hajj and *'umra* three times before I went. His first Hajj was with his work [as a religious guide and imam]. I performed Hajj in 2014; I applied in 2009 and could not go because my mother was sick, and I could not leave her behind . . .

Al-ḥājja Mariam's reflection on her Hajj experience echoes the stories of many women whom I came to know in Morocco, who often sacrificed the obligation to perform Hajj to fulfil other responsibilities.

Becoming a *Ḥājja*: Cultural and Religious Capital in Shared Narratives of the Hajj Experience

In the public sphere, being addressed as *al-ḥājja* is a form of cultural capital for women who have performed the Hajj. The term 'cultural capital' refers to non-financial social assets that promote social mobility beyond economic means. It also refers to a person's distinctive skills, knowledge and practices that promote social mobility and allow people to enhance their social position

(Crawford and Newcomb 2013, 66). While some female pilgrims, particularly younger ones, do not mind if people do not use the honorific title upon their return, others insist on it. For many women, the symbolic capital that comes with becoming *al-ḥājja* provides access to other forms of capital within Moroccan society.

One example of a young woman who was able to negotiate her position within the local community after performing the Hajj is Sawsan, a thirty-two-year-old woman from Fes. Born and raised within a financially comfortable family, as she characterised it, Sawsan performed the Hajj in 2012 together with her father. Since then, she has become one of the most respected young women in her neighbourhood. Younger and older women come to seek her advice on daily matters and request her religious guidance, as she enjoys social and religious status among the women of her neighbourhood.[14] Sawsan's privileged status as the daughter of a well-known official already provided her with access to large social networks. Her new title, *al-ḥājja*, allowed her to claim an additional higher moral stance and to exert religious influence on women in her family's network. I was told that Sawsan was already known as a wise young woman before she went on Hajj. Yet, only after the completion of her Hajj did women begin to come to her house and seek her advice. Her mother told me proudly:

> I felt that she was going to perform Hajj while young. Now, she is *al-ḥājja*, she has religious knowledge and many women come to seek her wise advice . . . The women ask her about daily issues they struggle with, and she is happy to give them advice.

The mother reconfirmed Sawsan's high religious reputation by calling her *al-ḥājja* when they talked about her to other people. For her part, Sawsan demonstrated her religious knowledge at woman's gatherings by giving advice and offering her opinion on different issues. During a women's meeting that I attended in October 2016, I noted that women asked Sawsan many questions about the Hajj and *ʿumra*. They wanted to hear her opinion when the Saudi government decided to increase the fees for the Hajj entry visa. Sawsan's extraordinary position as a young pilgrim helped her to accumulate indicators of distinction and prestige. However, it is important to recognise that such prestige or symbolic capital exists only insofar as it is recognised by others

(Bourdieu 1990). By increasing her religious knowledge through her performance of the Hajj, and subsequently sharing her knowledge and experiences with other women and helping them to overcome daily dilemmas, Sawsan gained respect in her local community.

Sawsan's case is not unique. I noted numerous occasions where having been on Hajj provided Moroccan women with self-confidence and a legitimate foundation from which to access power within their social networks. Some qualifications are in place here, however. First of all, this power predominantly applies in female networks where the subject is frequently present.[15] What characterises Sawsan's case is that her elevated religious status spilled over into other domains: she is often invited to participate in social events such as weddings, birth celebrations and women's gatherings, something that can also be related to her family's social position.[16] This illustrates the fact that, more broadly, the pilgrimage experience is also a social project, and that a valuable asset of pilgrimage concerns the fact that it also provides additional social capital in the sense of 'strategic positioning' (Bourdieu 1986). For Moroccan women, being able to perform the Hajj is considered a sign of success, which is also a major topic of discussion in women's social gatherings (Cooper 1999, 91; O'Brien 1999).

A second qualification that should be made relates to the ways in which social stratification in Morocco affects how the Hajj performance of female pilgrims from different socio-economic positions is assessed. The criteria that determine the symbolic capital that Hajj performance may generate change in each context, depending on cultural as well as socio-economic factors. While Sawsan gained much respect and religious capital in her social network after performing Hajj, this may not be the case for women from less privileged backgrounds. I will demonstrate this in the next section by discussing the Hajj stories of Lubna, a pilgrim from Mohammedia, who is only three years older than Sawsan, but has a quite different social background.

Social Capital, Pilgrimage and Financial Needs

The travel and accommodation costs involved make it almost impossible for people who have limited financial means, especially women, to perform the pilgrimage to Mecca.[17] Those who could afford it were often either women with affluent husbands (or fathers) who paid for them, or women who ran their own business or possessed financial capital through inheritance. Sawsan's mother was able to perform Hajj after the death of her father using her inheritance money, while Sawsan's pilgrimage was financed by her father. For women who have little or no financial capital, performing pilgrimage is much harder.

One of these women is Lubna, who grew up in an urban neighbourhood in Mohammedia as the eldest of four children. From an early age, Lubna shared in her parents' responsibilities for taking care of her younger siblings, the more so after the death of her father in 2004. Lubna was employed as a daily worker in a car-parts factory in Casablanca until it closed in 2016. She had wished to perform the Hajj, but financially, it seemed like a distant dream. The factory where she worked, however, had an annual lottery in which two employees are randomly selected to win 50,000 Moroccan dirhams (approx. 5,000 Euros) earmarked for a Hajj journey. In 2014, Lubna was the winner.

However, the responses Lubna received from her fellow factory workers and from family and friends in the neighbourhood when she won the prize money confronted her with her marginal position as a poor single woman. She vividly recalled how everyone coveted the prize:

> I still remember how everyone gathered, waiting to hear the next name. The manager took a folded piece of paper out of the box in front of him, and read the name aloud: 'Lubna, congratulations!' I could not believe it at first, but I acted indifferent. A female friend standing next to me touched my arm and congratulated me. A male colleague standing to my left said: 'If you do not want it, give it to me!'

While it is possible that her male colleague may have been joking, Lubna would soon learn that while they would not say so to her face, some people deemed it more appropriate that a young and poor woman like her should renounce the prize in favour of somebody else. Lubna decided to ignore the gossips that reached her ears and focused on overcoming the next obstacle to realising her dream.

Indeed, winning the lottery as such was no guarantee that Lubna would be able to perform the Hajj. When trying to register for a Hajj visa at the local government pilgrimage department, the local male governor informed her that, prize or no prize, like all Moroccans Lubna would have to go through the visa lottery system, the *qur'a*, before she could undertake the pilgrimage to Mecca.

Two problems occurred during this process. The first was that thousands of people had applied in Lubna's governorate and only 390 visas were available for people in that area. The chance that Lubna would be among the lucky ones selected in the *qurʿa* was therefore exceedingly small. The other, more serious, issue was that in accordance with Saudi Arabia's policy concerning male guardianship for women, Lubna could not even register without a *maḥram*, a legitimate male companion. She thus faced the task of finding a male relative who was willing and able to accompany her on the journey to Mecca.[18] She decided to ask her grandfather. At the age of 85, he belonged to the category of the eldest 15 per cent of registered applicants who are automatically selected to perform the pilgrimage without having to go through the lottery system.[19] Lubna's uncles stepped in to raise enough money to buy their father a Hajj package tour.

Ironically, while it was Lubna who needed a male companion to be able to perform the Hajj, in the official records she was eventually registered as the companion of her fragile grandfather rather than the other way round. Her grandfather was privileged because of his old age, while Lubna was disadvantaged because of both her gender and her age. Nonetheless, she told me that she was happy that her grandfather could perform the Hajj because of her. Having found a way to overcome the restrictions imposed on her as a female pilgrim, Lubna was now ready to prepare for her Hajj journey. She performed the Hajj in 2015, and safely returned to Morocco with her grandfather as *al-ḥājja*.

When I met her for the first time, Lubna had just come back from Mecca. Upon her return, she had expected that, in line with local etiquette, many visitors, including family members, friends and neighbours, would come to her house to congratulate her on her safe return. During the first few days following her return, indeed, some family members and close friends did visit her. Lubna's neighbours, however, and many women whom she considered her friends, never came to her house to congratulate her. Lubna explained this to me by referring to the gossip that her decision not to relinquish her prize had caused, and to being called 'a woman! ... unfit to perform Hajj because of poverty and age', as she put it. She suspected that, behind her back, her neighbours and friends accused her of being conceited and not knowing her place.

To understand the wilful breach of etiquette by Lubna's neighbours and her disappointment about their behaviour it is helpful to reflect on the socio-cultural context in which the views and experiences of the various parties that feature in her Hajj story are embedded. In a poor neighbourhood like Lubna's, it is exceedingly rare that people have the means to go to Mecca. The Hajj is conceived of as a privilege beyond the reach of one's own kind. A young woman with modest means who performs the Hajj defies social expectations. For this, she had to be punished: first, by being reminded of her place through accusations behind her back that she considered herself better than other women in the neighbourhood; and second, by breaching of the local etiquette of paying her a congratulatory visit upon her return from Mecca. However, by defying the unstated norms, Lubna showed that disadvantaged situations were not as 'set in stone' as people might think.

Fortunately, Lubna's recollections about the resentment of her neighbours and former friends were not the last of her Hajj stories. Thanks to the bonding that resulted from sharing similar experiences during Hajj, Lubna managed to build meaningful relationships with fellow female pilgrims, and thus was able to extend her social network beyond her daily environment. Not only did she feel appreciated by the women with whom she had performed the pilgrimage, but, through her contacts with them, she also gained access to the different layers of society to which many of her fellow pilgrims belonged. Cultivating her relationships with her new pilgrim friends thus compensated for the loss of former friendships and provided Lubna with social capital that allowed her to reach out to a world beyond her old social network. In a way, Lubna expressed feelings of being empowered by the pilgrimage and its aftermath.[20]

Lubna's story illustrates the significant impact socio-cultural context has on people's gendered perspectives and experiences of the Hajj. Her *habitus*, daily life, social background and economic status influenced her expectations and experiences of the Hajj as much as her gender did. The fact that her uncles financed her equally impoverished grandfather's Hajj, while Lubna faced social pressure to forgo her money prize, highlights the influence of patriarchal views and practices affecting Moroccan female and male pilgrims differently.

Women's Hajj, Power and Patriarchy

Although family structures and the recognition of women's rights have developed in Morocco over the years, patterns in familial power relations have not changed to the same extent (Sadiqi 2003; Ouguir 2013).[21] In general, men continue to have more authority than women, especially over their wives and unmarried daughters (Sadiqi 2003). As a result, female family members tend to be more restricted in their freedom of movement than male family members. Subsequently, women often meet with more obstacles than men when it comes to the ability to travel for pilgrimage. *Al-ḥājja* Zahra is one of them. Zahra is the first wife of a successful local businessman from Fes, with whom she had performed the Hajj several years previously. Since her pilgrimage, her husband had acquired a new, younger wife, who accompanied him in performing *'umra* on an annual basis to look after his needs whilst in Mecca. In Chapter Three, I quoted Zahra expressing her longing for Mecca and describing the pain burning in her chest due to her inability to go on *'umra*. Being financially dependent on her husband, she was unable to fulfil her wish.

As I had the opportunity to see Zahra on several occasions, I witnessed her mentioning the issue of her longing to return to Mecca repeatedly, and each time her words were accompanied by tears and sighs. One of her most repeated remarks was that she feared she would die before being able to set eyes on the Ka'ba again. Zahra's grievances are aggravated by the fact that, ever since her husband married his second wife, this younger woman gets to accompany him on his *'umra* trips. This privilege has become the focus of attention in the rivalry between the two wives. Zahra spoke to people who were close to her husband, such as his sister-in-law, her sons-in-law and her husband's elder brother, to mediate on her behalf. For many women, to go on pilgrimage with one's spouse was the simplest way of avoiding disagreements or restrictions imposed by the husband. It also reduces the risk of becoming the object of gossip: in the eyes of outsiders, the legitimacy of women who perform pilgrimage is enhanced if they do so in order to accompany their husbands as dutiful wives. Therefore, while in religious terms the Hajj of a woman equals that of a man, the symbolic capital that male pilgrims gain by Hajj performance tends to be more significant and weigh more than that of female pilgrims.[22]

Women, Symbolic Capital and the Male's Ability to Perform the Pilgrimage

Although pilgrimage to Mecca is obligatory for both Muslim men and women who can perform it, some women put male relatives – particularly their husbands – before themselves when it comes to performing the Hajj. In this sense, even women for whom the Hajj is beyond personal reach can influence travel to Hajj indirectly; creating or enhancing a relationship of indebtedness can be an effective way of exerting power over others, particularly for those who have limited access to formal power (O'Brien 1999). As mothers and housewives, women play a principal role in transmitting socio-cultural norms and values and providing encouragement and support. During my fieldwork I came across several examples of women who exerted this hidden power. In the next subsection I explore how a wife can play a pivotal role in the pilgrimage of her husband by focusing on the story of Najla, the mother of Yusra, whom I introduced in Chapter Four.[23] When I interviewed Najla about her husband's pilgrimage to Mecca, she began her story as follows:

> There was this time when I told my husband, 'I have a feeling you will go on Hajj.' He said: '*Min fummik li-Allāh* [May these words go directly from your mouth to God].'[24] I told him that I had a good feeling about it. I registered his name, attended the selection process, and there it was . . . They called the first name, then the second and . . . the third was his, the name of my husband.

Najla knew that her husband wished to perform the Hajj, but did not have the financial means and therefore kept postponing his registration year after year. Without consulting her husband, Najla decided to register his name for the *qur'a* at a local governmental office in Mohammedia where they lived and worked as schoolteachers.[25] In her view, her husband's intention, or *niyya*, to go on pilgrimage needed to be pushed forwards, and she was the one to make that step on his behalf. Smiling triumphantly, Najla told me:

> After every prayer, my husband would put his hands up and pray: 'Oh God, I hope that these hands will be washed with Zamzam water.' One day I was coming back from work when I saw a poster about the Hajj registration. I thought to myself, that is his opportunity . . . all I thought about is that I can help my husband in making his wish come true.

Although Najla had not performed the Hajj, she saw it as her responsibility to give practical support to her husband. She recalled that while walking back to her house, she wondered what other people would think when hearing that she had registered her husband for the Hajj lottery. She noted: 'They might think that I control my husband.' Once at home she told her husband what she had done. She clearly remembered the happiness she saw on his face when he realised what his wife had done for him. A few months later, when the husband was selected in the *qur'a*, Najla was overjoyed and phoned him to deliver the good news.

Having come this far, Najla faced a new responsibility: finding the necessary funds to make it possible financially for her husband to perform the Hajj. She told me:

> We did not have any *santīm*![26] Our savings amounted to around 4,000 dirhams in total [around 400 Euros]; not much at all compared to the 45,000 dirhams [4,500 Euros] that we needed for Hajj fees [at that time]. I told him, 'Let us ask the school for a loan of 20,000 [2,000 Euros] over our salaries.' Next, I called my sister in Italy and asked if she could give us 1,000 Euros. I was involved in a money-saving project with the teachers at my school and we had saved about 10,000 dirhams [1,000 Euros] in that group. We put all the money together and I went to pay. After making the payment at the bank, I only had 200 dirhams [20 Euros] left in my purse.

Najla's role did not end there; she next took on the responsibility of managing the salaries of her husband and herself to save the money needed to buy the necessary items for Hajj such as his *iḥrām* clothes, shoes and other necessaries. When her husband finally left for Mecca, she made sure to tell him how to spend the money he took with him and what gifts to buy. She herself spent days shopping in Casablanca for Hajj gifts for friends and family who would come to congratulate her husband upon his return. She bought prayer mats, beads, scarfs and other gifts. She also worked for many days preparing sweets and food for the return of her husband.

From Najla's story, I noted that Moroccan women who have not performed the pilgrimage can still be active agents in the process that leads their male relatives to perform pilgrimage to Mecca. Like Najla, women would take centre stage in their stories and speak about their roles confidently and in detail. The culturally specific nature of power and influence wielded by women thus came to the fore both in the performance of the Hajj itself and in the content of the Hajj stories that women told to me, either in person or at women's gatherings I attended. In these narratives, women claim authority by presenting themselves as the motor behind the success of male relatives' pilgrimage. This production of symbolic capital through narratives, and sometimes stories and songs, justified and acknowledged the position of those who could not go to Mecca vis-à-vis those who did perform the Hajj.

Conclusion

In this chapter I have examined how female agency comes to the fore in Moroccan women's stories about pilgrimage to Mecca. Focusing on the stories of women from diverse age groups and socio-economic backgrounds allowed me to relate women's Hajj experiences to their mobility in everyday life and to the various forms of capital needed for and generated by performance of the pilgrimage to Mecca. Until recently, because of the physical and social mobility implicit in visiting Mecca, most Moroccans tended to associate the Hajj performance with men rather than women, whom they associate with more local pilgrimages to saints' shrines. Although the number of female pilgrims from Morocco has grown over the last few decades, the stories presented in this chapter addressed the challenges that women continue to face before they are able to go on pilgrimage to Mecca.

Some challenges affect all women, such as restrictions on women's mobility due to patriarchal traditions, according to which women fall under the guardianship of men. A major obstacle for all female pilgrims is that, according to Saudi Hajj regulations, women under the age of 45 need to be accompanied by a male guardian. But, as the stories of Zahra illustrate, living in a polygamous marriage is a patriarchal Moroccan tradition that can become particularly painful when tensions between marriage partners are played out in relation to the issue of which wife gets to join the male head of household on his journey to Mecca. At the same time, framing marital tensions in terms of being thwarted in one's efforts to develop one's piety by revisiting Mecca, Zahra has a powerful tool with which to negotiate her position as first wife.

Culturally conditioned gender expectations may also result in women prioritising their domestic responsibilities as caregivers for family members over their ambition to fulfil the religious obligation of Hajj performance, as Mariam did. Women's choices, nonetheless, should not be interpreted one-sidedly as pointing to their lack of agency. For one thing, women often share in the religious prestige that comes from having a pilgrim in the family. Moreover, by putting such efforts into helping others to go to Mecca like Najla, women can lay claims on the same family members and thus improve their position in the family.

Besides factors that affect all women, Hajj performance can also be hampered by the specific ways in which women are positioned in different sets of power relations, for example on the basis of their age or socio-economic position. The stories I have discussed here thus illustrate the need to take an intersectional approach in order to understand how women's Hajj experiences are related to their mobilities. Class and gender play a role in the conceptions of women's experiences and in women's reflections on the worthiness of the social prestige involved in the use of the title *ḥājja*.

Notes

1. Fatima Mernissi was a Moroccan feminist writer and sociologist whose work largely addressed issues of gender and religion. The passage at the beginning of this chapter is quoted from Mernissi's *Dreams of Trespass: Tales of a Harem Girlhood* (1994).
2. Couscous is sometimes referred to as *siksu* or *sikuk* in Morocco.
3. 'Ḥanna' is a word used locally to address a grandmother as a sign of respect. The word is derived from the Arabic word *ḥanan*, meaning compassion and kindness. Although throughout this book names are not transliterated, I chose to transliterate the word here for reasons of pronunciation.

4. *Faqīh* normally refers to an Islamic jurist, an expert in *fiqh* or Islamic jurisprudence. In Morocco it is often used to refer to a person knowledgeable about the Qur'an, including an imam of a mosque (Elckeman 1976).
5. *Ḥāyik* is a traditional white outdoor cloak made of silk and wool, and is often worn by women in the colder regions of Morocco. This large garment is a symbol of modesty and discretion. 'Mellali' indicates that it was made in Beni Mellal, a city located in the centre of Morocco. For more information on Moroccan women's dress see Boulanouar (2010).
6. Fieldnotes, 23 September 2016.
7. There is no clear reason why the song specifies girls to be looked after, as probably all children need care, but it might relate to the fact that girls, like women, need to have a guardian looking after them so this makes it more urgent.
8. Up until the 1940s, while some caravans of Moroccan pilgrims travelled over land to Saudi Arabia, others went by steamship (Slight 2014, 55). Resources that I came across during my fieldwork include a short video from 1949 documenting the pilgrimage to Mecca from Morocco. The film states that 450 pilgrims were chosen among 2,500 from Morocco to sail towards Jeddah, from where they would continue to Mecca. Hajj flights did not commence until 1957 (Guttery 1998).
9. Pierre Bourdieu's concept of capital relates to his theoretical ideas on class. He identifies three dimensions of capital, each with its own relationship to class: economic, cultural and social capital (Bourdieu 1986). Bourdieu defines *habitus* as the experience and possession of a tradition by an agent (Bourdieu 1985, 13).
10. Field, in the conceptualisation of Bourdieu, is a competitive arena of social relations where agents or institutions deploy immense physical, mental, symbolic and strategic resources in the production, acquisition and control of forms of capital (Bourdieu 1991).
11. Maliki fatwas from the seventeenth and eighteenth centuries state safety, security and proper accompaniment as conditions for women's travel to Hajj (Hendrickson 2016).
12. According to Hanafi and Hanbali schools, it is not permissible for women to perform the Hajj without *maḥram* company. Yet, according to Shafi'i and Maliki schools (the Maliki school is dominant in North Africa, including Morocco), the condition of *maḥram* company, or that of the husband, is not an obligatory condition since *maḥram* company is a means of preserving a woman's safety, which can be achieved if women travel in a secured group (Maghniyyah 1997, 10–11).

13. According to a local official, there is no limit on the number of women that a male pilgrim can accompany as *rafīq* during Hajj.
14. I have classified the acquisition of religious knowledge through Hajj as both cultural and religious capital because the process strongly resembles an educational process. The power of religious capital lies in how it represents a form of power.
15. It must be noted that in Sawsan's case her father also showed great pride in her being a young pilgrim. I observed, for example, how he would also pay close attention to her when she was giving her views and that he also occasionally asked her advice.
16. Both men and women who have gone on Hajj enjoy social capital, yet my focus here is on women's perspectives.
17. For more information on gendered social and financial structures in Morocco (which might distinguish women from men in terms of financial independence), see e.g. Sadiqi (2010), Ennaji (2016), Booley (2016).
18. Also, when I accompanied a group of pilgrims on *'umra* in 2016 and 2018, my father acted as my male companion in order to be able to go on this minor pilgrimage.
19. In Morocco, the oldest 15 per cent of pilgrims do not go through the lottery system, so as to give more opportunities to older people to perform the pilgrimage to Mecca. In 2016, the oldest pilgrim among this 15 per cent group of oldest applicants was 95 and the youngest was born in 1933 and was 83. These oldest pilgrims were allowed to be accompanied by one person who would look after them, who also would not have to go through the lottery system.
20. Studies of other religious traditions also reflect on how pilgrims empower themselves through pilgrimage (Hermkens et al. 2009; Jansen and Notermans 2012). A few chapters of Hermkens et al., *Moved by Mary: The Power of Pilgrimage in the Modern World* discuss examples of gender empowerment through pilgrimage. Janine Klungel, for example, argues that Marian pilgrimage is integrated into women's efforts to stabilise their way of life. Similar cases of women's empowerment are observed by Lena Gemzöe, who shows how, by honouring Mary directly, women in Portugal avoid intermediaries and thus gain a sense of empowerment. Anna Fedele examines how the pilgrimage to the Mary Magdalene shrine in southern France helps women escape what they see as the patriarchy of established religion.
21. For more information on the Moroccan women's rights movement and reforms in family law, see, among others, Buskens (2003, 2006), Evrard (2014), Ouguir (2013), Sadiqi (2008), Weingartner (2005), Wuerth (2005).

22. According to my female interlocutors, male pilgrims participate in several community events such as resolving conflicts, mediation between people and witnesses to contracts. In family gatherings, they are often invited to make supplicatory prayers at the end of a gathering or following a meal for blessing. The women's role, however, is limited more to women's gatherings in more private settings.
23. I discuss the story of Najla further in Chapter Ten.
24. *Min fummik li-Allāh* (literally, 'From your mouth to God') is a local expression that indicates hopes for whatever has been said to be realised ('May God fulfil your wish' or 'May what you wish come true').
25. For more information about the *qur'a* process, see Chapter Two.
26. The word *santīm* comes from the French word *centime*, meaning 'one cent'. One *santīm* is worth one hundredth of a dirham. There is no smaller currency than a *santīm*, and although the coin is no longer minted, Moroccans sometimes refer to financial quantities in *santīm*. The smallest coins currency in today's Morocco is 10 centimes and 20 centimes. In daily conversation, Moroccans also refer to the *franc* (worth the same as a *santīm*) and the *riyal* (one dirham = 20 *riyal*) as units of financial measurement.

PART THREE

THE PILGRIMAGE: INFORMING EVERYDAY LIFE

Light-hearted Approach to Hajj Narratives: Hajj in Moroccan Humour

There was a Moroccan man who returned from Hajj. He went to a nearby shop in his neighbourhood where he was a regular customer. He asked the owner to show him the record of his debt in the shopkeeper's loan notebook. The man was excited thinking that *al-ḥājj* was about to pay the debt. He opened the notebook and pointed to one page. The pilgrim said: 'Where is my name?' The shop owner answered: 'Here it is, *al-ḥājj*!' The pilgrim nodded his head and said: 'Well, now you can write "*al-ḥājj*" in front of my name!' (told by Sarah, Ouezzane, 14 October 2016).

8

‘*ḤAJJ AL-MISKĪN*’: MOROCCAN LOCAL PILGRIMAGE

The power of the word in Morocco belonged to men and to the authorities. No one asked the point of view of poor people or women.

(Tahar Ben Jelloun)[1]

Introduction

On the ninth day of Dhū l-Ḥijja, pilgrims gather at the plain of Arafat as an obligatory rite of the Hajj.[2] On the same day, on 11 September 2016, I joined hundreds of people who gathered at a small coastline site in Morocco known as Sīdī Shāshkāl, where they performed rituals like those of the Hajj. Three Moroccan friends agreed to accompany me that morning. In a public taxi, leaving the centre of the city of Safi, we drove along the coastal road with other cars and trucks for around half an hour before we saw the place. As we walked down to the shore, dozens of people were putting up their small stalls to sell clothes, spices, coal, ceramic dishes and much more, all of which I learned were necessities for *ʿīd l-kbīr* taking place the following day. A large slaughtered calf was hanging for a local butcher's customers to see. Food vendors were scattered along the street that led down to the coast. We looked down at the golden sand, and then walked on, passing groups of people as we approached the beach itself. Within a matter of minutes, we had reached the only construction on the beach, the site of Sīdī Shāshkāl, which had been prepared for a pilgrimage ritual, locally known as *ḥajj al-miskīn*, which translates as the Pilgrimage of the Poor.

The pilgrimage took place around a small shrine located on large rocks near the shore. The shrine consisted of a four-sided packed-earth building with a distinctive structure, a *qubba* or dome. The rites of the Pilgrimage of the Poor continued from the early morning until the late afternoon as people gathered in groups around the old building commemorating the parallel pilgrimage far away near Mecca. I followed a group of women into the shrine. The woman in front of me wore a yellow *jellaba* and carried two candles. She removed her flip-flops – as a sign of respect, I was told – and stepped onto the old dusty floor. She placed her candles on the floor next to some others and a few coins. Next, she touched the walls to her right, whispering prayers for blessings. After this, she moved her hands over her own body, starting from her forehead down to her legs. The place was too small, so that two women who sat on the floor stood up and left. I followed them shortly afterwards.

As I walked out of the room, I came face to face with an old man wearing traditional clothes. As he walked up the broken steps, assisted by a long stick, he repeated: 'May God accept your pilgrimage! Oh, the Pilgrimage of the Poor!' As he made his prayer, men and women stopped to greet him and some handed him a few coins. He slipped the coins into the pocket of his *jellaba* and continued to make prayers. I stood next to him and asked him about the ritual taking place at the site of Sīdī Shāshkāl. He told me: 'This is our Hajj . . . Like those performing Hajj in Arafat near Mecca, we have our 'Arafa here . . . May God accept it . . . We all worship God.'[3]

During my research, I was able to participate in two local pilgrimages of people unable to undertake the Hajj to Mecca: the pilgrimage to Sīdī Shāshkāl on the west coast, and the pilgrimage to the site of Sīdī Bū Khiyār in the Rif mountains of northern Morocco. These pilgrimages are viewed, by those who undertake them, as alternative spiritual journeys, substitutions, out of necessity, for the Hajj proper; they are called *ḥajj al-miskīn*, or the Pilgrimage of the Poor. In my search for secondary resources discussing the Pilgrimage of the Poor, I was only able to find two sources. The first was a small booklet in Arabic by the Moroccan researcher and historian Ibrahim Kredya from Safi, containing some explanatory narratives about the site of Sīdī Shāshkāl, and the second account was within David Hart's ethnography, *The Aith Waryagher of the Moroccan Rif* (1976).[4] In a chapter discussing Islam in the Rif, Hart covers the local pilgrimage to Sīdī Bū Khiyār (ibid., 178–81). He narrates the story of Sidi Mhand (buried north of Sīdī Bū Khiyār), who had arranged with local people to perform a pilgrimage to his site in the Rif mountains, insisting that the whole ritual should resemble the pilgrimage to Mecca. Sidi Mhand, according to Hart, told local pilgrims that performing the poor man's pilgrimage is equal to half a pilgrimage to Mecca. On one occasion when the people present wanted to pray before noon, Sidi Mhand told them instead to wait until noon – at which point he miraculously opened the skies so that they could see Mecca and the holy places of Islam. David Hart attended this pilgrimage on 1 August 1955. Almost sixty-three years later, I attended the event, as documented in this chapter.

The belief in and veneration of local saints is seen by many authors as one of the central aspects of 'Moroccan Islam' (Hammoudi 1997; Eickelman 1976; Geertz 1969; Gellner 1968).[5] In Morocco, a saint is referred to as master, *walī* or *sayyid*, and, less commonly, as *marabout*, a French term, from the Arabic *murabiṭun* or 'tied to God' (Eickelman 1974, 220).[6] Such sanctified persons are popularly believed to possess the attribute of *baraka*.[7] The lodge or building associated primarily with a wali or with a religious order often qualifies as *zāwiya* (plural *zawāya*) and such places are visited by individuals and groups of Moroccans. The visit, *ziyāra*, to the *zāwiya* or to other tombs of saints can take place at any time of the year in addition to the annual festivals, called *mawāsim* (Eickelman 1976, 7).[8] It is not the mission of this chapter, however, to discuss the nature of sainthood in Morocco, a subject that has been treated in numerous academic works (such as Cornell 1998, Combs-Schilling 1989, Eickelman 1976, Gellner 1969 and Geertz 1968, to name but a few). The focus on the saints and their visits in this chapter is related to the practice of the Pilgrimage of the Poor which takes place at a specific time of the year and resonates with elements of the pilgrimage to Mecca.

In the next section of this chapter, I introduce, in narrative form, the two pilgrimages of the poor: that to the site of Sīdī Shāshkāl and the pilgrimage at the site of Sīdī Bū Khiyār. I discuss the ritual, along with its religious, social and economic dimensions, as well as its political messages, which make the study of this aspect of pilgrimage worthy of greater attention. Following this, I will offer a presentation of different views or perceptions of this pilgrimage in Moroccan society.

Sīdī Shāshkāl and Sīdī Bū Khiyār: Rituals that Imitate the Pilgrimage to Mecca

At Sīdī Shāshkāl, the rites of the pilgrimage included walking anti-clockwise around the four-sided packed-earth building, which can qualify as an imitation of the ritual of circumambulating the Kaʿba, which is a mandatory rite of the Meccan pilgrimage. Whilst a few pilgrims circled the shrine seven times, as in Mecca, most people seemed satisfied with one or two rounds, after which they sat at a distance observing the others. Some pilgrims then prayed at the site, standing on the ruins of a building which they called 'Arafah' (or 'Arafat'). This rite of standing entailed a reference to the Plain of Arafat near Mecca where pilgrims perform the rite of standing on the same day. Following these rites, many people washed themselves in the Atlantic Ocean. One of the pilgrims told me that in the past, before a nearby well which was called 'Zamzam', dried up some years ago, people used to drink its water and linked its significance to the holy water of the Zamzam Well from which pilgrims drink during the Hajj.

The rites of the pilgrimage at Sīdī Bū Khiyār were somewhat similar and took place on the day preceding *ʿīd l-kbīr*.[9] Pilgrims walked past a small rectangular structure of mud and stone, the outside wall of which was painted in white, the site where Sīdī Bū Khiyār is believed to be buried, towards the pinnacle of the Jbil Hmam at a point called Tamrabit where a female saint, Lalla Mannana, is said to be buried (Hart 1976, 195–6).[10] A man standing at the site told me that Lalla Mannana was Sīdī Bū Khiyār's lover and companion. She is an important figure in the ritual of the pilgrimage. He added that the pilgrimage rituals at the site include circulating, or standing near, the site of Lalla Manana on top of the hill. Some people circumambulated Lalla Mannana's tomb that morning, while many others were satisfied just standing between the ruined walls of what used to be a room. In this respect, what I observed contrasted with David Hart's recorded observations, where he noted: 'pilgrims made the circumambulation three times around her tomb prior to the noon prayer, and then using her pinnacles as a vantage point, they even stoned the devils' (Hart 1976, 178–81). On the day I attended the pilgrimage at Sīdī Bū Khiyār, there was no stoning of devils, something which was, according to another pilgrim, not practised any more, and people instead focused on making *du'ā'* prayers. Considering the tense political situation at the time, this may have also been due to the strong police surveillance.

Among those I met at the two sites, very little was known about the figures of Sīdī Shāshkāl and Sīdī Bū Khiyār beyond the fact that both were *awalī' ṣāliḥīn*, saints, and the site of their tombs is a place of pilgrimage.[11] Ahmad, an old man at the site, told me that 'Shāshkāl was a religious scholar who came from the East'.[12] According to Ahmad, 'Sīdī Shāshkāl was a wise, knowledgeable Islamic scholar who dedicated his life to the worship of God'. That is why, according to Ahmad, like many other Moroccan saints Shāshkāl lived in an isolated area, away from civilisation, to dedicate his time to fasting, prayer and meditation; consequently, this site became a place of pilgrimage after his death. In a booklet dedicated to the Pilgrimage of the Poor near Safi, local historian Ibrahim Kredya confirms this story, stating that Shāshkāl was regarded with immense respect, and over the years people developed the practice of visiting his shrine on the Day of Arafat.

Fouad Rehouma, a Moroccan anthropologist, offers another narrative. He explains, in a short video about the Pilgrimage of the Poor, that the rituals at the site of Sīdī Shāshkāl date back to the thirteenth century.[13] Rehouma states that Sīdī Ahmad Shāshkāl used to teach local pilgrims who intended to perform the Hajj the rituals and practices required once they reached Mecca. He used his rock to symbolise the Ka'ba to train people in how to perform the *ṭawāf* rite of Hajj. He also used a nearby rock to train future pilgrims on the rite of standing near Mount Arafat during the Hajj. Upon the death of Sīdī Shāshkāl, people who intended to perform the pilgrimage to Mecca continued to visit the place to practise the rites of the pilgrimage. By the seventeenth century, the place had become a popular destination for the Moroccan poor, who could not afford to travel to Mecca but instead came to Sīdī Shāshkāl to circumambulate it. According to the researcher, however, at the time the intention was never to provide a substitute for the pilgrimage to Mecca, as is the case for many of those who visit it nowadays.

The stories about the origins of the pilgrimage also included reference to the historical period between the eleventh and the nineteenth centuries, when some legal opinions discouraged or even prohibited the pilgrimage to Mecca (Hendrickson 2016).[14] These legal opinions were justified by references to the risks linked to long-distance travel from Morocco (and North Africa in general) to Mecca at the time. As a result of the prohibition of travel to Mecca, some interlocutors claimed, local citizens looked for alternatives and started performing local pilgrimages close to their communities.

Despite the uncertainty about their origin, Moroccans performing the pilgrimage at the two sites emphasised the validity of their ritual since all pilgrims, despite their location, worship the same God and seek His acceptance, forgiveness and blessings. Their understanding seemed to be that no one should be excluded from a ritual which accesses God's spiritual benefits, such as pilgrimage. Among pilgrims, the two sites were associated with good luck and *baraka*. For example, I was told about miracles that had happened to people who visited the two sites in the past. Osama, a man in his sixties, had come to Sīdī Shāshkāl from Casablanca to escape the noise of a large city and to enjoy the sacred site. He told me:

> The first time I came here was many years ago. I was young and wanted to swim in the sea, not realising how tricky the water can be. Once in the water, the waves were too strong and took me out further and further . . . I thought I was going to die and almost gave up. That was the last thing I remember before I woke up on the shore. The waves must have carried me back. People who were nearby ran to me and helped me recover. They told me that I was saved by the *baraka* of the saint.

Osama emphasised that even the money he carried in his pocket was not lost. 'This must be a place blessed as God has saved it from destruction all these years', he added.

At the site of Sīdī Bū Khiyār, the *baraka* was manifested in a healing ritual that took place in the room where the saint is believed to be buried.[15] Behind this tomb, which was covered in green cloth, two men stood reading verses from the Qur'an. On the opposite site stood a man and a woman after placing their baby girl on top of the tomb. They had explained to the Qur'an reciter that the child was extremely sick. One of the two men put his hand on the head of the baby and started reciting verses from the Qur'an and finished by saying *duʿāʾ* prayers. The woman handed over some money before carrying

Figure 8.1 The site of Sīdī Shāshkāl (top) and its visitors on the day of the Pilgrimage of the Poor (11 September 2016)

her daughter out of the room. I asked one of the visitors about the two men reciting the Qur'an and prayers. He said that they were *fuqahā'*, religious men who had been infused with *baraka* and offered their services during the day but were not necessarily related to the late saint.[16]

Outside the shrine of Sīdī Bū Khiyār a group of men, dressed in white, sat near the wall of what I was told was once a small mosque. Those men were the *ṭulba*, Qur'an reciters, who, since the morning, had gathered to recite from the Qur'an for the public. They stood in a half-circle in an open area, while hundreds of people surrounded them to hear their recitation.[17] Here, they went through the litany or *dhikr*. The following is one of the poems they delivered, *sīdī Ahmad yā Muhammad*:[18]

O Master, Ahmad, Muhammad,	*Sīdī Ahmad yā Muhammad*
Allah Allah Allah	*Allah Allah Allah*
May God bless you, Master;	*Ṣalla Allah 'alayka sīdī*
Allah Allah Allah	*Allah Allah Allah*
With you, my heart was supported,	*Yā man bika al-qalbu ta'ayyad*
Allah Allah Allah	*Allah Allah Allah*
And it was brought up on you, master;	*Wa tarabba 'alayka sīdī*
Allah Allah Allah	*Allah Allah Allah*
Do not deprive me, O Muhammad,	*Lā tiḥrimnī yā Muhammad*
Allah Allah Allah	*Allah Allah Allah*
from seeing your face, master;	*Min sanā wajhika sīdī*
Allah Allah Allah	*Allah Allah Allah*

Then, the *ṭulba* sat on the ground and began reciting the Qur'an. Later, a man in a light blue *jellaba* (unlike the others, who were dressed in white) stood up and collected some *ma'rūf* or *ṣadaqa*, financial support from the audience. The *ṭulba* numbered around forty men, a relatively small number when compared with the 421 men who were present at the time of David Hart's research in 1955 (Hart 1976, 196). Despite their number, the *ṭulba* were a distinct feature of the pilgrimage experience for many of the visitors. Describing the collective prayer that took place during the pilgrimage season of 1955, David Hart writes, 'The sight of this collective devotion was one I shall never forget, a magnificent example of both humility of the Aith Waryaghar before God, and of simple human dignity', and indeed, this is

Figure 8.2 The day of the Pilgrimage of the Poor at the site of Sīdī Bū Khiyār (21 August 2018)

the view I too formed of the overarching atmosphere. To quote David Hart: the 'keynotes of the annual pilgrimage to Sīdī Bū Khiyār are simplicity and orthodoxy' (Hart 1976, 189). Indeed, the rituals were unadorned, without unnecessary elaboration, and so was the gathering. So, a great deal of the religious tone and core ritual remains consistent, in the practices of this pilgrimage today, with Hart's observations. The image in Figure 8.2 documents the pilgrimage in 2018 (see Hart 1976, 179, for a photographic documentation of the pilgrimage in 1952).

Besides their religious function, the two sites were booming with social activities ranging from greeting strangers, to listening to their stories, to gathering around fortune-tellers, among others. Both sites also hosted a thriving impromptu market, with hundreds of people shopping for *ʿīd* necessities from the numerous stalls. Due to its multiple functions – as a shrine, a pilgrimage site and a vibrant market-place on the Day of Arafat – the two sites are visited by a variety of people, including local inhabitants and visitors from nearby villages. The diversity of visitors contributes also to a variety of ways of interpreting the Pilgrimage of the Poor and its performance: primarily taking place for the purpose of worshipping God, and paying respect to the saint, it also serves as a place for shopping for the upcoming *ʿīd l-kbīr* and as a space for leisure time, in order to chat, meet people or relax on the day preceding the *ʿīd*, and all this in addition to its specific political dimension (discussed later in the chapter).

Debating the Equivalence of the Pilgrimage of the Poor and the Hajj

When I visited the two sites of Sīdī Shāshkāl and Sīdī Bū Khiyār, I spoke to many visitors who insisted on the sacred nature of the site they visited and the value of the pilgrimage which takes place there on the Day of Arafat. Although I witnessed many similarities between the rites performed at the two sites and the Hajj taking place in Mecca, as an outsider, nonetheless, the rites of the Pilgrimage of the Poor looked unstructured and variable. For the people at the sites, nevertheless, the pilgrimage was very much alive, and the sacredness of the place was evident in the stories they shared. Logistical problems and the necessary expenses involved make Hajj prohibitive and, while not religiously obligated to perform the Hajj in Mecca if they are unable to do so, many Muslims continue to wish to perform pilgrimage in some meaningful manner.

What counts, for those who attend the Pilgrimage of the Poor, is that it has a connection to and resonates with the Hajj. Many people whom I met at the sites of Sīdī Shāshkāl and Sīdī Bū Khiyār had their own personal rationale for participating in the pilgrimage. They look at themselves as Muslims performing a pilgrimage inspired by the pilgrimage to Mecca. Many pilgrims to Sīdī Shāshkāl, for example, told me that they were aware of the difference between their local pilgrimage and the pilgrimage to Mecca. Yet they still hoped that God would accept their ritual. As a man whom I met at Sīdī Shāshkāl told me:

> Both those who make the pilgrimage to Mecca and those who make the pilgrimage to Sīdī Shāshkāl do it to seek God's blessings. The poor people who cannot afford to go to Mecca come here with the same motives . . . People come here and wash their sins in the sea and God is the One who accepts from His worshippers. God knows what people ardently desire and He forgives their sins. Indeed, we are all pilgrims!

This pilgrim asserts the primacy of sincere motivation and conformity to broader Islamic imperatives as factors which God will judge. In a sense, he asserts the concept of equality before God, the idea that God judges people through criteria which supersede material considerations; God is understood to accept the offerings of the poor – whatever they may be – as being just as valid as those of the more fortunate ones who can visit Mecca. It is also worth noting that the Muslim Pilgrimage of the Poor tradition freed local pilgrims from the obligations and restrictions advocated by orthodox teachings.[19] The ability to equate the Pilgrimage of the Poor with making Hajj in Mecca seems to be a spiritually liberating position for the poor – a small compensation, one might argue, for their material deprivation. Thus, they enjoy the opportunity to fulfil a religious obligation, address their personal needs and feel closer to God.

The most important criterion that visitors to Sīdī Shāshkāl and Sīdī Bū Khiyār repeatedly used, as suggested earlier, for determining whether their pilgrimage was acceptable as a devotional act, or *ʿibāda*, is the intention of that act, the *niyya*. The Arabic term *niyya* features prominently in texts about Islamic ritual law. *Niyya* is required in acts of worship and ritual duties including prayer, fasting and pilgrimage (Powers 2004, 425). Among Muslims, *niyya* is consistently treated as a formal focus that transforms or translates a given act into the specific named duty. In the pilgrimage to Mecca, *niyya* is verbalised at several points starting with the *niyya* of the overall performance of the Hajj or *ʿumra*, which is required when pilgrims reach one of the several approved entry sites into the precincts of Mecca and following the state of *iḥrām*. Similarly, those performing the local pilgrimage to Sīdī Shāshkāl claim to formulate their *niyya* to perform *ḥajj al-miskīn*. They, the pilgrims, recognise the primacy of Mecca, whilst also asserting that God – and God alone – will judge the quality of the pilgrim's prayer and intention during this alternative pilgrimage.

Those who perform the Pilgrimage of the Poor view it as an opportunity to ask God to strengthen their faith. As one man told me, 'We ask for a stronger *īmān*; we ask for halal food and life, and we ask for a solution to misfortune and perplexity'. Thus, the Pilgrimage of the Poor has a particular function and significance, that is, to offer a means by which the socio-economically disadvantaged may feel themselves able to approach God by performing pilgrimage. Those who visit the saint's shrine perceive this practice as a devotional bridge for the disadvantaged to claim the same access to sacred space as wealthier co-citizens, and use religious evidence to support their interpretation. Indeed, the pilgrims seem to have found a way to synthesise a theological interpretation of the conception of the intermediaries with their own traditions and aspirations.

It is worth mentioning here that when pilgrims perform prayers at the site, they turn their backs to the shrine and pray facing the *qibla* of the Kaʿba in Mecca (Bonine 1990, 50–70).[20] The site of the pilgrimage, therefore, is instrumental in 'reaching' or 'worshipping' God for those unable to reach Mecca, as pilgrims at the site would describe it. David Hart had documented that only three men from the Jbil Hmam in the Rif area had made the pilgrimage to Mecca in 1961, followed by four men in 1964 and three in 1966 (Hart 1974, 178). Although the number of pilgrims from the area who visit Mecca today has grown significantly, the pilgrimage to Mecca is still beyond reach for many people. The two sites, therefore, fill a 'religious void' for local pilgrims (Eade and Sallnow 1991, 15). As Eade and Sallnow assert, pilgrimage cannot be understood as a universal or homogeneous phenomenon, but should instead be deconstructed into historically and culturally specific instances (ibid. 1991, 3). The Pilgrimage of the Poor represents a shared heritage and is symptomatic of the materially impoverished daily lives of some groups of Moroccans. The poverty of my interlocutors at both pilgrimage sites became a unifying force among them, part of their shared identity, and a link with the place of the pilgrimage. There is a comfort in being removed from a social context in which the poor know themselves to be judged, explicitly or implicitly, as inferior by their richer fellow citizens, as well as in trying, at least, to compensate for failing to perform the much-coveted Hajj.

An illustration of the political connotation emerged from comments which drew a stark contrast with Mecca in terms of the state's position vis-à-vis the holy sites. Unlike Mecca, the site of Sīdī Bū Khiyār is neglected during the rest of the year, enjoying no material investment, so that, apart from on the days of the pilgrimage, it is effectively abandoned. As interpreted by Adil and Jawad, two men whom I joined to visit Sīdī Bū Khiyār, ignoring the site was part of the state's larger neglect of the Rif in general and of its people and their culture. The police forces, however, chose to be present at the site for the duration of the pilgrimage, unlike at the site Sīdī Shāshkāl, where no police monitored the gathering. The heavy police presence at the site was explained by the local pilgrims in two ways. The first explanation related to the nature of the pilgrimage. As I was told, in the previous year's pilgrimage a group of 'religious men', as the pilgrims termed them, visited the site and tried to prevent people from performing the Pilgrimage of the Poor, decreeing that there was no substitute for the pilgrimage to Mecca. This incident had resulted in a conflict among the pilgrims. The police were thought to be present this year in order to avoid similar incidents. The second explanation was related to the political unrest in the Rif, where all communal gatherings were monitored closely by the police. On the surface, however, the surveillance by the police did not seem to affect the proceedings of the pilgrimage: people seemed relaxed and close to each other, enjoying meeting others and performing the rites of their pilgrimage.

The pilgrimage at Sīdī Bū Khiyār represented not only a way for participants in it to connect with the spiritual meaning of the pilgrimage in connection to Mecca, but also a way of reflecting on the political reality on the ground. Sīdī Bū Khiyār was a site of safety and protection. Many studies have shown the historical role of saintly shrines as sacred sites and as a distinct locus where it becomes possible to reconcile social and political conflicts (El Mansour 1999, 185–98).[21] At the site Sīdī Bū Khiyār, Adil greeted pilgrims enthusiastically with '*ʿāsha l-rīf*' (Long live the Rif!), and several young people wore T-shirts with the Amazigh flag bearing the letter yaz (ⵣ).[22] These signs of local Amazigh identification were noteworthy, juxtaposed as they were with a national Moroccan flag which had been put on the shrine – possibly in an attempt to placate agents of the state in the form of the police, thereby avoiding any repercussions arising from the display of other symbols which might be seen as challenging the status quo.

When we sat under an oak tree to escape the heat of the sun, Adil and Jawad were busy discussing the significance of the gathering. Adil explained to the younger man: 'Every Riffian who comes to Sīdī Bū Khiyār wants to connect with our sacred land.' This connection, at least in its physical sense, came to a halt by mid-afternoon as people started to leave, as did we. By the evening, Adil commented: 'the site will be deserted once more, until the next year, when on the Day of Arafat, the devoted, pious pilgrims will return to perform the Pilgrimage of the Poor.'

Competing Framings of the Pilgrimage of the Poor

Travelling to Mecca to perform the Hajj is the dream of many pilgrims who performed the alternative Pilgrimage of the Poor. In addition to fulfilling a religious obligation, as I have argued throughout this book, the pilgrimage to Mecca reflects various aspirations regarding Moroccan social life, which combine a longing for piety with wider religious and social goals. Many of those who performed the Pilgrimage of the Poor remarked on this spiritual aspect that the closeness to the site of Sīdī Shāshkāl or the site of Sīdī Bū Khiyār evoked. They, however, would prioritise travelling to Mecca for pilgrimage if they could. The practice of the Pilgrimage of the Poor, nonetheless, is a matter of disagreement locally. Some deem it to be a sign of religious ignorance and, by definition, a ritual exclusive to the 'poor': obviously, the link made by some between poverty and ignorance is open to challenge and may simply reflect social prejudice. In the following narrative, I recount a conversation I witnessed between a few of my interlocutors in the city of Safi, a conversation which revealed some of the local opinions regarding the performance of this pilgrimage.

On return from Sīdī Shāshkāl on the day of the Pilgrimage of the Poor, I arrived in the city of Safi at sunset, just in time to join a local family in breaking their fast.[23] I sat in the living-room with aunt Fatiha and her sister Rasmiya, her son Musa and her elder brother Hassan. Fatiha brought in two types of dates on white plates and some water in a small decorated glass:

> **Fatiha:** [addressing me] This is *real* Zamzam water, and the dates are brought from Mecca by my brother, who performed *'umra* in Ramadan. [jokingly] Should I call you *al-ḥājja*, now that you performed the Pilgrimage of the Poor?
>
> **Musa:** [who had accompanied me throughout the day, answering his mother's question] Me too! You should call me *al-ḥājj*, [jokingly] now I have performed my Hajj even before you.
>
> **Fatiha:** One day, God willing, I will go to the *real* Hajj, to visit Mecca, Medina and the Prophet . . . What are people doing there, at this place of Sīdī Shāshkāl? You know that Mecca is the only place for pilgrimage recognised by God.

Hassan: It would be better for people to abandon such *bidʿa* [heretical] practices . . . That is not Islam. Not pilgrimage! I do not understand why people still do it, then.
Musa: People told us they pray to God to accept their visit and make prayers like those of pilgrims in Mecca.
Fatiha: it is all *jahl* [ignorance, or illiteracy]! Those who want to do the pilgrimage should go to Mecca; it is not obligatory to do the Hajj if one is not able, anyway.
Musa: An old man told us, 'This is our Hajj; God will accept it, because we all worship God!'
Fatiha: This is not Islam, this is *ḥarām* [taboo].

The opinions of Fatiha and Hassan illustrate the differing views on the Pilgrimage of the Poor. Their comments identify the practices of those who perform the Pilgrimage of the Poor as *ḥarām* and not Islamic. Fatiha's opinion also implies that those people who undertake this form of pilgrimage are unaware of what she identified as 'correct' religious practice, referring to them as 'illiterate' and 'ignorant'. In their argument, Fatiha and Hassan refer to Islam and Qur'anic verses, using such authorities to bolster their argument and prove that the Pilgrimage of the Poor is to be avoided.

Many others among my interlocutors also condemned the Pilgrimage of the Poor and described it as being *shirk* (polytheism), *jahl* (ignorance),[24] *tkharbīq* (foolish). These opinions resemble the stance taken towards local cults around Muslim saints in various parts of the world (Schielke and Stauth 2008). Another observation during my fieldwork was that those who condemned or looked down on the Pilgrimage of the Poor were reflecting the social order and class distinctions in Morocco. The emphasis on 'real Zamzam water', in its decorated glass, and the production of two types of dates on pristine plates, could be seen as signifiers of social status, rather than markers of religious decorum. The criticism of pilgrims using terms such as *jahl* (ignorance), and *tkharbīq* (foolish) by inference, seems to signify class differences. On several occasions I was told, mostly by middle-class Moroccans, that those who perform the Pilgrimage of the Poor are not educated and are financially poor.[25] In a strongly class-conscious society, this inevitably means associating Muslim practices with those who occupy a more elevated rank in the social hierarchy (Munson 1993).

Many Moroccans who have been to the Hajj in Mecca, as well as others from diverse backgrounds, shared a similar view to that of Fatiha and her family. The disapproval of the Pilgrimage of the Poor was, however, often articulated differently. Some people limited their negative analysis merely to saying: 'These practices do not reflect Islam'; 'God proclaimed pilgrimage only to Mecca'; and 'This is *shirk* (polytheism)'. Some people quoted the hadith which sanctioned journeying (*shadd al-riḥāl*) to no other mosques apart from al-Masjid al-Ḥarām in Mecca, the Prophet's Mosque in Medina and the Masjid al-Aqsa in Jerusalem.[26] However, it must be said that the permissibility of journeying to places other than the three mosques designated in this hadith was a point of contention even among theologians, not just Moroccans who opposed the Pilgrimage of the Poor. While these views are rooted in a strict adherence to doctrinal precision, they still convey a negative view of the religiously motivated practices of those whose economic circumstances prevent full doctrinal adherence, as it is interpreted within the more prescriptive readings of the Qur'an and Sunna.

Conclusion

To conclude, although the validity of local pilgrimages such as those performed at the sites of Sīdī Shāshkāl and Sīdī Bū Khiyār is rejected by many Moroccans, hundreds of people continue to practise the pilgrimage to local sites in Morocco, a fact which reflects how Islam is being negotiated in daily life. Those who perform the Pilgrimage of the Poor would state 'We all worship God'. Their pilgrimage can be interpreted as a response to non-negotiable social constraints and as an assertion of the value of the devotional activities of the socially marginalised. The Pilgrimage of the Poor, then, is a complex, possibly ambiguous practice that can take various forms and involves elements of ritual, belief, economics and, in some instances, also politics.

The question concerning the contemporary role of the Pilgrimage of the Poor should be seen in a wider context, in which the *msakīn*, as they refer to themselves and their pilgrimage practices, are trying to re-position themselves as devout Muslims in a wider sense, in relation to the pilgrimage in Mecca. In their local pilgrimage, they see themselves as part of a greater *umma*, while at the same time defining themselves as Moroccan pilgrims. The Pilgrimage of the Poor, in this sense, is part of a much wider public debate about Islam. In effect, it reveals how diverse groups of Muslims negotiate their positions with respect to different interpretations of the global discursive tradition of Islam, applying these interpretations within their local context.

While the Hajj is a universal ritual, the Pilgrimage of the Poor, or pilgrimage to saints' shrines, lacks the scriptural authority and the traditions of orthodox Islam. Consequently, unlike the Hajj, the Pilgrimage of the Poor is widely disputed. Theologically, any pilgrimage site other than Mecca is rejected by the major Islamic law schools. However, for those who perform the Pilgrimage of the Poor, it offers a much-needed sense of spiritual achievement which would otherwise be denied to them. It also asserts their egalitarian representation of divinity: a God who judges through scrutiny of intentions and quality of prayer, rather than by observance of established rituals only.

The pilgrims who make these local pilgrimages reconstruct their actions through a spiritual lens and assert the importance of what they do in God's eyes. They are indirectly challenging the social order which accepts that the wealthy will occupy high-rise Saudi suites, with privileged views over the Kaʿba, and at the same time questioning the views of some fellow Muslims who deem *them* to be ignorant and their practices at variance with 'normative' Islam. They seek to level out the social gradations which penalise them for their poverty. Such alternative pilgrimages, nonetheless, may be consolatory, enabling those who make them to cherish the hope of a better future, to be patient within the context of social and political frustrations, and to hope for the day when they can perform the pilgrimage to Mecca.

Finally, pushing my argument even further, I could imagine that the Pilgrimage of the Poor might be seen as a form of critique against the current commodification of the Hajj in Saudi Arabia, particularly its accessibility only to those who can afford it. In Chapter Six, I focused on the contestations of the Hajj management, as discussed by Moroccans. Given the absence of any such administrative oversight of the Pilgrimage of the Poor, an examination of it in the light of such criticism might provide a welcome counterpoint to the arguments put forward by its detractors.

Notes

1. Tahar Ben Jelloun is a Moroccan French novelist and writer who has written expressively about Moroccan culture and the immigrant experience.
2. Moroccans use Arafat (ʿArafāt) or ʿArafa interchangeably when they talk about the Day of Arafat and places related to it. In this chapter, I will maintain the same format as documented during the Pilgrimage of the Poor, using Arafat and ʿArafa interchangeably as they appear in context.
3. Fieldnotes, 11 September 2016.
4. Ait Waryaghar (or Ait Ouriaghel) is the largest Berber tribe in the Rif region of north-eastern Morocco. Ait Waryagher means 'those who do not back off' or 'those who do not retreat'. The tribe inhabits most of the territory around the city of El Hoceima (Hart 1976).
5. A saint is a person, elect in the eyes of God, whose life is an example to his or her people. For more on saints in Africa see, among many others, Soares (2004), Schulz (2003), O'Brien (1988).
6. In general, a *marabout* is a person who may have a special relationship with God which makes him serve as an intermediary between people and God (Eickelman 1974, 220).
7. Other *baraka*-endowed persons include figures claimed to be descendants of the prophet Muhammad (the *shurfa*) and the *ṭulba* (Qur'an reciters) (Eickelman 1976).
8. *Mawāsim* is the plural of *mawsim* (or *musim* in Moroccan Arabic), which refers to annual regional festivals that combine religious celebration (often in honour of a saint) with festive and commercial activities (Schielke 2006).
9. In 2018, the Day of Arafat was commemorated in Mecca a day earlier than in Morocco. Saudi Arabia declared that the Day of Arafat, which falls on the ninth of Dhū l-Ḥijja, would be on 20 August 2018 (making 21 August the first day of *ʿīd l-kbīr*). However, Moroccan officials declared that the first day of *ʿīd l-kbīr* would be celebrated on Wednesday, 22 August. Several countries celebrated *ʿīd l-kbīr* on 22 August, including, in addition to Morocco, Indonesia, Malaysia, Brunei, Singapore and Japan. The Pilgrimage of the Poor took place on Morocco's Day of Arafat, the same day as *ʿīd l-kbīr* in many parts of the world, including Saudi Arabia.
10. In David Hart's (1976) book, he describes the site of Sīdī Bū Khiyār and refers to Mannana as Aralla Yamna. Lalla is a prefix used with a woman's name as a sign of respect and means 'lady' in Tamazight or Berber. It is used for female saints in the same way 'Moulay' or 'Sīdī' is used for male saints.

11. According to Hart, it is not known whether Sīdī Bū Khiyār was a *sharīf* or a *mrabit*, but only that he was a student of great saints, among whom was Sidi Bu Midyan al-Ghawth (1126–98), and probably came from Tlemcen in Algeria (Hart 1976, 194). According to Hart, the pilgrims he met believed that Sīdī Bū Khiyār had possessed great *baraka*, which allowed them, among other things, to fly, on the Day of Arafat, from the Rif to Mecca and back during the same day; none of the people I met at the site recalled such stories.
12. The histories of many saints are unknown in Morocco. Most, however, are believed to have come from the east (of the Arab world), where the Muslim prophets came from (Eickelman 1976).
13. https://www.youtube.com/watch?v=89Zx2Jl9PUE (last accessed 21 March 2021).
14. Some Muslim jurists working within the Maliki school of law have been discouraging or prohibiting the pilgrimage to Mecca for Andalusian and North African Muslims since at least the eleventh century. When the Almoravid ruler asked Ibn Rushd al-Jadd if *jihād* or the Hajj was more meritorious for Andalusians, Ibn Rushd protested that the answer was obvious. He stated that the merits of *jihād* are innumerable, while Moroccans are all exempt from the Hajj because of their inability to perform it; furthermore, Muslims risking the dangerous journey would incur sin (Hendrickson 2016). The jurist Ibn al-Munayyir prohibited the pilgrimage for anyone who feared he might delay or mis-pray even one daily prayer on the journey. The voluminous *fatwā* compilation of another scholar, Aḥmad al-Burzulī', includes more opinions discouraging the Hajj than describing its proper performance (ibid.).
15. David Hart mentions other saints in addition to Sīdī Bū Khiyār as the saints of Jbil Hmam: Sidi l-Hajj Misa'ud, and his son Sidi Hand u-Musa of the Igzinnayen (ibid. 1976, 194). However, no pilgrimage is made to the tomb of the other saints, but is reserved only for Sīdī Bū Khiyār.
16. According to David Hart, Sīdī Bū Khiyār left no descendants (Hart 1976, 194).
17. This term *ṭulba* (sing. *ṭalib*), literally means 'students'. In Morocco, *ṭulba* refers to students of the Qur'an who specialise in group recitation at ceremonies such as weddings and funerals (Mateo Dieste 2013).
18. I was able to trace the poem to Ahmad al-'Alawī, an Algerian Sufi sheikh (Lings 1993).
19. There are other pilgrimages resembling the Pilgrimage of the Poor outside of Morocco, such as the pilgrimage to the Sheikh Nur Hussein Shrine in eastern Ethiopia and Yenihan Baba in Bulgaria (Zarcone 2012).

20. As was mentioned earlier, Muslims pray towards the Kaʿba in Mecca, which is the sacred direction for prayer (*qibla*). In Morocco, however, slight variations in *qibla* direction applied in the past, based on various calculations (Bonine 1990). At the time of the empire of the Almohads, for example, Islamic jurists (*fuqahā*) focused on making spiritual practice easier for the average practitioner to carry out rather than focusing on strict mathematical accuracy regarding the correct direction of Mecca (Stockstill 2018, 69). Mosques with inaccurate *qibla* directions at the time included those in Marrakech, Tlemcen and Fes, among others (Buresi 2018, 153).
21. *Zāwiya*s were granted the right of sanctuary (*ḥurum*) and the right to offer asylum to fugitives (El Mansour 1999, 185–98).
22. The Amazigh flag is composed of blue, green and yellow horizontal bands of the same height, and the letter yaz (ⵣ), which symbolises the 'free man', which is the meaning of the Berber word 'Amazigh'.
23. It is a recommended *sunna* for those who are not pilgrims to fast on the Day of Arafat. According to a hadith narrated from the prophet Muhammad, 'Fasting on the Day of Arafat expiates the sins of the year before and the year after' (Ibn Mājah, vol. 1, book 7, hadith 1730).
24. There are no universal definitions and standards of literacy. However, illiteracy rates in the Moroccan national census are based on the most common definition, the ability to read and write at a specific age, which estimates illiteracy rates at 32 per cent of the adult population according to the latest census of 2014. Illiteracy is more common in adults over 50 years old, at 61.1 per cent, and more common among females than among males (High Commission for Planning 2015).
25. Against a total population of 35.2 million in 2018, some 25 per cent of the population (nearly ten million Moroccans) can be considered financially poor (World Bank 2019).
26. In the hadith, it was narrated that the Prophet said: 'Do not set out on a journey except for to three Mosques, i.e. al-Masjid al-Ḥarām, the Mosque of God's Messenger (in Medina) and the al-Aqsa Mosque (Mosque of Jerusalem)' (Al-Bukhārī, book 20, hadith 2).

9

CONSTITUTED EVERYDAYNESS: SINGING OF MECCA AND THE PILGRIMAGE IN MOROCCO

. . . listening to music and singing is for the heart a true touchstone and a speaking standard.

(Al-Ghazali)[1]

Introduction

O God, bless the Prophet;
The rider of al-burāq;[2]
Muhammad, the essence of being, Ṭāhā[3]
O God, bless the Prophet;
The rider of al-burāq;
Muhammad, the essence of being, Ṭāhā

On the morning of a hot summer's day, I woke up to these lyrics, coming from somewhere outside the room where I had been asleep. The voice of the female singer was mixed with other sounds from outside: cars honking, doors opening, people chatting, chirping birds nesting on the windowsill, and a passing motorbike. I reached for my watch; it was 7:20 a.m. This was my first full day in Fes after arriving late in the afternoon the day before. I lay back on my mattress and continued to listen as the lyrics gently unfolded, praising God, the Prophet and the beauty of creation:

We begin with the name of the Generous,
the Living, and the Provider;
And embroider clothing for the listeners;
To say, would you understand why I cry?
For the beloved one who stole my heart and mind;
His love tore me apart;
I have no power but to believe!

Unable to sleep any more, I got up, searching for the source of the music. The gentle breeze of the night had been replaced by dry heat. The music was coming from a CD player in the living room. The girls were still sleeping, and one mattress had been folded and placed on the table. Fatima, the mother, was nowhere to be seen; she was on the roof, I thought.

Overwhelmed by the heat of Fes, I slid under the table, reaching for the tiles in search of some coolness. From under the table, I continued to listen to the lyrics as the song continued:

He was called al-Makkī . . .[4]
O God, may he be my companion on the day we meet You;
May I never face an ordeal or see one;
Praying in the name of the Hāshimī, the Arab prophet[5]
I pray in the name of Kaʿba and those who visited her

I soon learned that every morning *khāltī* Fatima turned on some music while she finished her morning chores, opening all the windows, folding the mattresses and covers used the night before, dusting and sweeping the floor. Every day I woke up to the same song, belonging to a popular genre of music known in Morocco as the *malḥūn*.[6] Other songs on the same CD included themes praising God, encouraging listeners to think about the Creation, the need to remember the Prophet and the pilgrimage to Mecca. Such songs with their religious themes were favourites for Fatima, and they also featured as part of the repertoire at wedding parties, private gatherings, radio broadcasts, celebrations honouring the birth of a new family member, or at performances in public spaces. Today, with the advent of the Internet, many similar songs can be heard on YouTube or on social media platforms shared by Moroccans.[7]

In this chapter, I examine Moroccan songs, the lyrics of which revolve around the theme of the pilgrimage to Mecca with a frequency which reveals the importance of this experience in the lives of Moroccans. I analyse how pilgrimage-inspired lyrics in various musical forms are perceived by listeners (Hirschkind 2006). Pilgrimage songs constitute a public display of piety, evoke a longing for Mecca and suggest images of the performance of the pilgrimage, for both pilgrims and non-pilgrims alike, reaffirming a bond between Moroccans and Mecca. This emotional response acts to maintain a vital connection to the religious centre, Mecca, even if that centre is physically inaccessible, through messages of Muslim virtue and morality. Meanwhile, for those yet to perform Hajj, the lyrics act as a reminder of the pilgrimage as an ultimate religious goal.

Songs and music are part of everyday life in Morocco, where people listen to them in public and private spheres in both religious and mundane sittings (Ter Laan 2016; Kapchan 2007).[8] The interest in music of a religious nature is not confined to a specific age profile in Morocco – it is a universal phenomenon. A study conducted by El-Ayadi, Rachik and Tozy (2007), based on a 2006 survey of religious values and practices among young people in Morocco, demonstrates the growing interest of youth in music as a form of pious entertainment.[9] In the same survey, the researchers describe this taste in religious music as a compromise between the religious and the profane (El-Ayadi et al. 2007, 78). My argument, however, places the emphasis elsewhere. Compromise can suggest a concession, a lessening of principles or beliefs to create harmony between conflicting standpoints. However, rather than being a compromise, I suggest that in the daily lives of Moroccans, the sacred and profane intertwine (to say the least), and even co-constitute each other. It seems to me that my interlocutors in Morocco strive to be pious in their daily lives; the expression of a longing for Mecca is one central aspect of those values or ideals that energise and motivate them day to day. In celebrations of significant and important life events like marriage and birth, one can see a concentration or an intensification of those ideals. Mecca, I suggest, does not represent access to the sacred simply metaphorically, but represents also a state of pure bliss and abundance for many Moroccan Muslims. Therefore, references to the holy city and to the Hajj in songs, as I shall show in this chapter, stimulate feelings of happiness, blissfulness and joy.

To address this topic, I first discuss some reasons why music and songs are relevant to the discussion of pilgrimage in the everyday life of Moroccans. Next, I present ethnographic sketches of various settings in which the songs of the pilgrimage were heard and performed during my fieldwork, to show how these songs form an intrinsic part of Moroccan everyday life, in both religious and non-religious contexts. Then, I will discuss the different themes represented in the songs in relation to the pilgrimage to Mecca. I will also discuss how Moroccans celebrate their piety, sensations, longing for Mecca and religiosity when listening to these songs. Finally, I will reflect on the role of these songs as a cultural element of everyday life in Morocco.

Why Songs of Pilgrimage?

Music occupies an important place in everyday life and popular culture in Morocco and, indeed, throughout Muslim-majority countries (Ter Laan 2016; Kapchan 2007).[10] The performance of religiously inspired music is a long-standing and diverse tradition in Morocco (Kapchan 2008; Waugh 2005; Schuyler 1985).[11] Much of the existing literature discusses the Sufi influence on religiously inspired music, which has become popular in music festivals and public performances in Morocco over the last decades (Maréchal and Dassetto 2014; Kapchan 2007; Schuyler 2007).[12] Moroccan music reflects the range of cultures and groups that have passed through the country, leaving behind a rich and varied legacy, as is documented by both locals and foreigners and performed in public and private settings (Bentahar 2010, 41–8; cf. Kapchan 2007; Lortat-Jacob 1979, 62–72).[13]

Music can also be seen as a unifying marker of social, cultural and religious solidarity among listeners (Ronström 1992, 181). Ronström asserts that music is powerful because it can function as a symbol of a community or social group even if it is charged with various, sometimes contested, meanings. In his article 'The Gnawa of Oujda: Music and contending identities in the Maghreb', Tony Langlois argues:

> Music provides a medium for the expression, open or obliquely, of shared sentiments and normative values. At the same time a range of social elements compete for ownership of musical genres as potent symbolic property. Whether looking at performance or more general forms of social use, musical activity

> involves an interaction between the individual and the group, which in turn involves specific cultural restraints and possibilities. (Langlois 1996, 203)

Therefore, it is important to look at how the lyrics and the performance setting affect different groups of listeners in order to fully appreciate the complex role music plays (Ter Laan 2016).[14] In an analogous manner, Moroccans celebrate the return of pilgrims from Mecca by singing songs, a tradition practised in many other places, for example the Nubian women's songs for pilgrims (Frishkropf 2008, 492) and those performed among Hausa women (Cooper 1999; cf. Waterman 1990, 31). However, the songs discussed below are sung or heard well beyond the confines of celebrations for specific events. They permeate the everyday lives of Moroccans deeply, including on special occasions like engagement and wedding parties and family gatherings of many varieties, as well as during the routines of daily life itself, as exemplified by Fatima's early morning ritual. Music, as has frequently been demonstrated, is capable of evoking powerful emotions (Ter Laan 2016; Schuyler 2002), sensations (Meyer 2006), and represents a site for raising a pious Muslim subject through the 'ethics of listening' (Schulz 2006; 2003; Hirschkind 2001). In a way, songs can also mediate religious experiences and help listeners establish a connection to their longing for Mecca.

In the following section, I present three songs with a thematic focus on the pilgrimage to Mecca, considering the settings in which I heard each of them, and then discuss their significance within Moroccan daily life. The songs will be given in translation, with explanatory notes and discussions of the text.

Mapping Out the Scene: Three Songs

Amdāḥ Maghribiya

I heard this song for the first time in a shop that sold men's clothes in the old *medina* of Fes. I went to the shop with *khāltī* Fatima, who seemed familiar with the seller as he stood up to greet her with 'Oh, *al-ḥājja*! Welcome! Welcome!'. After politely asking about her health, the man reached into the drawer of his desk and took out some CDs. 'I have prepared some nice songs for you', he said. He then invited her to sit on a small chair and listen as he placed one CD in an old computer and the music began:

May God grant you peace, O prophet Muhammad
Rise up to praise God,
O lovers of the Messenger of God;
This is an hour of God's,
in which the prophet, the Messenger of God, is present . . .
O visitors of Mecca and Medina,
Ask *ḥabīb-Allah* [the beloved of God] for intercession;[15]
Between Mecca and Medina,
Ask the beloved of God for intercession;
Between Mecca and Medina there is a scent of frankincense[16]
O prophet, O Muhammad, O *al-'Arabī*
O visitors of Mecca and Medina,
Ask the beloved of God, for his intercession

The shop owner showed *khāltī* Fatima the list of songs on the CD while the song continued:

In my dream I saw *al-Madanī*[17]
And my mind was taken by his love;
Let us visit him; let us visit him;
Our prophet is a shining light . . .
Mecca is a bride covered with white silk;
If we are hungry, from the food of God we will be satisfied;
If we are thirsty, from the well of Zamzam we will drink,
If we are tired, we will ride on camel . . .
God is our Lord; may You forgive us!

Two weeks later, I attended a henna party where these lyrics were played by a DJ while girls and women danced, shaking their shoulders and hips. Some women swayed from side to side in their chairs, snapped their fingers, tapped their feet and repeated the lyrics aloud. A friend of mine commented: 'When a song about the prophet is performed, we should stand as a sign of respect to the theme of the song and join with singing along and dancing.' On a third occasion, I heard the song in a short video of a wedding party in Fes, shared with me by a Moroccan friend via WhatsApp. In the video, a lead singer, dressed in a white *jellaba* and green hat, sang parts of the song while groups of people gathered around him singing along, clapping and dancing. The highlight of the video was the section where the singer said 'O visitors of Mecca and Medina' and all the gathering dancers replied, 'Ask the prophet of God for his intercession.' This form of call and response was repeated.

Al-Ḥajja[18]

I heard this song for the first time on 15 September 2016, the third day of *ʿīd l-kbīr*. Najat invited me to her house in Temara. Her mother, grandmother and father sat in their living room watching a musical performance on Channel 1, the national TV channel. Najat's mother brought some mint tea to enjoy following a heavy dinner. The evening music programme on Channel 1 offered a mixture of modern and traditional songs. Then, a band was shown, comprising around forty men dressed in traditional long, loose, hooded white *jellaba*s with full sleeves and red caps. The men played different instruments, including the *kamanja*, which is a violin played while being held vertically on the knee, the three-string traditional instrument *gimbrī*, also known as the *sintīr* or *hajhūj*, the five-stringed *oud* and the *bindīr*, a frame drum played with the fingers. The musicians sat in three rows and in the middle of the front row was the singer. With no instrument to play, he was easily distinguishable from the rest of the men with his cream-coloured *jellaba*. After a couple of minutes of unaccompanied music, the singer started to perform:

Stanza 1

We take refuge in your house . . .
O be generous, O Muhammad, O Ṭāhā;[19]
A sea of glory . . . of favour, O Messenger of God
My soul was taken away by longing for the prophet;
Between ice and fire my heart is resilient;
My body in the land of Fes . . . Its situation only known by its Master;
But the soul is in Ṭayba and my brain is puzzled[20]
My pain is one that no doctor can heal
But only the Seal of the prophets can . . .[21]
O birds in the sky, I ask you by the *sulka* and those who read it[22]
Lend me your wings to reach the prophet and see him . . .

At this point, Najat's father, *al-ḥājj* Abdullah, turned to me to introduce the song. I learned that the song was originally a poem composed by Abdel Hadi Bennani, a spice merchant from Fes, whose lyrics are celebrated in Morocco even today although the song might be a hundred years old.[23] He informed me that the lyrics were deeply moving, especially given the style in which the song is played, *malḥūn*, and the language itself was very rich in metaphors. He invited us to listen carefully as the song continued:

Stanza 3[24]

Who knows, I may see you in my dream while people are asleep,
And greet you . . . O Master of those who transcend;
My fragmentation will be gathered by you . . .
And my thirst will be quenched . . .
We come to Mecca, the place of beauty, glory, and dignity
In Rabigh we enter the state of *iḥrām*,[25]
in the way directed by our messenger, Ṭāha
We will recite *talbiya* and perform *ṭawāf*,
like previous worshippers of God[26]
We kiss the stone of happiness; and our wishes will be complete
And we will be full of the water of Zamzam that we miss;
Between the Ṣafā and the Marwā, my soul will remain there;
We will plead to the Listener of prayers when our aim is complete . . .

The song continued with more stanzas highlighting the experience on Mount Arafat, in Minā, when visiting the prophet in Medina, and ended with a dedication of the poem to the prophet. Najat pointed out that her father liked this musical genre, and later she played me a new cover of the song, available on YouTube, performed by a young popular singer called Sanaa Mrahti.[27] *Al-ḥājj* Abdullah pointed that this song was significant for him, as it reminded him of the pilgrimage to Mecca:

> Any pilgrim . . . even any Muslim can relate to the lyrics . . . When the poet says his body is in Fes, but his soul is in *Medina* where the prophet is . . . He longs to be next to the prophet and visit him . . . May God never prevent anyone from [accessing] those Holy Places! . . . Being near the prophet

means the person would be healed from any sickness . . . That is why the poet wishes he can fly and reach the prophet . . .

In many versions of the song, *al-ḥājj* Abdullah added, the original mention of Fes was omitted, and was replaced with 'My body is *among the people*, and its situation is only known by its Master'. This change in the lyrics 'was made so that the listeners, wherever they were in Morocco, could relate to the song and the expression of longing [in it]'.

Allah Yā Mawlānā

This encounter took place at a party held by Najat's cousin, Asma. Asma had become mother to a baby boy and invited us to attend a celebration of the occasion for family and friends. We arrived in the early afternoon in the neighbourhood where Asma lived. On the street, alongside Asma's house, a big white marquee had been put up by a caterer, who also provided food and drinks. Najat told me that the men of the family and their male friends would have their celebration at the same place, but later in the evening. The men's gathering would be accompanied by *ṭulba*, reciters of the Qur'an, and *munshidīn*, singers who would perform religiously themed songs. For the women, however, the music was performed by a male DJ who was stationed outside the tent. The tent was almost full of women and girls of different ages, taking their place at the decorated tables. Najat, who sat next to me at a table that accommodated eight women, assured me that the songs played by the DJ would be like those performed live by the band members who would arrive later for the men's celebration, 'Maybe with the exception of the more *sha'bī*, popular upbeat songs [in the women's] celebration', she added.

The songs varied in their themes: a song of praise of God was followed by a song about the prophet, and these filled the time until Asma entered the tent carrying her new-born baby. Asma was welcomed with the popular prayer in Moroccan Arabic: *Ṣalāt wa-salām 'la rasūl Allah; lā jāh ila jāh sayidnā Muhammad; Allah ma'āhu al-jāh al-'alī* (Prayer and peace be with the messenger of God. There is no glory but the glory of our prophet Muhammad; God, with him is the highest glory). After the women had collectively recited this chanting, they ululated and applauded. Asma greeted the guests and welcomed them. Then she was led to the middle of the tent where she joined in dancing when the iconic song of Nass El Ghiwane, *Allah yā Mawlānā*, was played:

> *Allah yā Mawlānā* [God, O our Master]
> Allah, Allah, *Allah Mawlānā*
> *Allah yā Mawlānā*
> My condition is not hidden from You,
> O *al-Wāḥid*, my Lord![28]
> Praises to the Living, the Infinite[29]
> Praises to You, O God, be generous to me
> Thanks to You my rivers are full of water
> and in Your flowers, my bees are foraging . . .
>
> The prophet, O my neighbours,
> If I have enough food, I will walk to him tomorrow
> I will see with my own eyes
> Visit the Kaʿba, circle it and recite *talbiya* . . .

As the song continued, women joined in chanting, repeating 'Allah, Allah, Allah' after each of the following lines:

> People have visited Muhammad;
> I housed [him] in my heart
> The people visited him . . .
> The prophet, the Arab Messenger
> Ask the angels, ask the soul! . . .
> My heart is attached to the Qurashī[30]
> Who would blame me? . . .
> Those who tried would understand me.

The song, with its devotional lyrics and distinctive melody, appealed to a wide age-range and I heard it in several social gatherings and in a wide range of contexts.

Moroccans Discuss the Themes of Pilgrimage Songs

In addition to discussing the pilgrimage to Mecca, the themes of the songs described in this chapter share some characteristics, including the praise of

God and of the prophet. In many ways, these songs do not differ much from songs praising God or the prophet Muhammad which are common in many other Muslim societies and in Sufi chanting (Ernst 1997, 186–8). In conversations with interlocutors around the meaning of these songs, they highlighted the fondness for Mecca and Medina, in addition to the awe experienced while visiting them. The songs are densely packed with a series of emotion-evoking images and metaphorical expressions of the salvation and hope offered to pilgrims through Hajj. The lyrics reflect a depth of experience, from striving to travel until accomplishment of the pilgrimage: illness and pain caused by the distance from the holy sites are healed when those sites are reached; thirst is quenched with Zamzam water; longing is satisfied once pilgrimage is achieved. It seems as if these linguistic patterns reflect and reinforce people's established attitudes to the Hajj and may additionally also help to reinforce their position in society and view of pilgrimage.

The first song, *Amdāḥ maghribiya*, belongs, as its name indicates, to the genre of *amdāḥ*, plural of *madīḥ*, which is also known as *madīḥ nabawī* in reference to the prophet Muhammad as it is often devoted to eulogising or praising the prophet and his family.[31] Discussing the song, *Khāltī* Fatima emphasised the meanings of love and longing towards the prophet highlighted in the lyrics. According to *al-ḥājj* Omar, a pilgrim from Safi, this love was part of the love a Muslim expresses towards God. 'The path to the love of God is bound with the love of His Messenger', he would say. The traditional motif of awe for the prophet is apparent in Moroccan religious and cultural traditions beyond music. Moroccan Sufi traditions, for example, use blessings upon the prophet as part of the practice of remembrance of God, often performed after prayers. These traditions continue in Morocco today as groups of artists and performers practise a variety of sonic expressions, including not only *madīḥ*, but also *malḥūn* and pop songs about the love of the prophet. In their prayers and even daily conversations, I heard Moroccans refer to the prophet with various names such as *ḥabīb-Allah* (the beloved of God) and *sīdī rasūl-Allah* (my master Messenger of God), which were also featured in songs.

The fondness for the prophet expressed in both the *al-Ḥajja* and the *Amdāḥ maghribiya* songs was further expressed in wishing to see the prophet in one's dreams. To see the prophet in a dream or a vision – to have an intimate quasi-visual encounter with the messenger of God in Islam – is seen as a good omen. The longing to see the prophet (whether by seeing him in a dream or by visiting his mosque and tomb in Medina), therefore, is an ultimate wish for many people.

The first two songs, *Amdāḥ maghribiya* and *Al-Ḥajja*, are of a different nature from *Allah yā Mawlānā*, a song that is popular in Morocco and beyond. *Allah yā Mawlānā* is a well-known Moroccan folk song, which has been reinterpreted by the famous Moroccan band Nass El Ghiwane (Bentahar 2010).[32] Since the band's formation in 1971, this group of four working-class young men from Casablanca have produced not only songs that championed social justice during the 1970s, but have also revived traditional Moroccan lyrics (Fernández Parrilla and Islán Fernández 2009, 152). The group composed their songs in *dārīja* and gained popularity with audiences across Morocco (Schaefer 2012). Politically, Nass El Ghiwane voiced the socio-political and economic concerns of average Moroccans in addition to cultural and religious themes (Aadnani 2006, 25; Schuyler 2007).[33] The themes of their songs range from love songs, to revolutionary songs criticising corruption, to others that encourage a pious life, including performing the pilgrimage to Mecca: a diverse thematic repertoire.[34]

The performance of pilgrimage songs at seemingly non-religious celebrations and weddings was deemed appropriate by the organisers, who wished thereby to create a certain ambience and effect on the listeners, elevating the significance of the occasion by association with pious subject matter. Such is the centrality of Hajj to their life journey for many Moroccans that there is no separation or segregation between profane songs of celebration and religious ones; they may occupy various places on the musical spectrum, but are relevant for all occasions. Thus, it was interesting to see that at an event such as the celebration of a birth, the pure joy felt towards new life can be celebrated by evoking the spirit of pilgrimage. Asma, for example, told me that songs like *Allah yā Mawlānā* and similar ones played at the celebration were emblematic of the desire to protect the new child, to ward off the evil eye by reminding the guests of the prophet, Mecca and the pilgrimage, and thus bring some of their *baraka* and protective power into everyday occasions and public celebrations (Tammam and Haenni 2004).

Pilgrimage Songs as Expressions of Longing and Piety

When I asked Moroccans about the songs of pilgrimage to which we listened, often their answer was that they heard them so frequently that they normalised them and did not reflect much on them. Nonetheless, I found that the very act of listening to these songs was sometimes seen by those listeners as a form of religious practice. *Khālti* Fatima pointed out that listening to *Amdāḥ maghribiya* made her feel closer to Mecca and Medina, remembering the times when she had performed Hajj and *ʿumra*, and so made her feel closer to God. When I heard this song at an engagement party together with *khālti* Fatima, a cousin who sat at our table commented: 'I can recall my pilgrimage when I hear this song; the *ṭawāf*, the Kaʿba, the Rawḍa . . . Oh how much I long for those places!' In response, Fatima commented: 'I will go on *ʿumra* this year, *in-shāʾ-Allāh*, and see those places again.' For both women listening to the song, the experience produced a vital connection with the sacred space of Mecca, even if the city was physically far away. Moreover, listening to this song was also seen by both women as a valuable practice in and of itself, as the lyrics were encouraging listeners to perform religious acts, shown in Fatima's response to her cousin and in the song's final prayer: 'O, God, our Master; have mercy on us'.[35] Asking for God's mercy was a popular theme within prayer that I frequently heard in Morocco. In a sense, this longing for mercy relates strongly to the Hajj, a pilgrimage act which offers forgiveness of sins and the opportunity to begin afresh, with a tabula rasa, as it were. Therefore, the longing expressed in the songs for mercy and forgiveness carries with it this implicit longing for the blessing of the Hajj.

Al-ḥājj Abdullah saw in the second song, *al-Ḥajja*, a 'reminder of the importance of holy sites and therefore a reminder of [a Muslim's] religious duties including the pilgrimage to Mecca'. It seemed to me that listening to the song was a performative practice that created pious dispositions in the listening audience (Hirschkind 2006). Somewhat like the Egyptians in the piety movement that Charles Hirschkind studied, many listeners to the three songs with whom I spoke claimed that they moved them to cultivate a spiritual self and community with others (Hirschkind 2006; Shannon 2015). Unlike those in the piety movement, however, the audiences in Fes and Temara did not limit themselves doctrinally but were encouraged to listen in order to bridge and even transcend ideologies. The songs indeed represent devotional opportunities for listeners, and form part of the everyday social fabric of shared values which supersede narrow doctrinal boundaries. This process is facilitated by the Internet, which has enlarged the possibilities of buying and downloading music and gives people the opportunity to search for very particular songs that they would like to hear and share, outside religiously delineated demarcations of sect.

This interweaving of pilgrimage-themed songs and everyday settings may transfer religious discipline from the exclusive sphere of the spiritual and emphasise a central Islamic concept: that being a Muslim must be actively lived out in every aspect of existence. It is not a habit to be adopted in some contexts and later discarded; it can 'legitimise' mundane activities with a 'religious' air. Thus, in a way, such songs offer listeners constant reminders of the central truths and core practices of their religion.

For listeners to them, the songs induced an effect in them which was often manifested in bodily reactions such as tears, smiles and sighs. When listening to these songs, listeners are active agents who respond to the song with direct sensory expression. Addressing the senses, feelings and the religious imagination at the same time, pilgrimage songs can mediate religious experiences, as already stated by *al-ḥājj* Abdullah, *khāltī* Fatima and Najat, who, in diverse ways, expressed how these songs helped establish a connection to the holy places, the pilgrimage, God and the prophet. The power of these songs, therefore, was reflected in terms of the senses, sentiments and emotions evoked by the religious themes. The writers/singers seek to evoke the sublime through references to shared human experiences, such as those connected with the senses or with daily life.

In addition to the meanings of the songs expressed so far, sometimes the pilgrimage songs carried social and political messages interwoven with the religious message. For example, in Nass El Ghiwane's *Allah yā Mawlānā*, the singers expressed to God their plea that is rooted in lived experience and daily concerns. The lyrics that affirm 'O my condition is not hidden from You; You are the One, God' do not only refer to a plea, or prayer, rooted in a religious condition, but refer to daily injustice in the form of poverty or specific hardships that people face in their daily lives. As Najat stated, 'In their songs, Nass El Ghiwane spoke of social and political meanings, especially the social injustice and oppression that people [of Morocco] faced at the time'.

During the reign of King Hassan II (1961–99), the audio-visual landscape was controlled by the state and heavy censorship was placed on television, cinema, radio channels and printed media (Boum 2012).[36] Thus, Nass El Giwane and their songs were part of an alternative artistic movement that developed at the time.[37] This situation might contribute towards references to Mecca as a symbol of an ideal Muslim *umma*, or even a *watan* (homeland) to which Muslims aspire in the face of injustice and their daily struggles. These songs offered consolation in times of hardship and oppression. In *Allah yā Mawlānā*, visiting the Prophet and going to Mecca is expressed as a way of facing the hazards of everyday life. The Hajj songs have acquired a national resonance, above that of local group identity. Thus, people in Morocco today can still relate to the themes of these songs, which reach back in time and continue to be popular. Whatever the social context or the additional layers of meaning attached to them, the core element remains unchanged.

Conclusion

This chapter has reflected on how songs play a role in highlighting the presence of Hajj and Mecca in the lives of Moroccans, either as a personal memory or as part of a collective story of an ideal world for which everybody longs. The chapter demonstrates how pilgrimage songs provide a socio-cultural space in which people can express their longing not only for pilgrimage but also for the perfection represented by Mecca, and offer a medium in which to express and evoke emotions and piety. These songs reveal a conceptual and structural orientation towards pilgrimage as being central in the everyday lives of Muslims in Morocco. The songs are functional both for those who have completed Hajj and for those who aspire to do so. For the former, the combination of music and evocative lyrics regenerates some of the positive emotions associated with Hajj; for the latter, the songs act as inspiration prompts to fulfil this pillar of the faith.

Holy sites, especially Mecca and Medina, are referenced in many popular songs and pilgrimage is often present as a theme, even when the celebration was not related to the Hajj. The diverse natures of the settings for these songs underscore the fact that Hajj permeates all aspects of social and religious life; there is no strict demarcation between what is appropriate for the religious domain and what suits the everyday realm. As a form of popular expression, the ultimate role of popular pilgrimage songs in Morocco is to provide a reflection of, and a meditation on, the importance of pilgrimage to Mecca in the lives of Moroccans. In return, the spiritual elements of songs inform the mundane occasions during which they are performed, in a reciprocal and seamless cycle of integration.

Notes

1. See al-Ghazali (1853, Vol. 2, Book 8, 237).
2. Al-burāq is the name of a mule-like white beast which according to Islamic tradition carried the prophet Muhammed from Mecca to Jerusalem, where he ascended into heaven, and back in the night known as *laylat al-'isrā' wal-mi'rāj* (the Nocturnal Journey and Ascension) (Morris 1987).
3. *Ṭāhā* consists of two Arabic letters, Ṭā' and Hā', which form a unique letter combination that appears in the beginning of the twentieth *sūra* (chapter) of the Qur'an (also called Ṭā-Hā). The *sūra* begins with God addressing the prophet Muhammad and thus is used to refer to the prophet (Déclais 2005).
4. 'Makkī' literally means 'Meccan', meaning something or someone coming from Mecca. 'Makkī' or 'al-Makkī' is a common reference to the prophet Muhammad.
5. 'Hāshimī' refers to people descended from the Banū Hāshim clan of Quraysh, of which Muhammad was a member. The name Hāshimī, as well as al-'Arabī ('The Arab/Arabic [one]'), is a common reference to the prophet Muhammad.
6. *Malḥūn* is a genre of music that developed in Morocco in the fifteenth century, with origins in the Tafilalt-region of south-eastern Morocco, an area on the edge of the desert (Schuyler 2002, 799). In Morocco, *malḥūn* circulated among urban artists, craftspeople and Sufi groups throughout the sixteenth and seventeenth centuries (Jirari 1970, 562–7). By the eighteenth and nineteenth centuries, *malḥūn* began to reflect Morocco's increased unification, and came to represent national pride (Ter Laan 2016).
7. Fieldnotes, 26 July 2019.
8. For general information on music in Morocco, see, among others, Ter Laan (2016), Witulski (2009, 2014), Kapchan (2007), Waugh (2005), Aydoun (2001), Schuyler (1985, Crapanzano (1981).
9. There is much debate about music and the permissibility of musical performance in Islam, a subject which is beyond the scope of this chapter. For more on these debates see, among others, Gazzah (2008) and Al-Qaradawi (1994).
10. See also Shannon (2015), Harnish and Rasmussen (2011), Stokes (2010), Rasmussen (2010), Nooshin (2009), Frishkopf (2008), Waugh (2005), Shiloah (1997, 1995).

11. See also Witulski (2018, 2016), Ter Laan (2016), Kapchan (2008), Schuyler (1981).
12. Ritual musical practices from the Sufi brotherhoods have different repertoires but generally can be divided into chants (with or without instruments) dedicated to God (*dhikr*), songs of praise dedicated to the Prophet (*madīḥ*) and religious poetry (*sama'*) (Kapchan 2007). According to the Sufi mystic al-Makki, 'the [singing] voice is an instrument said to carry and communicate meaningful ideas; when the listener perceives the meaning of the message without being distracted by the melody, his listening (*sama'*) is lawful; otherwise, and when the content expresses physical love, simple desire and simple futilities, the listening (*sama'*) is pure diversion and must be banished (al-Makki, *Food of Hearts*, quoted in Shiloah, 1997, 149). The decline in the popularity of Sufi orders in the post-independence era affected the popularity of Sufi music. However, since the 1980s, Sufi music has regained popularity and undergone a national revival, mostly because of the reforms of Mohammed VI (Ter Laan 2016).
13. Each year the Ministry of Culture sponsors more than a dozen festivals and musical events such as the Festival of Andalusian Music, which is held in Chefchaouen, the Essaouira Gnawa Festival of World Music and the Fes Festival of World Sacred Music (Ter Laan 2016; Kapchan 2008).
14. My interlocutors in Morocco frequently referred to numerous musical genres to describe their own musical preferences. These genres include *gnawa* (originally brought to Morocco by West African slaves) (Jankowsky 2010); Andalusian music and the musical traditions of medieval Islamic Spain (Aydoun 2014 [1995]); *malḥūn*, which consists of dialect sung poetry (Schuyler 2002, 799); *raï*, which emerged in the early twentieth century in Algeria and uses vivid dance rhythms and a combination of electric (synthesisers) and traditional instruments (Gazzah 2008; Howe 2005); *sha'bi*, which refers to a combination of rural and urban festive folk music (Aydoun 2014, 141–2); Amazigh music in many styles, both traditional and contemporary (Ter Laan 2016); Sufi music (Kapchan 2007); *sharqī* (Middle Eastern music) (Gazzah 2008); and *anashīd*, translated as the chanting or reciting of poetry (Ter Lann 2016). Variations in the style and rhythm of the same songs are sometimes to be found in different geographical regions of Morocco.
15. Intercession (*shafā'a* in Arabic) of prophets is the process of seeking authority to intercede (for protection, blessing or forgiveness) on behalf of believing members of the Muslim community. There is much debate on *shafā'a* in Islam between scholars who deny it entirely, believing that only God has the power to protect people, and others who believe that prophets and angels have authority

to intercede on behalf of Muslims. In some Sufi traditions intercession can be realised by or through saints. There is general consent that the intercession of the prophet Muhammad on the Day of Resurrection is accepted by God (Heck 2012; Muslim, book 1, hadith 400).

16. Frankincense (*al-jawi* or *lubaan* in Arabic) consists of aromatic yellow resin grains produced by a certain genus of trees grown mainly in Somalia and South Arabia (including Yemen and Oman), and is traditionally used in perfumes and incense and as a medicine (Dietrich 2012).
17. *Al-Madanī* refers to someone living in Medina, a reference to the prophet Muhammad.
18. *Al-ḥajja* in the name of the song is a feminine reference to the pilgrimage to Mecca, which is common when speaking about one pilgrimage in the singular form in Arabic.
19. The song's title is also given as its opening lyrics, 'We take refuge in your house' (*zāwagnā fi-ḥimāk*).
20. Ṭayba is one of the names of Medina.
21. *Tāj al-mursalīn* or 'Seal of the prophets' is a metaphorical term used to mean the last prophet or the final prophet. It is used to designate the prophet Muhammad (Aḥmad 2011).
22. *Sulka* is an Amazigh expression that refers to group gatherings that aim at collective reciting of the Qur'an and making *du'ā'* prayers.
23. Abdel Hadi Bennani was a merchant and poet from Fes who died in 1925 (Danielson, Reynolds and Marcus 2001).
24. Versions of the song can be found on YouTube: https://youtu.be/W6XhE_YfzaY?si=7X4XsTScUYtE_tSM (last accessed 12 March 2024).
25. Rabigh is a town north-west of Mecca, near which pilgrims can enter the state of *iḥrām*.
26. The 'stone of happiness' refers to the black stone at the Ka'ba.
27. Sanaa Mrahti is a popular Moroccan *malḥūn* singer. See https://www.youtube.com/watch?v=rPClx344CqI (last accessed 12 December 2023).
28. *Al-Wāḥid* is one of the ninety-nine names of God in Islam and means the One or Absolute One (Reynolds 2020).
29. The Living (al-Ḥayy) and the Infinite (al-Bāqi) are among the ninety-nine names of God in Islam.
30. Qurashī (belonging to the Quraysh tribe, which was a noble tribe in Mecca around the time of the birth of the Prophet, and to which he belonged); in the text, it is used as a nickname for the Prophet.

31. *Madīḥ* poetry is similar to the genre of *sama*ʿ, attentive and active listening, which is derived from traditional Sufi chanting practices (Waugh 2005). *Sama*ʿ is used as a method of spiritual discipline in Sufi doctrine, that leads to the development of what may be called 'higher senses and emotions' (Becker 2004, 29). While *madīḥ* is associated with the praise of the Prophet, *sama*ʿ is based on poems of the Sufi shaykhs. Popular Sufi shaykhs in Morocco include al-Imam al-Harraq, Ibn al-Farid, Abu al-Hassan al-Shustari, Abd al-Ghani an-Nabulsy and Ibn al-Arabi (Waugh 2005).
32. Some research participants told me that the song itself has older roots than its performance by Nass El Ghiwane, yet none of those people could tell who sang it first.
33. The group plays a diverse selection of traditional instruments in untraditional combinations, including the *sentir*, a gut-stringed bass lute, banjo, kettledrums, frame drums, tambourines and cymbals.
34. Nass El Ghiwane are still very popular not only in Morocco but also among second- and third-generation descendants of Moroccans in Europe.
35. *Madīḥ* songs often end with a prayer such as 'O God, have mercy on us!'.
36. The new Moroccan pop music culture emerged during a period of intense political and social unrest (1956–73), in which the political stage was dominated by a confrontation between the king and the nationalist movement (Istiqlal). Following two military coups (in 1971 and 1972), the state censored all kinds of cultural production and political oppression in a period known as the Years of Lead (Miller 2013).
37. The music of Nass El Ghiwane and other bands was monitored by the state and was thought to be a vehicle for shaping opinions dangerous for the political establishment (Aadnani 2006).

10

THE PILGRIMAGE OF THE CAT AND OTHER HAJJ STORIES: PERFORMING PIETY AND MORAL TRANSFORMATION THROUGH STORYTELLING

So relate the story; perchance they may reflect.

(Qur'an 7, 176)

Introduction

Yusra and her mother Najla were delighted that Souad, Yusra's grandmother, had come to Mohammedia from Meknes a few weeks in advance of *ʿīd l-kbīr*, which she liked to spend with her daughter's family. The three women and I gathered in the kitchen to prepare lunch. Yusra put a kettle on, opened the fridge and took out a large bag of fresh mint to make Moroccan tea. Next to her stood her mother, stirring a steaming pot of chicken stew on the stove. On a small chair, I sat next to Yusra's grandmother, Souad, facing a small cooker, comprising a single gas tank and burner placed on the floor. Souad first placed a large eggplant directly in the flame and waited for a while before turning it to the other side. Skinned, the roasted eggplant, together with similarly skinned tomatoes, bell peppers and spices, were necessary to make *zaʿlūk*, a popular Moroccan side dish. By the side of the only kitchen window, a small radio was placed on a wooden table. The sound of Moroccan songs was reaching us, yet not distracting us from our conversation.

Souad was telling us a story about her neighbour when the radio podcast stopped for an announcement break. From the radio, we heard a familiar chant: '*Labbayka Allahumma labbayk; labbayka lā sharīka laka, labbayk . . .*' Well-known to the four of us, the *talbiya* is the prayer invoked by pilgrims as an expression of their determination to perform the Hajj. We stopped our conversation to hear what came next: 'Dear pilgrims', a female voice announced, and it continued: 'if your first destination is Mecca, remember to carry your *iḥrām* on the airplane with you . . . And make sure you follow the instructions of the Ministry of Religious Affairs regarding pilgrimage ritual.' The voice faded into the *talbiya* again, indicating the end of the message. This announcement was around thirty seconds long, after which Moroccan songs continued. Commenting on the announcement, Souad said:

> My father used to tell us about his grandfather, who, wanting to go to Mecca, walked on his feet all the way from Morocco . . . When he returned, he had so many stories to tell about people he met on the way; daily jobs he had to do to make money and feed himself, and stories of those he met in Mecca. It took him about a year to reach Mecca . . . I learned a lot from my father through these stories . . .

Upon hearing her mother's comment, Najla turned to us and assured us that she too had heard many pilgrimage stories from her own parents. She told her mother: 'Yes! Tell the girls the story my dad told us.' 'Which one?', the mother asked. Najla answered: 'The one about the man who never went to Hajj . . . It was one of my favourites!' The older woman placed another eggplant on the fire in front of her, and began the storytelling . . .[1]

Storytelling about the Hajj is the main theme of this chapter, a strand of enquiry prompted by many exchanges such as that with Yusra, Najla and Souad. Therefore, I look at storytelling practices in Morocco as a widespread activity, including the genres of family anecdote, folktale and historical account, focusing particularly on stories with the pilgrimage theme which I encountered in the context of Moroccan everyday life. Some of these stories were narratives of individual experiences that related to the pilgrimage. Others were tales orally transmitted from one generation to the next as folk tales, whilst a third group of stories were shared electronically, either on social media platforms or through mobile communication applications like WhatsApp. By reflecting on stories of pilgrimage, both personal stories and fables I was told during my fieldwork, I will show that sharing stories in Morocco is a communicative strategy for illustrating Muslim identities, discussing morality and re-affirming the narrator's commitment to Muslim piety. I will show also how the telling of effective, relevant stories becomes a vital attribute of influential social practice. The stories people tell offer insights into how they make sense of themselves and their social world. Stories, in this view, are not only narratives that people tell, but also things people live (Polletta et al. 2011). Sometimes, the stories reveal a common wisdom that questions the elevated ambience surrounding pilgrims, and at other times these stories reflect on historical and personal events. However, all are laced with moral messages, such as the call to the way of God, or guiding people towards being more compassionate towards others, with the eventual aim of showing them the light, enabling them to believe in God and submitting to Him. I shall show how sometimes particular tales and stories are repeated in more than one version, and argue that this is the case because they have a bearing, as a whole or in part, on the context and the message the narrator wants to transmit.

The entire Moroccan tradition of storytelling is too rich to describe for the purpose of the argument put forward in this chapter. My focus, therefore, is on three specific stories which I will examine after briefly discussing traditions of storytelling, past and present, in Morocco in relation to the promulgation of a particular morality as my theoretical point of departure.

Storytelling: A Historic Means of Discussing Shared Morals, Attitudes and Values

My point of departure in the analysis of storytelling is the power of *lkelma/awal* (the oral word in Moroccan Arabic and Berber, respectively), which is evident in many deep aspects of Moroccan culture (Sadiqi 2003). Storytelling in Morocco was, up to relatively recent times, based almost exclusively on the oral medium, similar to other forms of knowledge transmission which are still dominant, as opposed to the written.[2] Storytelling is a powerful force in the lives, experiences and identities of people across the globe where legends, myths, epic folk tales and sagas are told, and Morocco is no exception (Rahmouni 2015; Hamilton 2011). Historical accounts of Morocco refer to the oral traditions of storytelling, including *al-ḥalqa*, a gathering in a circle where people gather around storytellers who narrate their tales in market squares, as public entertainment that extends back to the ninth century (Amine and Carlson 2008, 72) and probably well before, taking the pre-existing Amazigh culture into consideration (Hamilton 2011). In the seventeenth century, the theologian El Hassan Al Youssi documented his encounter on arriving in Marrakech in 1650 (1060 in the hijri calendar), where he listened to comic stories told in public in the major square of the city. Al Youssi recognised the tales as a means of teaching religious doctrine and disseminating local customs and traditions. In Morocco, as in other places, storytelling is a necessary framework for discussing the past, and at times it can become a palpable foundation for understanding the present (Rahmouni 2015). Narratives assume a special importance as a conduit for the communal reception of information and values which are not necessarily conveyed in written form. Therefore, in present-day Moroccan society, the oral word still holds sway and has authority in personal narratives.

The oral tradition in Morocco is one that infuses daily life and is still strong, from the tradition of *al-ḥalqa*, to casual accounts shared at breakfast tables or around evening mint tea in family gatherings, to daily conversations among people who meet for the first time on a train or in a taxi. The enjoyment of stories and in the spoken word was very noticeable everywhere I went in Morocco. I listened to accounts of the country's historical figures, the arrival of Islam, colonisation and resistance, the hundreds of saints, and much more. Some stories covered personal events, while others were transmitted by parents or grandparents, collective narratives, or repositories of cultural traditional folklore, that have been passed down the generations. These stories, when not connected to the current daily lives of narrators or their audience, are selected, organised and evaluated for certain occasions and events. Among these stories, the Hajj was present both as a thematic backdrop and as a subject of discussion.

In *The Politics of Storytelling* (2002), Michael Jackson defines storytelling as a 'coping strategy that involves making words stand for the world, and then, by manipulating them, changing one's experience of the world' (Jackson 2002, 18). This hints at a different function of the narrative: a transformative, operational function. Stories do not simply transmit a stream of events, but the narrator can actively manipulate the narrative content, structure and style in such a way as to superimpose upon it a view of the world, or indeed, as Jackson says, to change one's perception of that world. In the following, I first present each of the three pilgrimage stories and describe the setting in which they were told, and then discuss their significance for both the narrators and listeners, recognising Abu-Lughod's reminder that 'a story is always situated; it has both a teller and an audience' (Abu-Lughod 1993, 15).

The Hajj of Fadila and her Husband

Al-ḥājj Yousef had been working in a government office for administration of pilgrimage affairs for around twenty years. During those years he had had many encounters with pilgrims. One of the stories that he shared with me one afternoon, as we were discussing his work, was the story of Fadila. One reason for Yousef's sharing of this story was his insistence that a person's ability to perform the Hajj is linked with fate and destiny. What follows is my translation of Yousef's story:

> It was three months before the Hajj season of 2007. There was a woman who came to my office to ask for a favour. The woman, who had previously registered for Hajj along with her husband, and had been successfully selected in the *qur'a*, and had paid the expenses of Hajj, wanted to cancel her journey to Mecca. 'Why?', I asked her. I wanted to understand. The woman said: 'My husband has had an accident, a car accident. He was taken to hospital, and he is in a critical condition . . . Doctors say that he has many broken bones and they do not even know if he will ever wake up! I do not think we can go to Hajj!'
>
> I was going on Hajj in 2007 too; I was excited and eagerly awaiting the experience. I told her that to give up their right to a Hajj visa, they would have to fill in an application and, upon its approval, she could reclaim her money. I also, however, told her to wait. 'Who knows, let's hope your husband will get better', I told her.
>
> The woman agreed to wait and left. Three weeks later she showed up in my office again. She had a large file that contained her husband's medical report, signed by five doctors who were responsible for his treatment. The report stated that the man had fallen into a coma following the accident and would need several months to recover. I asked the woman again: 'Are you sure you want to do this? Do you need the money for your husband's treatment?' The woman said that her husband had enough funds to cover his treatment. 'If you do not need the money', I told her, 'then wait some more!' The woman looked reluctant, but she just nodded her head in agreement and left.

It was two weeks later that she returned to my office, this time with her daughter. She said that her husband was still in a coma and that she had little hope that he would recover. The daughter asked why I was against her mother's decision. I told her that I hoped they would wait because if they withdrew their Hajj registration, they would lose their opportunity to perform Hajj that year. I told her: 'I cannot take off the name of someone who was selected for Hajj. It feels wrong to do so! I do not want to be a reason for their failure to perform Hajj that year.' The daughter said that she understood my point and asked her mother to wait a few more days.

It was the third of December 2007 when the woman came to my office again, together with her daughter. I was worried; I thought to myself, she must have come to ask me to withdraw her registration and claim her money back again. I was worried that she carried sad news about her husband; May God have mercy on him, I thought to myself.

Without introduction, she said: 'We will go on Hajj!' On 27 November, just one week earlier, her husband had woken up. He stood on his feet five days later and the doctors said that his bones were healed. 'It was miraculous', she said, and told me that her husband insisted on going on Hajj.

On the day of travel, we travelled on the same plane. The man who had had the accident stayed in the same hotel, and in Minā he was in the same tent with me. He completed the ritual of the Hajj and we returned to Morocco on Friday, 11 January 2008.

On Thursday I went to work, when, in the afternoon, the wife of the man and his daughter came to my office. I welcomed them with

> *'Allah yataqabbal'* [May Allah accept your Hajj]. I noticed that the woman was wearing a white *jellaba*, normally worn either by women going on Hajj or by widows. She said: 'May God have mercy on him; he passed away.'
>
> I remember that we returned on the same flight on 11 January, and on Monday the fourteenth day of the same month he died in his house. It was for a *ḥikma* [reason] that only God knows.[3] It was his destiny to perform the Hajj, return home and then die . . . Before he went on Hajj, five doctors had said that he would not be able to stand before the season of the Hajj and would not be able to perform the ritual but with the will of God he was able to stand, go on Hajj, perform it and return to his house where he died . . . for a *ḥikma* that only God knows . . .

The Pilgrimage of the Cobbler

In the kitchen with Najla, Yusra and Souad, mentioned in the introductory vignette, the conversation continued with the grandmother commenting on present-day Hajj procedures. She remarked that even though Hajj was accessible for people who did not need visas, for example, it was still challenging, as it involved inherent difficulties and required significant preparation. She noted that although travel itself may have become easier, pilgrims still encounter problems associated with the modern management of the Hajj (see Chapters Two and Six). She said that when she was a child, her father had told her a story about a man who always prayed to go on Hajj but was never able to make the journey. The following is the oral narrative of the story of the cobbler, in my translation:

> A long time ago, a cobbler lived in a small village with his family. For thirty years the cobbler lived in the hope of performing the Hajj. 'This year I have saved enough to go for Hajj', he told himself. He bought his *iḥrām* and got ready to leave for Mecca. Before leaving, he went to the local market to buy his family a sheep to be slaughtered on the day of *ʿīd*. On his way back, the sheep entered a wrong house; it was the house of his neighbour. He knocked on the door to ask for his sheep, but an excited little girl came out and thanked him for his gift. Looking inside the house, he saw the sheep and three other young girls gathering around it. The house was almost empty

apart from an old carpet where the girls sat. The girl's mother came out and apologised for her daughter's excitement. The man learned that the family had been without food for three days and the hungry girls were happy to see the sheep.

Surprised by the neighbour's acute poverty and their hunger, the man's heart bled, and he shed compassionate tears. He went home, took the three hundred dirhams he had saved for the Hajj pilgrimage, and gave the poor widow the money.

All the same, the man still desired to go on Hajj and prayed for God to accept his deed.

Days and months passed, and it was time for those who had left for Hajj to return home. After the pilgrimage season was over, the cobbler joined the people of the village to welcome the pilgrims. Those who had already returned from the Hajj approached him saying, *Hajj mabrūr in-shā'Allah!* [May God accept your pilgrimage].

The man was surprised and did not understand. One of the returning pilgrims told him that when they were performing their *ṭawāf* in Mecca, they had seen him there. They had seen him circling the Ka'ba with other pilgrims. Even though the cobbler told them he had never been on Hajj, the pilgrims swore that, with their own eyes, they had seen him there, in Mecca.

The Pilgrimage of the Cat

In addition to the story of the cobbler, narrated by Souad, Najla related a second story, which fits into the tradition of fable, in which anthropomorphism ascribes to the animal kingdom the attributes, including the speech and moral values, of the human world. It is worth including, as it contains another lesson, different from that of the story of the cobbler. My translation:

> There once was a cat that went on pilgrimage to Mecca. The cat was known as a troublemaker, chasing and hunting mice. When he returned from the Hajj, the mice thought he had changed to be better-mannered. Since tradition demands welcoming the safe return of pilgrims, the leader of the mice decided to pay the cat a visit. The other mice, however, were not convinced. 'That cat is our enemy; how can we trust him?' they asked. The leader mouse explained: 'Now that he has been to Mecca, and become an *al-ḥājj* cat, he is no longer free to do what he used to do in the past. These days, he prays and does virtuous deeds.'
>
> The other mice were not persuaded. 'You go and see him, and check if he has changed', they said. 'We will wait for you here and hear what you say upon your return.'
>
> The leader mouse set out for the home of the cat. When he reached it, he entered through a crack in the wall. When he poked his head out the other side and looked round, he saw the cat sitting on a mat, murmuring prayers and glorifying his Maker.
>
> The mouse decided that the cat had really changed his ways and moved confidently towards it with customary greetings. But as soon as the cat caught sight of the mouse, he bounded towards the latter and chased him!

After he had run back to his fellow mice, they asked him: 'How is the cat after his Hajj?'

'Never mind the Hajj', said the leader of the mice: 'He may have performed the Hajj, but he still pounces like his old self, a cat!'

The Three Stories: Themes and Discussions

The three Hajj stories just presented reflect on moral themes that relate to everyday situations. One of the moral themes discussed in the stories is the role of pre-ordained fate, a sense of the hand of God working behind life's random events, transforming or shaping what happens into a pattern which is beyond human understanding.[4] On the surface of it, the story told by *al-ḥājj* Yousef about Fadila's husband, who recovered from an accident just in time to perform Hajj and died upon return, is of a different nature from the other stories. The other stories were told to me in the form of hearsay, an example of collectively shared popular stories.

Several factors made the story of Fadila important for *al-ḥājj* Yousef on an individual level. *Al-ḥājj* Yousef met the woman and knew the story of her husband and felt responsible for their Hajj performance. In his words:

> I did not want to be a reason for them not going on Hajj . . . If they withdrew their registration, that meant they would miss the Hajj . . . I never wanted to be a reason to stop anyone from going on Hajj . . .

The experiences of *al-ḥājj* that Yousef had had through his work, and the stories of the pilgrims he had dealt with, were crucial factors in his own development of piety. Through them, he reflected on the virtue of patience and 'trusting God's will'. He described how the stories of pilgrims had taught him to think about the wisdom underlying life's occurrences and the reason behind certain events in one's life:

> The story of Fadila and her husband made me realise that there was a reason behind it that only God knew; there was the explanation in the story . . . Five doctors said that the man would not be able to stand on his feet, not even perform Hajj . . . He, however, stood, travelled to Mecca, performed the rituals, and returned home . . . God's wisdom was behind these events . . .

Another variant on this interpretation was suggested in *al-ḥājj* Yousef's story of Fadila when he shared it with one of his male colleagues, Hamza, who agreed with the stance regarding *al-ḥājj* that Yousef adopted towards Fadila. Addressing his colleague, Hamza said:

> You might have had a feeling that the man would get better in time to be able to perform the Hajj . . . It is a great responsibility to oversee taking such a decision . . . You had to take a moral stance to help the woman . . .

Indeed, for the two men, the action of *al-ḥājj* Yousef originated from a moral responsibility both as a Muslim and as an official responsible for the Hajj application process. Thus, in addition to being motivated by deep faith in God's plan, *al-ḥājj* Yousef felt a religious and professional moral imperative to try to enable prospective pilgrims to complete the Hajj. Even if the obstacles seemed insurmountable, his duty was to facilitate the Hajj.

Just as the story of Fadila did for *al-ḥājj* Yousef, the story of the cobbler held much meaning for Najla. She told me that she had heard it from her father, who in turn had heard it from his parents: it is thus a transgenerational narrative. According to the grandmother, the cobbler was a poor man, who could not afford to perform the pilgrimage to Mecca. He saved money for a long time, but when he was finally able to pay for his travel expenses he faced the dilemma of opting for the Hajj or helping his needy widow neighbour. That he chose to do the latter was an indication in the eyes of Souad of the importance of performing honourable deeds for one's family, neighbours and community that will be judged and rewarded by God, who in the story granted the cobbler the Hajj without him travelling from Morocco to Mecca to perform the ritual.

This narrative contains elements of magical realism which evoke other traditional tales, across all cultures, in which virtue is rewarded in a sometimes mysterious, superhuman manner. Then, it is a morality tale, conveying the idea that virtuous deeds will be seen by the Almighty and rewarded. It serves the social and religious function of underscoring the central tenets of faith, including charity and morality. Although the theme of the story is related to the pilgrimage to Mecca, for Souad it was the question of ethics, in Arabic *akhlāq*, that was significant in the story. According to Souad, a Muslim's duties towards God, such as the daily prayers, fasting in Ramadan and performing the pilgrimage to Mecca, may be overruled by the duty of being good to other people, including family members and neighbours. Souad explained the story's message as follows:

> The right actions towards God are not limited to performing rituals, but ensuring that one's actions are done in a way that maintains virtues at their optimum level . . . The man in the story found that helping a destitute neighbour in tough times is important, so decided to give to the poor . . . God is Merciful and showers His sublime mercy on those of his creatures who show compassion to others and solve the problems of others, as the cobbler had done . . .

Following the theme of the story, Souad considered faith and moral behaviour as two sides of the same coin. The story about the cobbler touched on an ethical question that I observed being discussed on many occasions: what is more important – fulfilling one's ritual religious duty to perform Hajj, or fulfilling one's moral religious duty to help one's neighbour? Najla, for example, was critical of both Moroccans who borrow money to be able to perform the Hajj and those who would go to Mecca several times whilst others around them are in financial need. For her, performing the pilgrimage is not an obligation for those who cannot financially afford its expenses. In her opinion:

> The cobbler in the story did not go to Mecca but God rewarded him for being good to his neighbour . . . [The Prophet] ordered people to help each other; people should take the money of Hajj and give it to the poor . . . To me, people should make the Hajj here, not go on Hajj in Mecca.

Najla insisted that there are many ways people can earn God's mercy and forgiveness. She asserted that the answer would be 'helping students, poorer Moroccans in general or helping the less advantaged such as the people of Syria and Iraq'. She asserted that with the money millions of pilgrims pay every year, the treasuries of the Saudi government are already overflowing, and this money would be better used to help those in need.

Telling the cobbler's story can be seen as part of Souad's positioning, revealing key aspects of the narrator's social contexts. Due to Souad's financial inability to perform the Hajj, she used the story of the cobbler to reflect on her view about prioritising other religious duties above the Hajj. This could be seen as a consolatory narrative for her, assuaging her inability to perform the Hajj, or asserting a more nuanced moral debate regarding competing religious imperatives.

It has been said that a story must be heard to exist, and only acquires meaning through narration and reception (Jackson 2002). However, it could be argued that modern technologies and social media allow many Moroccans to share stories of the pilgrimage without the need of face-to-face oral transmission. During my fieldwork, several interlocutors shared stories about the Hajj via WhatsApp and Facebook. Lubna, one of my interlocutors, shared via WhatsApp the story of Saed, a man who helped a poor patient at a private hospital where he worked by giving away his Hajj savings and was later rewarded with a free Hajj with a rich patient who needed a companion. Lubna claimed that the story is one of real people. As a reader, I was led to wonder whether the story of Saed might be an appropriated and modified version of other tales, like that of the cobbler, since the moral message in the two stories is similar. Regardless of whether they are rooted in verifiable facts or are more apocryphal creations, in integrating the importance of pilgrimage with charitable giving in the local imagination, the stories are laden with moral messages and serve to reinforce and perpetuate the central beliefs and values of those who tell, re-tell and absorb them with great eagerness.

For Lubna, and other interlocutors, digital spaces made it possible to share religiously-themed stories and discuss their meaning within a Muslim perspective (Al-Ajarma and Buitelaar 2022; Rozehnal 2022). When receiving a story via WhatsApp, she has the option of only reading it, or sharing it with friends. In doing so, she exercises a degree of moral and religious authority, determining what messages to share as a tool of mobilisation (Ammerman 2013, 7–10).

The shared stories influenced the listeners or readers and allowed them to reflect on their themes and messages (Alimi 2018; Powers 2010). For example, when I retold the story of the cat's pilgrimage to Fatiha, who hosted me in Safi, she told me that she was hearing the story for the first time.[5] Nonetheless, she asserted that 'it is correct that everyone wishes to be called *al-ḥājj* without the internal abandonment of wrong habits and corrupt morals'.[6] There is no doubt that Hajj confers social kudos on those who complete it, signalled via the honorific naming but also having more widespread effects on a person's standing in the community. However, simultaneously, Muslims are aware that surface attributes and signals of piety are no guarantee of deep spiritual commitment. The story of the cat, for Fatiha as for Najla, underscores the idea that spiritual transformation of the Hajj can only be achieved through genuine personal effort and committed religious practice; the mere fact of making a pilgrimage will not change a person in and of itself. In Chapter Four, I showed how Moroccans reflected on the impossibility of complete change in the lives of pilgrims as their everyday lives are marked by imperfection, uncertainty and moral failure (Beekers and Kloos 2017; Schielke 2015; 2009). In life, as in the story of the cat who went on Hajj, many people return to their old habits following the pilgrimage.[7]

Hajj Narratives as they Relate to Lived Experiences

The previously discussed act of telling and sharing stories reflects real-life issues that the narrators, or sometimes their listeners, must deal with. For example, the personal story that *al-ḥājj* Yousef shared reflected aspects of his work with pilgrims and the struggles that prospective pilgrims may go through before they are able to go on Hajj. When I visited *al-ḥājj* Yousef's office, several residents came in to ask about the Hajj procedure or to express concerns about not being able to perform the Hajj due to the long process.[8] It is reassuring and comforting in such cases to hear stories like that of Fadila. By sharing these stories, *al-ḥājj* Yousef was projecting a sense of his own satisfaction in his job as facilitator of the Hajj process for people in his constituency. He derived both professional satisfaction and religious reward, or *ajr*, through his ability to assist future pilgrims by facilitating their application and preparation process before the Hajj.

Najla and Souad touched upon the idea of God's reward from a unique perspective; they emphasised that it is not restricted to performing the Hajj or fulfilling one's other religious obligations only. In her study of Ramadan in Morocco, Marjo Buitelaar describes the ways women can gain *ajr* during Ramadan in particular: visiting mosques and graves, praying, giving alms, distributing food to the poor, painting others' hands and feet with henna (1993, 120).[9] Although these acts are (merely) recommended rather than obligatory as is the case with the Hajj, Souad, found in the story a way of expressing her evaluation of the performance of Hajj relative to wider charitable behaviour. The story Souad narrated helped her (and her daughter) to come to terms with not having been able to perform the Hajj by offering an alternative source of religious reward and personal satisfaction.

Najla went as far as forwarding an alternative spiritual route to Hajj by advocating the performance of virtuous deeds for people in need as another type of Hajj, what she referred to as 'Hajj *in* Morocco'. However, as I have already discussed in Chapter Seven, when Najla's husband expressed his wish to perform the Hajj, Najla was the one to register his name for the national Hajj lottery and supported his travel to Mecca. She offered some of her savings from her teaching job, and borrowed money from her sister to help her husband pay the pilgrimage fees.[10] Thus there existed two distinct forces for Najla, pulling in different directions: Hajj as the performance of charity at home versus the doctrinal Hajj in Mecca. These irreconcilable positions illustrate how we tend to resolve an impossible dilemma, in this case the inability to go on Hajj to Mecca, by adopting a consolatory narrative which suggests an equally valid alternative.

Even though she helped her husband to fulfil his wish to perform the Hajj, sacrificing her own ambitions because of deference to or love for her husband, Najla nevertheless continued to maintain a parallel attitude, preferring almsgiving and other kinds of charity to spending tens of thousands of dirhams to go on Hajj. What she learned from the story of the cobbler is that a person does not need to travel to Mecca to gain God's mercy and acceptance as a pilgrim. If a person is a good Muslim, a charitable neighbour, and performs virtuous deeds, God will reward them and accept them as pilgrims without them making pilgrimage to Mecca. In her words:

> The Hajj can be done here *in Morocco* . . . Someone who wants to do the pilgrimage can give the money to a poor student who wants to study . . . Or give the money of the Hajj to a person who needs to have surgery . . . God would reward those people, just as He rewarded the cobbler.

Both charitable giving and Hajj are fundamental obligations prescribed for Muslims, but if she could manage only one of the two, Najla would choose the former.[11] Najla considered *ṣadaqa* (benevolence or charity) to be an integral part of Muslim religiosity. She insisted that, in the same way that Hajj is a religious duty, charitable acts are likewise a sign of religious devotion and care of the poor and needy in society. Najla's husband, nonetheless, did not share the opinion of his wife and mother-in-law regarding pilgrimage *in* Morocco. For him, every Muslim longs to perform the Hajj, much as he himself did before going to Mecca. He pointed out that eventually, God rewarded the cobbler by accepting his wish to fulfil his obligation of Hajj performance, even though he had not actually travelled to Mecca. These differences of approach and attitude to religious duty within the same close family – and even within the minds of individuals – represent the balancing of competing priorities and religious imperatives within a pragmatic context of costs, opportunities and alternative options.

Souad offers a different case, as she lives alone in the city of Meknes, apart from the times she travels to visit her children, as was the case when I met her. At the age of 85, she knows that her opportunities to perform the pilgrimage are extremely limited. She can afford to perform the pilgrimage neither physically nor financially. Although she is strong for her age, if she ever decided to perform the Hajj she would need a companion to look after her. The story of the cobbler can be seen as a way of responding to her social situation and her related psychological needs (Linde 1993; Counted and Zock 2019). Indeed, Souad seemed to have found attachment in the story about the cobbler and consolation for her own inability to perform the Hajj herself.

Listening to how stories like the ones under discussion here were narrated, I noted that often they are jointly constructed. The listener tended to play a subtly active role, encouraging and prompting the narrator, and – most crucially – endorsing the moral code at the end. It seemed that a religious blessing, a saying carrying approbation, support and deep appreciation, is often the rejoinder that finalises the narrative. In a sense, the community reception of the tale's thematic concerns is prefigured in the listener's individual reactions. The very act of telling a religiously themed story to a specific listener also rests on a set of assumptions regarding shared values. Such an assumption, that the listener and narrator share a moral framework of reference, licenses the latter to expand the story fully. Also, short interjections during the story, questions, exclamations or other supportive comments encourage the narrator to continue. Without the assumed commonality of reference points and the supportive attitude of the listener, narratives would lose a considerable amount of their power and narrators would be inhibited in their narrations.

Why, then, do people share Hajj narratives? There are many motives: to inspire others, to underscore a spiritual message, to emphasise the benevolence of God and to seek to resolve the tensions between competing Islamic imperatives. Additionally, there is the consolatory motive for those for whom the Hajj is out of reach.

My own interpretation of the overriding message is that the stories are affirmative of core Islamic principles and virtues, reinforcing community values. Suggesting that there are more ways of obtaining *ajr* than Hajj performance, these stories influence people's decisions and suggest that by helping a person in need, rather than thinking of one's individual desire to perform Hajj, one can achieve a greater reward. In such a reading, such an outcome is due to the benevolence of an all-seeing God who accepts the self-sacrifice of forgoing the Hajj made by the devout would-be pilgrim who, seeing the needs of fellow Muslims, chooses to priorities these above their own individual spiritual ambition.

Conclusion

In this chapter on pilgrimage-themed storytelling practices in Morocco, I have shown that the Hajj and stories about the Hajj are deeply integrated into practices of faith in the daily lives of people. Three stories were presented. The first was a personal experience that I heard about from a local employee concerning a sick man who was able to perform Hajj before his death. The second was associated with a cobbler, a pious man who through his exceptional piety achieved the faculty of translocating in his body to Mecca, where his fellow countryman saw him performing the pilgrimage with them. This narrative was followed by a third fable, which presented a core message about people's true nature not changing because of going or not going on Hajj, the fable of the cat. I looked at the position of the characters in the stories, the stories' themes, and the position of the storytellers.

For most Muslims, the performance of the Hajj represents a powerful experience of spiritual transformation. It is therefore not surprising that it is a regular topic of conversation among Moroccans. One of the functions and purposes of these stories is to provide guidance and moral lessons related not only to the pilgrimage but also to how Muslims should behave in their everyday lives. In the story of the cobbler, for example, the moral of the story is to help one's neighbours and to give to those less fortunate, even if that giving comes at the expense of a dear wish, such as making the pilgrimage to Mecca. In the same story, one sees how the pilgrimage to Mecca was, in a mystical, magical manner, given as a reward to the cobbler upon his performing a charitable act.

Another function of the Hajj stories is the offering of exemplary acts which function as a model for the good life. The purpose of telling those stories was – as many Moroccans explained – to give the audience the opportunity to assess their position with regard to different matters and to correct their actions and behaviours. Further, the telling of the stories is not an act carried out in isolation, but is very much part of an interactive, socially dynamic construction of community and the re-affirmation of shared values. The content of these stories involves an embodiment of active religious values and negotiation of the tensions between religious and mundane life. Thus, from the fable of the cat, and magical realism and mystical events in the cobbler's story, to grittily realistic shared stories, the urge to tell stories which embody, discuss and present religious values and competing imperatives is a profound one, as is amply illustrated in my experience of Moroccan narratives.

Notes

1. Fieldnotes, 4 September 2015.
2. Statistics from the 2014 census showed that the illiteracy rate was 32 per cent of the population (High Commission for Planning 2015). This means that a significant number of Moroccans are not fully comfortable with the written word, and the spoken narrative continues to assume a far greater social importance than in societies with a long tradition of large-scale literacy.
3. *Ḥikma* refers to reason, wisdom or philosophy.
4. Muslims use different expressions when talking about fate, including *qadar* or *qaḍā' wa qadar*, meaning the decree of God or predetermination (Gardet 2012), and *qisma* or *naṣīb*, meaning share (or 'one's share in life') and destiny (Bosworth, 2012). Moroccans mainly use *qadar*, meaning destiny, *al-miktāb*, meaning 'what has been written [by God]' and *qaddar-Allāh*, meaning 'God so determined'. They also use the expression '*qaddara Allāh wa mā-shā'a fa'al*', meaning 'God

so determined and did as He willed', which is derived from hadith (Muslim, book 1, hadith 100), and *'al-miktāb mā minnu hurūb'*, meaning 'destiny cannot be escaped'.

5. See Chapter Eight.
6. Although they are not known to many Moroccans besides Najla's family, I have also heard versions of the fable of the cat who went on Hajj in Palestine, Jordan and Tunisia.
7. For more information on change in pilgrims following the Hajj, see Chapter Four.
8. See Chapter Two for particulars of the pilgrimage application process in Morocco.
9. In Arabic, *ajr* (pl. *ujūr*) means 'wages, pay, honorarium, price, rate, or fee'. For additional ethnographic accounts which discuss *ajr* see Buitelaar (1993) and Benthall (2012).
10. For more information about Najla's role in her husband's pilgrimage, see Chapter Seven.
11. For further analysis of charity in Islam see, among others, Bensaid and Grine (2013); Bonner (2003); Ibrahim and Sherif (2008).

CONCLUSION
MECCA IN MOROCCO: MANIFESTATIONS OF THE HAJJ IN MOROCCAN EVERYDAY LIFE

During five specific days of the year, around thirty-two thousand Moroccans join at least two million Muslim men and women from over one hundred different countries in Mecca for the Hajj. At other times of the year, tens of thousands of Moroccans also visit Mecca to perform the *'umra*, the non-mandatory pilgrimage. Leaving their country, family and friends, Moroccan pilgrims embark on the journey to Mecca where they perform the ritual of the Hajj, mixing with Muslims from other countries and with pilgrims whose nationalities, languages and traditions might be foreign to them. For the duration of the Hajj season, the pilgrims are physically separated from their daily routines in Morocco. Throughout this research, my central argument has been that, although the Hajj removes Moroccans from their everyday lives with its rhythms and customs, nevertheless the distinctive Hajj practices – experiences as well as the meanings that pilgrims attach to the Hajj – are shaped by, and in return shape, their daily life-worlds.

Approaching pilgrimage from the perspective of 'lived religion', this book is informed by the overarching question: how does Hajj pilgrimage feature in the everyday lives of Moroccans, and how are Moroccan views of Hajj reflected in the micro-practices of pilgrims and their wider networks? To answer this overarching research question, I spent three Hajj seasons and a total of eighteen months in Morocco between the summer of 2015 and the winter of 2017. I participated in the daily lives of Moroccans across the full spectrum of life's rich tapestry: I observed their actions, listened to their stories and interacted with them in their homes, and in their places of work and of leisure. I joined pilgrims during their daily chores, on their shopping trips, and at weddings and birthday celebrations. I followed the pilgrimage application process, and the preparations pilgrims took before embarking on their Hajj journey. I accompanied families as they said farewell to departing pilgrims at the airport and as they welcomed them on their return. My conversations were many and varied on all these occasions, and I discussed at length people's experiences in Mecca and the rich ramifications of the pilgrimage. Thus, I have witnessed the intertwining of rituals and social practices that took place every day, paying particular attention to the activities and topics of conversation around the season of the Hajj.

The structure I chose for this study in a sense echoes the conclusions I have reached about the significance of the Hajj in Morocco: the Hajj experience is a logistical and concrete one, occupying a discrete period of time, yet its lasting ramifications move outwards into ever-widening circles, getting entangled in both the religious and mundane life of the pilgrims before they go on Hajj and after they return home. Similarly, my study begins by documenting the practicalities of preparation and the actual rituals and practices of the Hajj. In this part I also examined the pilgrims' varied experiences and encounters with other pilgrims, and the concept of the *umma*, as well as various aspects of homecoming.

In the three chapters that followed, I examined the wider political domain of Morocco and considered the Hajj as a channel for the expression of political and personal identification with the homeland. Despite the experience of the *umma*, the wider Muslim community which Moroccans experience during the pilgrimage and which they highly esteem, providing them with a sense of belonging, I demonstrated that an awareness of national identity within this wider grouping also occurs. In Chapter Five, for example, I explored the impact of forces external to the pilgrims, such as the state and the media, on this process of identification. I also discussed, in Chapter Six, the impact of the Saudi government's control over the Hajj, the modernisation and commercialisation taking place in Mecca and the way in which Saudi economic power and political orientation impact on the religious experience of the Hajj. In this same part, Chapter Seven discussed gender politics, examining the specific ways in which being a woman informed the Hajj experience. I was interested in the limitations placed on women as aspirant and actual pilgrims, as well as the opportunities offered to women by the Hajj in terms of enhancing social prestige and status; significantly, I explored the intersection of class and gender, showing how the benefits of being a female pilgrim are not automatically conferred on a woman of lower social status.

For the third and final ethnographic part of this book, Chapter Eight to Ten, the focus shifted from pilgrims themselves to the cultural and social embeddedness of the Hajj in domains of Moroccan everyday life. Here, I explored three specific local social and cultural practices, each with its own special connection to the Hajj. In Chapter Eight, I discussed 'the Pilgrimage of the Poor', a practice rooted in religious observation, but nevertheless contested by many in Morocco, who remain unconvinced of its authenticity. I showed how, for many people who cannot afford the pilgrimage to Mecca, the local alternative of the Pilgrimage of the Poor was a technique enabling them to connect with the pilgrimage happening simultaneously in Mecca, in addition to discussing the social and political dimensions of these local pilgrimages. This topic gave insights into social structure, attitudes and values in relation both to class and religious practices. In Chapter Nine, I discussed pilgrimage songs, which people often listen to in Morocco. I reflected on the significance of these songs as reminders of the pilgrimage and the aspiration to visit Mecca, revealing how people strive to cultivate pious selves through the portrayal of Mecca as an ideal place. These songs occur in contexts that might seem mundane or distanced from the central religious experience, such as parties and celebrations, or simply in the routines of daily life. Their occurrence in these situations, however, demonstrates that the religious and mundane cannot be neatly separated but intertwine. Finally, in Chapter Ten, I discussed storytelling as an aspect of Moroccan daily life and showed how Hajj stories carry moral lessons about what is considered proper Muslim behaviour. The power of these stories lies not least in that they reflect the struggles Moroccans face and the decisions they must make in their everyday lives. Such stories reveal the depth of penetration of the Hajj into the imagination of Moroccans and serve as a re-enforcement of community values.

How, then, does this book fit within larger anthropological debates on pilgrimage, questions of personal piety and ethical formation, and the everyday lives of Muslims, and their agency? The next section outlines how my findings speak to the theoretical framework that informed the research questions posed at the beginning of the book.

Pilgrimage to Mecca as a Component within the Broader Anthropology of Pilgrimage

In the presentation of my theoretical framework at the beginning of this book, I reflected on the importance of Mecca as a pilgrimage centre. Despite the increase in interest in pilgrimage studies, attention has traditionally often focused on two dimensions of a pilgrimage: (1) the site itself, and what takes place at it and within that area; and (2) a focus on the concept of *communitas*, as outlined in Victor Turner's writings on the subject. During my research in Morocco, I found that, indeed, many people focused on experiences which from an etic point of view would broadly fall within the phenomenon of *communitas*. In Chapter Two, for example, I demonstrated how pilgrims aspire to visit Mecca, a journey some must wait several years to be able to take owing to financial and administrative constraints. Once they successfully travel to Mecca, however, as we see in Chapter Three, they express their devotion to performing the Hajj ritual and being emotionally moved by being in holy spaces and interacting with other pilgrims. While discussing their performance of the pilgrimage, Moroccans often speak of feelings of Islamic unity in the space occupied by the pilgrims, very much emphasising aspects of *communitas*.

Also, we see how Moroccans often refer to the *umma*, the Muslim community, when reflecting on performing the Hajj. For many Moroccan pilgrims, their journey to Mecca was a momentous event, being the first time they had ever left their home country, let alone a journey to the most sacred place for Muslims. To a considerable extent, therefore, my research data confirms that, although the pilgrimage to Mecca is an experience shared by differing Muslim groups, pilgrims tend to emphasise, first, that differences within Islam and among Muslims are re-synthesised into Muslim unity in Mecca. Many people who shared their stories with me also dwelled on the significance to them of experiencing difference within unity, of encountering 'otherness', having experienced the *umma* by mingling with other Muslims, and sometimes literally tasting the *umma* when trying foods that belong to people of other nationalities, all of which might fall into what Turner called *existential communitas*, spontaneous feelings of mutual communion and harmony among pilgrims (Turner 1969, 131–40).

The findings of this research, however, show that the ideal of *communitas* as expressed by Moroccan pilgrims did not always seem to be spontaneous; pilgrims are informed by their own expectations about the experience, so one can see a strong *normative* component to it. As set out in Chapter Three, people often reported expecting to experience certain feelings of mutual acceptance and recognition of unity based on the narratives of previous pilgrims, and based therefore on a shared discourse that sketches idealistic images of the pilgrimage experience. These references to unity and harmony on encountering the global Muslim community in Mecca are also propagated in strategic ways: the Moroccan polity, for example, appropriates these ideas during the pilgrimage season to embrace and promote the ideals of unity and harmony that the Hajj stands for, and advocates for similar ideals not only in Morocco but also for Moroccans in Mecca, who should act as 'ambassadors' for their country, as shown in Chapter Five.

Furthermore, the stories of my interlocutors indicate that their actual feelings were not always in line with normative expectations, sometimes causing disappointment, feelings of shame, or even anxiety. For example, pilgrims spoke about disputes, arguments, and dissatisfaction with some aspects of their pilgrimage experience. In Chapters Six and Seven, we see how pilgrims sometimes complain, argue, and challenge discrepant elevated expectations that have been pre-formed at home about the pilgrimage. An interesting point, for further future study, is how the character of the narratives of the Hajj, on which both pilgrims and their 'audiences' had to rely in the past, will change because of people's current access to modes of communication such as mobile phones and social media. Whereas in the past, during the long journey to – and return home from – Hajj, pilgrims had much time to process their experiences into narratives that resonate with ideal representations of the Hajj, today's pilgrims, by contrast, can instantly share their experiences and voice their satisfaction or dissatisfaction with those at home. More than before, therefore, Moroccan pilgrims' narratives of their pilgrimage to Mecca encompass, and speak to, more than one 'grand scheme'.

It is not surprising for such conflicted opinions to occur, as expectations and experiences differ from person to person. Over time, aspects of the physical reality of the various Hajj sites themselves have changed, even if the rites carried out there as such may have remained the same. Thus, while the main sites that the pilgrims visit, like the Kaʿba, Arafat and the tomb of the Prophet, have not changed significantly throughout the centuries, in recent years some drastic measures have been taken to modernise the Hajj and to accommodate the enormous increase in the numbers of pilgrims. Various changes have taken place, including the expansion of the mosques, the introduction of air-conditioned tents and new modes of modern transportation, and pilgrims do not physically point out a sacrificial animal any more. Therefore, we see pilgrims producing different narratives, which sometimes conflict with those of others who preceded them. While their overall narratives may be similar, the views of recent pilgrims are influenced by such alterations.

A theoretical perspective that I found particularly useful in my analysis was to approach the pilgrimage as a site of sensory experiences. In Chapter Three, I demonstrate how pilgrims' narratives concerning their pilgrimage experience are profoundly related to the senses. In addition to moving physically through space to seek contact with the sacred sites, pilgrims use touch, sight, hearing and taste to relate to these sites. Seeing the Kaʿba for the first time, which moves almost everyone to tears, touching the Kaʿba or the pillars of the mosque, drinking Zamzam water and experiencing renewed bodily health, were all moments which pilgrims described with an intensity of expression, often drawing on sensory vocabulary, to convey the overwhelming sensations experienced during the pilgrimage. The sacred and the bodily sensations which evoke emotions mingle in a complex relationship, and this is emphasised by pilgrims, who often claimed that the pilgrimage experience itself is beyond words, if not beyond comprehension.

In their pursuit of conveying what they regard as the ineffable experience of Hajj, pilgrims reach for the most readily available linguistic fields, the senses, suggesting that for many, the impact of the Hajj can best be understood through the emotions evoked by bodily experiences. The idea that the experiences of pilgrims cannot be described in words, and that one must personally go to Mecca and live the experience through the sensations, may well reflect a desire to convey authenticity, as well as the 'purity' and singularity of the experience. Being moved to tears when seeing the Kaʿba, for example, as shown in Chapter Three, seems to point to an elevated level of religiosity on the part of the narrator.

Most significantly, in looking at the Hajj as a gender-mediated experience, as in Chapter Seven for example, one can see the need to take aspects such as gender and class into consideration. Being a woman, especially a young woman, means that fewer advantages accrue in terms of the process of application, the possibility and experience of travel, and even the performance of the Hajj ritual and recognition of this by others. Other examples of contested regulations and practices relate to women's inability, due to the prohibitions placed upon them, to reach the tomb of the Prophet in Medina, which I point to in Chapter Six and in Chapter Three. This book shows, instead, that we should look at the ways in which pilgrims' experiences are diverse, unpredictable, and contingent on personal projects of ethical improvement.

Pilgrimage has always been a complex endeavour that is highly dependent on the relationship between the pilgrims' search for meaning and the environment in which they have been operating. It is not positioned exclusively at the pilgrimage site and within the ritual itself, but also is situated within, and is fashioned by, the movement of people, objects and ideas involved in pilgrimage. To contextualise, or frame, pilgrimage fully, it is essential to focus on the longer-term effects of the Hajj, once pilgrims return home, on their religious, social and political everyday lives. This is the contribution that this study aims to provide to the existing body of research.

Two strands of thought are especially relevant to my analysis. The first is the analytical primacy of moral, ethical self-formation in the construction of pious subjects within the authorised framework of a religious tradition – that is, in the cultivation of religious virtues and the pursuit of moral perfection, a concept associated especially with scholars in the tradition of Talal Asad and Saba Mahmood. The second strand of thought calls attention to the inevitability of ambivalence in a multiplex everyday life, where religious concerns exist alongside a plethora of competing priorities and 'grand schemes', a concept particularly associated with Samuli Schielke.

Ethical Self-formation away from Mecca

A key focus of my discussion is on the fact that while pilgrimage is a journey to and through sacred space, it usually also includes a journey *back or away from* that space. Following their contact with the sacred, pilgrims return home, inevitably carrying some new quality or capital – moral, spiritual or even material – as part of the pilgrimage memory and experience. This movement back and the return home itself form a ritualised process of the journey and mark, in a way, the beginning of a new journey, aspects of which are addressed in Chapter Four. Upon their return, pilgrims have a new status within their social networks, but also – if their pilgrimage is deemed to have been accepted by God – they believe that they are now free from sin and can begin or continue their lives in a more observant manner. Pilgrimage, in a way, provides an opportunity for the presumption, or the hope, that pilgrims may lead transformed lives upon their return. This fact underscores the importance of studying the lives of pilgrims not exclusively within the sphere of their contact with the sacred, but how their pilgrimage becomes a significant part of their everyday life upon return.

Pilgrims focus on the importance of talking, behaving and dealing with others in accordance with authoritative Islamic teachings about refashioning themselves as virtuous Muslims subjects (Mahmood 2005; Hirschkind 2006). Pilgrims speak of virtuous behaviour which one should maintain during the pilgrimage, and in accordance with which they should continue to live when they return home. As demonstrated in Chapter Two, they also focus on remembering God's goodness and remembering that, having answered God's call, they should always humbly recall and be grateful for the fact that God has chosen them to visit His house in Mecca. The pilgrimage itself is a rare experience for Muslims, in which they exclusively encounter fellow members of the faith community. Being able to perform the Hajj in itself, I suggest, acts to distinguish, in the minds of the pilgrims, Muslims from non-Muslims, reinforcing the geographically extensive nature of their religion and bolstering people with a sense of security in their beliefs. Physically, access to Mecca is limited to Muslims only, and those gathered to perform the pilgrimage all represent the Muslim *umma*, a fact which gives pilgrims the opportunity to share ideas but also to situate themselves, in distinctive groupings from a specific cultural background, among other Muslim communities. I show how these two contradictory impulses, to unite universally within the *umma* and yet also to distinguish one's distinctive regionality, coexist.

Being a Moroccan, then, is a highly significant marker of identity, just as being part of the *umma* is. Although pilgrims strive to visit Mecca and express their longing for the holy places, and voice this in terms of a visit to the Prophet, they nonetheless also express their longing for Morocco once they are in Mecca. In Chapter Five, we saw Muna, the *ḥājja* from Casablanca who thanked God she was Moroccan after meeting people from other nationalities in Mecca, an incongruous experience which on one level goes against the grain of the *umma*. For her, the experience made her value her national identity in a way she never experienced before going to Mecca. Does this negate the *umma* experience of unity? Or do pilgrims sense an overarching Muslim identity of *umma* manifested in regional variations, in such a way that it enables them to reassess and re-evaluate their own distinctive thread within the tapestry of the faith? The answer can be either, or both simultaneously.

One can also see the active self-formation of pilgrims in Morocco in Chapter Four, where it is illustrated in the way pilgrims strive to live up to their new title of *al-ḥājj/al-ḥājja*, honorific titles that come with special prestige, but at the same time are laden with the responsibility of being 'faithful' to the new status of someone who has visited Mecca. My study demonstrates that the spiritual transformation implied by the honorific title of *al-ḥājj/al-ḥājja* is imbued with significant social capital in Moroccan society. I have referenced the enhanced expectations associated with the title: enduring religious devotion, enhanced moral conduct, and even heightened judgement and wisdom outside the religious sphere. In Chapter Four I discuss the interior struggle some pilgrims face to realise these expectations, and the way some pilgrims use their religious title to gain social prestige. For many pilgrims, Hajj is an opportunity for spiritual and moral cultivation that helps to create a committed Muslim personality and, subsequently, to contribute to a society which is oriented towards individual and collective self-improvement.

Within the complexities of everyday life, we see how pilgrims try – sometimes successfully and at other times not – to live up to high moral standards. In this process, we see individuals constantly making and remaking themselves into what they consider to be good Muslims (Deeb and Harb 2013; Fernando 2014; Jacobsen 2011). This aspiration to be able to be good Muslims, leading a morally meaningful life, might be the reason some people delay their pilgrimage to the later years of their lives, hoping that age will naturally incline them toward greater observance.

Whilst I have tried to take seriously the inner processes through which religiosities are shaped as pilgrims strive to cultivate personal piety and ethical formation, I have not sought to focus specifically on the pursuit of pious perfection. Conversations with my interlocutors and participation in their daily activities concentrated on a variety of everyday life concerns including work, family, financial issues and social relationships, as well as people's aspirations and disappointments – simply put, their 'ordinary lives' (Schulte Nordholt and Steijlen 2007). For instance, the very fact that pilgrims want to go back to Mecca, a desire which was expressed by many Moroccans (see especially Chapters Four and Seven), shows that everyday life has an impact on religiosity in one way or another; this fact lends weight to the significance of studying ordinary Muslims' ambivalent commitment to both religious and non-religious concerns (e.g. Marsden 2005; Schielke 2015). Therefore, to arrive at a nuanced view about the relation between pilgrimage and self-formation, it is important to understand how pilgrims express ambivalence, moral failure and imperfection.

Hajj in Everyday Life

Moroccan pilgrims negotiate their status as pilgrims, both while they are at the sacred sites in Mecca and when they return to the more mundane reality of daily life, through a complex process of self-formation. However, everyday life, as shown in Chapter Four, presents various challenges that require decision-making. Should one ask others to address one with the honorific title *al-ḥājj or al-ḥājja*? Should a person conduct business which might entail a religious compromise, such as the inability to perform prayers on time? Should all those who have performed Hajj expect to be treated with the exact same regard as the more financially fortunate and socially elevated fellow pilgrims? Should a person who has already been to Hajj go repeatedly to Mecca for *'umra*? These challenges are not only limited to the everyday lives of pilgrims after the Hajj, but present themselves even before the journey itself and are, in fact, part of everyday Muslim life. Therefore, it is important to participate in the lives of pilgrims on a long-term basis, as this allows a closer examination of how they negotiate religious issues and dilemmas in their everyday lives (see e.g. Marsden 2005; Marsden and Retsikas 2012; Schielke 2015; Schielke and Debevec 2012).

By mapping the everyday lives of pilgrims in Morocco, I have not only focused on the processes that take place before, during and after the Hajj, but have also looked at the variety of ways in which the pilgrimage to Mecca, and the idea of Mecca itself, are appropriated into everyday life in practice. In studies of religion in everyday life, one often sees analysis based on a discrepancy between moral norms and individual behaviours (Schielke 2009; Debevec 2012). The lives of pilgrims after returning from the Hajj, however, are characterised by complex ambiguity. Indeed, ambivalence, ambiguity and contradiction are, in any case, part of the complexities of Muslims' everyday religiosity.

Processes of ethical improvement, therefore, are not only rooted in expressions of piety but also, importantly, emerge from responses to self-perceived setbacks and feelings of inability, weakness and error. Thus, I have drawn into the analysis a notion of moral failure (Beekers and Kloos 2018). Many pilgrims in Morocco identify and acknowledge the perception of moral failure, and, crucially, one's reaction to it, as part of the process of becoming a better Muslim. Within an acknowledgement of the notion of failure, and a willingness to learn from failures, pilgrims simultaneously speak of their hopes for future improvement of the self, and subsequently may strive to lead more pious lives. Acknowledgements of moral failure and imperfection were seen by many pilgrims as contributing to, rather than obstructing and detracting from, personal projects of ethical improvement. Pilgrims were emphatic and asserted that they would try to change themselves for the better as they dealt with setback, doubts and conflicts.

Although within this book I have focused on those who have been successful in performing the pilgrimage and who return from Mecca to their everyday life, it is also important to pay attention to the constraints in everyday life that prevent many other Moroccans from 'going there' and reaching Mecca. In Chapter Two, for example, I discussed the large numbers (hundreds of thousands) of Moroccans registering for Hajj every year, while the numbers selected are significantly smaller. This leaves people disappointed. The relationship between ordinary lives and piety comes to the fore here in the ways in which people who experience such disappointment often voice this disappointment in religious terms, labelling their failure 'destiny', or speaking of it not yet being their time, or as 'hearing' God's call to visit His house in Mecca but being unable to fulfil it. In addition to those not selected through the bureaucratic selection process, hundreds of poor Moroccans, who are unable to even apply for the Hajj, choose to perform local pilgrimage, known in Morocco as the Pilgrimage of the Poor. In my research, I examined how such local practices form part of the rhythms of daily life, which adapt to, respond to, reshape and are reshaped by, the circumstances of both religious and other living conditions. I demonstrate that Moroccan pilgrims exercise individual religious agency, and how this enables them, some more than others, to negotiate the changes in their status as pilgrims among their community, or in their status as aspirant pilgrims, unable to achieve their ambition through the usual route, but finding spiritual satisfactions in an alternative manner.

Openly acknowledging failure, and accommodating that failure within a religious context, was sometimes described by Moroccans as a means of realising and accepting the fact that humans are not perfect and that failure – and the admission of failure – is part of being a good Muslim in itself. On the basis of my fieldwork, and taking into consideration the previously mentioned studies of ethical self-formation and everyday life, I have shown that processes of ethical improvement are based not only on expressions of piety but also, importantly, on self-perceived setbacks and on feelings of inability, weakness and error, as discussed earlier. Thus, I have drawn into the analysis a notion of moral failure (Beekers and Kloos 2018). Senses of failure are a crucial factor, therefore, in the constitution of religious agency.

For many Moroccans who wish to perform the pilgrimage, Mecca is beyond reach. Their gender, their financial situation, health issues, or the quota and *qur'a* systems, do not work in their favour. In these cases, I show how the everyday is always open to contestations and innovations as mechanisms by which people manage their spiritual ambitions and religiosity. I show that, while Islamic scriptures clearly provide 'scripts', or authoritative reference points, releasing those who are unable to perform the pilgrimage to Mecca from that religious duty, the ways in which Muslim interpret their inability to perform the pilgrimage can vary widely. My work illustrates that such dramatic differences in opinion reflect the way people still struggle to accommodate such variations in religious practice and feel the lack of absolute religious knowledge or guidance in catering for the complexities of everyday life, and the truth that not everyone has equal access to opportunities, the Hajj included.

Particularly while thinking of Mecca and the pilgrimage in general, the tendency might be to concentrate on situations that might readily and obviously be conceived of as 'religious'. However, participant observation of the everyday lives of pilgrims allows access to study settings in which religion might not necessarily have a primary presence. I hope to have demonstrated in this study that such approach provides rich opportunities to study the religious within the mundane, an interesting and complex area of investigation. For example, in Chapter Nine, I examine musical genres in Morocco. I found that in some musical forms, Mecca as a place and the Hajj as an experience take centre stage. In the themes of these songs, one can perceive the importance of the pilgrimage and the idealisation of Mecca as a place of perfection, formulations which, in return, stimulate feelings of happiness and provoke memories of Mecca among the listeners. Those same songs, nonetheless, are equally concerned with the struggles of everyday life, such as with poverty or social discord.

Everyday life is complex and filled with ambiguities, leading pilgrims, and Muslims in general, to navigate multiple social and cultural contexts. In doing so, they move between – and combine – religious and mundane moral registers simultaneously. In this context, storytelling is one means of dealing with ambiguity and delivering moral lessons to listeners. In Chapter Ten, I present three short stories in which pilgrimage to Mecca is discussed. In addition to their giving a glimpse into the cultural and oral traditions in Morocco, the importance of these stories revolves around the fact that by citing the pilgrimage, they provide moral lessons that sometimes go beyond the religious teachings related to the Hajj, and contain social messages related to wealth and class issues as well. In the story of the cobbler, for example, we see the dilemma of a man with savings: should he give them to his poor neighbour, or go to Hajj himself, using the money for the purpose he intended? When the cobbler chooses the charitable giving, we also see how he is then rewarded by God, in that people saw him circumambulating the Kaʿba with them in some miraculous form, although he never left for Mecca. The moral lesson of the story, I suggest, is about revealing important social norms we should observe. These include the importance of being good to one's neighbour, the importance of charity, and, for that storyteller, an acceptance of and reconciliation to the fact that she herself was unable to perform the pilgrimage to Mecca. Such narratives illustrate that Mecca has indeed a powerful presence in everyday life, even when that presence is articulated through a channel which is non-religious and has ramifications within the realm of daily life and social morality.

Another way in which this comes to the fore in Morocco, as demonstrated in Chapter Five, is that, besides the religious impetus behind the journey for individual Muslims, normative authorisation is clearly also political, and group pilgrimages may well be promoted by the Moroccan polity to reinforce nationalism or a sense of civic pride, quite a different impulse from the individual's devotional drive. The annual departure of the pilgrimage is an opportunity for the central government to assert its management of the process, and as already mentioned, an opportunity for the king to assert his authority. This conflation of religious and political motives also manifests itself in the Saudi measures regarding the Hajj governance in Chapter Six.

Indeed, that many pilgrims feel an ever-increasing tension between the materialism of the modern age and the Hajj manifested in luxurious accommodation for the elite, contrasting with the simplicity of the facilities experienced by the majority. However, I have also demonstrated that the pilgrims – using their own agency – act to work through tensions and to manipulate the imposed procedures. This came to the fore in my observation, described in Chapter Seven, of the female pilgrims who insisted on visiting the tomb of the prophet, and yet were prevented from seeing the tomb itself. In defiance of the Saudi regulations, the women voiced, in loud ululations and extra prayers, their satisfaction once they reached the Rawḍa. Nonetheless, contestations around the management of the Hajj are becoming ever more apparent, and I would propose that another investigation might monitor how future developments in Saudi policies impact the Hajj experiences of pilgrims and inform their choices of pilgrimage.

To sum up: an approach that focuses on the socio-cultural embeddedness of religion in everyday life provides a rich avenue of exploration and allows us to conclude that, depending on the specific circumstances in which pilgrims find themselves, there are always threads to be found with which to weave a tapestry to portray one's own view of conflicting events. No clear distinction can be made, nor can a hierarchical order be discerned, between the 'everyday' and the devotional practices of 'ordinary' Muslims, those who strive for pious ethical selves.

BIBLIOGRAPHY

Aadnani, Rachid. 2006. 'Beyond Raï: North African Protest Music and Poetry'. *World Literature Today* 80 (4): 21–6.

Abdel Haleem, M. A. S. 2012. 'The Importance of the Hajj: Spirit and Rituals'. In *Hajj: Journey to the Heart of Islam*, edited by V. Porter, with M. A. S. Abdel Haleem et al., 26–67. Cambridge MA: Harvard University Press.

Abdel Haleem, M. A. S. 2005. *The Qur'an: A New Translation by M. A. S. Abdel Haleem*. Oxford World's Classics. New York: Oxford University Press.

Abel, A. 2012. 'Dār al-Islām'. In *Encyclopaedia of Islam, Second Edition*. Leiden: Brill Online. http://dx.doi.org/10.1163/1573-3912_islam_SIM_1703

Abū al-Makārim, Thammām Faysal. 2013. *Muthakkirāt Riḥlat Hajj li-Amīra Būbāl al-Nawāb Sikandar Bīghum* [The Pilgrimage Journey of Princess Nawab Sikandar Begum Abū al-Makārim]. New Delhi.

Abū al-Naṣr Ǧamīl M. 1975. *A History of the Maghrib*. 2nd edn. Cambridge: Cambridge University Press.

Abu-Lughod, Lila. 1993. *Writing Women's Worlds: Bedouin Stories*. Berkeley: University of California Press.

Abu-Lughod, Lila. 1991. 'Writing Against Culture'. In *Recapturing Anthropology: Working in the Present*, edited by Richard G. Fox, 466–79. Santa Fe: School of American Research Press/University of Washington Press.

Abu-Lughod, Lila. 1986. *Veiled Sentiments: Honor and Poetry in a Bedouin Society*. Berkeley: University of California Press.

Abu-Rabiʿ, Ibrahim M. 1996. *Intellectual Origins of Islamic Resurgence in the Modern Arab World*. Albany: State University of New York Press.

Abun-Nasr, Jamil M. 1987. *A History of the Maghrib in the Islamic Period*. Cambridge: Cambridge University Press.

Adama, Hamadou. 2009. 'The Hajj: Between a Moral and a Material Economy'. *Afrique Contemporaine* (3): 119–38.

Adams, Kathleen M. and Kathleen Gillogly (eds). 2011. *Everyday Life in Southeast Asia*. Bloomington: Indiana University Press.

Aḥmad, Ḥaḍrat Mirzā Bashīr. 2011. *The Life and Character of the Seal of Prophets*. Surrey: Islam International.

Ahmad, Mahjabeen and Shamsul Khan. 2016. A Model of Spirituality for Ageing Muslims. *Journal of Religion and Health*, 55: 830–43.

Aitsiselmi, Farid and Dawn Marley. 2008. 'The Role and Status of the French Language in North Africa'. In *Studies in French Applied Linguistics*, edited by Dalila Ayoun, 185–222. Amsterdam: John Benjamins.

Al-ʿAbdarī, Muhammad. 1999. *Riḥlat al-ʿAbdarī – al-Riḥla al-Maghribiyya* [The Journey of al-ʿAbdarī – The Moroccan Journey]. Damascus: Dār Saʿd al-Dīn.

Al-ʿAyāshī. 2006. *Al-riḥla al-ʿayyashiyya 1661–1663* [The Journey of ʿAyyashī 1661–1663]. UAE: Sawidi.

Al-Ajarma, Kholoud. 2018. 'Cadeaus, souvenirs en verhalen van Palestijnse pelgrims naar Mekka'. *ZemZem* 14 (1): 62–71.

Al-Ajarma, Kholoud and Marjo Buitelaar. 2021. 'Social Media Representations of the Pilgrimage to Mecca: Challenging Moroccan and Dutch Mainstream Media Frames'. *Journal of Muslims in Europe*, 10 (2), 146–67.

Al-Alawi, Irfan. 2006. 'The Destruction of Holy Sites in Mecca and Medina', *Islamic Magazine*, 15.

Alalou, Ali. 2009. 'Francophonie in the Maghreb: A Study of Language Attitudes among Moroccan Teachers of French'. *The French Review* 82 (3): 558–79.

Al-Atawneh, Muhammad. 2009. 'Is Saudi Arabia a Theocracy? Religion and Governance in Contemporary Saudi Arabia'. *Middle Eastern Studies* 45 (5): 721–37.

Al-Baṣīrī, Abdullah bin Muhammad. 2002. *Al-ḥajj wa al-ʿumra wa al-ziyāra* [*Hajj, ʿumra* and *ziyāra*]. King Fahad Library: Riyadh.

Al-Bukhārī, Muḥammad b. Ismāʿīl. n.d. *Ṣaḥīḥ al-Bukhārī*. Beirut: Dar al-Arabia.

Al-Faruqi, Lois Ibsen. 1985. 'Music, Musicians and Muslim Law'. *Asian Music* 17 (1): 3–36.

Al-Manuni, Muhammad. 1953. *Min Ḥadīth al-Rakb al-Maghribī* [The Moroccan Hajj Caravan]. Tetouan: Maṭbaʿat al-Makhzan.

Al-Maqarrī, Ahmad. 1986. *Nafḥ al-Ṭīb Min Ghuṣn al-Andalus al-Raṭīb* [Narratives from Al-Andalus]. Beirut: Dar al-Fikr.

Al-Nawawī, Yaḥya. 2007. *Riyāḍ al-Ṣāliḥīn* [The Meadows of the Righteous]. Beirut: Dar Ibn-Katheer.

Al-Nisā'ī, Ahmad. 1964. *Sunan Al-Nisā'ī*. Beirut: Scientific Books.

Al-Qaradawi, Yusuf. 1994. *The Lawful and the Prohibited in Islam (Al-Halal Wal Haram Fil Islam)*. Plainfield: American Trust Publications.

Al-Qaysī, Abu Abdullah Muhammad. 1968. *Uns al-sārī wa al-sārib, min aqṭar al-Maghārib ila muntahā al-Āmāl wa al-Ma'ārib sayyid al-A'ājim wa al-a'ārib* [Delight of Travellers from the Lands of the West to the Essence of Hope and Master of Arabs and Foreigners]. Fes: Ministry of State in Charge of Cultural Affairs and Traditional Teaching.

Al-Rasheed, Madawi. 2007. *Contesting the Saudi State: Islamic Voices from a New Generation*. Cambridge: Cambridge University Press.

Al-Rasheed, Madawi. 2002. *A History of Saudi Arabia*. Cambridge: Cambridge University Press.

Al-Tahiri, Ahmad. 2005. *Al-Maghrib al-Aqṣa wa Mamlakat Banī Ṭarīf al-Burghwaṭiyya* [Morocco and the Kingdom of Bani Tarif of Barghawata]. Casablanca: Najah.

Al-'Ulaymī, Mujīr al-Dīn. 1973. *Al-Uns al-Jalīl bi-Tārīkh al-Quds wa al-Khalīl* [The Glorious History of Jerusalem and Hebron]. Amman: al-Muhtaseb.

Al-Yāsīnī Ayman. 1985. *Religion and State in the Kingdom of Saudi Arabia*. Westview Special Studies on the Middle East. Boulder, CO: Westview Press.

Ali, Kecia. 2014. *The Lives of Muhammad*. Cambridge, MA: Harvard University Press.

Alimi, Moh Yasir. 2018. 'Muslims through Storytelling: Islamic Law, Culture and Reasoning in South Sulawesi'. *Komunitas: International Journal of Indonesian Society and Culture* 10 (1): 131–46.

Altorki, Soraya. 1986. *Women in Saudi Arabia: Ideology and Behavior among the Elite*. New York: Columbia University Press.

Altorki, Soraya and Camillia Fawzi El-Solh. 1988. *Arab Women in the Field: Studying Your Own Society*. 1st edn. Contemporary Issues in the Middle East. Syracuse, NY: Syracuse University Press.

Amine, Khalid and Marvin A. Carlson. 2008. 'Al-halqa in Arabic Theatre: An Emerging Site of Hybridity'. *Theatre Journal* 60 (1): 71–85.

Amiri, Reza Ekhtiari, Ku Hasnita Binti Ku Samsu and Hassan Gholipour Fereidouni. 2011. 'The Hajj and Iran's Foreign Policy towards Saudi Arabia'. *Journal of Asian and African Studies* 46 (6): 678–90.

Ammerman, Nancy Tatom. 2013. *Sacred Stories, Spiritual Tribes: Finding Religion in Everyday Life*. New York: Oxford University Press.

Ammerman, Nancy Tatom. 2007. *Everyday Religion: Observing Modern Religious Lives*. Oxford: Oxford University Press.

'Anānī Khalīl. 2016. *Inside the Muslim Brotherhood: Religion, Identity, and Politics*. Religion and Global Politics. New York: Oxford University Press.

Anderson, Benedict. 1983. *Imagined Communities. Reflections on the Origin and Spread of Nationalism*. London: Verso.

Aourid, Hassan. 2019. *Riwā'u Makka* [The Waves of Mecca]. Beirut: al-Markaz al-Thakafi.

Appadurai, Arjun. 1996. *Modernity at Large: Cultural Dimensions of Globalization*. Public Worlds, V. 1. Minneapolis, MN: University of Minnesota Press.

Arendonk, C. van and D. Gimaret 2012. 'Salām'. In *Encyclopaedia of Islam, Second Edition*. Leiden: Brill Online. http://dx.doi.org/10.1163/1573-3912_islam_SIM_6520

Armbruster, Heidi and Anna Lærke. 2008. *Taking Sides: Ethics, Politics and Fieldwork in Anthropology*. Oxford: Berghahn.

Asad, Talal. 2003. *Formations of the Secular: Christianity, Islam, Modernity*. Stanford, CA: Stanford University Press.

Asad, Talal. 1993. *Genealogies of Religion. Discipline and Reasons of Power in Christianity and Islam*. Baltimore: Johns Hopkins University Press.

Asad, Talal. 1986. *The Idea of an Anthropology of Islam*. Washington, DC: Center for Contemporary Arab Studies.

Asad, Talal. 1983. 'Anthropological Conceptions of Religion: Reflections on Geertz'. *Man* 18 (2): 237–59.

Asani, Ali S. and Carney E. S. Gavin. 1998. 'Through the Lens of Mirza of Delhi: The Debbas Album of Early-Twentieth-Century Photographs of Pilgrimage Sites in Mecca and Medina'. *Muqarnas* (15): 178–99.

Aydoun, Ahmed. 2014 [1995]. *Musique du Maroc*. Casablanca: Éditions EDDIF/Autre temps.

Aziz, Heba. 2001. 'The Journey: An Overview of Tourism and Travel in the Arab/Islamic Context'. In *Tourism and the Less Developed World: Issues and Case Studies*, edited by D. Harrison, 151–60. Cambridge: CABI.

Azraqī, Muhammad ibn 'Abd Allāh, 1964. *Kitab Akhbar Makkah* [Reports about Mecca]. B'einit: Khayats.

Baderoon, Gabeba. 2012. '"The Sea Inside Us": Narrating Self, Gender, Place and History in South African Memories of the Hajj'. *Social Dynamics* 38 (2): 237–52.

Bamberg, Michael. 1997. 'Positioning between Structure and Performance'. *Journal of Narrative and Life History* 7 (1–4): 335–42.

Bayram, Aydın. 2014. 'The Rise of Wahhabi Sectarianism and Its Impact in Saudi Arabia/Vehhabi Fırkasının Doğuşu ve Suudi Arabistan'a Etkisi'. *Atatük Üniversitesi İlahiyat Fakültesi Dergisi* (42): 245–61.

Bazzaz, Sahar. 2010. *Forgotten Saints. History, Power, and Politics in the Making of Modern Morocco*. Cambridge, MA: Harvard Middle Eastern Monographs, 41.

Beekers, Daan and David Kloos (eds). 2017. *Straying from the Straight Path: How Senses of Failure Invigorate Lived Religion*. New York and Oxford: Berghahn.

Benjamin, Medea. 2018. *Inside Iran: The Real History and Politics of the Islamic Republic of Iran*. London: OR Books.

Benomar, Jamal. 1988. 'The Monarchy, the Islamist Movement and Religious Discourse in Morocco'. *Third World Quarterly* 10 (2): 539–55.

Bensaid, Benaouda and Fadila Grine. 2013. 'Ethico-Spiritual Dimensions of Charity: An Islamic Perspective'. *Middle-East Journal of Scientific Research* 13: 65–77.

Bentahar, Ziad. 2010. 'The Visibility of African Identity in Moroccan Music'. *Wasafiri* 25 (1): 41–8.

Benthall, Jonathan. 2012. '"Cultural Proximity" and the Conjuncture of Islam with Modern Humanitarianism'. In *Sacred Aid: Faith and Humanitarianism*, edited by Michael Barnett and Janice Stein, 65–88. Oxford: Oxford University Press.

Beránek, Ondřej and Pavel Ťupek. 2018. *The Temptation of Graves in Salafi Islam: Iconoclasm, Destruction and Idolatry*. Edinburgh: Edinburgh University Press.

Beránek, Ondřej and Pavel Ťupek. 2009. *From Visiting Graves to Their Destruction: The Question of Ziyāra through the Eyes of Salafis*. Waltham: Brandeis University, Crown Center for Middle East Studies.

Berger, Peter. 2018. 'Closeness and Disjuncture: On Friendship in the Field'. In *Empirical Anthropology: Issues of Academic Friends and Friends in the Field*, edited by Georg Pfeffer and Nibedita Nath, 232–50. New Delhi: Concept.

Berriane, Johara. 2015. 'Pilgrimage, Spiritual Tourism and the Shaping of Transnational "Imagined Communities": The Case of the Tidjani Ziyara to Fez'. *International Journal of Religious Tourism and Pilgrimage* 3 (2): 1–10.

Berriane, Johara. 2012. 'Ahmad Al-Tijânî and His Neighbors: The Inhabitants of Fez and their Perceptions of the Zâwiya'. In *Prayer in the City: The Making of Muslim Sacred Places and Urban Life. Global Local Islam*, edited by Patrick Desplat and Dorothea Elisabeth Schulz, 57–76. Bielefeld: Transcript.

Biagi, Francesco. 2014. 'The 2011 Constitutional Reform in Morocco: More Flaws than Merits'. *Jean Monnet Occasional Papers*, Institute for European Studies (Malta) 7: 1–19.

Bianchi, Robert R. 2017. 'The Hajj and Politics in China'. In *Muslim Pilgrimage in the Modern World*, edited by Babak Rahimi and Peyman Eshaghi, 68–88. Durham, NC: University of North Carolina Press.

Bianchi, Robert R. 2016. 'Hajj By Air'. In *The Hajj: Pilgrimage in Islam*, edited by Eric Tagliacozzo and Shawkat M. Toorawa, 131–51. New York: Cambridge University Press.

Bianchi, Robert R. 2015. 'The Hajj and Politics in Contemporary Turkey and Indonesia'. In *Hajj: Global Interactions through Pilgrimage*, edited by Luitgard Mols and Marjo Buitelaar, 65–82. Leiden: National Museum of Ethnology.

Bianchi, Robert R. 2014. 'The Hajj in Everyday Life'. In *Everyday Life in the Muslim Middle East*, edited by Donna Lee Bowen, Evelyn A. Early and Becky Schulthies, 319–28. Bloomington: Indiana University Press.

Bianchi, Robert R. 2013. *Islamic Globalization: Pilgrimage, Capitalism, Democracy, and Diplomacy*. Singapore and London: World Scientific.

Bianchi, Robert R. 2007. 'Travel for Religious Purposes'. *Oxford Encyclopedia of the Islamic World*. Oxford Islamic Studies Online. http://bridgingcultures.neh.gov/muslimjourneys/items/show/187

Bianchi, Robert R. 2004. *Guests of God: Pilgrimage and Politics in the Islamic World*. New York: Oxford University Press.

Bilaʿraj, Abdul-Rahman. 2016. *Dawr Riḥrāt al-Hajj fi-Ṭawāsul al-Thaqāfī bayn al-Maghrib wa al-Mashriq* [The Role of the Pilgrimage in Cultural Communication between the East and the West]. Algeria: Mu'assasat Kunūz al-Ḥikma li-Nashr wa al-Tawzīʿ.

Birks, J. Stace. 1977. 'The Mecca Pilgrimage by West African Pastoral Nomads'. *The Journal of Modern African Studies* 15 (1): 47–58.

Black, Kathy, Bishop Kyrillos, Jonathan L. Friedmann, Tamar Frankiel, Hamid Mavani and Jihad Turk. 2018. 'The Islamic Calendar'. In *Rhythms of Religious Ritual: The Yearly Cycles of Jews, Christians, and Muslims*, 125–54. Claremont, CA: Claremont Press.

Bligh, Alexander. 1985. 'The Saudi Religious Elite (Ulema) as Participant in the Political System of the Kingdom'. *International Journal of Middle East Studies* 17 (1): 37–50.

Bogaert, Koenraad and Project Muse. 2018. *Globalized Authoritarianism: Megaprojects, Slums, and Class Relations in Urban Morocco*. Globalization and Community, 27. Minneapolis: University of Minnesota Press.

Boissevain, Katia. 2012. 'Preparing for the Hajj in Contemporary Tunisia: Between Religious and Administrative Ritual'. In *Ethnographies of Islam: Ritual Performances and Everyday Practices*, edited by Baudouin Dupret, Thomas Pierret, Paulo G. Pinto and Kathryn Spellman-Poots, 21–30. Edinburgh: Edinburgh University Press.

Bonine, Michael E. 1990. 'The Sacred Direction and City Structure: A Preliminary Analysis of the Islamic Cities of Morocco'. *Muqarnas* 7: 50–72.

Bonner, Micheal. 2003. 'Poverty and Charity in the Rise of Islam'. In *Poverty and Charity in Middle Eastern Contexts*, edited by Michael Bonner, Mine Ener and Amy Singer, and University of Michigan, 13–30. Albany: State University of New York Press.

Booley, Ashraf. 2016. 'The Rights and Freedoms of Moroccan Women: Has the 2004 Reforms Benefited Moroccan Women?' *Potchefstroom Electronic Law Journal/ Potchefstroomse Elektroniese Regsblad* (19): 1–23.

Borneman, John and Abdellah Hammoudi. 2009. *Being There: The Fieldwork Encounter and the Making of Truth*. Berkeley: University of California Press.

Boulanouar, Aisha Wood. 2010. *Myths and Reality: Meaning in Moroccan Muslim Women's Dress*. PhD thesis, University of Otago.

Boum, Aomar. 2013. *Memories of Absence: How Muslims Remember Jews in Morocco*. Stanford, CA: Stanford University Press.

Boum, Aomar. 2012. 'Festivalizing Dissent in Morocco'. *Middle East Report* 42 (263): 22–5.

Bourdieu, Pierre. 1990 [1980]. *The Logic of Practice* (trans. Richard Nice). Stanford, CA: Stanford University Press.

Bourdieu, Pierre. 1986. 'The Forms of Capital'. In *Handbook of Theory and Research for the Sociology of Education*, edited by J. Richardson (trans. Richard Nice), 241–58. New York: Greenwood.

Bourdieu, Pierre. 1985. 'The Genesis of the Concepts of Habitus and Field'. *Sociocriticism* 2 (2): 11–24.

Bourdieu, Pierre. 1977. *Outline of a Theory of Practice*. Cambridge: Cambridge University Press.

Bourdieu, Pierre and Lois Wacquant. 1992. *An Invitation to Reflexive Sociology*. Chicago: University of Chicago Press.

Bourqia, Rahma and Susan Gilson Miller (eds). 1999. *In the Shadow of the Sultan: Culture, Power, and Politics in Morocco*. Cambridge, MA: Harvard University Press.

Bowen, Donna Lee and Evelyn A. Early. 1993. *Everyday Life in the Muslim Middle East*. Indiana Series in Arab and Islamic Studies. Bloomington: Indiana University Press.

Bowen, John R. 1993. *Muslims through Discourse: Religion and Ritual in Gayo Society*. Princeton, NJ: Princeton University Press.

Brower, Benjamin Claude. 2015. 'The Hajj by Land'. In *The Hajj: Pilgrimage in Islam*, edited by Eric Tagliacozzo and Shawkat M. Toorawa, 87–112. Cambridge: Cambridge University Press.

Brubaker, Rogers and Cooper, Frederick. 2000. 'Beyond "Identity"'. *Theory and Society* 29 (1): 1–47.

Bruner, Jerome. 2004. 'Life as Narrative'. *Social Research* 71 (3): 691.

Buhl, F. 2012. 'Ṭawāf'. In *Encyclopaedia of Islam, Second Edition*. Leiden: Brill Online. http://dx.doi.org/10.1163/1573-3912_islam_SIM_7446

Buitelaar, Marjo. 2018. 'Comparing Notes: An Anthropological Approach to Contemporary Islam'. Inaugural lecture, Groningen: University of Groningen. https://www.rug.nl/staff/m.w.buitelaar/inauguralmbcontemporaryislam.pdf

Buitelaar, Marjo. 2017. 'Moved by Mecca: The Meanings of the Hajj for Present-day Dutch Muslims'. *Muslim Pilgrimage in Europe*. Routledge, 2017. 29–42.

Buitelaar, Marjo. 2009. *Islam en het dagelijks leven. Religie en cultuur onder Marokkanen*. Amsterdam: Atlas.

Buitelaar, Marjo. 1993. *Fasting and Feasting in Morocco: Women's Participation in Ramadan*. Oxford: Berg.

Buitelaar, Marjo and Khadija Kadrouch-Outmany. 2023. 'Patience and Pilgrimage: Dutch Hajj Pilgrims' Emergent and Maturing Stories about the Virtue of ṣabr'. In *Narrating the Pilgrimage to Mecca*, edited by Marjo Buitelaar and Richard van Leeuwen, 323–53. Leiden: Brill.

Buitelaar, Marjo and Richard van Leeuwen (eds). 2023. *Narrating the Pilgrimage to Mecca*. Leiden: Brill.

Buitelaar, Marjo, Manja Stephan-Emmrich and Viola Thimm (eds). 2020. Muslim *Women's Pilgrimage to Mecca and Beyond. Reconfiguring Gender, Religion and Mobility*. London and New York: Routledge.

Buresi, Pascal. 2018. 'Preparing the Almohad Caliphate: the Almoravids'. *Al-'Usur al-Wusta: The Journal of Middle East Medievalists* (26): 151–68.

Buskens, Léon. 2006. 'Sharia en nationaal recht in Marokko' [Sharia and National Law in Morocco] In *Sharia en nationaal recht in twaalf moslimlanden* [Sharia and National Law in Twelve Muslim Countries], edited by J. M. Otto, A. J. Dekker and L. J. van Soest-Zuurdeeg, 43–84. Amsterdam: WRR, Amsterdam University Press.

Buskens, Léon. 2003. 'Recent Debates on Family Law Reform in Morocco: Islamic Law as Politics in an Emerging Public Sphere'. *Islamic Law and Society* 10 (1): 70–131.

Caidi, Nadia, Susan Beazley and Laia Colomer Marquez. 2018. 'Holy Selfies: Performing Pilgrimage in the Age of Social Media'. *The International Journal of Information, Diversity, & Inclusion* 2 (1–2): 1–24.

Campo, Juan. 1991. *The Other Sides of Paradise: Explorations into the Religious Meanings of Domestic Space in Islam*. Columbia, SC: University of South Carolina Press.

Campo, Juan. 1991. 'The Mecca Pilgrimage in the Formation of Islam in Modern Egypt'. In *Sacred Places and Profane Spaces*, edited by J. Scott and P. Simpson-Housley, 145–61. New York: Greenwood Press.

Carra de Vaux, B. and L. Gardet. 2012. 'Basmala'. In *Encyclopaedia of Islam, Second Edition*. Leiden: Brill Online. http://dx.doi.org/10.1163/1573-3912_islam_COM_0102

Certeau, Michel de and Steven Rendall. 1988. *The Practice of Everyday Life*. Berkeley: University of California Press.

Chabbi, Jacqueline. 2012. 'Zamzam'. In *Encyclopaedia of Islam, Second Edition*. Leiden: Brill Online. http://dx.doi.org/10.1163/1573-3912_islam_SIM_8112

Champion, Daryl. 2003. *The Paradoxical Kingdom: Saudi Arabia and the Momentum of Reform*. New York: Columbia University Press.

Classen, Constance. 1991. 'Creation by Sound/Creation by Light: A Sensory Analysis of Two South American Cosmologies'. In Th*e Varieties of Sensory Experience: A Sourcebook in the Anthropology of the Senses*, edited by David Howes, 239–56. Toronto: University of Toronto Press.

Clingingsmith, David, Asim Ijaz Khwaja and Michael Kremer. 2009. 'Estimating the Impact of the Hajj: Religion and Tolerance in Islam's Global Gathering'. *The Quarterly Journal of Economics* 124 (3): 1,133–70.

Cohen, Jeffrey H. 2000. 'Problems in the Field: Participant Observation and the Assumption of Neutrality'. *Field Methods* 12 (4): 316–33.

Cohen, Shana. 2004. *Searching for a Different Future: The Rise of a Global Middle Class in Morocco*. Durham, NC: Duke University Press.

Coleman, Simon. 2023. 'Narrating Mecca: Between Sense and Presence'. In *Narrating the Pilgrimage to Mecca*, edited by Marjo Buitelaar and Richard van Leeuwen, 422–9. Leiden: Brill.

Coleman, Simon. 2002. 'Do You Believe in Pilgrimage?: Communitas, Contestation and Beyond'. *Anthropological Theory* 2 (3): 355–68.

Coleman, Simon and John Eade. 2004. *Reframing Pilgrimage: Cultures in Motion*. European Association of Social Anthropologists. London: Routledge.

Coleman, Simon and John Elsner. 1995. *Pilgrimage: Past and Present: Sacred Travel and Sacred Space in the World Religions*. London: British Museum Press.

Combs-Schilling, M. E. 1989. *Sacred Performances: Islam, Sexuality, and Sacrifice*. New York: Columbia University Press.

Cook, Michael. 2000. *The Koran: A Very Short Introduction*. Oxford: Oxford University Press.

Cooke, Miriam and Bruce B. Lawrence. 2005. *Muslim Networks from Hajj to Hip Hop*. Islamic Civilization and Muslim Networks. Chapel Hill: University of North Carolina Press.

Cooper, Barbara. 1999. 'The Strength in the Song: Muslim Personhood, Audible Capital, and Hausa Women's Performance of the Hajj'. *Social Text* 60: 87–110.

Cornell, Vincent J. 1998. *Realm of the Saint: Power and Authority in Moroccan Sufism*. Austin: University of Texas Press.

Counted, Victor and Hetty Zock. 2019. 'Place Spirituality: An Attachment Perspective'. *Archive for the Psychology of Religion* 41 (1): 12–25.

Coward, Harold G. 1997. *Life After Death in World Religions*. Faith Meets Faith Series. Maryknoll, NY: Orbis.

Cragg, Kenneth and R. Marston Speight. 1980. *Islam from Within: Anthology of a Religion*. Belmont, CA: Wadsworth.

Crapanzano, Vincent. 1985. *Tuhami, Portrait of a Moroccan*. Chicago: University of Chicago Press.

Crawford, David and Rachel Newcomb. 2013. *Encountering Morocco. Fieldwork and Cultural Understanding*. Public Cultures of the Middle East and North Africa. Bloomington: Indiana University Press.

Crumrine, N. Ross and E. Alan Morinis. 1991. *Pilgrimage in Latin America*. Contributions to the Study of Anthropology, No. 4. New York: Greenwood Press.

Dallu, Burhan al-Din. 2004. *Jazirat al-ʿArab Qabl al-Islam* [The Arabian Peninsula before Islam]. Beirut: All Prints Distributors and Publishers.

Danforth, Loring M. 2016. *Crossing the Kingdom: Portraits of Saudi Arabia*. Oakland, CA: University of California Press.

Davidson, Joyce and Christine Milligan. 2004. 'Embodying Emotion, Sensing Space: Introducing Emotional Geographies'. *Social and Cultural Geography* 5 (4): 523–32.

Davies, James and Dimitrina Spencer (eds). 2010. *Emotions in the Field: The Psychology and Anthropology of Fieldwork Experience*. Stanford, CA: Stanford University Press.

Davies, Stephen. 2011. 'Infectious Music: Music – Listener Emotional Contagion'. In *Empathy: Philosophical and Psychological Perspectives*, edited by A. Coplan and P. Goldie, 134–48. Oxford: Oxford University Press.

Davis, Susan Schaefer. 1983. *Patience and Power: Women's Lives in a Moroccan Village*. Cambridge, MA: Schenkman.

De Koning, Martijn. '"I'm a Weak Servant": The Question of Sincerity and the Cultivation of Weakness in the Lives of Dutch Salafi Muslims'. In *Straying from the Straight Path: How Senses of Failure Invigorate Lived Religion*, edited by Daan Beekers and David Kloos, 37–53. New York and Oxford: Berghahn.

Debevec, Liza. 2012. 'Postponing Piety in Urban Burkina Faso: Discussing Ideas on When to Start Acting as a Pious Muslim'. In *Ordinary Lives and Grand Schemes: An Anthropology of Everyday Religion*, edited by Joska Samuli Schielke and Liza Debevec, 33–47. New York: Berghahn.

Déclais, Jean-Louis. 2005. 'Names of the Prophet'. In *Encyclopaedia of the Qur'an*, edited by Jane Dammen McAuliffe. Washington, DC: Georgetown University.

Deeb, Lara. 2015. 'Thinking Piety and the Everyday Together: A Response to Fadil and Fernando'. *Hau: Journal of Ethnographic Theory* 5 (2): 93–6.

Deeb, Lara. 2011. *An Enchanted Modern: Gender and Public Piety in Shi'i Lebanon*. Princeton: Princeton University Press.

Deeb, Lara. 2006. *An Enchanted Modern: Gender and Public Piety in Shi'i Lebanon*. Princeton: Princeton University Press.

Deeb, Lara and Mona Harb. 2007. 'Sanctioned Pleasures: Youth, Piety and Leisure in Beirut'. *Middle East Report* 245 (1): 2–19.

Delaney, Carol. 1990. 'The "Hajj": Sacred and Secular'. *American Ethnologist* 17 (3): 513–30.

Dellal, Mohamed and Amar Sellam. 2013. *Moroccan Culture in the 21st Century: Globalization, Challenges and Prospects*. African Political, Economic, and Security Issues. Hauppauge, NY: Nova.

Denny, F. M. 2012. 'Umma'. In *Encyclopaedia of Islam, Second Edition*. Leiden: Brill Online. http://dx.doi.org/10.1163/1573-3912_islam_COM_1291

Dessing, Nathal M, Nadia Jeldtoft, Jørgen Schøler Nielsen and Linda Woodhead (eds). 2013. *Everyday Lived Islam in Europe*. Ashgate Ahrc/Esrc Religion and Society Series. Farnham: Ashgate.

Dietrich, A. 2012. 'Lubān'. In *Encyclopaedia of Islam, Second Edition*. Leiden: Brill Online. http://dx.doi.org/10.1163/1573-3912_islam_SIM_4681

Donnan, Hastings. 1995. 'Pilgrimage and Islam in Rural Pakistan: The Influence of the 'Haj''. *Etnofoor* 8 (1): 63–82.

Dorsey, James M. 2017. 'Think that 2016 Was a Tough Year for Saudi Arabia? Wait Till You See 2017'. *International Policy Digest*, 2 January. https://intpolicydigest.org/2017/01/02/think-2016-tough-year-saudi-arabia-wait-till-see-2017/

Doumato, Eleanor Abdella. 2009. 'Obstacles to Equality for Saudi Women'. In *The Kingdom of Saudi Arabia, 1979–2009: Evolution of a Pivotal State, A Special Edition of Viewpoints*, 23–7. Washington, DC: The Middle East Institute. https://www.voltairenet.org/IMG/pdf/Kingdom_of_Saudi_Arabia_1979-2009.pdf

Dresch, Paul, Wendy James and David J. Parkin (eds). 2000. *Anthropologists in a Wider World: Essays on Field Research*. Methodology and History in Anthropology, 7. New York: Berghahn.

Driessen, Henk. 1998. 'The Notion of Friendship in Ethnographic Fieldwork'. *Anthropological Journal on European Cultures* 7 (1): 43–62.

Dubisch, Jill. 1996. 'Anthropology as Pilgrimage'. *Etnofoor* 9 (2): 66–77.

Dubisch, Jill. 1995. *In a Different Place: Pilgrimage, Gender, and Politics at a Greek Island Shrine*. Princeton Modern Greek Studies. Princeton, NJ: Princeton University Press.

Dupret, Baudouin, Thomas Pierret, Paulo G. Pinto and Kathryn Spellman-Poots (eds). 2012. *Ethnographies of Islam: Ritual Performances and Everyday Practices*. Edinburgh: Edinburgh University Press. http://www.jstor.org/stable/10.3366/j.ctt3fgtj5

Dwyer, Kevin. 2013. 'Afterword: Anthropologists among Moroccans'. In *Encountering Morocco: Fieldwork and Cultural Understanding*, edited by David Crawford and Rachel Newcomb, 213–56. Bloomington: Indiana University Press.

Dwyer, Kevin and Faqir Muhammad. 1982. *Moroccan Dialogues: Anthropology in Question*. Baltimore: Johns Hopkins University Press.

Eade, John and Michael J. Sallnow. 1991. *Contesting the Sacred: The Anthropology of Christian Pilgrimage*. London: Routledge.

Egan, Martyn. 2012. 'Halal Ignorance: Religion and Domination in Saudi Arabia'. Paper presented at *BRISMES Graduate Conference*. London: LSE. https://me.eui.eu/wp-content/uploads/sites/264/2016/03/Egan_Halal-Ignorance_AOM.pdf

Eickelman, Dale F. 2009. 'Not Lost in Translation: The Influence of Clifford Geertz's Work and Life on Anthropology in Morocco'. *The Journal of North African Studies* 14 (3–4): 385–95.

Eickelman, Dale F. 1985. *Knowledge and Power in Morocco: The Education of a Twentieth-Century Notable*. Princeton, NJ: Princeton University Press.

Eickelman, Dale F. 1976. *Moroccan Islam: Tradition and Society in a Pilgrimage Center*. Austin: University of Texas Press.

Eickelman, Dale F. 1974. 'Islam and the Impact of the French Colonial System in Morocco: A Study in Historical Anthropology'. *Humaniora Islamica* 2: 215–35.

Eickelman, Dale F. and Armando Salvatore. 2002. 'The Public Sphere and Muslim Identities'. *European Journal of Sociology/Archives Européennes De Sociologie/Europäisches Archiv Für Soziologie* 43 (1): 92–115. http://www.jstor.org/stable/23999100

Eickelman, Dale F. and James Piscatori. 1990. *Muslim Travellers: Pilgrimage, Migration, and the Religious Imagination*. London: Routledge.

Eickelman, Dale F. and Jon W. Anderson. 1999. 'Redefining Muslim Publics'. In *New Media in the Muslim World*, edited by Dale Eickelman and Jon Anderson, 1–19. Bloomington: Indiana University Press.

Eisenlohr, Patrick. 2012. 'Media and Religious Diversity'. *Annual Review of Anthropology* 41 (1): 37–55.

El-Ayadi, Mohammed, Hassan Rachik and Mohamed Tozy. 2007. *L'islam Au Quotidien: Enquête Sur Les Valeurs et Les Pratiques Religieuses Au Maroc* [Daily Islam: Survey of Values and Religious Practices in Morocco]. Casablanca: Éditions Prologues.

Elliot, Alice. 2016. 'The Makeup of Destiny: Predestination and the Labor of Hope in a Moroccan Emigrant Town'. *American Ethnologist* 43 (3): 488–99.

El Mansour, Mohammed. 2020. *The Power of Islam in Morocco: Historical and Anthropological Perspectives*. Abingdon: Routledge.

El Mansour, Mohammed. 1999. 'The Sanctuary (hurum) in pre-colonial Morocco'. In *In the Shadow of the Sultan: Culture, Power and Politics in Morocco*, edited by Rahma Bourqia and Susan Gilson Miller, 185–98. Harvard Center for Middle Eastern Studies. Cambridge, MA: Harvard University Press.

EI Moudden, Abderrahmane. 1990. 'The Ambivalence of Rihla: Community Integration and Self-definition in Moroccan Travel Accounts, 1300–1800'. In *Muslim Travelers*, edited by Dale F. Eickelmen and James Piscatori, 69–84. London: Routledge.

Ende, Werner. 2010. 'Baqīʿ al-Gharqad'. In *Encyclopaedia of Islam, Third Edition*. Leiden: Brill Online. http://dx.doi.org/10.1163/1573-3912_ei3_COM_23494

Ennaji, Moha. 2008. 'Representations of Women in Moroccan Arabic and Berber Proverbs'. *International Journal of the Sociology of Language* (190): 167–81.

Ergun, Ayça and Aykan Erdemir. 2010. 'Negotiating Insider and Outsider Identities in the Field: "Insider" in a Foreign Land; "Outsider" in One's Own Land'. *Field Methods* 22 (1): 16–38.

Erlmann, Veit (ed.). 2004. *Hearing Cultures: Essays on Sound, Listening and Modernity*. Oxford: Berg.

Esin, E and Haluk Doganbey. 1963. *Mecca the Blessed, Medinah the Radiant*. London: Elek.

Evrard, Amy. 2014. *The Moroccan Women's Rights Movement*. Syracuse, NY: Syracuse University Press.

Ewing, Katherine P. 1990. 'The Illusion of Wholeness: Culture, Self, and the Experience of Inconsistency'. *Ethos* 18 (3): 251–78.

Fadil, Nadia and Mayanthi Fernando. 2015. 'Rediscovering the "Everyday" Muslim: Notes on an Anthropological Divide'. *Hau: Journal of Ethnographic Theory* 5 (2): 59–88.

Farghal, Mohammed. 1995. 'The Pragmatics of inšallah in Jordanian Arabic'. *Multilingua* 14 (3): 253–70.

Faroqhi, Suraiya. 1994. *Pilgrims and Sultans: The Hajj Under the Ottomans, 1517–1683*. London: I. B. Tauris.

Fechter, Anne-Meike. 2003. 'Cultures in the Classroom: Teaching Anthropology as a "Foreigner" in the UK'. *Anthropology Matters* 5 (1). https://www.anthropologymatters.com/index.php/anth_matters/article/view/128

Feld, Steven. 1991. 'Sound as a Symbolic System: The Kaluli Drum'. In *Varieties of Sensory Experience: A Sourcebook in the Anthropology of the Senses*, edited by David Howes, 79-99. Toronto: University of Toronto Press.

Feld, Steven. 1982. *Sound and Sentiment: Birds, Weeping, Poetics and Song in Kaluli Expression*. Philadelphia: University of Pennsylvania.

Fernández Molina, Irene. 2011. 'The Monarchy vs. the 20 February Movement: Who Holds the Reins of Political Change in Morocco?' *Mediterranean Politics* 16 (3): 435–41.

Fernández Parrilla, Gonzalo and Helio Islán Fernández. 2009. 'La Leyenda Nass El Ghiwane'. *Al-Andalus Magreb* 16: 149–61. https://www.academia.edu/5181185/La_leyenda_Nass_El_Ghiwane

Fewkes, Jacqueline H. 2020. 'Considering the Silences: Understanding Historical Narratives of Women's Indian Ocean Hajj Mobility'. *Muslim Women's Pilgrimage to Mecca and Beyond*, edited by Marjo Buitelaar, et al., 127–46. London: Routledge.

Fewkes, Jacqueline H. and Megan Adamson Sijapati (eds). 2020. *Muslim Communities and Cultures of the Himalayas: Conceptualizing the Global Ummah*. London: Routledge.

Fischer, Michael M. J. and Mehdi Abedi. 1990. *Debating Muslims: Cultural Dialogues in Postmodernity and Tradition*. New Directions in Anthropological Writing. Madison, WI: University of Wisconsin Press.

Flaskerud, Ingvild and Richard J. Natvig. 2018. *Muslim Pilgrimage in Europe*. London: Routledge.

Foucault, Michel. 1988. 'Technologies of the Self'. In *Technologies of the Self: A Seminar with Michel Foucault*, edited by Luther H. Martin, Huck Gutman and Patrick H. Hutton, 16–49. London: Tavistock.

Fox, James. 1989. 'Ziarah Visits to the Tombs of the Wali, the Founders of Islam in Java'. In *Islam in the Indonesian social context*, edited by Merle Calvin Ricklefs, 19–36. Clayton, Victoria: Monash University Press.

Frey, Nancy Louise. 1998. *Pilgrim Stories: On and Off the Road to Santiago*. Berkeley: University of California Press.

Frishkopf, Michael. 2008. 'Islamic Music in Africa as a Tool for African Studies'. *Canadian Journal of African Studies/Revue Canadienne Des Études Africaines* 42 (2–3): 478–507.

Gardet, L. 'Karāma'. 2012. In *Encyclopaedia of Islam, Second Edition*. Leiden: Brill Online. http://dx.doi.org/10.1163/1573-3912_islam_COM_0445

Gatrad, Abdul Rashid and Aziz Sheikh. 2005. 'Hajj: Journey of a Lifetime'. *BMJ* 330 (7,483): 133–7.

Gazzah, Miriam. 2008. *Rhythms and Rhymes of Life: Music and Identification Processes of Dutch-Moroccan Youth*. Amsterdam: Amsterdam University Press.

Geel, Annemarie van. 2018. *'For Women Only'. Gender, Segregation, Islam, and Modernity in Saudi Arabia*. PhD thesis, Radboud University.

Geertz, Clifford. 1975. *The Interpretation of Cultures: Selected Essays*. London: Hutchinson.

Geertz, Clifford. 1973. *The Interpretation of Cultures: Selected Essays*. New York: Basic.

Geertz, Clifford. 1971. *Islam Observed: Religious Development in Morocco and Indonesia*. Chicago: University of Chicago Press.

Geertz, Clifford. 1968. *Islam Observed: Religious Development in Morocco and Indonesia*. New Haven: Yale University Press.

Geertz, Clifford, Hildred Geertz and Lawrence Rosen. 1979. *Meaning and Order in Moroccan Society: Three Essays in Cultural Analysis*. Cambridge: Cambridge University Press.

Gellner, Ernest. 1981. *Muslim Society*. Cambridge Studies in Social Anthropology, 32. Cambridge: Cambridge University Press.

Gellner, Ernest. 1969. *Saints of the Atlas*. Nature of Human Society Series. London: Weidenfeld & Nicolson.

Gemzöe, Lena. 2005. 'The Feminization of Healing in Pilgrimage to Fatima'. In *Pilgrimage and Healing*, edited by Jill Dubisch and Michael Winkelman, 25–48. Tucson: University of Arizona Press.

Gennep, Arnold van. 1960. *The Rites of Passage*. Chicago: University of Chicago Press.

Ghazali, Muhammad. 1853. *Iḥyā' 'Ulūm al-Dīn* [The Revival of the Religious Sciences]. Cairo: s.n. Vol. 2, Book 8, 237.

Gibb, H. A. R. 1929. *Ibn Battuta, Travels in Asia and Africa, 1325–1354*. London: Routledge.

Glaser, Barney G. and Anselm L. Strauss. 1967. *The Discovery of Grounded Theory: Strategies for Qualitative Research*. Chicago: Aldine.

Goldberg, Jacob. 2013. *Foreign Policy of Saudi Arabia: The Formative Years*. Harvard Middle Eastern Studies, V. 19. Cambridge, MA: Harvard University Press.

Green, Joel. 2018. 'Sufis in a "Foreign" Zawiya: Moroccan Perceptions of the Tijani Pilgrimage to Fes'. *Independent Study Project (ISP) Collection*. https://digitalcollections.sit.edu/isp_collection/3002/

Gregory, Stanford and Kessem Wehbe. 1986. 'The Contexts of Inshallah in Alexandria Egypt'. *Anthropological Linguistics* 28 (1): 95–105.

Guillemin, Marilys and Lynn Gillam. 2004. 'Ethics, Reflexivity, and "Ethically Important Moments" in research'. *Qualitative Inquiry* 10 (2): 261–80.

Gupta, Akhil and James Ferguson. 1997. *Anthropological Locations: Boundaries and Grounds of a Field Science*. Berkeley: University of California Press.

Habermas, Jürgen and Max Pensky. 2001. *The Postnational Constellation: Political Essays*. Studies in Contemporary German Social Thought. Cambridge: Polity Press.

Hall, David D. 1997. *Lived Religion in America: Toward a History of Practice*. Princeton, NJ: Princeton University Press.

Hamilton, Richard. 2011. *The Last Storytellers: Tales from the Heart of Morocco*. London: I. B. Tauris.

Hammoudi, Abdellah. 2009. 'Textualism and Anthropology: On the Ethnographic Encounter, or an Experience in the Hajj', In *Being There: The Fieldwork Encounter and the Making of Truth*, edited by John Borneman and Abdellah Hammoudi, 25–54. Berkeley: University of California Press.

Hammoudi, Abdellah. 2006. *A Season in Mecca: Narrative of a Pilgrimage*. Cambridge: Polity Press.

Hammoudi, Abdellah. 1997. *Master and Disciple: The Cultural Foundations of Moroccan Authoritarianism*. Chicago: University of Chicago Press.

Hammoudi, Abdellah. 1993. *The Victim and its Masks: An Essay on Sacrifice and Masquerade in the Maghreb* (trans. Paula Wissing). Chicago: University of Chicago Press.

Hammoudi, Abdellah. 1974. 'Segmentarité, Stratification Sociale, Pouvoir Politique et Saintete: Reflections sur les Theses de Gellner'. *Hesperis-Tamuda* 15 (1): 147–80.

Haq, Farooq and John Jackson. 2009. 'Spiritual Journey to Hajj: Australian and Pakistani Experience and Expectations'. *Journal of Management, Spirituality & Religion* 6 (2): 141–56.

Harb, Mona and Sami Atallah. 2014. 'Decentralization in the Arab World Must be Strengthened to Provide Better Services'. *IE-Med Mediterranean Yearbook 2015*. Barcelona: European Institute of the Mediterranean. https://www.iemed.org/publicacions/historic-de-publicacions/anuari-de-la-mediterrania/sumaris/iemed-mediterranean-yearbook-2015

Harnish, David D. and Anne K. Rasmussen. 2011. *Divine Inspiration: Music and Islam in Indonesia*. New York: Oxford University Press.

Harris, Max. 2019. *Christ on a Donkey: Palm Sunday, Triumphal Entries, and Blasphemous Pageants*. Early Social Performance. Kalamazoo: Arc Humanities Press.

Hart, David. 1976. *The Aith Waryaghar of the Moroccan Rif: An Ethnography and History*. Tucson: University of Arizona Press.

Havard, Megan E. 2018. 'When Brother Becomes Other: Communitas and Conflict along the Camino de Santiago'. *International Journal of Religious Turism and Pilgrimage* 6 (2): 89–97.

Hearn, Dana. 1998. 'Fatawa and Religious Discourse as an Avenue of Participation'. *The Arab Studies Journal* 6–7: 84–97.

Heck, Paul L. 2012. 'An Early Response to Wahhabism from Morocco: The Politics of Intercession'. *Studia Islamica* 107 (2): 235–54.

Hemer, Susan R. and Alison Dundon (eds). 2016. *Emotions, Senses, Spaces: Ethnographic Engagements and Intersections*. Adelaide: University of Adelaide Press.

Hendrickson, Jocelyn. 2016. 'Prohibiting the Pilgrimage: Politics and Fiction in Mālikī "Fatwās"'. *Islamic Law and Society* 23 (3): 161–238.

Hirschkind, Charles. 2006. *The Ethical Soundscape: Cassette Sermons and Islamic Counterpublics*. New York: Columbia University Press.

Hirschkind, Charles. 2001. 'The Ethics of Listening: Cassette-Sermon Audition in Contemporary Egypt'. *American Ethnologist* 28 (3): 623–49.

Hissouf, Abdellatif. 2016. 'The Monarchy and the Islam-oriented PJD: Pragmatic Cohabitation and the Need for Islamic Political Secularism'. *All Azimuth* 5 (1): 43–56.

Hlaoua, Aziz and Cedric Baylocq. 2016 'Spreading a "Moderate Islam"? Morocco's New African Religious Diplomacy'. *Afrique contemporaine* 257(1): 113–28.

Hmimnat, Salim. 2020. '"Spiritual Security" As a (Meta-)Political Strategy to Compete over Regional Leadership: Formation of Morocco's Transnational Religious Policy Towards Africa'. *The Journal of North African Studies* 25 (2): 189–227.

Hmimnat, Salim. 2018. *Al-Siyāsa al-Dīniyya bi l-Maghrib 1984–2002* [Religious Policy in Morocco 1984–2002]. Casablanca: Afrique Orient.

Hobday, Peter. 1979. *Saudi Arabia Today: An Introduction to the Richest Oil Power*. New York: St. Martin's Press.

Hoffman, Bernard G. 1967. *The Structure of Traditional Moroccan Rural Society*. Studies in Social Anthropology, Vol. 2. The Hague: Mouton.

Hoffman, Valerie J. 1999. 'Annihilation in the Messenger of God: The Development of a Sufi Practice'. *International Journal of Middle East Studies* 31(3): 351–69.

Hoffman-Ladd, Valerie J. 1992. 'Devotion to the Prophet and His Family in Egyptian Sufism'. *International Journal of Middle East Studies* 24 (4): 615–37.

Hoisington, William A. 1978. 'Cities in Revolt: The Berber Dahir (1930) and France's Urban Strategy in Morocco'. *Journal of Contemporary History* (13) 3: 433–48.

Howes, David. 2003. *Sensual Relations: Engaging the Senses in Culture and Social Theory*. Ann Arbor: University of Michigan Press.

Howes, David. 1991. *The Varieties of Sensory Experience: A Sourcebook in the Anthropology of the Senses*. Toronto: University of Toronto Press.

Howe, Marvine. 2005. The Islamist Awakening and Other Challenges. New York: Oxford University Press.

Hrbek, Ivan. 2020. 'Ibn Battuta'. In *Encyclopædia Britannica, Inc.* https://www.britannica.com/biography/Ibn-Battuta

Hurgronje, Christiaan Snouck. 2007. *Mekka in de tweede helft van de negentiende eeuw. Schetsen uit het dagelijks leven*. Amsterdam: Uitgeverij Atlas.

Hyndman-Rizk, Nelia. 2012. *Pilgrimage in the Age of Globalisation: Constructions of the Sacred and Secular in Late Modernity*. Newcastle upon Tyne: Cambridge Scholars.

Ibn Jubayr, Muhammad. 2012. *Riḥlat ibn Jubayr* [The Travels of Ibn Jubayr]. Beirut: Dar Sader.

Ibn Kathīr, Ismāʿīl. 1986. *Tafsīr Ibn Kathīr* [Ibn Kathīr's Interpretations of the Qur'an]. Beirut: Dār al-Fikr.

Ibn Mājah, Muhammad. 1999. *Sunan Ibn Mājah*. Mecca: Maktabat Nizār Muṣṭafa al-Bāz.

Ibrahim, Barbara and Dina H. Sherif (eds). 2008. *From Charity to Social Change Trends in Arab Philanthropy*. Cairo: The American University in Cairo Press.

Ibrahim, Barbara and Dina H. Sherif (eds). 1991. *Varieties of Sensory Experience: A Sourcebook in the Anthropology of the Senses*. Toronto: University of Toronto Press.

Ilahiane, Hsain. 2006. *Historical Dictionary of the Berbers (Imazighen)*. Lanham: Scarecrow Press.

Iskander, John. 2007. 'Devout Heretics: The Barghawata in Maghribi Historiography'. *The Journal of North African Studies* 12 (1): 37–53.

Ismail, Salwa. 2006. *Political Life in Cairo's New Quarters: Encountering the Everyday State*. Minneapolis: University of Minnesota Press.

Jackson, Michael. 2002. *Politics of Storytelling: Violence, Transgression and Intersubjectivity*. Copenhagen: Museum Tusculanum Press.

Jamal, Ahmad, Razaq Raj and Kevin A. Griffin (eds). 2018. *Islamic Tourism: Management of Travel Destinations*. Boston, MA: CABI.

James, William. 2012. *Essays in Radical Empiricism*. Auckland: Floating Press.

Jankowsky, Richard C. 2010. *Stambeli: Music, Trance, and Alterity*. Chicago: University of Chicago Press.

Jansen, Willy and Catrien Notermans. 2012. *Gender, Nation and Religion in European Pilgrimage*. Farnham: Ashgate.

Jenkins, Richard. 1997. *Rethinking Ethnicity: Arguments and Explorations*. London: SAGE.

Johnson, Andrew. 2014. 'Mecca under Threat: Outrage at Plan to Destroy the "Birthplace" of the Prophet Mohamed and Replace It with a New Palace and Luxury Mall'. http://www.islamicpluralism.org/2425/mecca-under-threat

Joll, Christopher M. 2011. Muslim Merit-Making in Thailand's Far-South. Muslims in Global Societies Series 4. Springer. https://www.academia.edu/1975047/Muslim_Merit-making_in_Thailands_Far-south_Springer_2011_

Jones, Delmos. 2008. 'Anthropology and the Oppressed: A Reflection of "Native" Anthropology'. *NAPA Bulletin* 16 (1): 58–70.

Joseph, Suad (ed.). 2018. *Arab Family Studies: Critical Reviews*. Syracuse, NY: Syracuse University Press.

Joseph, Suad and Marilyn Booth (eds). 2013. *Women and Islamic Cultures: Disciplinary Paradigms and Approaches, 2003–2013*. Leiden: Boston.

Joseph, Suad and Afsaneh Najmabadi. 2003. *Encyclopedia of Women and Islamic Cultures*. Gale Virtual Reference Library. Leiden: Brill.

Joseph, Suad and Susan Slyomovics (eds). 2001. *Women and Power in the Middle East*. Upcc Book Collections on Project Muse. Philadelphia, PA: University of Pennsylvania Press.

Kadrouch Outmany, Khadija. 2016. 'Religion at the Cemetery: Islamic Burials in the Netherlands and Belgium'. *Contemporary Islam: Dynamics of Muslim Life* 10 (1): 87–105.

Kadrouch-Outmany, Khadija and Marjo Buitelaar. 2020. 'Young Moroccan-Dutch Women on Hajj'. In *Muslim Women's Pilgrimage to Mecca and Beyond: Reconfiguring Gender, Religion and Mobility*, edited by Marjo Buitelaar, Manja Stephan-Emmrich and Viola Thimm, 36–55. London and New York: Routledge.

Kandiyoti, Deniz. 1991. *Women, Islam and the State*. Basingstoke: Macmillan.

Kapchan, Deborah A. 2008. 'The Promise of Sonic Translation: Performing the Festive Sacred in Morocco'. *American Anthropologist* 110 (4): 467–83.

Kapchan, Deborah A. 2007. 'Memory, Music and Religion: Morocco's Mystical Chanters'. *Religion* 37 (1): 104–6.

Kapferer, Bruce. 2019. 'Crisis and Communitas: Victor Turner and Social Process'. *Anthropology Today* 35 (5): 1–2.

Kateman, Ammeke. 2023. 'Experiencing the Hajj in an Age of Change: Tuning the Emotions in Several Hajj Accounts of Pilgrims Travelling from Morocco and Egypt in the First Half of the Twentieth Century'. In *Narrating the Pilgrimage to Mecca*, edited by Marjo Buitelaar and Richard van Leeuwen, 183–203. Leiden: Brill.

Katz, Marion Holmes. 2013. *Prayer in Islamic Thought and Practice*. Cambridge: Cambridge University Press.

Katz, Marion Holmes. 2004. 'The Hajj and the Study of Islamic Ritual'. *Studia Islamica* 98– 9: 95–129.

Kaye, Dalia Dassa. 2008. *More Freedom, Less Terror?: Liberalization and Political Violence in the Arab World*. Santa Monica, CA: RAND Corp. https://www.jstor.org/stable/10.7249/mg772rc

Kazi, Abdul Khaliq. 1966. 'The Meaning of Īmān and Islām in the Qur'an'. *Islamic Studies* 5 (3): 227–37. www.jstor.org/stable/20832845

Kechichian, Joseph. 1986. 'The Role of the "Ulama" in the Politics of an Islamic State: The Case of Saudi Arabia'. *International Journal of Middle East Studies* 18 (1): 53–71.

Kelly Spurles, Patricia L. 2004. *Henna for Brides and Gazelles: Ritual, Women's Work, and Tourism in Morocco*. Montréal: Université de Montréal.

Kenny, Erin. 2007. 'Gifting Mecca: Importing Spiritual Capital to West Africa'. *Mobilities* 2 (3): 363–81.

Khan, Naveeda. 2012. *Muslim Becoming: Aspiration and Skepticism in Pakistan*. Durham, NC: Duke University Press.

Khan, Naveeda. 2006. 'Of Children and Jinn: An Inquiry into an Unexpected Friendship during Uncertain Times'. *Cultural Anthropology* 21 (2): 234–64.

Khel, Muhammad Nazeer Ka Ka, 1981. 'Bayʿa and its Political Role in the Early Islamic State'. *Islamic Studies* 20 (3): 227–38. http://www.jstor.org/stable/20847171

King, Judith. 2023. 'The Struggle to Define Pilgrimage'. *Religions* 14 (1): 79.

King, Mike. 2007. *Secularism: The Hidden Origins of Disbelief*. Cambridge: James Clarke.

Kioumgi, Farid and and Robert Graham. 2009. *A Photographer on the Hajj: The Travels of Muhammad 'Ali Effendi Sa'udi (1904/1908)*. Cairo: The American University in Cairo Press.

Kloos, David and Daan Beekers. 2017. 'Introduction: The Productive Potential of Moral Failure in Lived Islam and Christianity'. In *Straying from the Straight Path: How Senses of Failure Invigorate Lived Religion*, edited by Daan Beekers and David Kloos, 1–20. New York and Oxford: Berghahn.

Kramer, Martin. 1990. 'Khomeini's Messengers: The Disputed Pilgrimage of Islam'. In *Religious Radicalism and Politics in the Middle East*, edited by Emmanuel Sivan and Menachem Friedman, 177–94. Albany, NY: State University of New York Press.

Kraus, Wolfgang. 1998. 'Contestable Identities: Tribal Structures in the Moroccan High Atlas'. *The Journal of the Royal Anthropological Institute* 4 (1): 1–22.

Kruk, Remke. 1995. 'Ibn Battuta: Travel, Family Life and Chronology'. *Al-Qantara* 16 (2): 369–84.

Kruk, Remke and Frans Oort. 2015. 'Hajj Murals in Dakhla Oasis (Egypt)'. In *Hajj: Global Interactions through Pilgrimage*, edited by Luitgard E. M. Mols and Marjo Buitelaar, 163–84. Leiden: Sidestone Press.

Kurin, Richard. 1984. 'Morality, Personhood and the Exemplary Life: Popular Conceptions of Muslims in Paradise'. In *Moral Conduct and Authority: The Place of Adab in South Asian Islam*, edited by Barbara Metcalf, 196–220. Berkeley: University of California Press.

Laan, Nina Ter. 2016. 'Dissonant Voices: Islam-Inspired Music in Morocco and the Politics of Religious Sentiments'. PhD thesis, Radboud University Nijmegen.

Lakoff, George and Mark Johnson. 2003. *Metaphors We Live By*. Chicago: University of Chicago Press.

Lakoff, George and Mark Johnson. 1999. *Philosophy in the Flesh: The Embodied Mind and its Challenge to Western Thought*. New York: Basic Books.

Lambek, Michael. 2000. 'The Anthropology of Religion and the Quarrel between Poetry and Philosophy'. *Current Anthropology* 41 (3): 309–20.

Landau, Rom. 1962. *Hassan II King of Morocco*. Edinburgh: Edinburgh University Press.

Larsson, Göran and Simon Sorgenfrei. 2021. '"How Is One Supposed to Sleep When the Ka'ba Is Over There?"'. *Journal of Muslims in Europe* 10 (3): 309–30.

Larsson, Göran and Simon Sorgenfrei. Langlois, Tony. 1996. 'Music and Contending Identities in the Maghreb'. In *Nationalism, Minorities and Diasporas: Identities and Rights in the Middle East*, edited by Kirsten E. Schulze, Martin Stokes and Colm Campbell, 203–16. London: I. B. Tauris.

Laughlin, Charles and John McManus. 1995. 'The Relevance of the Radical Empiricism of William James to the Anthropology of Conciousness'. *Anthropology of Consiousness* 6 (3): 34–46.

Law, Bill. 2015. 'Hajj Stampede: Strain on al-Sauds amid Feuds, War and Incompetence'. *Independent*. http://www.masjidtucson.org/submission/practices/hajj/foursacredmonths.html

Lecomte, G. 2012. 'al-Saḳīfa'. In *Encyclopaedia of Islam, Second Edition*. Leiden: Brill Online. http://dx.doi.org/10.1163/1573-3912_islam_COM_0980

Linde, Charlotte. 1993. *Life Stories: The Creation of Coherence*. Oxford Studies in Sociolinguistics. New York: Oxford University Press.

Lortat-Jacob, Bernard. 1979. 'Music as a Collective Enterprise: The Case of Berber Music of the High Atlas'. *The World of Music* 21 (3): 62–77.

Lövheim, Mia. 2013. *Media, Religion and Gender: Key Issues and New Challenges*. New York: Routledge.

Lövheim, Mia. 2011. 'Young Women's Blogs as Ethical Spaces'. *Information, Communication & Society* 14 (3): 338–54.

Lücking, Mirjam. 2017. 'Working in Mecca: How Informal Pilgrimage-Migration from Madura, Indonesia, to Saudi Arabia Challenges State Sovereignty'. *European Journal of East Asian studies* 16 (2): 248–74.

Lutz, Catherine and Lila Abu-Lughod. 1990. *Language and the Politics of Emotion*. Studies in Emotion and Social Interaction. Cambridge: Cambridge University Press.

Macdonald, D. B. 2012. 'Fiṭra'. In *Encyclopaedia of Islam, Second Edition*. Leiden: Brill Online. http://dx.doi.org/10.1163/1573-3912_islam_SIM_2391

Madani, Mohamed, Driss Maghraoui and Saloua Zerhouni. 2012. 'The 2011 Moroccan Constitution: A Critical Analysis'. International Institute for Democracy and Electoral Assistance. Stockholm: IDEA. https://www.idea.int/sites/default/files/publications/the-2011-moroccan-constitution-critical-analysis.pdf

Maghniyyah, Muhammad Jawad. 1997. *The Hajj According to Five Schools of Islamic Law*. Tehran: Department of Translation and Publication, Islamic Culture and Relations Organization.

Maghraoui, Abdeslam M. 2019. 'From Authoritarian Pluralism to Centralized Autocracy in Morocco'. In *The Lure of Authoritarianism: The Maghreb after the Arab Spring*, edited by Stephen J. King and Abdeslam Maghraoui, 264–82. Indiana Series in Middle East Studies. Bloomington, IN: Indiana University Press. www.jstor.org/stable/j.ctvfc54tb.14

Maghraoui, Abdeslam M. 2001. 'Political Authority in Crisis: Mohammed VI's Morocco'. *Middle East Report* (218): 12–17. www.jstor.org/stable/1559304

Mahmood, Saba. 2005. *Politics of Piety: The Islamic Revival and the Feminist Subject*. Anthropology Online. Princeton, NJ: Princeton University Press.

Makris, G. P. 2007. *Islam in the Middle East: A Living Tradition*. Oxford: Blackwell.

Maqsood, Ruqaiyyah. 2008. *Need to Know: Islam*. London: HarperCollins.

Marcus, George. 1998. *Ethnography through Thick and Thin*. Princeton, NJ: Princeton University Press.

Marcus, George and Michael Fisher. 1986. *Anthropology as Cultural Critique*. Chicago: University of Chicago Press.

Maréchal, Brigitte and Felice Dassetto. 2014. *Hamadcha du Maroc. Rituels musicaux, mystiques et de possession*. Louvain-la-Neuve: Presses Universitaires de Louvain.

Marsden, Magnus. 2005. *Living Islam: Muslim Religious Experience in Pakistan's North-West Frontier*. Cambridge: Cambridge University Press.

Marshall, Patricia A. 1992. 'Research Ethics in Applied Anthropology'. *IRB: Ethics & Human Research* 14 (6): 1–5.

Masbah, Mohammed. 2017. 'A New Generation of Protests in Morocco? How Hirak al-Rif Endures'. *Policy Alternatives: Arab Reform Initiative*. https://archives.arab-reform.net/en/node/1102

Mateo Dieste, Josep Lluís. 2013. *Health and Ritual in Morocco: Conceptions of the Body and Healing Practices*. Social, Economic, and Political Studies of the Middle East and Asia, V. 109. Boston: Brill.

Matthews, Anis and Daud R. Matthews. 1996. *A Guide to Hajj-'Umrah*. Riyadh: Dar Al-Hadyah.

Mawdudi, Sayyid A. 1982. *Origin and Significance of the Hajj*. http://www.islamicity.com/mosque/hajj/letsbemuslims.htm

Mazumdar, Shampa and Sanjoy Mazumdar. 2002. 'In Mosques and Shrines: Women's Agency In Public Sacred Space'. *Journal of Ritual Studies* 16 (2): 165–79.

Mazumdar, Shampa and Sanjoy Mazumdar. 1999. 'Ritual Lives of Muslim Women: Agency in Everyday Life'. *Journal of Ritual Studies* 13 (2): 58–70.

McGuire, Meredith B. 2008. *Lived Religion: Faith and Practice in Everyday Life*. Oxford: Oxford University Press.

McIntosh, Ian, E. Moore Quinn and Vivienne Keely (eds). 2018. *Pilgrimage in Practice: Narration, Reclamation and Healing*. Cabi Religious Tourism and Pilgrimage Series. Wallingford: CABI.

McIntyre, Ronald R. 2015. 'Saudi Arabia'. In *The Politics of Islamic Reassertion*, edited by Mohammed Ayoob, 9–29. New York: Routledge.

McLoughlin, Leslie. 1993. *Ibn Saud: Founder of a Kingdom*. London: Palgrave Macmillan.

McLoughlin, Sean. 2013. 'Organizing Hajj-going from Contemporary Britain: A Changing Industry, Pilgrim Markets and the Politics of Recognition'. In *The Hajj: Collected Essays*, edited by V. Porter and Liana Saif, 241–52. London: The British Museum Press.

McLoughlin, Sean. 2010. 'Muslim Travellers: Homing Desire, the Umma, and British-Pakistanis'. In *Diasporas: Concepts, Identities, Intersections*, edited by Kim Knott and Sean McLoughlin, 223–9. London: Zed Books.

McLoughlin, Sean. 2009a. 'Holy Places, Contested Spaces: British-Pakistani Accounts of Pilgrimage to Makkah and Madinah'. In *Muslims in Britain: Identities, Places and Landscapes*, edited by Peter Hopkins and Richard Gale, 132–49. Edinburgh: Edinburgh University Press. www.jstor.org/stable/10.3366/j.ctt1r2820

McLoughlin, Sean. 2009b. 'Contesting Muslim Pilgrimage: British-Pakistani Identities, Sacred Journeys to Makkah and Madinah, and the Global Postmodern'. In *The Pakistani Diaspora*, edited by Virinder S. Kalra, 233–65. Karachi and Oxford: Oxford University Press.

Meijer, Roel. 2010. 'Reform in Saudi Arabia: The Gender-Segregation Debate'. *Middle East Policy* 17 (4): 80–100. http://mepc.org/journal/middle-east-policy-archives/reform-saudi-arabia-gender- segregation-debate

Mernissi, Fatima. 1994. *Dreams of Trespass: Tales of a Harem Girlhood*. Reading, MA: Addison-Wesley.

Metcalf, Barbara D. 1990. 'The Pilgrimage Remembered: South Asian Accounts of the Hajj'. In *Muslim Travelers*, edited by Dale F. Eickelmen and James Piscatori, 85–107. London: Routledge.

Metcalf, Barbara D. 1984. *Moral Conduct and Authority: The Place of Adab in South Asian Islam*. Berkeley: University of California Press.

Meyer, Birgit. 2011. 'Religious Sensations: Media, Aesthetics, and the Study of Contemporary Religion'. In *Religion, Media and Culture: A Reader*, edited by Gordon Lynch et al., 159–70. London: Routledge.

Meyer, Birgit. 2009. *Aesthetic Formations: Media, Religion, and the Senses*. New York: Palgrave Macmillan.

Meyer, Birgit. 2006. 'Religious Sensations: Why Media, Aesthetics, and Power Matter in the Study of Contemporary Religion'. Inaugural lecture, Vrije Universiteit Amsterdam. http://www.fsw.vu.nl/nl/Images/Oratietekst%20Birgit%20Meyer_tcm30-36764.pdf

Meyer, Birgit and Annelies Moors (eds). 2006. *Religion, Media, and the Public Sphere*. Bloomington: Indiana University Press.

Migdadi, Fathi, Muhammad A. Badarneh and Kawakib Momani. 2010. 'Divine Will and its Extensions: Communicative Functions of maašaallah in Colloquial Jordanian Arabic'. *Communication Monographs* 77 (4): 480–99.

Miller, Susan Gilson. 2013. *A History of Modern Morocco*. New York: Cambridge University Press.

Mines, Diane P. and Sarah Lamb (eds). 2010. *Everyday Life in South Asia*. Bloomington: Indiana University Press.

Mols, Luitgard and Marjo Buitelaar (eds). 2015. *Hajj: Global Interactions through Pilgrimage*. Mededelingen van het Rijksmuseum voor Volkenkunde Leiden, vol. 43. Leiden: Sidestone.

Morris, James Winston. 1987. 'The Spiritual Ascension: Ibn 'Arabī and the Mi'rāj Part I'. *Journal of the American Oriental Society* 107 (4): 629–52.

Motadel, David (ed.). 2014. *Islam and the European Empires*. Oxford: Oxford University Press.

Munson, Henry. 1993. *Religion and Power in Morocco*. New Haven: Yale University Press.

Munson, Henry. 1984. *The House of Si Abd Allah: The Oral History of a Moroccan Family*. New Haven: Yale University Press.

Munt, Harry. 2014. *The Holy City of Medina: Sacred Space in Early Islamic Arabia*. New York: Cambridge University Press.

Murata, Sachiko and William Chittick. 1994. *The Vision of Islam*. London: Paragon House.

Muslim, Ibn al-Ḥajjāj. 1983. *Ṣaḥīh Muslim*. Edited by Muḥummad Fu'ād 'Abd al-Bāqī. Beirut: Dār al-Fikr.

Narayan, Kirin. 1993. 'How Native is "Native" Anthropologist?'. *American Anthropologist* 95 (3): 671–86.

Nasr, Ahmad. and Abu Bakar Bagader. 2001. 'Al-Gēs: Women's Festival and Drama in Mecca'. *Journal of Folklore Research* 38 (3): 243–62.

Nasrawi, Salah. 2007. 'Mecca's Ancient Heritage Is Under Attack'. *Los Angeles Times*. http://articles.latimes.com/2007/sep/16/news/adfg-mecca16

Naṣṣār, Husayn. 1991. *Adab al-Riḥla* [The Literature of Travel Writing]. Beirut: Librairie Du Liban.

Nehme, Michel G. 1994. 'Saudi Arabia 1950–80: Between Nationalism and Religion'. *Middle Eastern Studies* 30 (4): 930–43.

Nelson, Harold D. 1978. *Morocco, a Country Study*. Washington, DC: US Government Printing Office.

Nevo, Joseph. 1998. 'Religion and National Identity in Saudi Arabia'. *Middle Eastern Studies* 34 (3): 34–53.

Newcomb, Rachel. 2017. *Everyday Life in Global Morocco*. Bloomington: Indiana University Press.

Newcomb, Rachel. 2010. *Women of Fes: Ambiguities of Urban Life in Morocco*. Pennsylvania: University of Pennsylvania Press.

Nieuwkerk, Karin van. 2011. *Muslim Rap, Halal Soaps, and Revolutionary Theater: Artistic Developments in the Muslim World*. Austin: University of Texas Press.

Nooshin, Laudan. 2009. *Music and the Play of Power in the Middle East, North Africa and Central Asia*. Farnham: Ashgate.

O'Brien, Susan. 1999. 'Pilgrimage, Power, and Identity: The Role of the Hajj in the Lives of Nigerian Hausa Bori Adepts'. *Africa Today* 46 (3–4): 10–40.

O'Connor, Paul James. 2012. *Islam in Hong Kong: Muslims and Everyday Life in China's World City*. Hong Kong China: Hong Kong University Press.

Obdeijn, Herman, Paolo De Mas and Philip Hermans. 1999. *Geschiedenis van Marokko* [History of Morocco]. Amsterdam: Bulaaq.

Ochsenwald, William. 1984. *Religion, Society, and the State in Arabia: The Hijaz under Ottoman Control, 1840–1908*. Columbus: Ohio State University Press.

Ochsenwald, William. 1980. *The Hijaz Railroad*. Charlottesville, VA: University Press of Virginia.

Orsi, Robert A. 2003. 'Is the Study of Lived Religion Irrelevant to the World We Live In?'. Special Presidential Plenary Address, Society for the Scientific Study of Religion, Salt Lake City, 2 November 2002. *Journal for the Scientific Study of Religion* 42 (2): 169–74.

Osella, Filippo and Benhamin Soares. 2009. 'Islam, Politics, Anthropology'. *Journal of the Royal Anthropological Institute* 15 (1): S1–S23.

Ouguir, Aziza. 2013. *Female Religious Agents in Morocco: Old Practices and New Perspectives*. PhD thesis, Universiteit van Amsterdam.

Page, Simon. 2014. 'Mecca: The "Blessed Heart" of Islam'. In *Between Cultural Diversity and Common Heritage; Legal and Religious Perspectives on the Sacred Places of the Mediterranean*, edited by Silvio Ferrari and Andrea Benzo, 319–30. Farnham: Ashgate.

Parker, Anne and Avon Neal. 1995. *Hajj Paintings: Folk Art of the Great Pilgrimage*. Washington, DC and London: Smithsonian Institution Press.

Pearson, M. N. 1994. *Pious Passengers: The Hajj in Earlier Times*. London: Hurst.

Pennell, C. R. 2002. *Morocco: From Empire to Independence*. Oxford: Oneworld.

Perecman, Ellen and Sara R. Curran. 2006. *A Handbook for Social Science Field Research: Essays and Bibliographic Sources on Research Design and Methods*. Thousand Oaks, CA: Sage.

Peters, Francis Edward. 2017. *Mecca: A Literary History of the Muslim Holy Land*. Princeton, NJ: Princeton University Press.

Peters, Francis Edward. 2017 [1984]. *Jerusalem: The Holy City in the Eyes of Chroniclers, Visitors, Pilgrims, and Prophets from the Days of Abraham to the Beginnings of Modern Times*. Princeton, NJ: Princeton University Press.

Peters, Francis Edward. 1994. *The Hajj: The Muslim Pilgrimage to Mecca and the Holy Places*. Princeton, NJ.: Princeton University Press.

Peterson, John. 2003. *Historical Dictionary of Saudi Arabia*. Lanham, MD: Scarecrow Press.

Podeh, Elie. 2010. 'The "Bayʿa": Modern Political Uses of Islamic Ritual in the Arab World'. *Die Welt Des Islams* 50 (1): 117–52.

Poliakov S. P and Martha Brill Olcott. 1992. *Everyday Islam: Religion and Tradition in Rural Central Asia*. Armonk, NY: M. E. Sharpe.

Polletta, Francesca and James M Jasper. 2001. 'Collective Identity and Social Movements'. *Annual Review of Sociology* 27 (1): 283–305.

Polletta, Francesca, Pang Ching Bobby Chen, Beth Gharrity Gardner and Alice Motes. 2011. 'The Sociology of Storytelling'. *Annual Review of Sociology* 37: 109–30.

Porcello, Thomas, Louise Meintjes, Ana Maria Ochoa and David W. Samuels. 2010. 'The Recognition of the Sensory World'. *Annual Review of Anthropology* 39: 51–66.

Porter, Geoffrey D. 2001. 'From Madrasa to Maison D'hôte: Historic Preservation in Mohammed VI's Morocco'. *Middle East Report* 218: 34–7.

Porter, Venetia (ed.). 2012. *Hajj: Journey to the Heart of Islam*. London: British Museum Press.

Powers, David S. 2010. 'Demonizing Zenobia: The Legend of al-Zabba' in Islamic Sources'. In *Histories of the Middle East: Studies in Middle Eastern Economy, Society, and Law* in Honor of A. L. Udovitch, edited by Petra M. Sijpesteijn, Roxani Eleni Margariti and Adam Sabra, 127–82. Leiden and Boston: Brill.

Powers, Paul R. 2004. 'Interiors, Intentions, and the "Spirituality" of Islamic Ritual Practice'. *Journal of the American Academy of Religion* 72 (2): 425–59.

Rabinow, Paul. 1977. *Reflections on Fieldwork in Morocco*. Berkeley: University of California Press.

Rahimi, Babak and Peyman Eshaghi (eds). 2019. *Muslim Pilgrimage in the Modern World*. Chapel Hill: University of North Carolina Press.

Rahman, M. Raisur. 2015. *Locale, Everyday Islam and Modernity: Qasbah Towns and Muslim Life in Colonial India*. New Delhi: Oxford University Press.

Rahmouni, Aicha. 2015. *Storytelling in Chefchaouen Northern Morocco: An Annotated Study of Oral Performance with Transliterations and Translations*. Leiden: Brill.

Rasanayagam, Johan. 2017. 'Anthropology in Conversation with an Islamic Tradition: Emmanuel Levinas and the Practice of Critique'. *Journal of the Royal Anthropological Institute* 24 (1): 90–106.

Rashid, Hussein. 2017. 'Hajj: The Pilgrimage'. In *The Practice of Islam in America: An Introduction*, edited by Edward E. Curtis, 60–80. New York: NYU Press. http://www.jstor.org/stable/j.ctt1pwtb7t

Rasmussen, Anne K. 2010. *Women, the Recited Qur'an, and Islamic Music in Indonesia*. Berkeley: University of California Press.

Reader, Ian. 2007. 'Positively Promoting Pilgrimage: Media Representations of Pilgrimage in Japan'. *Nova Religio: The Journal of Alternative and Emergent Religions* 10 (3): 13–31.

Reynolds, Gabriel Said. 2020. *Allah: God in the Qur'an*. New Haven: Yale University Press. http://www.jstor.org/stable/j.ctvxkn7q4

Rhani, Zakaria. 2014. 'The Genealogy of Power and the Power of Genealogy in Morocco: History, Imaginary and Politics'. In *Genealogy and Knowledge in Muslim Societies: Understanding the Past*, edited by Bowen Savant Sarah and De Felipe Helena, 37–52. Edinburgh: Edinburgh University Press. w.jstor.org/stable/10.3366/j.ctt9qdr4r.7

Rippin, Andrew and Teresa Bernheimer. 2018. *Muslims: Their Religious Beliefs and Practices*. London: Routledge.

Rius Pinies, Monica. 2000. *La Alquibla en al-Andalus y al-Magrib al-Aqṣa*. Barcelona: Institut Millas Vallicrosa d'Historia de la Ciencia Arab.

Rizqiyah, Nena Siti and Maman Lesmana. 2018. 'Islamic Religious Values in Maher Zain's Songs'. *IOSR Journal of Humanities and Social Science* 23 (1): 17–24.

Roberson, Jennifer. 2014. 'The Changing Face of Morocco under King Hassan II'. *Mediterranean Studies* 22 (1): 57–87.

Robinson, C. F. 2012. 'Uḥud'. In *Encyclopaedia of Islam, Second Edition*. Leiden: Brill Online. http://dx.doi.org/10.1163/1573-3912_islam_SIM_7685

Rodman, Margaret C. 2003. 'Empowering Place: Multivocality and Multilocality'. In *The Anthropology of Space and Place: Locating Culture*, edited by Setha M. Low and Denise Lawrence-Zúñiga, 204–23. Malden: Blackwell.

Ronström, Owe. 1992. 'On Music and the Rhetoric of Multiculturality'. In *Ethnicity in Youth Culture*, edited by Lövgren Palmgren and Bolin, 179–94. Botkyrka: Invandrarminnesarkivet.

Rosen, Lawrence. 2016. *Two Arabs, a Berber, and a Jew: Entangled Lives in Morocco*. Chicago: University of Chicago Press.

Rosen, Lawrence. 2011. *The Culture of Islam: Changing Aspects of Contemporary Muslim Life*. Chicago: University of Chicago Press.

Ross, Fiona C. 2004. 'Sense-scapes: Senses and Emotions in the Making of Place'. *Anthropology Southern Africa* 27 (1–2): 35–42.

Roy, Olivier. 2013. *Holy Ignorance: When Religion and Culture Part Ways* (trans. Ros Schwartz). New York: Oxford University Press.

Rozehnal, Robert (eds). 2022. *Cyber Muslims: Mapping Islamic Digital Media in the Internet Age*. London: Bloomsbury Academic.

Ruchti, Jefri J. (trans.). 2012. *Morocco's Constitution of 2011*. Getzville, NY: Hein. https://www.constituteproject.org/constitution/Morocco_2011.pdf

Rustomji, Nerina. 2008. *The Garden and the Fire: Heaven and Hell in Islamic Culture*. New York: Columbia University Press.

Ryad, Umar (ed.). 2017. *The Hajj and Europe in the Age of Empire*. Leiden: Brill.

Sadiqi, Fatima. 2018. 'Female Perceptions of Islam in Today's Morocco'. *Journal of Feminist Scholarship* 11: 48–60.

Sadiqi, Fatima. 2010. 'Women's Rights in the Middle East and North Africa'. Freedom House, Morocco. https://www.refworld.org/docid/4b990120c.html

Sadiqi, Fatima. 2008. 'The Central Role of the Family Law in the Moroccan Feminist Movement'. *British Journal of Middle Eastern Studies* 35 (3): 325–37.

Sadiqi, Fatima. 2006. 'The Impact of Islamization on Moroccan Feminisms'. *Signs: Journal of Women in Culture and Society* 32 (1): 32–40.

Sadiqi, Fatima. 2003. *Women, Gender, and Language in Morocco*. Leiden: Brill.

Sadiqi, Fatima and Aziza Ouguir. 2018. 'Reflecting on Feminisms in Africa'. *Meridians* 17 (2): 269–78.

Safran, Nadav. 1988. *Saudi Arabia: The Ceaseless Quests for Security*. Ithaca: Cornell University Press.

Sakr, Naomi. 2008. 'Women and Media in Saudi Arabia: Rhetoric, Reductionism and Realities'. *British Journal of Middle Eastern Studies* 35 (3): 385–404. http://www.jstor.org/stable/20455617

Salamé, Ghassan. 1987. 'Islam and Politics in Saudi Arabia'. *Arab Studies Quarterly* 9 (3): 306–26. http://www.jstor.org/stable/41857933

Sallnow, Michael J. 1987. *Pilgrims of the Andes: Regional Cults in Cusco*. Washington, DC: Smithsonian Institution Press.

Sallnow, Michael J. 1981. 'Communitas Reconsidered: The Sociology of Andean Pilgrimage'. *Man*, New Series 16 (2): 163–82.

Samman, Khaldoun. 2007. *Cities of God and Nationalism: Mecca, Jerusalem, and Rome as Contested World Cities*. Boulder: Paradigm.

Sardar, Ziauddin. 2014. *Mecca: The Sacred City*. New York: Bloomsbury.

Sardi, Maria. 2013. 'Weaving for the Hajj under the Mamluks'. In *The Hajj: Collected Essays*, edited by Venetia Porter and Liana Saif, 169–74. London: The British Museum Press.

Sater, James. 2016. *Morocco: Challenges to Tradition and Modernity*. London: Routledge.

Schaefer, John Philip Rode. 2012. 'Protest Song Marocaine'. *Middle East Report* 263: 26–32.

Scherer-Rath, Michael, Maaike de Haardt and Reinder Ruard Ganzevoort. 2014. *Religious Stories We Live By: Narrative Approaches in Theology and Religious Studies*. Leiden: Brill.

Schielke, Samuli. 2015. *Egypt in the Future Tense: Hope, Frustration, and Ambivalence Before and After 2011*. Bloomington, IN: Indiana University Press.

Schielke, Samuli. 2012. *The Perils of Joy: Contesting Mulid Festivals in Contemporary Egypt*. Syracuse, NY: Syracuse University Press.

Schielke, Samuli. 2010. 'Second Thoughts on the Anthropology of Islam'. ZMO Working Papers. http://zmo.de/publikationen/WorkingPapers/schiel- ke_2010.pdf

Schielke, Samuli. 2009. 'Being Good in Ramadan: Ambivalence, Fragmentation, and the Moral Self in the Lives of Young Egyptians'. *The Journal of the Royal Anthropological Institute* 15: S24–40. www.jstor.org/stable/20527687

Schielke, Samuli. 2008. 'Policing Ambiguity: Muslim Saints-Day Festivals and the Moral Geography of Public Space in Egypt'. *American Ethnologist* 35 (4): 539–52.

Schielke, Samuli and Liza Debevec (eds). 2012. *Ordinary Lives and Grand Schemes: An Anthropology of Everyday Religion*. New York: Berghahn.

Schimmel, Annemarie. 1994. *Deciphering the Signs of God: A Phenomenological Approach to Islam*. Albany: State University of New York Press.

Schulte Nordholt, Henk and Fridus Steijlen. 2007. 'Don't Forget to Remember Me: An Audiovisual Archive of Everyday Life in Indonesia in the 21st Century'. *Indonesian Studies Working Papers*, University of Sydney, No. 1.

Schulz, Dorothea E. 2012. *Muslims and New Media in West Africa: Pathways to God*. Book Collections on Project Muse. Bloomington: Indiana University Press.

Schulz, Dorothea E. 2008. 'Soundscape'. In *Key Words in Religion, Media, and Culture*, edited by David Morgan, 172–86. New York: Routledge.

Schulz, Dorothea E. 2006. 'Promises of (Im)mediate Salvation: Islam, Broadcast Media, and the Remaking of Religious Experience in Mali'. *American Ethnologist* 33 (2): 210–29.

Schulz, Dorothea E. 2003. '"Charisma and Brotherhood" Revisited: Mass-mediated Forms of Spirituality in Urban Mali'. *Journal of Religion in Africa* 33 (2): 146–71.

Schuyler, Philip D. 1985. 'The Rwais and the Zawia: Professional Musicians and the Rural Religious Elite in Southwestern Morocco'. *Asian Music* 17 (1): 114–31.

Schuyler, Philip D. 1981. 'Music and Meaning among the Gnawa Religious Brotherhood of Morocco'. *The World of Music* 23 (1): 3–13.

Scupin, Raymond. 1982. 'The Social Significance of the Hajj for Thai Muslims'. *The Muslim World* 72 (1): 25–33.

Shaikh, Fazlur Rehman. 2001. *Chronology of Prophetic Events*. London: Ta-Ha.

Shair, I. M. and P. P. Karan. 1979. 'Geography of the Islamic Pilgrimage'. *GeoJournal* 3 (6): 599–608. http://www.jstor.org/stable/41142335

Shannon, Jonathan Holt. 2015. *Performing Al-Andalus: Music and Nostalgia across the Mediterranean*. Bloomington: Indiana University Press.

Shannon, Jonathan Holt. 2006. *Among the Jasmine Trees: Music and Modernity in Contemporary Syria*. Middletown, CT: Wesleyan University Press.

Shatzmiller, Maya. 2005. *Nationalism and Minority Identities in Islamic Societies*. Montreal: McGill-Queen's University Press.

Sherif, Bahira. 2001. 'The Ambiguity of Boundaries in the Fieldwork Experience: Establishing Rapport and Negotiating Insider/Outsider Status'. *Qualitative Inquiry* 7 (4): 436–47.

Shiloah, Amnon. 1997. 'Music and Religion in Islam'. *Acta Musicologica* 69 (2): 143–55.

Shiloah, Amnon. 1995. *Music in the World of Islam: A Socio-Cultural Study.* Aldershot: Scolar Press.

Shoemaker, Stephen J. 2012. *The Death of a Prophet: The End of Muhammad's Life and the Beginnings of Islam.* Philadelphia: University of Pennsylvania Press. http://www.jstor.org/stable/j.ctt3fh8r9

Sijapati, Megan Adamson. 2021. 'Everyday Religiosity and Extraordinary Experiences: Nepali Muslim Narratives of Hajj'. In *Muslim Communities and Cultures of the Himalayas: Conceptualizing the Global Ummah.* New York: Routledge.

Sijapati, Megan Adamson. 2018. 'Preparing for the House of God: Nepali Muslim Narratives of the Hajj'. *Himalaya (Portland, Or.)* 38 (2): 106–15.

Simon, Gregory M. 2014. *Caged in on the Outside: Moral Subjectivity, Selfhood, and Islam in Minangkabau, Indonesia.* Honolulu: University of Hawai'i Press.

Simpson, Andrew. 2008. *Language and National Identity in Africa.* Oxford: Oxford University Press.

Skeiker, Fadi F. 2010. 'Once Upon a Time'. *Storytelling, Self, Society* 6 (3): 223–30.

Slight, John. 2015. *The British Empire and the Hajj, 1865–1956.* Cambridge, MA: Harvard University Press.

Smith, Jane I. 1980. *Women in Contemporary Muslim Societies.* Lewisburg, PA: Bucknell University Press.

Soares, Benjamin F. 2004. 'Muslim Saints in the Age of Neoliberalism'. In *Producing African Futures: Ritual and Reproduction in a Neoliberal Age,* edited by Brad Weiss, 79–105. Leiden: Brill.

Soares, Benjamin F. 2000. 'Notes on the Anthropological Study of Islam and Muslim Societies in Africa'. *Culture & Religion* 1 (2): 227–85.

Sparkes, Andrew C. 2009. 'Ethnography and the Senses: Challenges and Possibilities'. *Qualitative Research in Sport and Exercise* 1 (1): 21–35.

Sparkes, Jason Idriss. 2022. 'Morocco as a Hub of Globalised Traditional Islam'. *Religions* 13 (5): 392.

Spiegel, Avi. 2015. *Young Islam: The New Politics of Religion in Morocco and the Arab World.* Princeton: Princeton University Press.

Spiro, Melford E. 1997. *Gender Ideology and Psychological Reality: An Essay on Cultural Reproduction.* New Haven, CT: Yale University Press.

Stanton, Andrea. 2022. 'From Mecca with Love: Muslim Religious Apps and the Centering of Sacred Geography'. In *Cyber Muslims: Mapping Islamic Digital Media in the Internet Age,* edited by Robert Rozehnal, 161–75. London: Bloomsbury Academic.

Stauth, Georg and Samuli Schielke (eds). 2008. *Dimensions of Locality: Muslim Saints, Their Place and Space*. Bielefeld: Transcript.

Stockstill, Abbey. 2018. 'A Tale of Two Mosques: Marrakesh's Masjid al-Jamiʿ al-Kutubiyya'. *Muqarnas* 35 (1): 65–82.

Stokes, Martin. 2010. *The Republic of Love: Cultural Intimacy in Turkish Popular Music*. Chicago: University of Chicago Press.

Stoller, Paul. 1997. *Sensuous Scholarship*. Philadelphia: University of Pennsylvania Press.

Stoller, Paul. 1989. *The Taste of Ethnographic Things: The Senses in Anthropology*. Philadelphia: University of Pennsylvania Press.

Sunier, Thijl. 2018. 'Between Islam as a Generic Category and Muslim Exceptionalism'. In *Exploring the Multitude of Muslims in Europe: Essays in Honor of Jorgen N. Nielsen*, edited by Niels Valdemar Vinding, Egdūnas Račius and J. Thielmann, 1–19. Leiden: Brill.

Sunier, Thijl. 2017. 'Moral Failure, Everyday Religion and Islamic Authorization'. In *Straying from the Straight Path: How Senses of Failure Invigorate Lived Religion*, edited by Daan Beekers and David Kloos, 107–24. New York: Berghahn.

Sunier, Thijl. 2014. 'Domesticating Islam: Exploring Academic Knowledge Production on Islam and Muslims in European Societies'. *Ethnic and Racial Studies*, 37 (6): 1,138–55.

Sunier, Thijl and Nico Landman. 2014. 'Turkse islam. Actualisatie van kennis over Turkse religieuze stromingen en organisaties in Nederland. Een literatuurstudie in opdracht van het Ministerie van Sociale Zaken en Werkgelegenheid [Turkish Islam. Updating of Knowledge about Turkish Religious Movements and Organizations in the Netherlands. A Literature Study Commissioned by the Ministry of Social Affairs and Employment]'. Den Haag: Ministerie van Sociale Zaken en Werkgelegenheid. https://fsw.vu.nl/en/Images/TRSO_rapport_SunierLandman_2014_tcm250-421419.pdf

Ṭabarānī, Sulaymān Ibn Ahmad. 1995. *Al-Muʿjam al-Awṣaṭ* [Intermediate Dictionary]. Cairo: Dar Al-Haramayn.

Tagliacozzo, Eric and Shawkat Toorawa (eds). 2015. *The Hajj: Pilgrimage in Islam*. Cambridge: Cambridge University Press.

Tammam, Husam and Patrick Haenni. 2004. 'De retour dans les rythmes du monde: Une petite histoire du chant (ex)islamiste en Égypte. Vingtième siècle'. *Revue d'histoire* 82: 91–102.

Tapper, Nancy. 1990. 'Ziyaret: Gender, Movement and Exchange in a Turkish Community'. In *Muslim Travelers: Pilgrimage, Migration, and the Religious*

Imagination, edited by Dale Eickelman and James Piscatori, 236–55. Berkeley: University of California Press.

Taylor, Charles. 2002. *Varieties of Religion Today: William James Revisited*. Institute for Human Sciences Vienna Lecture Series. Cambridge, MA: Harvard University Press.

Taylor, Jerome. 2011. 'Mecca for the Rich: Islam's Holiest Site "Turning into Vegas"'. *The Independent*. https://www.independent.co.uk/news/world/middle-east/mecca-for-the-rich-islams-holiest-site-turning-into-vegas-2360114.html

Teitelbaum, Joshua. 2020. 'Hashemites, Egyptians and Saudis: The Tripartite Struggle for the Pilgrimage in the Shadow of Ottoman Defeat'. *Middle Eastern Studies*, 56 (1): 36–47.

Thimm, Viola (ed.). 2018. *Understanding Muslim Mobilities and Gender*. MDPI AG (Multidisciplinary Digital Publishing Institute). https://www.mdpi.com/books/pdfview/book/535

Timmerman, Christiane, Nadia Fadil, Idesbald Goddeeris, Noel Clycq and Karim Ettourki (eds). 2017. *Moroccan Migration in Belgium: More Than 50 Years of Settlement*. Leuven: Leuven University Press.

Timothy, Dallen J. and Daniel H. Olsen. 2006. *Tourism, Religion, and Spiritual Journeys*. London: Routledge.

Toguslu, Erkan (ed.). 2015. *Everyday Life Practices of Muslims in Europe*. Leuven: Leuven University Press.

Tolmacheva, Marina. 2013. 'Medieval Muslim Women's Travel: Defying Distance and Danger'. *World History Connected* 10 (2): n.p. https://worldhistoryconnected.press.uillinois.edu/10.2/forum_tolmacheva.html

Tolmacheva, Marina. 1998. 'Female Piety and Patronage in the Medieval Hajj'. In *Women in the Medieval Dar al-Islam: Power, Patronage, and Piety*, edited by Gavin Hambly, 161–78. New York: St. Martin's Press.

Tolmacheva, Marina. 1993. 'Ibn Battuta on Women's Travel in the Dar al-Islam'. In *Women and the Journey: The Female Travel Experience*, edited by Bonnie Frederick and Susan McLeod, 119–40. Pullman, WA: Washington State University Press.

Tonkin, Elizabeth. 1992. *Narrating our Pasts: The Social Construction of Oral History*. Manchester: Manchester University Press.

Touhtou, Rashid. 2014. *Civil Society in Morocco under the New 2011 Constitution: Issues, Stakes and Challenges*. Doha: Arab Center for Research and Policy Studies. www.jstor.org/stable/resrep12647

Trofimov, Yaroslav. 2007. *The Siege of Mecca: The Forgotten Uprising in Islam's Holiest Shrine and the Birth of al-Qaeda*. New York: Doubleday.

Turner, Edith. 2012. *Communitas: The Anthropology of Collective Joy*. London: Palgrave Macmillan.

Turner, Victor W. and Edith L. B. Turner. 1978. *Image and Pilgrimage in Christian Culture: Anthropological Perspectives*. New York: Columbia University Press.

Tweed, Thomas A. 2006. *Crossing and Dwelling: A Theory of Religion*. Cambridge, MA: Harvard University Press.

Valdes, Mario J. 2004. 'Story-telling and Cultural Identity in Latin America'. In *Latin American Narratives and Cultural Identity: Selected Readings*, edited by Irene Blayer and Mark Anderson, 9–27. New York: Peter Lang.

Valentine, Simon Ross. 2021. 'The Ahmadiyya Jama'at: A Question of Muslim Identity'. In *Handbook of Contemporary Islam and Muslim Lives*, Vol. 2, pp. 1,211–32. Cham: Springer.

Van Leeuwen, Richard. 2023. 'Hajj Narratives as a Discursive Tradition'. In *Narrating the Pilgrimage to Mecca*, edited by Marjo Buitelaar and Richard van Leeuwen, 45–73. Leiden: Brill.

Vandendorpe, Florence. 2011. 'When Myth Shows What the Mind Does Not Reach'. *Storytelling, Self, Society* 7 (2): 91–109.

Vogel, Frank E. 2012. 'Shariʿa in the Politics of Saudi Arabia'. *The Review of Faith & International Affairs* 10 (4): 18–27.

Vogel, Frank E. 2000. *Islamic Law and Legal System: Studies of Saudi Arabia*. Leiden: Brill.

Waines, David. 2015. *Odyssey of Ibn Battuta, The: Uncommon Tales of a Medieval Adventurer*. London and New York: I. B. Tauris.

Waterbury, John. 1970. *The Commander of the Faithful: The Moroccan Political Elite. A Study in Segmented Politics*. New York: Columbia University Press.

Waterman, Christopher Alan. 1990. *Jùjú: A Social History and Ethnography of an African Popular Music*. Chicago: University of Chicago Press.

Watt, W. Montgomery. 2012. 'Hidj̲ra'. In *Encyclopaedia of Islam, Second Edition*. Leiden: Brill Online. http://dx.doi.org/10.1163/1573-3912_islam_SIM_2860

Waugh, Earle H. 2005. *Memory, Music and Religion: Morocco's Mystical Chanters*. Columbia: University of South California Press.

Wegley, Andrew C. 2006. 'Ritually Failing: Turner's Theatrical Communitas'. In *Ritual and Event*, 66–84. London: Routledge.

Weingartner, Laura A. 2005. 'Family Law and Reform in Morocco – the Mudawana: Modernist Islam and Women's Rights in the Code of Personal Status'. *University of Detroit Mercy Law Review* 82: 687–713.

Wensinck, A. J. and H. A. R. Gibb. "Arafa'. In *Encyclopaedia of Islam, Second Edition*. Leiden: Brill Online. http://dx.doi.org/10.1163/1573-3912_islam_SIM_0701

Wensinck, A. J. and J. Jomier. 2012. 'Iḥrām'. In *Encyclopaedia of Islam, Second Edition*. Leiden: Brill Online. http://dx.doi.org/10.1163/1573-3912_islam_SIM_3506

Werbner, Pnina. 2003. *Pilgrims of Love: The Anthropology of a Global Sufi Cult*. London: Hurst.

Werbner, Pnina. 2001. 'Murids of the Saints: Occupational Guilds and Redemptive Sociality'. In *Muslim Traditions and Modern Techniques of Power*, edited by Armando Salvatore, 265–89. New Brunswick, NJ: Transaction.

Werbner, Richard P. 1989. *Ritual Passage, Sacred Journey: Form, Process and Organization of Religious Movement*. Manchester: Manchester University Press.

Werenfels, Isabelle. 2014. 'Beyond Authoritarian Upgrading: The Re-emergence of Sufi Orders in Maghrebi Politics'. *Journal of North African Studies* 19 (3): 275–95.

Whyte, William Foote. 2016. 'Light Rhythms and Heavy Spirits: Entertaining Listeners through Gnawa Musical and Ritual Adaptations in Morocco'. *Ethnomusicology Forum* 25 (2): 172–90.

Whyte, William Foote. 1984. *Learning from the Field: A Guide from Experience*. Beverly Hills, CA: Sage.

Winegar, Jessica. 2006. *Creative Reckonings: The Politics of Art and Culture in Contemporary Egypt*. Stanford, CA: Stanford University Press.

Witte, Marleen de. 2011. 'Touched by the Spirit: Converting the Senses in a Ghanaian Charismatic Church'. *Ethnos* 76 (4): 489–509.

Witulski, Christopher. 2018. *The Gnawa Lions: Authenticity and Opportunity in Moroccan Ritual Music*. Bloomington, IN: Indiana University Press.

Wolf, Anne. 2019. 'Morocco's Hirak Movement and Legacies of Contention in the Rif'. *Journal of North African Studies* 24 (1): 1–6.

Wolfe, Michael. 1997. *One Thousand Roads to Mecca: Ten Centuries of Travelers Writing about the Muslim Pilgrimage*. New York: Grove.

Wuerth, Oriana. 2005. 'The Reform of the Moudawana: the Role of Women's Civil Society Organisations in Changing Status Code in Morocco'. *Hawwa* 3 (3): 309–33.

Wyrtzen, Jonathan. 2016. *Making Morocco: Colonial Intervention and the Politics of Identity*. Ithaca, NY: Cornell University Press.

X, Malcolm and Alex Haley. 1965. *The Autobiography of Malcolm X*. New York: Grove Press.

Yamba, C. Bawa. 1995. *Permanent Pilgrims: The Role of Pilgrimage in the Lives of West African Muslims in Sudan*. Edinburgh: Edinburgh University Press.

Zadeh, Travis. 2015. 'The Early Hajj: Seventh–Eighth Centuries CE'. In *The Hajj: Pilgrimage in Islam*, edited by Eric Tagliacozzo and Shawkat Toorawa, 42–64. Cambridge: Cambridge University Press.

Zarcone, Thierry. 2012. 'Pilgrimage to the "Second Meccas" and "Kaʿbas" of Central Asia'. In *Central Asian Pilgrims: Hajj Routes and Pious Visits between Central Asia and the Hijaz*, edited by Alexandre Papas, Thomas Welsford and Thierry Zarcone, 251–77. Berlin: Klaus Schwarz Verlag.

Zeghal, Malika. 2008. *Islamism in Morocco: Religion, Authoritarianism, and Electoral Politics*. Princeton, NJ: Markus Wiener.

INDEX

Note: *f* indicates a figure, *t* indicates a table

'abāyas, 138–9
al-'Abdarī, Muhammad, 13–14
Abdullah (*al-ḥājj* from Temara), 220–1, 225
Abu Bakr (*al-ḥājj*), 102–3, 104, 114–16
aesthetic formation, 79
Aith Waryagher of the Moroccan Rif, The (Hart, David), 28, 195
Allah Yā Mawlānā (Nass El Ghiwane), 221–2, 224, 226, 227
Amdāḥ maghribiya, 217–19, 223, 224, 225
Amina (*al-ḥājja*), 74, 79–80, 87
Aourid, Hassan, 46
Arafat, Day of, 10, 11*f*, 75, 132, 193, 210n
Asad, Talal
  'Idea of an Anthropology of Islam, The', 20
Āshūrā, 160
Asma (new mother), 221–2, 224
El-Ayadi, Mohammed, Rachik, Hassan and Tozy, Muḥammad, 215
'Ayyāḍ, Qadī, 168n
Ayyub (from Mohammedia), 57–8

baraka, 195, 198–9
bay'a, 126–7
Beekers, Dann and Kloos, David, 117–18
'Being Good in Ramadan' (Schielke, Samuli), 22–3
Bennani, Abdel Hadi, 220
Boissevain, Katia, 49–50
Bourdieu, Pierre, 175
Bū Khiyār *see* Sīdī Bū Khiyār
Buitelaar, Marjo, 79, 245–6
  Fasting and Feasting, 30
Buitelaar, Marjo and Leeuwen, Richard van
  Narrating the Pilgrimage to Mecca: Historical and Contemporary Accounts, 19
Buitelaar, Marjo, Stephan-Emmrich, Manja and Thimm, Violet
  Muslim Women's Pilgrimage to Mecca d Beyond: Reconfiguring Gender, Religion and Mobility, 19
bukhūr, 89

Cairo caravan, 13
capital, 175, 177–9
  cultural, 177–9
  religious, 177–9
  social, 112, 113–15, 179–83
  symbolic, 184–6
  women, 175, 177–83, 184–6

censorship, 227
Certeau, Michel de
Practice of Everyday Life, The, 21–2
charity, 246–7
Clingingsmith, David; Khwaja, Asim Ijaz; Kremer, Michael, 107
clothing, 74
distinctive Moroccan, 138–9
Hajj, 138–9
iḥrām clothing, 2, 39n, 54, 68
women, restrictions on, 39n, 166*f*, 174
Coleman, Simon, 18–19
Coleman, Simon and Eade, John
Reframing Pilgrimage: Cultures in Motion, 19
Combs-Schilling, M. E., 28
communitas, 17–19, 20, 254–5
contestation, 18–19, 20
Contesting the Sacred (Eade, John and Sallnow, Michael), 17–18
Crawford, David and Newcomb, Rachel
Encountering Morocco: Fieldwork and Cultural Understanding, 30
cultural capital, 177–9
culture, 35

dangers/tragedies, 146, 150, 160–4
death/dying, 109–10, 120n
Deeb, Lara, 25
dialect, 87
diversity, 30, 31, 136–9
du'ā' prayer, 66, 68, 86
Durkheim, Émile
Elementary Forms of the Religious Life, The, 16
durūs al-Ḥassaniyya, 128

Eade, John and Sallnow, Michael
Contesting the Sacred, 17–18
Egan, Martyn, 159
Eickelman, Dale
Moroccan Islam: Tradition and Society in a Pilgrimage Center, 28
Eickelman, Dale F. and Andersen, Jon W., 134
Elementary Forms of the Religious Life, The (Durkheim, Émile), 16
emotions 76–9, 95–6, 97, 99; *see also* senses
Encountering Morocco: Fieldwork and Cultural Understanding (Crawford, David and Newcomb, Rachel), 30
ethics, 242–3
ethical improvement, 261–2
ethical self-formation, 257–60, 262
ethnographic methods, 27–31
everyday life, 21–6, 251–64
al-ḥājj/al-ḥājja, 29
Hajj in, 260–4
religion, 112
songs, 217
stories, 235
studies, 30–1
Everyday Life in Global Morocco (Newcomb, Rachel), 30

Fadil, Nadia and Fernando, Mayanthi, 24
Fasting and Feasting (Buitelaar, Marjo), 30
fate, 241
Fatiha (from Safi), 206–7, 244–5
Fatima (*al-ḥājja* from Fes), 1, 31–2, 214, 217, 225
Fes el Bali, 1
fieldwork, 31–7
Foucault, Michel, 108
Frankincense, 230n
free speech, 140
Friday sermons, 132–3

Geertz, Clifford, 28
Islam Observed, 28
Gellner, Ernest
Saints of the Atlas, 28
gender *see* women
Gennep, Arnold van, 16
'Gnawa of Oujda: Music and contending identities in the Maghreb, The' (Langlois, Tony), 216–17
God
duties towards, 242–3
equality before, 203
mercy of, 225
signs of, 156–7

Grand Mosque of Mecca
cleanliness, 88–9
Kaʿba, the, 8–9*f*, 79–81, 83–4*f*
model of, 83–4*f*
siege, 166
grave visiting, 156, 157–60, 195
Guide to Performing Hajj and ʿumra, The, 54

habitus, 175
Hajj, 15, 25–6, 254–7
ambivalence towards, 147–8
bureaucracy, 29–30
clothing, 138–9
communication of narratives, 255
communitas, 20
conditions, 88–9, 134–5, 150
constraints, 261–2
contestation, 20
dangers/tragedies, 146, 150, 160–4
dissatisfaction, 255
diversity, 136–7, 138–9
duty to perform, 29, 48, 114–15
equality, 155
in everyday life, 251–64
experience sharing, 76
food, 67, 89–90, 103, 134–5
Friday sermons, 132
future, of, 165–6
gifts/souvenirs, 65, 82*f*–4*f*, 89, 96
harmony, 86, 255, 135
humour, 191–2
inability to perform, 62–3, 262
Iran boycott, 150, 157, 163, 171n
judgement, 137, 139–40
liminality, 16, 17
linguistic essence of, 45–6
Mecca, expansion/remodelling, 146, 150–60*f*
in the media, 97–8, 132, 133–4
modernisation, 146, 150–60*f*, 256
Mohammed VI, 128–35
monarchy, 128–35
Moroccan history of 12–15
motivation, 62–6
Muslim unity, 254, 255
Muslims in the West, 19
national identity, 123–41
nostalgia, 164–5
numbers performing, 15, 49*t*, 51–2*f*, 53*t*, 251
as the performance of charity at home, 246
politics, 163
prayer requests, 65
prohibition, 198
reflections on, 135–42
religious commitment, 63–4
retelling narratives, 95
returning from, 102–7, 109, 110–16, 135–42, 257–60
rites of passage, 16
ritual, 7–12, 17, 66, 68, 86
Saudi control of, 59, 147, 148, 149–50, 156, 159–60, 163–5
significance of, 2–3, 12
sins, cleansing of, 110, 111, 258
social status, 29, 64
songs, 47, 174–5, 213–28
stages of, 16
state role, 132
stories/storytelling, 232–49
time taken, 13
transformative qualities of, 105–6, 110–13, 115–18
types of, 9n
unity, 86, 255
wealth disparity, 151, 154, 167, 179–80, 185–6, 203–4
see also al-ḥājj/al-ḥājja; Hajj, preliminaries to; Hajj, as sensory experience
al-ḥājj/al-ḥājja, 1–2, 12, 259
capital, 177–8, 259
self-fashioning as, 102–19
status, 29, 64, 113–15
see also pilgrims
Hajj, preliminaries to, 48–70, 147
application process, 48, 49, 50–1, 261–2
corruption, 56–9
documentation, 53*t*
example of Zahra (*al-ḥājja*), 53–6
farewell practices, 64–5, 115, 128–35, 174–5

fees, 52, 146, 147*f*, 166–7, 179–80, 185
medical examination, 53
mujāmala visas, 56–9
pilgrimage lessons, 66–9, 197
qurʿa, 49, 50–6, 61, 180–1
qurʿa, avoiding, 56–60
ṣadaqa, 65
women supporting men, 185–6
Hajj, self-fashioning as *al-ḥājj*/*al-ḥājja*, 102–19
Abu Bakr, 114–16
completing one's faith, 110
death/dying, 109–10, 120n
human failings, 116–18
pilgrim's moral quest, 107–9, 112–13, 116
religious and social life, 111–13
social capital, 112, 113–15
spiritual transformation, 110–13, 115–18
Hajj, as sensory experience, 74–99
emotions, 76–9, 95–6, 97, 99
gifts/souvenirs, 82*f*–4*f*, 89, 96
media, the, 97–8
memories, 97, 98
morality, 95
pilgrimage accounts, 96, 97
religious education, 96, 97
retelling narratives, 95, 99
sight, 79–85
smell, 88–9
soundscapes and feelings, 85–8
spontaneity, 96
taste and touch, 80–1, 89–91
Hajj, The (Peters, Francis Edward), 19
ḥajj al-miskīn see Pilgrimage of the Poor
Hajj of Fadila and Her Husband, The, 236–8*f*, 241–2
al-ḥajja, 219–21, 223–4, 225
halal, 58, 159
Hammoudi, Abdellah, 46
Season in Mecca: Narrative of a Pilgrimage, A, 18, 29, 94
Hamza (colleague of Yousef), 242
Hanan (tailor), 74–5, 79–80, 87
Ḥanna (from Temara), 174, 176
ḥarām, 58, 159
Hart, David, 200, 201
Aith Waryagher of the Moroccan Rif, The, 28, 195
Hassan (pilgrim from Safi), 87, 90, 139, 140, 206–7
Hassan II (king of Morocco), 126, 128
ḥāyik, 174
Hirschkind, Charles, 20, 21
holy ignorance, 159
humour, 191–2

Ibn Battuta, 14, 45
Rihla, 14, 29
Ibn Jubayr, 97
Ibn Saud, Abd al-Aziz (king of Saudi Arabia), 149
ʿīd l-kbīr, 11, 193
'Idea of an Anthropology of Islam, The' (Asad, Talal), 20
identity, 37, 108, 258–9
national, 123–41, 259
Idriss I (emir of Morocco), 156
iḥrām, 7–8
iḥrām clothing, 2, 39n, 54, 68, 109
Image and Pilgrimage in Christian Culture (Turner, Victor and Turner, Edith), 17
Indonesia, 60, 71n
intercession, 229n
Iran, 150, 157, 163, 171n
Islam, 226, 247, 258
Five Pillars of, 7, 110
Friday sermons, 132–3
as a lived religion, 16–27
in the media, 133–4
Mohammed VI, 128, 129–30
in Morocco, 40n, 29, 30, 32, 125–8, 130, 132–4, 195
Salafi, 170n
training, 127
virtuous behaviour, 258
see also prayers
Islam Observed (Geertz, Clifford), 28

Jackson, Michael
Politics of Storytelling, The, 235
Jamal (*al-ḥājj*), 47–8, 51, 63, 64

janāza prayer, 87
Jannat al-Baqīʿ, 157, 158*f*
jellabas, 138
Jordan, 71n

Kaʿba, the, 8–9*f*, 79–81
  model of, 83–4*f*
Khadija (wife of Muhammad), 156, 157
Khawla (3D modeller), 84
Kloos, David and Beekers, Daan
  Straying from the Straight Path: How Senses of Failure Invigorate Lived Religion, 23–4
Kraus, Wolfgang, 28
Kredya, Ibrahim, 194, 197

Langlois, Tony
  'Gnawa of Oujda: Music and contending identities in the Maghreb, The', 216–17
language, 87
  orality, 95
  retelling narratives, 95
liminality, 16, 17
literacy, 249n
Lived Religion: Faith and Practice in Everyday Life (McGuire, Meredith), 22
Lubna (*al-ḥājja* from Mohammedia), 180–2, 244
Lücking, Mirjam, 60

McGuire, Meredith
  Lived Religion: Faith and Practice in Everyday Life, 22
madīḥ, 223
Mahmood, Saba, 20
  Politics of Piety, 21
maḥram, 36, 71n, 72n, 177, 181
makhzen, 126
male privilege, 94; *see also* patriarchy, the
malḥūn, 214
Mannana, Lalla ,196
maqam Ibrāhīm, 9
marriage, 183–4, 187
Maysa (pilgrim), 137
Mecca, 7–8, 25, 133, 146–8, 156
  abrāj al-bayt project, 150–1, 152*f*
  clock tower, 146, 150–1, 154–5
  dying in, 162
  expansion/remodelling, 146, 150–60*f*
  heritage, destruction of, 150–1, 155–60
  Jabal ʿUmar project, 151, 153*f*
  longing for, 215
  in songs, 263
  see also Hajj
media, the, 97–8, 132, 133–4; *see also* social media
Medina, 12, 91–4, 146–7, 148, 156
  Jannat al-Baqīʿ, 157, 158*f*
  Mount Uḥud, 157–9
Meyer, Birgit, 78, 79
Mhand *see* Sidi Mhand
Minā, 88–9, 137–8
  diversity, 137–8
  stampede of, 2015, 109–10, 160–4
mīqāt, 39n
miracles, 198–9
miskīna, 33
Mohammed VI (king of Morocco), 124, 127, 128–35
monarchy, 125–35
morality, 259–60
  moral failure, 261, 262
  moral quest, 107–9, 112–13, 116
  story themes, 241–5
Moroccan Islam: Tradition and Society in a Pilgrimage Center (Eickelman, Dale), 28
Morocco, 27–9
  bayʿa, 126–7
  bureaucracy, 29–30
  diversity, 30, 31
  history, 40n, 125–8
  Islam, 40n, 29, 30, 31, 125–8, 130, 132–4, 195
  literacy, 249n
  longing for, 140, 259
  makhzen, 126
  monarchy, 125–35
  national identity, 123–41, 259
  Palestine, 32–3
  politics, 125–8
  population, 15

religion, 28, 29–30, 31, 124, 125–8, 132
sacred sites, 159
self, concept of, 108
social class, 34
Mount Uḥud, 157–9
Muhammad, Prophet, 133, 156
fondness for, 223–4
living places, 157
relations of, 156
tomb of, 12
Muna (from Casablanca), 135–7, 138–9, 145–6, 164, 259
Musa (from Safi), 206–7
music, 215, 216–17, 263; *see also* songs
genres, 229n
Muslim Pilgrimage in the Modern World (Rahimi, Babak and Eshaghi, Peyman), 19
Muslim Women's Pilgrimage to Mecca d Beyond: Reconfiguring Gender, Religion and Mobility (Buitelaar, Marjo, Stephan-Emmrich, Manja and Thimm, Violet), 19

Najat (from Temara), 173–4, 220, 221
Najla (from Mohammedia), 115–16, 117, 184–6, 232, 233, 242, 243–4, 245–7
Narrating the Pilgrimage to Mecca: Historical and Contemporary Accounts (Buitelaar, Marjo and Leeuwen, Richard van), 19
Nass El Ghiwane, 224, 226
Allah Yā Mawlānā, 222, 224, 226, 227
national identity, 123–41
Newcomb, Rachel
Everyday Life in Global Morocco, 30
Women of Fes: Ambiguities of Urban Life in Morocco, 30–1
Nisrin (Moroccan woman), 113, 114
niyya, 8, 203
Nuha (pilgrim), 145–6, 164, 165

Omar (*al-ḥājj* from Safi), 223
orality, 95, 234–5
Organization of Islamic Cooperation (OIC), 51, 150
Osama (artist), 83
Osama (from Casablanca), 198
otherness, 254

Palestine, 32–3
participant observation, 33, 35
patriarchy, the, 183–4
Peters, Francis Edward
Hajj, The, 19
piety, 21, 24–5
interior, 111
performance of, 111
songs, 225–7
pilgrimage, 15, 204, 254, 257
anthropology of, 16–20
communitas, 17–19, 20
contestation, 18–19, 20
inscriptions, 94–5
liminality, 16, 17
Muslims in the West, 19
rites of passage, 16
songs of, 213–28
theoretical model of, 16–17
'umra, 10, 15, 59, 60–1, 90–4, 118, 146
women's empowerment through, 182
see also Hajj; Medina; Mina; Pilgrimage of the Poor
pilgrimage lessons, 66–9, 197
Pilgrimage of the Cat, The, 240*f*–1, 244
Pilgrimage of the Cobbler, The, 238–9*f*, 242–4, 246, 247
Pilgrimage of the Poor, 194–209
criticisms, 206–8
Hajj, equivalence with, 202–5
Sīdī Bū Khiyār, 194, 195, 196–7, 198–202, 204–5
Sidi Mhand, 195
Sīdī Shāshkāl, 193–4, 196, 197, 198, 200*f*, 201–2, 203–4
pilgrims, 262
as ambassadors, 130–1, 140, 141
challenges, 260–1
connecting with, 132
diversity, 136–9
everyday life, 260–4
expectations of, 111, 130–1
human failings, 116–18, 262
judgement, 137, 139–40

pilgrims (*cont.*)
in the media, 134
moral failure, 261, 262
moral quest, 107–9, 112–13, 116
praiseworthy, 139–40
spiritual transformation, 110–13, 115–18
status, 113–15
wealth disparity, 151, 154, 167, 179–80, 185–6, 203–4
policing, 204–5
politics, 125–8, 163, 204–5, 264
Politics of Piety (Mahmood, Saba), 21
Politics of Storytelling, The (Jackson, Michael), 235
poverty, 204, 206; *see also* wealth disparity
Practice of Everyday Life, The (Certeau, Michel de), 21–2
prayers, 10, 39n, 86, 87
du'ā', 66, 68, 86
janāza, 87
for the king, 130
requests, 65
ṣalāt, 39n
talbiya, 8, 86, 233
protests, 127, 162–3

al-Qaysī, Abu Abdullah Muhammad, 45
qur'a, 49, 50–6, 61, 180–1
avoiding, 56–60

Rahimi, Babak and Eshaghi, Peyman
Muslim Pilgrimage in the Modern World, 19
rajm, 10–11
Ramadan, 90, 128, 245–6
Rashid (shop owner), 109, 110, 114–15, 116, 117, 151
Morocco, longing for, 140
al-rawḍa al-nabawiya, 91–4
Reframing Pilgrimage: Cultures in Motion (Coleman, Simon and Eade, John), 19
Rehouma, Fouad, 197
religion, 25
duties, 243
lived, 22
in Morocco, 28, 29–30, 31, 124, 125–8, 132
religious merit, 105
sense of failure, 118
training, 127
see also Islam
religious capital, 177–9
'Revolution of the King and the People, The', 124
Rif, the, 204, 205
Rihla (Ibn Battuta), 14, 29
al-Risāla (Akkad, Moustapha), 35
rites of passage, 16
ritual, 7–12, 17, 66, 68, 86, 193–4, 196–7, 198–9
Roy, Olivier, 159
Ruqayya (pilgrim from Fes), 80–1, 88, 90

sacrifice, 11
Sadiqi, Fatima, 95, 108
Saed (benefactor), 244
sa'ī, 9–10
saints, 195, 197
Saints of the Atlas (Gellner, Ernest), 28
Salah (*al-ḥājj*), 154, 156–7, 160, 164
ṣalāt, 39n
Salim (*al-ḥājj*), 56–7, 59, 161
Sallnow, Michael, 17–18
Salma (from Temara), 177
sama', 231n
Sami (*al-ḥājj*), 81
Samira (pilgrim), 145–6, 164
Samiya (pilgrim from Fes), 111–12, 123–4, 135–6, 138
Saqifat Banī Sā'ida, 169n
Saudi Arabia, 59, 145–68
criticisms of, 146, 161–7
economy, 153, 166–7, 243
grave visiting, 156, 157, 159–60
Hajj control, 59, 147, 148, 149–50, 156, 159–60, 163–5
holy ignorance, 159
Mecca, expansion/remodelling, 146, 150–60*f*
qur'a, 51, 56, 57
reform, 149–50
women, restrictions on, 44n, 166*f*, 177
Sawsan (*al-ḥājja* from Fes), 178–9

Schielke, Samuli, 21
'Being Good in Ramadan', 22–3
'Second Thoughts about the Anthropology of Islam, or How to Make Sense of Grand Schemes in Everyday Life', 23
Season in Mecca: Narrative of a Pilgrimage, A (Hammoudi, Abdellah), 18, 29, 94
'Second Thoughts about the Anthropology of Islam, or How to Make Sense of Grand Schemes in Everyday Life' (Schielke, Samuli), 23
sensational forms, 78, 79
senses, the, 77–9, 256–7
sight, 79–85
smell, 88–9
soundscapes and feelings, 85–8, 226
taste and touch, 80–1, 89–91
'umra, 91–4
Shāshkāl *see* Sīdī Shāshkāl
Sīdī Bū Khiyār, 194, 195, 196–7, 198–202, 204–5
Sidi Mhand, 195
Sīdī Shāshkāl, 193–4, 196, 197, 198, 200*f*, 201–2, 203–4
social capital, 112, 113–15, 179–83; *see also* capital
social class/status, 29, 64, 112, 113–15, 167, 182, 207–8, 244; *see also* capital; wealth disparity
social media, 85*f*, 98, 134, 244, 255
socio-cultural community, 108, 182
patriarchy, the, 183–4
songs, 47, 74, 174–5, 213–28, 263
Allah Yā Mawlānā, 221–2, 224, 226, 227
Amdāḥ maghribiya, 217–19, 223, 224, 225
as expressions of longing and piety, 225–7
al-ḥajja, 219–21, 223–4, 225
listening as religious act, 225–6
Mecca in, 263
non-religious uses, 224
social and political, 225
themes, 222–4
Souad (from Meknes), 232, 233, 238, 242–3, 245–6, 247
spirituality, 80
stories/storytelling, 232–49, 263–4
community reception, 247–8
Hajj of Fadila and Her Husband, The, 236–8*f*, 241–2
lived experiences, 245–8
moral themes, 241–5
Pilgrimage of the Cat, The, 240*f*–1, 244
Pilgrimage of the Cobbler, The, 238–9*f*, 242–4, 246, 247
shared, 244
social media, 244
traditions, 234–6
Straying from the Straight Path: How Senses of Failure Invigorate Lived Religion (Kloos, David and Beekers, Daan), 23–4
supernatural, the, 88
symbolic capital, 184–6

talbiya, 8, 86, 233
ṭawāf, 8–9*f*, 10, 11, 12, 67
ṭawāf al-wadāʿ, 68
Taylor, Charles, 95
thabāt, 110
theoretical framework, 15–37
ethnographic methods, 27–31
fieldwork, 31–7
Islam, as a lived religion, 16–27
pilgrimage, anthropology of, 16–20
tourism, 159
travel, 13–15, 175
duʿāʾ prayer, 66, 68
Trench, Battle of the, 156
ṭulba, 200
Turner, Victor, 16–17
Turner, Victor and Turner, Edith
Image and Pilgrimage in Christian Culture, 17
20 February Movement, 127

umma, 254–5, 258–9
'umra, 10, 15, 59, 60–1, 118
fees, 146
food, 90
sensory experiences, 91–4
uprisings, 127, 162–3

wealth disparity, 151, 154, 167, 179–80, 185–6, 203–4, 212n
women, 64, 173–87, 257
capital, 175, 177–83, 184–6
clothing restrictions, 39n, 165, 166*f*, 174
empowerment, 182, 184–6
face covering, 39n
Hajj, participation in, 176–7
al-ḥājja, 177–9
henna parties, 145
patriarchy, the, 183–4
pilgrimage documentation, 53*t*
al-rawḍa al-nabawiya, 92–4
responsibilities, 177
restrictions, 36, 50, 92–4, 157, 165, 166*f*, 176–7, 181, 183, 264
supporting men, 184–6
wealth, 179–81, 185–6
Women of Fes: Ambiguities of Urban Life in Morocco (Newcomb, Rachel), 30–1
wuqūf, 10

Yasir (shop owner), 61, 155
Yassin (*al-ḥājj*), 57–8, 62
Yousef (*al-ḥājj*), 236, 241–2, 245
Al Youssi, El Hassan, 235
Yusra (from Mohammedia), 232

Zahra (*al-ḥājja* from Fes), 53–6, 95–6, 183
Zamzam water, 90–1, 94f, 154*f*–5, 196
ziyāra see grave visiting

EU representative:
Easy Access System Europe
Mustamäe tee 50, 10621 Tallinn, Estonia
Gpsr.requests@easproject.com

www.ingramcontent.com/pod-product-compliance
Lightning Source LLC
Chambersburg PA
CBHW050202240426
43671CB00013B/2222
9781399520720